PACIFIC BASI

Editor: Kaori O'Connor

MRS. BISHOP'S TRAVELING PARTY.

KOREA

AND HER NEIGHBOURS

BY ISABELLA BIRD

INTRODUCTION BY PAT BARR

KPI

LONDON, BOSTON, SYDNEY AND HENLEY

First published in 1897
This edition published in 1985 by KPI Limited
14 Leicester Square, London WC2H 7PH, England,

Distributed by
Routledge & Kegan Paul plc
14 Leicester Square, London WC2H 7PH, England,

Routledge & Kegan Paul Inc
9 Park Street, Boston, Mass., 02108, USA,

Routledge & Kegan Paul
c/o Methuen Law Book Company
44 Waterloo Road
North Ryde, NSW 2113, Australia and

Routledge & Kegan Paul plc
Broadway House, Newtown Road,
Henley-on-Thames, Oxon RG9 1EN, England

Printed in Great Britain by
St Edmundsbury Press, Bury St Edmunds, Suffolk

© this edition KPI Limited 1985

No part of this book may be reproduced in
any form without permission from the publisher,
except for the quotation of brief passages
in criticism

ISBN 0-7103-0135-9

INTRODUCTION

THE AUTHOR of this book, who describes herself as 'an experienced muleteer' also capable of 'leaping over deep crevices', eluding piratical attack and 'flying down' rapids in a ramshackle *sampan* was, at the time of writing, a dumpy doctor's widow of sixty-three. She was, of course, much else besides. Born in 1831 into a well-connected clerical family, she had spent much of her youth languishing on rectory sofas sick in body and oppressed in spirit by the educational and social restrictions imposed on her sex. She didn't really break free from this convention-bound life till she was forty, when she took off for the Hawaiian Islands in a desperate search for health and happiness.

By the time she went to Korea in 1894 however, Isabella had accomplished much. She had travelled adventurously in parts of America, in Malaya, Japan, Tibet, Persia and Kurdistan and the books she wrote about her journeys had been widely acclaimed; she was well-known as an expert on contemporary Asian affairs, as a champion of Christian medical missions, as the first woman to be elected a member of the Royal Geographical Society. However, these public activities never gave her much private pleasure and it was partly to escape their demands and obligations that she left England again at an age when most middle-class women of her kind were settled by the fireside. But, as Isabella wrote to a friend, she was 'constitutionally incapable of settling', even less so now those she had most loved – her parents, her younger sister Henrietta, her husband, John Bishop – had all pre-deceased her. In the hope of recapturing that spiritual buoyancy

I

and physical well-being that travel had always given her in the past, she sailed back to her beloved East and stayed there for three years.

The Korea that Isabella saw at that time was a paradigm of what we are now pleased to call 'an under-developed country', a demon-haunted, tiger-infested land saddled with a weak ruler, a coinage so devalued that six men or one pony were required to carry £10 worth of it, a hierarchy of rapacious officials too idle even to support the full weight of their own bodies. Mrs Bishop's account doesn't spare her readers a single detail of the tribulations and discomforts that awaited any westerner intrepid enough to travel in such a benighted land, and certainly was not calculated to put Korea on the track beaten by the average nineteenth-century 'globe-trotter'.

Inn-rooms (often adjoining pig-pens) were flea- and rat-ridden; boats were leaky and perilous; ponies bony and pugnacious; crowds pestering and sometimes hostile. But there were compensations: the 'barbaric' splendour of a royal procession in Seoul; the tranquil seclusion of monasteries in the Diamond Mountains; the sheer oddity of Korean men whose precious top-knots of hair were covered in horse-hair gauze and who could be incited to near riot by an edict demanding they be cut off! Such splendours, seclusions, eccentricities were soon to pass away forever, and this gives Mrs Bishop's book special value, for nineteenth-century western accounts of 'The Hermit Nation' are rare anyway, and none others (as far as I know) describe so thoroughly the condition of Korea at this crucial point in its own and Asia's history.

In the period of Isabella's visits between 1894 and '97 China's long-held suzerainty of the country ended and drastic social and political reforms were precipitately imposed by the Japanese – the first stage in their ambitious plans for the domination of Asia that were to come to dust in Hiroshima fifty years later. Other major powers also became aware at this time of the country's strategic importance as a buffer state, an unenviable role that has brought it much suffering and conflict ever since. Isabella's vivid first-hand accounts of what was going on – the landing of Japanese troops at Chemulpo before the actual declaration of the Sino-Japanese war, the King's formal renunciation of Chinese suzerainty for instance – are worthy of any foreign correspondent, had there been one on the spot, which there wasn't. She also provides some fascinating insights into the characters of the royal family (especially the ill-fated Queen) with whom she established unusually informal and friendly contact.

Although Isabella became increasingly engrossed in Korean affairs she didn't 'settle' there, and part of this book describes her northward journeys to parts of Manchuria, Vladivostock and beyond – presented here as mere side-trips, but sufficiently adventurous to be counted as pioneering expeditions in themselves by lesser mortals! The professed object of her latter journey was to visit the Korean settlements in Siberia, from which she deduced that, given the right incentives and social conditions, Koreans *were* capable of developing habits of industry, honesty and self-discipline and therefore that the corrupt and oppressive government was largely responsible for the parlous state of their home country.

On several other occasions Isabella advocates the adoption of sterling Victorian-Christian virtues as a cure for the 'backwardness' and 'immorality' of eastern lands. But her thinking on the issue is woolly. She recognises the need for western-style development, yet is appalled by the vulgar, selfish materialism that follows the importation of foreign customs and goods. The dilemma is, of course, a common one among those who share her concern for the world's "poor primitives": that their simplicity, trust, contentment, traditionalism (the very stuff of their attraction) is invariably destroyed by the processes of modernisation that bring material betterment. Isabella believed that Christianity might solve this problem in Korea, but she is nevertheless realistic, indeed occasionally caustic, in her assessment of missionary work there and its possible future influence. Her personal commitment to Christianity is clearly stated in this book, but it was always practically rooted in her conviction that medical and educational missions could alleviate the sorry lot of peasant women, the sick and destitute.

Moving alongside, often in uneasy tandem with the resolutely-Christian, socially-concerned Mrs Bishop was always the freedom-loving, carefree Isabella Bird who, many years before, had galloped across the Rocky Mountains and fallen half in love with her 'dear desperado', Jim Nugent. By this point in Isabella's career she is subdued but by no means vanquished and her voice is clearly heard in passages that celebrate her joy in nature's beauty, in reaching inaccessible, little-known places, in the exercise of her lively, insatiable curiosity. And her powers of observation are as keen as they ever were when she describes, for example, how Koreans trained falcons, grew ginseng, worshipped spirits, hunted tigers, and how absolutely splendid was the scenery around the high pass of Tan-pa Ryong.

It was always with considerable regret that Isabella left such wild and isolated places to return to the 'civilisation' about which she felt so ambivalent and where she had to justify her existence through good works, writing books, giving lectures. She worked diligently at these pursuits after her final departure from the East in 1897, her first task being the composition of *Korea and Her Neighbours* which appeared the following year and received reviews that she ungratefully termed 'monotonously favourable' (though one critic did venture to enquire why on earth Mrs Bishop chose to visit countries which she found so squalid, comfortless and decadent). But in the main the book considerably enhanced her professional reputation and after its publication she found herself '. . . transplanted into the ranks of political writers and quoted as an authority on the political situation in the Far East', as she put it.

The popular success of her voluminous works on Korea and China gave her some satisfaction and a greater degree of financial security, but neither fame nor fortune could really make Mrs Bishop happy. In her last years she was still unable to 'settle' or to form any new emotional ties. So she moved restlessly from one unsuitable house to another – and made a last madcap expedition to the Atlas Mountains in her seventieth year – before coming to a reluctant halt in Edinburgh, where she died in 1904.

PAT BARR

Author's Prefatory Note.

My four visits to Korea, between January, 1894, and March, 1897, formed part of a plan of study of the leading characteristics of the Mongolian races. My first journey produced the impression that Korea is the most uninteresting country I ever traveled in, but during and since the war its political perturbations, rapid changes, and possible destinies, have given me an intense interest in it; while Korean character and industry, as I saw both under Russian rule in Siberia, have enlightened me as to the better possibilities which may await the nation in the future. Korea takes a similarly strong grip on all who reside in it sufficiently long to overcome the feeling of distaste which at first it undoubtedly inspires.

It is a difficult country to write upon, from the lack of books of reference by means of which one may investigate what one hopes are facts, the two best books on the country having become obsolete within the last few years in so far as its political condition and social order are concerned. The traveler must laboriously disinter each fact for himself, usually through the medium of an interpreter; and as five or six versions of each are given by apparently equally reliable authorities, frequently the "teachers" of the foreigners, the only course is to hazard a bold guess as to which of them has the best chance of being accurate.

Accuracy has been my first aim, and my many foreign friends in Korea know how industriously I have labored to attain it. It is by these, who know the extreme difficulty of the task, that I shall be the most leniently criticised wherever, in spite of carefulness, I have fallen into mistakes.

Circumstances prevented me from putting my traveling experiences, as on former occasions, into letters. I took careful notes, which were corrected from time to time by the more prolonged observations of residents, and as I became better acquainted with the country; but, with regard to my journey up the South Branch of the Han, as I am the first traveler who has reported on the region, I have to rely on my observation and inquiries alone, and there is the same lack of recorded notes on most of the country on the Upper Tai-döng. My notes furnish the travel chapters, as well as those on Seoul, Manchuria, and Primorsk; and the sketches in contemporary Korean history are based partly on official documents, and are partly derived from sources not usually accessible.

I owe very much to the kindly interest which my friends in Korea took in my work, and to the encouragement which they gave me when I was disheartened by the difficulties of the subject and my own lack of skill. I gratefully acknowledge the invaluable help given me by Sir Walter C. Hillier, K.C.M.G., H.B.M.'s Consul-General in Korea, and Mr. J. M'Leavy Brown, LL.D., Chief Commissioner of Korean Customs; also the aid generously bestowed by Mr. Waeber, the Russian Minister, and the Rev. G. Heber Jones, the Rev. James Gale, and other missionaries. I am also greatly indebted to a learned and careful volume on *Korean Government*, by Mr. W. H. Wilkinson, H.B.M.'s Acting Vice-Consul at Chemulpo, as well as to the *Korean Repository* and the *Seoul Independent*, for information which has enabled me to correct some of my notes on Korean customs.

Various repetitions occur, for the reason that it appears to me impossible to give sufficient emphasis to certain facts without them; and several descriptions are loaded with details, the result of an attempt to fix on paper customs and ceremonies destined shortly to disappear. The illustrations, with the exceptions of three, are reproductions of my own photographs. The transliteration of Chinese proper names was kindly undertaken by a well-known Chinese scholar, but unfortunately the actual Chinese characters were not in all cases forthcoming. In justice to the kind friends who have so generously aided me, I am anxious to claim and accept the fullest measure of personal responsibility for the opinions expressed, which, whether right or wrong, are wholly my own.

I am painfully conscious of the demerits of this work, but believing that, on the whole, it reflects fairly faithfully the regions of which it treats, I venture to present it to the public; and to ask for it the same kindly and lenient criticism with which my records of travel in the East and elsewhere have hitherto been received, and that it may be accepted as an honest attempt to make a contribution to the sum of the knowledge of Korea and its people, and to describe things as I saw them, not only in the interior but in the troubled political atmosphere of the capital.

ISABELLA L. BISHOP.

November, 1897.

Contents

7

8 Contents

List of Illustrations.

Korea and Her Neighbors

INTRODUCTORY CHAPTER

IN the winter of 1894, when I was about to sail for Korea (to which some people erroneously give the name of "The Korea"), many interested friends hazarded guesses at its position,—the Equator, the Mediterranean, and the Black Sea being among them, a hazy notion that it is in the Greek Archipelago cropping up frequently. It was curious that not one of these educated, and, in some cases, intelligent people came within 2,000 miles of its actual latitude and longitude!

In truth, there is something about this peninsula which has repelled investigation, and until lately, when the establishment of a monthly periodical, carefully edited, *The Korean Repository*, has stimulated research, the one authority of which all writers, with and without acknowledgment, have availed themselves, is the Introduction to Père Dallet's *Histoire de l' Église de Korée*, a valuable treatise, many parts of which, however, are now obsolete.

If in this volume I present facts so elementary as to provoke the scornful comment, "Every schoolboy knows that," I venture to remind my critics that the larger number of possible readers were educated when Korea was little more than "a geographical expression," and had not the advantages of the modern schoolboy, whose "up-to-date" geographical textbooks have been written since the treaties of 1883 opened the Hermit Nation to the world; and I will ask the minority to be

patient with what may be to them "twice-told tales" for the
sake of the majority, specially in this introduction, which is
intended to give something of lucidity to the chapters which
follow.

The first notice of Korea is by Khordadbeh, an Arab geog-
rapher of the ninth century, A.D., in his *Book of Roads and
Provinces*, quoted by Baron Richofen in his work on China,
p. 575. Legends of the aborginal inhabitants of the peninsula
are too mythical to be noticed here, but it is certain that it
was inhabited when Kit-ze or Ki-ja, who will be referred to
later, introduced the elements of Chinese civilization in the
twelfth century B.C. Naturally that conquest and subsequent
immigrations from Manchuria have left some traces on the
Koreans, but they are strikingly dissimilar from both their
nearest neighbors, the Chinese and the Japanese, and there
is a remarkable variety of physiognomy among them, all the
more noticeable because of the uniformity of costume. The
difficulty of identifying people which besets and worries the
stranger in Japan and China does not exist in Korea. It is
true that the obliquity of the Mongolian eye is always present,
as well as a trace of bronze in the skin, but the complexion
varies from a swarthy olive to a very light brunette.

There are straight and aquiline noses, as well as broad and
snub noses with distended nostrils; and though the hair is
dark, much of it is so distinctly a russet brown as to require
the frequent application of lampblack and oil to bring it to a
fashionable black, while in texture it varies from wiriness to
silkiness. Some men have full moustaches and large goatees,
on the faces of others a few carefully tended hairs, as in China,
do duty for both, while many have full, strong beards. The
mouth is either the wide, full-lipped, gaping cavity constantly
seen among the lower orders, or a small though full feature, or
thin-lipped and refined, as is seen continually among patricians.

The eyes, though dark, vary from dark brown to hazel; the
cheek bones are high; the brow, so far as fashion allows it to

be seen, is frequently lofty and intellectual; and the ears are small and well set on.   The usual expression is cheerful, with a dash of puzzlement.   The physiognomy indicates, in its best aspect, quick intelligence, rather than force or strength of will.   The Koreans are certainly a handsome race.

The physique is good.   The average height of the men is five feet four and a half[1] inches, that of the women cannot be ascertained, and is *dis*proportionately less, while their figureless figures, the faults of which are exaggerated by the ugliest dress on earth, are squat and broad.   The hands and feet of both sexes and all classes are very small, white, and exquisitely formed, and the tapering, almond-shaped finger-nails are carefully attended to.   The men are very strong, and as porters carry heavy weights, a load of 100 pounds being regarded as a moderate one.   They walk remarkably well, whether it be the studied swing of the patrician or the short, firm stride of the plebeian when on business.   The families are large and healthy. If the Government estimate of the number of houses is correct, the population, taking a fair average, is from twelve to thirteen millions, females being in the minority.

Mentally the Koreans are liberally endowed, specially with that gift known in Scotland as " gleg at the uptak."   The foreign teachers bear willing testimony to their mental adroitness and quickness of perception, and their talent for the rapid acquisition of languages, which they speak more fluently and with a far better accent than either the Chinese or Japanese. They have the Oriental vices of suspicion, cunning, and un-

[1] The following are the measurements of 1,060 men taken at Seoul in January, 1897, by Mr. A. B. Stripling:—

	Highest.	Lowest.	Average.
Height . . .	5 ft. 11¼ in.	4 ft. 9½ in.	5 ft. 4½ in.
Size round chest .	39¼ in.	27 in.	31 in.
" head .	23¼ "	20 "	21½ "

truthfulness, and trust between man and man is unknown. Women are secluded, and occupy a very inferior position.

The geography of Korea, or Ch'ao Hsien ("Morning Calm," or "Fresh Morning"), is simple. It is a definite peninsula to the northeast of China, measuring roughly 600 miles from north to south and 135 from east to west. The coast line is about 1,740 miles. It lies between 34° 17' N. to 43° N. latitude and 124° 38' E. to 130° 33' E. longitude, and has an estimated area of upwards of 80,000 square miles, being somewhat smaller than Great Britain. Bounded on the north and west by the Tu-men and Am-nok, or Yalu, rivers, which divide it from the Russian and Chinese empires, and by the Yellow Sea, its eastern and southern limit is the Sea of Japan, a "silver streak," which has not been its salvation. Its northern frontier is only conterminous with that of Russia for 11 miles.

Both boundary rivers rise in Paik-tu San, the "White-Headed Mountain," from which runs southwards a great mountain range, throwing off numerous lateral spurs, itself a rugged spine which divides the kingdom into two parts, the eastern division being a comparatively narrow strip between the range and the Sea of Japan, difficult of access, but extremely fertile; while the western section is composed of rugged hills and innumerable rich valleys and slopes, well watered and admirably suited for agriculture. Craters of volcanoes, long since passed into repose, lava beds, and other signs of volcanic action, are constantly met with.

The lakes are few and very small, and not many of the streams are navigable for more than a few miles from the sea, the exceptions being the noble Am-nok, the Tai-döng, the Nak-tong, the Mok-po, and the Han, which last, rising in Kang-wön Do, 30 miles from the Sea of Japan, after cutting the country nearly in half, falls into the sea at Chemulpo on the west coast, and, in spite of many and dangerous rapids, is a valuable highway for commerce for over 170 miles.

Owing to the configuration of the peninsula there are few good harbors, but those which exist are open all the winter. The finest are Fusan and Wön-san, on Broughton Bay. Che-mulpo, which, as the port of Seoul, takes the first place, can hardly be called a harbor at all, the "outer harbor," where large vessels and ships of war lie, being nothing better than a roadstead, and the "inner harbor," close to the town, in the fierce tideway of the estuary of the Han, is only available for five or six vessels of small tonnage at a time. The east coast is steep and rocky, the water is deep, and the tide rises and falls from 1 to 2 feet only. On the southwest and west coasts the tide rises and falls from 26 to 38 feet!

Off the latter coasts there is a remarkable archipelago. Some of the islands are bold masses of arid rock, the resort of sea-fowl; others are arable and inhabited, while the actual coast fringes off into innumerable islets, some of which are im-mersed by the spring tides. In the channels scoured among these by the tremendous rush of the tide, navigation is oft-times dangerous. Great mud-banks, specially near the mouths of the rivers, render parts of the coastline dubious.

Korea is decidedly a mountainous country, and has few plains deserving the name. In the north there are mountain groups with definite centres, the most remarkable being Paik-tu San, which attains an altitude of over 8,000 feet, and is re-garded as sacred. Farther south these settle into a definite range, following the coast-line at a moderate distance, and throwing out so many ranges and spurs to the west as to break up northern and central Korea into a congeries of corrugated and precipitous hills, either denuded or covered with *chap-paral*, and narrow, steep-sided valleys, each furnished with a stony stream. The great axial range, which includes the "Diamond Mountain," a region containing exquisite moun-tain and sylvan scenery, falls away as it descends towards the southern coast, disintegrating in places into small and often infertile plains.

The geological formation is fairly simple. Mesozoic rocks occur in Hwang-hai Do, but granite and metamorphic rocks largely predominate. Northeast of Seoul are great fields of lava, and lava and volcanic rocks are of common occurrence in the north.

The climate is undoubtedly one of the finest and healthiest in the world. Foreigners are not afflicted by any climatic maladies, and European children can be safely brought up in every part of the peninsula. July, August, and sometimes the first half of September, are hot and rainy, but the heat is so tempered by sea breezes that exercise is always possible. For nine months of the year the skies are generally bright, and a Korean winter is absolutely superb, with its still atmosphere, its bright, blue, unclouded sky, its extreme dryness without asperity, and its crisp, frosty nights. From the middle of September till the end of June, there are neither extremes of heat nor cold to guard against.

The summer mean temperature at Seoul is about 75° Fahrenheit, that of the winter about 33°; the average rainfall 36.03 inches in the year, and the average of the rainy season 21.86 inches.[1] July is the wettest month, and December the driest. The result of the abundant rainfall, distributed fairly through the necessitous months of the year, is that irrigation is necessary only for the rice crop.

The fauna of Korea is considerable, and includes tigers and leopards in great numbers, bears, antelopes, at least seven species of deer, foxes, beavers, otters, badgers, tiger-cats, pigs, several species of marten, a sable (not of much value, however), and striped squirrels. Among birds there are black eagles, found even near Seoul, harriers, peregrines (largely used for hawking), pheasants, swans, geese, spectacled and common teal, mallards, mandarin ducks, turkey buzzards (very shy), white and pink ibis, sparrow-hawks, kestrels, imperial

[1] These averages are only calculated on observations taken during a period of three and a half years.

cranes, egrets, herons, curlews, night-jars, redshanks, buntings, magpies (common and blue), orioles, wood larks, thrushes, redstarts, crows, pigeons, doves, rooks, warblers, wagtails, cuckoos, halcyon and bright blue kingfishers, jays, snipes, nut-hatches, gray shrikes, pheasants, hawks, and kites. But until more careful observations have been made it is impossible to say which of the smaller birds actually breed in Korea, and which make it only a halting-place in their annual migrations.

The denudation of the hills in the neighborhood of Seoul, the coasts, the treaty ports, and the main roads, is impressive, and helps to give a very unfavorable idea of the country. It is to the dead alone that the preservation of anything deserving the name of timber in much of southern Korea is owing. But in the mountains.of the northern and eastern provinces, and specially among those which enclose the sources of the Tu-men, the Am-nok, the Tai-döng, and the Han, there are very considerable forests, on which up to this time the woodcutter has made little apparent impression, though a good deal of timber is annually rafted down these rivers.

Among the indigenous trees are the *Abies excelsa, Abies microsperma, Pinus sinensis, Pinus pinea*, three species of oak, the lime, ash, birch, five species of maple, the *Acanthopanax ricinifolia, Rhus semipinnata, Elæagnus*, juniper, mountain ash, hazel, *Thuja Orientalis* (?), willow, *Sophora Japonica* (?), hornbeam, plum, peach, *Euonymus alatus*, etc. The flora is extensive and interesting, but, with the exception of the azalea and rhododendron, it lacks brilliancy of color. There are several varieties of showy clematis, and the *mille-fleur* rose smothers even large trees, but the climber *par excellence* of Korea is the *Ampelopsis Veitchi*. The economic plants are few, and, with the exception of the *Panax quinquefolia* (ginseng), the wild roots of which are worth $15 per ounce, are of no commercial value.

The mineral wealth of Korea is a vexed question. Probably

between the view of the country as an El Dorado and the scepticism as to the existence of underground treasure at all, the mean lies.   Gold is little used for personal ornaments or in the arts, yet the Korean declares that the dust of his country is gold ; and the unquestionable authority of a Customs' report states that gold dust to the amount of $1,360,279 was exported in 1896, and that it is probable that the quantity which left the country undeclared was at least as much again.   Silver and galena are found, copper is fairly plentiful, and the country is rich in undeveloped iron and coal mines, the coal being of excellent quality.   The gold-bearing quartz has never been touched, but an American Company, having obtained a concession, has introduced machinery, and has gone to work in the province of Phyŏng-an.

The manufactures are unimportant.   The best productions are paper of several qualities made from the *Brousonettia Papyrifera*, among which is an oiled paper, like vellum in appearance, and so tough that a man can be raised from the ground on a sheet of it, lifted at the four corners, fine grass mats, and split bamboo blinds.

The arts are *nil*.

Korea, or Ch'ao Hsien, has been ruled by kings of the present dynasty since 1392.   The monarchy is hereditary, and though some modifications in a constitutional direction were made during the recent period of Japanese ascendency, the sovereign is still practically absolute, his edicts, as in China, constituting law.   The suzerainty of China, recognized since very remote days, was personally renounced by the king at the altar of the Spirits of the Land in January, 1895, and the complete independence of Korea was acknowledged by China in the treaty of peace signed at Shimonoséki in May of the same year.   There is a Council of State composed of a chancellor, five councillors, six ministers, and a chief secretary.   The decree of September, 1896, which constitutes this body, announces the king's absolutism in plain terms in the preamble.

There are nine ministers—the Prime Minister, Minister of the Royal Household, of Finance, of Home Affairs, Foreign Affairs, War, Justice, Agriculture, and Education, but the royal will (or whim) overrides their individual or collective decisions.

The Korean army consists of 4,800 men in Seoul, drilled by Russians, and 1,200 in the provinces; the navy, of two small merchant steamers.

Korea is divided into 13 provinces and 360 magisterial districts.

The revenue, which is amply sufficient for all legitimate expenses, is derived from Customs' duties, under the able and honest management of officers lent by the Chinese Imperial Maritime Customs: a land tax of $6 on every fertile *kyel* (a fertile *kyel* being estimated at about 6⅓ acres), and $5 on every mountain *kyel;* a household tax of 60 cents per house, houses in the capital enjoying immunity; and a heavy excise duty of $16 per *cattie* on manufactured ginseng.

Up to 1876 Korea successfully preserved her isolation, and repelled with violence any attempt to encroach upon it. In that year Japan forced a treaty upon her, and in 1882 China followed with "Trade and Frontier Regulations." The United States negotiated a treaty in 1882, Great Britain and Germany in 1884, Russia and Italy in 1886, and Austria in 1892, in all which, though under Chinese suzerainty, Korea was treated with as an independent state. By these treaties, Seoul and the ports of Chemulpo (Jenchuan), Fusan, and Wön-san (Gensan) were opened to foreign commerce, and this year (1897) Mok-po and Chinnam-po have been added to the list.

After the treaties were signed, a swarm of foreign representatives settled down upon the capital, where three of them are housed in handsome and conspicuous foreign buildings. The British Minister at Peking is accredited also to the Korean Court, and Britain has a resident Consul-General. Japan, Russia, and America are represented by Ministers, France by a Chargé d'Affaires, and Germany by a Consul. China, which has been tardy in entering upon diplomatic relations with Korea since the war, placed her subjects under the protection of the British Consul-General.

Until recently, the coinage of Korea consisted of debased copper *cash*, 500 to the dollar, a great check on business transactions; but a new fractional coinage, of which the unit is a 20-cent piece, has been put into circulation, along with 5-cent nickel, 5-*cash* copper, and 1-*cash* brass pieces. The fine Japanese *yen* or dollar is now current everywhere. The *Dai Ichi Gingo* and Fifty-eighth Banks of Japan afford banking facilities in Seoul and the open ports.

In the treaty ports of Fusan, Wön-san, and Chemulpo, there were in January, 1897, 11,318 foreign residents and 266 foreign business firms. The Japanese residents numbered 10,711, and their firms 230. The great majority of the American and French residents are missionaries, and the most conspicuous objects in Seoul are the Roman Cathedral and the American Methodist Episcopal Church. The number of British subjects in Korea in January, 1897, was 65, and an agency of a British firm in Nagasaki has recently been opened at Chemulpo. The approximate number of Chinese in Korea at the same time was 2,500, divided chiefly between Seoul and Chemulpo. There is a newly-instituted postal system for the interior, with postage stamps of four denominations, and a telegraph system, Seoul being now in communication with all parts of the world.

The roads are infamous, and even the main roads are rarely more than rough bridle tracks. Goods are carried everywhere on the backs of men, bulls, and ponies, but a railroad from Chemulpo to Seoul, constructed by an American concessionaire, is actually to be opened shortly.

The language of Korea is mixed. The educated classes introduce Chinese as much as possible into their conversation, and all the literature of any account is in that language, but it is of an archaic form, the Chinese of 1,000 years ago, and differs completely in pronunciation from Chinese as now spoken in

China. *En-mun*, the Korean script, is utterly despised by the educated, whose sole education is in the Chinese classics. Korean has the distinction of being the only language of Eastern Asia which possesses an alphabet. Only women, children, and the uneducated used the *En-mun* till January, 1895, when a new departure was made by the official Gazette, which for several hundred years had been written in Chinese, appearing in a mixture of Chinese characters and *En-mun*, a resemblance to the Japanese mode of writing, in which the Chinese characters which play the chief part are connected by *kana* syllables.

A further innovation was that the King's oath of Independence and Reform was promulgated in Chinese, pure *En-mun*, and the mixed script, and now the latter is regularly employed as the language of ordinances, official documents, and the Gazette ; royal rescripts, as a rule, and despatches to the foreign representatives still adhering to the old form.

This recognition of the Korean language by means of the official use of the mixed, and in some cases of the pure script, the abolition of the Chinese literary examinations as the test of the fitness of candidates for office, the use of the " vulgar " script exclusively in the *Independent*, the new Korean newspaper, the prominence given to Korean by the large body of foreign missionaries, and the slow creation of scientific textbooks and a literature in *En-mun*, are tending not only to strengthen Korean national feeling, but to bring the " masses," who can mostly read their own script, into contact with Western science and forms of thought.

There is no national religion. Confucianism is the official cult, and the teachings of Confucius are the rule of Korean morality. Buddhism, once powerful, but " disestablished " three centuries ago, is to be met with chiefly in mountainous districts, and far from the main roads. Spirit worship, a species of *shamanism*, prevails all over the kingdom, and holds the uneducated masses and the women of all classes in complete bondage.

Christian missions, chiefly carried on by Americans, are beginning to produce both direct and indirect effects.

Ten years before the opening[1] of Korea to foreigners, the Korean king, in writing to his suzerain, the Emperor of China, said, "The educated men observe and practice the teachings of Confucius and Wen Wang," and this fact is the key to anything like a correct estimate of Korea. Chinese influence in government, law, education, etiquette, social relations, and morals is predominant. In all these respects Korea is but a feeble reflection of her powerful neighbor ; and though since the war the Koreans have ceased to look to China for assistance, their sympathies are with her, and they turn to her for noble ideals, cherished traditions, and moral teachings. Their literature, superstitions, system of education, ancestral worship, culture, and modes of thinking are Chinese. Society is organized on Confucian models, and the rights of parents over children, and of elder over younger brothers, are as fully recognized as in China.

It is into this archaic condition of things, this unspeakable grooviness, this irredeemable, unreformed Orientalism, this parody of China without the robustness of race which helps to hold China together, that the ferment of the Western leaven has fallen, and this feeblest of independent kingdoms, rudely shaken out of her sleep of centuries, half frightened and wholly dazed, finds herself confronted with an array of powerful, ambitious, aggressive, and not always overscrupulous powers, bent, it may be, on overreaching her and each other, forcing her into new paths, ringing with rude hands the knell of time-honored custom, clamoring for concessions, and bewildering her with reforms, suggestions, and panaceas, of which she sees neither the meaning nor the necessity.

And so "The old order changeth, giving place to new," and many indications of the transition will be found in the later of the following pages.

[1] See appendix A.

CHAPTER I

FIRST IMPRESSIONS OF KOREA

IT is but fifteen hours' steaming from the harbor of Nagasaki to Fusan in Southern Korea. The Island of Tsushima, where the *Higo Maru* calls, was, however, my last glimpse of Japan; and its reddening maples and blossoming plums, its temple-crowned heights, its stately flights of stone stairs leading to Shinto shrines in the woods, the blue-green masses of its pines, and the golden plumage of its bamboos, emphasized the effect produced by the brown, bare hills of Fusan, pleasant enough in summer, but grim and forbidding on a sunless February day. The Island of the Interrupted Shadow, Chŏl-yong-To, (Deer Island), high and grassy, on which the Japanese have established a coaling station and a quarantine hospital, shelters Fusan harbor.

It is not Korea but Japan which meets one on anchoring. The lighters are Japanese. An official of the *Nippon Yusen Kaisha* (Japan Mail Steamship Co.), to which the *Higo Maru* belongs, comes off with orders. The tide-waiter, however, is English—one of the English *employés* of the Chinese Imperial Maritime Customs, lent to Korea, greatly to her advantage, for the management of her customs' revenue. The foreign settlement of Fusan is dominated by a steep bluff with a Buddhist temple on the top, concealed by a number of fine cryptomeria, planted during the Japanese occupation in 1592. It is a fairly good-looking Japanese town, somewhat packed between the hills and the sea, with wide streets of Japanese shops and various Anglo-Japanese buildings, among which the Consulate and a Bank are the most important. It has substantial retain-

23

ing and sea walls, and draining, lighting, and roadmaking
have been carried out at the expense of the municipality.
Since the war, waterworks have been constructed by a rate of
100 *cash* levied on each house, and it is hoped that the present
abundant supply of pure water will make an end of the frequent epidemics of cholera.   Above the town, the new Japanese military cemetery, filling rapidly, is the prominent
object.

Considering that the creation of a demand for foreign goods
is not thirteen years old, it is amazing to find how the Koreans
have taken to them, and that the foreign trade of Fusan has
developed so rapidly that, while in 1885 the value of exports
and imports combined only amounted to £77,850, in 1892 it
had reached £346,608.   Unbleached shirtings, lawns, mus-
lins, cambrics, and Turkey reds for children's wear have all
captivated Korean fancy; but the conservatism of wadded cotton garments in winter does not yield to foreign woollens, of
which the importation is literally *nil*.   The most amazing
stride is in the importation of American kerosene oil,
which has reached 71,000 gallons in a quarter; and which,
by displacing the fish-oil lamp and the dismal rushlight in
the paper lantern, is revolutionizing evening life in Korea.
Matches, too, have "caught on" wonderfully, and evidently
have "come to stay."   Hides, beans, dried fish, *bêche de
mer*, rice, and whale's flesh are among the principal exports.   It was not till 1883 that Fusan was officially opened to
general foreign trade, and its rise has been most remarkable.
In that year its foreign population was 1,500; in 1897 it was
5,564.

In the first half of 1885 the Japan Mail Steamship Co. ran
only one steamer, calling at Fusan, to Wladivostok every five
weeks, and a small boat to Chemulpo, calling at Fusan, once a
month.   Now not a day passes without steamers, large or
small, arriving at the port, and in addition to the fine vessels
of the *Nippon Yusen Kaisha*, running frequently between

Kobe and Wladivostok, Shanghai and Wladivostok, Kobe and Tientsin, and between Kobe Chefoo, and Newchang, all calling at Fusan, three other lines, including one from Osaka direct, and a Russian mail line running between Shanghai and Wladivostok, make Fusan a port of call.

It appears that about one-third of the goods imported is carried inland on the backs of men and horses. The taxes levied and the delays at the barriers on both the overland and river routes are intolerable to traders, a hateful custom prevailing under which each station is controlled by some petty official, who, for a certain sum paid to the Government in Seoul, obtains permission to levy taxes on all goods.[1] The Nak-Tong River, the mouth of which is 7 miles from Fusan, is navigable for steamers drawing 5 feet of water as far as Miriang, 50 miles up, and for junks drawing 4 feet as far as Sa-mun, 100 miles farther, from which point their cargoes, transhipped into light draught boats, can ascend to Sang-chin, 170 miles from the coast. With this available waterway, and a hazy prospect that the much disputed Seoul-Fusan railway may become an accomplished fact, Fusan bids fair to become an important centre of commerce, as the Kyöng-sang Province, said to be the most populous of the eight (now for administrative purposes thirteen), is also said to be the most prosperous and fruitful, with the possible exception of Chul-la.

Barren as the neighboring hills look, they are probably rich in minerals. Gold is found in several places within a radius of 50 miles, copper quite near, and there are coal fields within 100 miles.

To all intents and purposes the settlement of Fusan is Japanese. In addition to the Japanese population of 5,508, there

[1] According to Mr. Hunt, the Commissioner of Customs at Fusan, in the Kyöng-sang province alone there are 17 such stations. Fusan is hedged round by a cordon of them within a ten-mile radius, and on the Nak-tong, which is the waterway to the provincial capital, there are four in a distance of 25 miles.

is a floating population of 8,000 Japanese fishermen. A Japanese Consul-General lives in a fine European house. Banking facilities are furnished by the Dai Ichi Gingo of Tokio, and the post and telegraph services are also Japanese. Japanese too is the cleanliness of the settlement, and the introduction of industries unknown to Korea, such as rice husking and cleaning by machinery, whale-fishing, *sake*-making, and the preparation of shark's fins, *bêche de mer*, and fish manure, the latter an unsavory fertilizer, of which enormous quantities are exported to Japan.

But the reader asks impatiently, "Where are the Koreans? I don't want to read about the Japanese!" Nor do I want to write about them, but facts are stubborn, and they are the outstanding Fusan fact.

As seen from the deck of the steamer, a narrow up and down path keeping at some height above the sea skirts the hillside for 3 miles from Fusan, passing by a small Chinese settlement with official buildings, uninhabited when I last saw them, and terminating in the walled town of Fusan proper, with a fort of very great antiquity outside it, modernized by the Japanese after the engineering notions of three centuries ago.

Seated on the rocks along the shore were white objects resembling pelicans or penguins, but as white objects with the gait of men moved in endless procession to and fro between old and new Fusan, I assumed that the seated objects were of the same species. The Korean makes upon one the impression of novelty, and while resembling neither the Chinese nor the Japanese, he is much better-looking than either, and his physique is far finer than that of the latter. Though his average height is only 5 feet 4½ inches, his white dress, which is voluminous, makes him look taller, and his high-crowned hat, without which he is never seen, taller still. The men were in winter dress—white cotton sleeved robes, huge trousers, and socks; all wadded. On their heads were black silk wadded caps with pendant sides edged with black fur, and on the top of these, rather high-crowned, somewhat broad-brimmed hats of black "crinoline" or horsehair gauze, tied under the chin with crinoline ribbon. The general effect was grotesque. There were a few children on the path, bundles of gay clothing, but no women.

I was accompanied to old Fusan by a charming English "Una," who, speaking Korean almost like a native, moved serenely through the market-day crowds, welcomed by all. A miserable place I thought it, and later experience showed that it was neither more nor less miserable than the general run of Korean towns. Its narrow dirty streets consist of low hovels built of mud-smeared wattle without windows, straw roofs, and deep eaves, a black smoke hole in every wall 2 feet from the ground, and outside most are irregular ditches containing solid and liquid refuse. Mangy dogs and blear-eyed children, half or wholly naked, and scaly with dirt, roll in the deep dust or slime, or pant and blink in the sun, apparently unaffected by the stenches which abound. But market day hid much that is repulsive. Along the whole length of the narrow, dusty, crooked street, the wares were laid out on mats on the ground, a man or an old woman, bundled up in dirty white cotton, guarding each. And the sound of bargaining rose high, and much breath was spent on beating down prices, which did not amount originally to the tenth part of a farthing. The goods gave an impression of poor buyers and small trade. Short lengths of coarse white cotton, skeins of cotton, straw shoes, wooden combs, tobacco pipes and pouches, dried fish and sea-weed, cord for girdles, paper rough and smooth, and barley-sugar nearly black, were the contents of the mats. I am sure that the most valuable stock-in-trade there was not worth more than three dollars. Each vendor had a small heap of *cash* beside him, an uncouth bronze coin with a square hole in the centre, of which at that time 3,200 *nominally* went to the dollar, and which greatly trammelled and crippled Korean trade.

A market is held in Fusan and in many other places every fifth day. On these the country people rely for all which they do not produce, as well as for the sale or barter of their productions. Practically there are no shops in the villages and small towns, their needs being supplied on stated days by travelling pedlars who form a very influential guild.

Turning away from the bustle of the main street into a narrow, dirty alley, and then into a native compound, I found the three Australian ladies who were the objects of my visit to this decayed and miserable town. Except that the compound was clean, it was in no way distinguishable from any other, being surrounded by mud hovels. In one of these, exposed to the full force of the southern sun, these ladies were living. The mud walls were concealed with paper, and photographs and other European knickknacks conferred a look of refinement. But not only were the rooms so low that one of the ladies could not stand upright in them, but privacy was impossible, invasions of Korean women and children succeeding each other from morning to night, so that even dressing was a spectacle for the curious. Friends urged these ladies not to take this step of living in a Korean town 3 miles from Europeans. It was represented that it was not safe, and that their health would suffer from the heat and fetid odors of the crowded neighborhood, etc. In truth it was not a "conventional thing" to do.

On my first visit I found them well and happy. Small children were clinging to their skirts, and a certain number of women had been induced to become cleanly in their persons and habits. All the neighbors were friendly, and rude remarks in the streets had altogether ceased. Many of the women resorted to them for medical help, and the simple aid they gave brought them much good-will. This friendly and civilizing influence was the result of a year of living under very detestable circumstances. If they had dwelt in grand houses 2½ miles off upon the hill, it is safe to say that the result would have been *nil*. Without any fuss or blowing of trumpets, they quietly helped to solve one of the great problems as to "Missionary Methods," though why it should be a "problem" I fail to see. In the East at least, every religious teacher who has led the people has lived among them, knowing if not sharing their daily lives, and has been easily accessible at all times. It is not easy to imagine a Buddha or One greater than Buddha only reached by favor of, and possibly by feeing, a gate-keeper or servant.

On visiting them a year later I found them still well and happy. The excitement among the Koreans consequent on the Tong-hak rebellion and the war had left them unmolested. A Japanese regiment had encamped close to them, and, by permission, had drawn water from the well in their compound, and had shown them nothing but courtesy. Having in two years gained general confidence and good-will, they built a small bungalow just above the old native house, which has been turned into a very primitive orphanage.

The people were friendly and kind from the first. Those who were the earliest friends of the ladies are their staunchest friends now, and they knew them and their aims so well when they moved into their new house that it made no difference at all. Some go there to see the ladies, others to see the furniture or hear the organ, and a few to inquire about the "Jesus doctrine." The "mission work" now consists of daily meetings for worship, classes for applicants for baptism, classes at night for those women who may not come out in the daytime, a Sunday school with an attendance of eighty, visiting among the people, and giving instruction in the country and surrounding villages. About forty adults have professed Christianity, and regularly attend Christian worship.

I mention these facts not for the purpose of glorifying these ladies, who are simply doing their duty, but because they fall in with a theory of my own as to methods of mission work.

There is a very small Roman Catholic mission-house, seldom tenanted, between the two Fusans. In the province of Kyöng-sang in which they are, there are Roman missions which claim 2,000 converts, and to promulgate Christianity in thirty towns and villages. There are two foreign priests, who spend most of the year in teaching in the provincial villages, living in Korean huts, in Korean fashion, on Korean food.

A coarse ocean with a distinct line of demarcation between the blue water of the Sea of Japan and the discoloration of the Yellow Sea, harsh, grim, rocky, brown islands, mostly unin-habited—two monotonously disagreeable days, more islands, muddier water, an estuary and junks, and on the third after-noon from Fusan the *Higo Maru* anchored in the roadstead of Chemulpo, the seaport of Seoul. This cannot pretend to be a harbor, indeed most of the roadstead, such as it is, is a slimy mud flat for much of the day, the tide rising and falling 36 feet. The anchorage, a narrow channel in the shallows, can accommodate five vessels of moderate size. Yet though the mud was *en évidence*, and the low hill behind the town was dull brown, and a drizzling rain was falling, I liked the look of Chemulpo better than I expected, and after becoming ac-quainted with it in various seasons and circumstances, I came to regard it with very friendly feelings. As seen from the roadstead, it is a collection of mean houses, mostly of wood, painted white, built along the edge of the sea and straggling up a verdureless hill, the whole extending for more than a mile from a low point on which are a few trees, crowned by the English Vice-Consulate, a comfortless and unworthy build-ing, to a hill on which are a large decorative Japanese tea-house, a garden, and a Shinto shrine. Salient features there are none, unless the house of a German merchant, an English church, the humble buildings of Bishop Corfe's mission on the hill, the large Japanese Consulate, and some new municipal buildings on a slope, may be considered such. As at Fusan, an English tide-waiter boarded the ship, and a foreign harbor-

HARBOR OF CHEMULPO.

master berthed her, while a Japanese clerk gave the captain his orders.

Mr. Wilkinson, the acting British Vice-Consul, came off for me, and entertained me then and on two subsequent occasions with great hospitality, but as the Vice-Consulate had at that time no guest-room, I slept at a Chinese inn, known as "Steward's," kept by Itai, an honest and helpful man who does all he can to make his guests comfortable, and partially succeeds. This inn is at the corner of the main street of the Chinese quarter, in a very lively position, as it also looks down the main street of the Japanese settlement. The Chinese settlement is solid, with a handsome *yamen* and guild hall, and rows of thriving and substantial shops. Busy and noisy with the continual letting off of crackers and beating of drums and gongs, the Chinese were obviously far ahead of the Japanese in trade. They had nearly a monopoly of the foreign "custom"; their large "houses" in Chemulpo had branches in Seoul, and if there were any foreign requirement which they could not meet, they procured the article from Shanghai without loss of time. The haulage of freight to Seoul was in their hands, and the market gardening, and much besides. Late into the night they were at work, and they used the roadway for drying hides and storing kerosene tins and packing cases. Scarcely did the noise of night cease when the din of morning began. To these hard-working and money-making people rest seemed a superfluity.

The Japanese settlement is far more populous, extensive, and pretentious. Their Consulate is imposing enough for a legation. They have several streets of small shops, which supply the needs chiefly of people of their own nationality, for foreigners patronize Ah Wong and Itai, and the Koreans, who hate the Japanese with a hatred three centuries old, also deal chiefly with the Chinese. But though the Japanese were outstripped in trade by the Chinese, their position in Korea, even before the war, was an influential one. They gave "postal facilities " between the treaty ports and Seoul and carried the foreign mails, and they established branches of the First National Bank[1] in the capital and treaty ports, with which the resident foreigners have for years transacted their business, and in which they have full confidence. I lost no time in opening an account with this Bank in Chemulpo, receiving an English check-book and pass-book, and on all occasions courtesy and all needed help. Partly owing to the fact that English cottons for Korea are made in bales too big for the Lilliputian Korean pony, involving reduction to more manageable dimensions on being landed, and partly to causes which obtain elsewhere, the Japanese are so successfully pushing their cottons in Korea, that while they constituted only 3 per cent. of the imports in 1887, they had risen to something like 40 per cent. in 1894.[2] There is a rapidly growing demand for yarn to be woven on native looms. The Japanese are well to the front with steam and sailing tonnage. Of 198 steamers entered inwards in 1893, 132 were Japanese; and out of 325 sailing vessels, 232 were Japanese. It is on record that an English merchantman was once seen in Chemulpo roads, but actually the British mercantile flag, unless on a chartered steamer, is not known in Korean waters. Nor was there in 1894 an English merchant in the Korean treaty ports, or an English house of business, large or small, in Korea.

Just then rice was in the ascendant. Japan by means of pressure had induced the Korean Government to consent to suspend the decree forbidding its export, and on a certain date the sluices were to be opened. Stacks of rice bags covered the beach, rice in bulk being measured into bags was piled on mats in the roadways, ponies and coolies rice-laden filed in strings down the streets, while in the roadstead a number of Japanese steamers and junks awaited the taking off the embargo at midnight on 6th March. A regular rice babel

[1] Now the *Dai Ichi Gingo.*
[2] For latest trade statistics see appendix B.

prevailed in the town and on the beach, and much disaffection prevailed among the Koreans at the rise in the price of their staple article of diet. Japanese agents scoured the whole country for rice, and every *cattie* of it which could be spared from consumption was bought in preparation for the war of which no one in Korea dreamed at that time. The rice bustle gave Chemulpo an appearance of a thriving trade which it is not wont to have except in the Chinese settlement. Its foreign population in 1897 was 4,357.

The reader may wonder where the Koreans are at Chemulpo, and in truth I had almost forgotten them, for they are of little account. The increasing native town lies outside the Japanese settlement on the Seoul road, clustering round the base of the hill on which the English church stands, and scrambling up it, mud hovels planting themselves on every ledge, attained by filthy alleys, swarming with quiet dirty children, who look on the high-road to emulate the *do-lessness* of their fathers. Korean, too, is the official *yamen* at the top of the hill, and Korean its methods of punishment, its brutal flagellations by *yamen* runners, its beating of criminals to death, their howls of anguish penetrating the rooms of the adjacent English mission, and Korean too are the bribery and corruption which make it and nearly every *yamen* sinks of iniquity. The gate with its double curved roofs and drum chamber over the gateway remind the stranger that though the capital and energy of Chemulpo are foreign, the government is native. Not Korean is the abode of mercy on the other side of the road from the *yamen*, the hospital connected with Bishop Corfe's mission, where in a small Korean building the sick are received, tended, and generally cured by Dr. Landis, who himself lives as a Korean in rooms 8 feet by 6, studying, writing, eating, without chair or table, and accessible at all times to all comers. The 6,700 inhabitants of the Korean town, or rather the male half of them, are always on the move. The narrow roads are always full of them, sauntering along in their dress hats, not apparently doing anything. It is old Fusan over again, except that there are permanent shops, with stocks-in-trade worth from one to twenty dollars; and as an hour is easily spent over a transaction involving a few *cash*, there is an appearance of business kept up. In the settlement the Koreans work as porters and carry preposterous weights on their wooden packsaddles.

GATE OF OLD FUSAN

CHAPTER II

CHEMULPO, being on the island-studded estuary of the Han, which is navigable for the 56 miles up to Ma-pu, the river port of Seoul, it eventually occurred to some persons more enterprising than their neighbors to establish steam communication between the two. Manifold are the disasters which have attended this simple undertaking. Nearly every passenger who has entrusted himself to the river has a tale to tell of the boat being deposited on a sandbank, and of futile endeavors to get off, of fretting and fuming, usually ending in hailing a passing *sampan* and getting up to Ma-pu many hours behind time, tired, hungry, and disgusted. For the steam launches are only half powered for their work, the tides are strong, the river shallows often, and its sandbanks shift almost from tide to tide. Hence this natural highway is not much patronized by people who respect themselves, and all sorts of arrangements are made for getting up to the capital by "road." There is, properly speaking, no road, but the word serves. Mr. Gardner, the British acting Consul-General in Seoul, kindly arranged to escort me the 25 miles, and I went up in seven hours in a chair with six bearers, jolly fellows, who joked and laughed and raced the Consul's pony. Traffic has worn for itself a track, often indefinite, but usually straggling over and sterilizing a width enough for three or four highways, and often making a new departure to avoid deep mud holes. The mud is nearly bottomless. Bullock-carts owned by Chinese attempt the transit of goods, and two or three embedded in the mud till the spring showed with what success. **Near**

Ma-pu all traffic has to cross a small plain of deep sand. Pack bulls, noble animals, and men are the carriers of goods. The redoubtable Korean pony was not to be seen. Foot passengers in dress hats and wadded white garments were fairly numerous.

The track lies through rolling country, well cultivated. There are only two or three villages on the road, but there are many, surrounded by fruit trees, in the folds of the adjacent low hills; stunted pines (*Pinus sinensis*) abound, and often indicate places of burial. The hillsides are much taken up with graves. There are wooden sign or distant posts, with grotesque human faces upon them, chiefly that of Chang Sun, a traitor, whose misdemeanors were committed 1,000 years ago. The general aspect of the country is bare and monotonous. Except for the orchards and the spindly pines, there is no wood. There is no beauty of form, nor any of those signs of exclusiveness, such as gates or walls, which give something of dignity to a landscape. These were my first impressions. But I came to see on later journeys that even on that road there can be a beauty and fascination in the scenery when glorified and idealized by the unrivalled atmosphere of a Korean winter, which it is a delight even to recall, and that the situation of Seoul for a sort of weird picturesqueness compares favorably with that of almost any other capital, but its orientalism, a marked feature of which was its specially self-asserting dirt, is being fast improved off the face of the earth.

From the low pass known as the Gap, there is a view of the hills in the neighborhood of Seoul, and before reaching the Han these, glorified and exaggerated by an effect of atmosphere, took on something of grandeur. Crossing the Han in a scow to which my chair accommodated itself more readily than Mr. Gardner's pony, and encountering ferry boats full of pack bulls bearing the night soil of the city to the country, we landed on the rough, steep, filthy, miry river bank, and were at once in the foul, narrow, slimy, rough street of Ma-pu, a twisted alley full of mean shops for the sale of native commodities, of bulls carrying mountains of brushwood which nearly filled up the roadway; and with a crowd, masculine solely, which swayed and loafed, and did nothing in particular. Some quiet agricultural country, and some fine trees, a resemblance to the land of the Bakhtiari Lurs, in the fact of one man working a spade or shovel, while three others helped him to turn up the soil by an arrangement of ropes, then two chairs with bearers in blue uniforms, carrying Mrs. and Miss Gardner, accompanied by Bishop Corfe, Mr. M'Leavy Brown, the Chief Commissioner of Korean Customs, and Mr. Fox, the Assistant Consul, then the hovels and alleys became thick, and we were in extra-mural Seoul. A lofty wall, pierced by a deep double-roofed gateway, was passed, and ten minutes more of miserable alleys brought us to a breezy hill, crowned by the staring red brick buildings of the English Legation and Consular offices.

The Russian Legation has taken another and a higher, and its loftly tower and fine façade are the most conspicuous objects in the city, while a third is covered with buildings, some Korean and tasteful, but others in a painful style of architecture, a combination of the factory with the meeting-house, belonging to the American Methodist Episcopal Mission, the American Presbyterians occupying a humbler position below. A hill on the other side of the town is dedicated to Japan, and so in every part of the city the foreigner, shut out till 1883, is making his presence felt, and is undermining that which is Korean in the Korean capital by the slow process of contact.

One of the most remarkable indications of the changes which is stealing over the Hermit City is that a nearly finished Roman Catholic Cathedral, of very large size, with a clergy-house and orphanages, occupies one of the most prominent positions in Seoul. The King's father, the Tai-Won-Kun, still actively engaged in politics, is the man who, thirty years ago, persecuted the Roman Christians so cruelly and persistently as to raise up for Korea a "noble army of martyrs."

I know Seoul by day and night, its palaces and its slums, its unspeakable meanness and faded splendors, its purposeless crowds, its mediæval processions, which for barbaric splendor cannot be matched on earth, the filth of its crowded alleys, and its pitiful attempt to retain its manners, customs, and identity as the capital of an ancient monarchy in face of the host of disintegrating influences which are at work, but it is not at first that one "takes it in." I had known it for a year before I appreciated it, or fully realized that it is entitled to be regarded as one of the great capitals of the world, with its supposed population of a quarter of a million, and that few capitals are more beautifully situated.[1] One hundred and twenty feet above the sea, in Lat. 37° 34′ N. and Long. 127° 6′ E., mountain girdled, for the definite peaks and abrupt elevation of its hills give them the grandeur of mountains, though their highest summit, San-kak-San, has only an altitude of 2,627 feet, few cities can boast, as Seoul can, that tigers and leopards are shot within their walls! Arid and forbidding these mountains look at times, their ridges broken up into black crags and pinnacles, ofttimes rising from among distorted pines, but there are evenings of purple glory, when every forbidding peak gleams like an amethyst with a pink translucency, and the shadows are cobalt and the sky is green and gold. Fair are the surroundings too in early spring, when a delicate green mist veils the hills, and their sides are flushed with the heliotrope azalea, and flame of plum, and blush of cherry, and tremulousness of peach blossom appear in unexpected quarters.

Looking down on this great city, which has the aspect of a lotus pond in November, or an expanse of overripe mush-

[1] By a careful census taken in February, 1897, the intra-mural population of Seoul was 144,636 souls, and the extra-mural 75,189, total 219,815, males predominating to the extent of 11,079.

JAPANESE MILITARY CEMETERY, CHEMULPO.

rooms, the eye naturally follows the course of the wall, which is discerned in most outlandish places, climbing Nam-San in one direction, and going clear over the crest of Puk-han in another, enclosing a piece of forest here, and a vacant plain there, descending into ravines, disappearing and reappearing when least expected. This wall, which contrives to look nearly as solid as the hillsides which it climbs, is from 25 to 40 feet in height, and 14 miles in circumference (according to Mr. Fox of H.B.M.'s Consular Service), battlemented along its entire length, and pierced by eight gateways, solid arches or tunnels of stone, surmounted by lofty gate houses with one, two, or three curved tiled roofs. These are closed from sunset to sunrise by massive wooden gates, heavily bossed and strengthened with iron, bearing, following Chinese fashion, high-sounding names, such as the "Gate of Bright Amiability," the "Gate of High Ceremony," the "Gate of Elevated Humanity."

The wall consists of a bank of earth faced with masonry, or of solid masonry alone, and is on the whole in tolerable repair. It is on the side nearest the river, and onwards in the direction of the Peking Pass, that extra-mural Seoul has expanded. One gate is the Gate of the Dead, only a royal corpse being permitted to be carried out by any other. By another gate criminals passed out to be beheaded, and outside another their heads were exposed for some days after execution, hanging from camp-kettle stands. The north gate, high on Puk-han, is kept closed, only to be opened in case the King is compelled to escape to one of the so-called fortresses on that mountain.

Outside the wall is charming country, broken into hills and wooded valleys, with knolls sacrificed to stately royal tombs, with their environment of fine trees, and villages in romantic positions among orchards and garden cultivation. Few Eastern cities have prettier walks and rides in their immediate neighborhood, or greater possibilities of rapid escape into sylvan solitudes, and I must add that no city has environs so safe, and that ladies without a European escort can ride, as I have done, in every direction outside the walls without meeting with the slightest annoyance.

I shrink from describing intra-mural Seoul.[1] I thought it the foulest city on earth till I saw Peking, and its smells the most odious, till I encountered those of Shao-shing ! For a great city and a capital its meanness is indescribable. Etiquette forbids the erection of two-storied houses, consequently an estimated quarter of a million people are living on " the ground," chiefly in labyrinthine alleys, many of them not wide enough for two loaded bulls to pass, indeed barely wide enough for one man to pass a loaded bull, and further narrowed by a series of vile holes or green, slimy ditches, which receive the solid and liquid refuse of the houses, their foul and fetid margins being the favorite resort of half-naked children, begrimed with dirt, and of big, mangy, blear-eyed dogs, which wallow in the slime or blink in the sun. There too the itinerant vendor of "small wares," and candies dyed flaring colors with aniline dyes, establishes himself, puts a few planks across the ditch, and his goods, worth perhaps a dollar, thereon. But even Seoul has its " spring cleaning," and I encountered on the sand plain of the Han, on the ferry, and on the road from Ma-pu to Seoul, innumerable bulls carrying panniers laden with the contents of the city ditches.

The houses abutting on these ditches are generally hovels with deep eaves and thatched roofs, presenting nothing to the street but a mud wall, with occasionally a small paper window just under the roof, indicating the men's quarters, and invariably, at a height varying from 2 to 3 feet above the ditch, a

[1] *Nous avons changé tout cela.* As will be seen from a chapter near the end of the book, the Chief Commissioner of Customs, energetically seconded by the Governor of Seoul, has worked surprising improvements and sanitary changes which, if carried out perseveringly, will redeem the capital from the charges which travellers have brought against it.

blackened smoke-hole, the vent for the smoke and heated air, which have done their duty in warming the floor of the house. All day long bulls laden with brushwood to a great height are entering the city, and at six o'clock this pine brush, preparing to do the cooking and warming for the population, fills every lane in Seoul with aromatic smoke, which hangs over it with remarkable punctuality. Even the superior houses, which have curved and tiled roofs, present nothing better to the street than this debased appearance.

The shops partake of the general meanness. Shops with a stock-in-trade which may be worth six dollars abound. It is easy to walk in Seoul without molestation, but any one standing to look at anything attracts a great crowd, so that it is as well that there is nothing to look at. The shops have literally not a noteworthy feature. Their one characteristic is that they have none! The best shops are near the Great Bell, beside which formerly stood a stone with an inscription calling on all Koreans to put intruding foreigners to death. So small are they that all goods are within reach of the hand. In one of the three broad streets, there are double rows of removable booths, in which now and then a small box of Korean *niello* work, iron inlaid with silver, may be picked up. In these and others the principal commodities are white cottons, straw shoes, bamboo hats, coarse pottery, candlesticks, with draught screens, combs, glass beads, pipes, tobacco pouches, spittoons, horn-rimmed goggles, much worn by officials, paper of many kinds, wooden pillow-ends, decorated pillowcases, fans, inkcases, huge wooden saddles with green leather flaps bossed with silver, laundry sticks, dried persimmons, loathsome candies dyed magenta, scarlet, and green, masses of dried seaweed and fungi, and ill-chosen collections of the most trumpery of foreign trash, such as sixpenny kerosene lamps, hand mirrors, tinsel vases, etc., the genius of bad taste presiding over all.

Plain brass dinner sets and other brass articles are made,

and some mother-of-pearl inlaying in black lacquer from old designs is occasionally to be purchased, and embroideries in silk and gold thread, but the designs are ugly, and the coloring atrocious. Foreigners have bestowed the name Cabinet Street on a street near the English Legation, given up to the making of bureaus and marriage chests. These, though not massive, look so, and are really handsome, some being of solid chestnut wood, others veneered with maple or peach, and bossed, strapped, and hinged with brass, besides being ornamented with great brass hasps and brass padlocks 6 inches long. These, besides being thoroughly Korean, are distinctly decorative. There are few buyers, except in the early morning, and shopping does not seem a pastime, partly because none but the poorest class of women can go out on foot by daylight.

In the booths are to be seen tobacco pipes, pipestems, and bowls, coarse glazed pottery, rice bowls, Japanese lucifer matches, aniline dyes, tobacco pouches, purses, flint and tinder pouches, rolls of oiled paper, tassels, silk cord, nuts of the edible pine, rice, millet, maize, peas, beans, string shoes, old crinoline hats, bamboo and reed hats in endless variety, and coarse native cotton, very narrow.

In this great human hive, the ordinary sightseer finds his vocation gone. The inhabitants constitute the "sight" of Seoul. The great bronze bell, said to be the third largest in the world, is one of the few "sights" usually seen by strangers. It hangs in a bell tower in the centre of the city, and bears the following inscription :—

" Sye Cho the Great, 12th year Man cha [year of the cycle] and moon, the 4th year of the great Ming Emperor Hsüan-hua [A.D. 1468], the head of the bureau of Royal despatches, Sye Ko chyeng, bearing the title Sa Ka Chyeng, had this pavilion erected and this bell hung."

This bell, whose dull heavy boom is heard in all parts of Seoul, has opened and closed the gates for five centuries.

The grand triple gateway of the Royal Palace with its double roof, the old audience hall in the Mulberry Gardens, and the decorative roofs of the gate towers, are all seen in an hour. There remains the Marble Pagoda, seven centuries old, so completely hidden away in the back yard of a house in one of the foulest and narrowest alleys of the city, that many people never see it at all. As I was intent on photographing some of the reliefs upon it, I visited it five times, and each time with fresh admiration; but so *wedged* in is it, that one can only get any kind of view of it by climbing on the top of a wall. Every part is carved, and the flat parts richly so, some of the tablets representing Hindu divinities, while others seem to portray the various stages of the soul's progress towards Nirvana. The designs are undoubtedly Indian, modified by Chinese artists, and this thing of beauty stands on the site of a Buddhist monastery. It is a thirteen-storied pagoda, but three stories were taken off in the Japanese invasion three centuries ago, and placed on the ground uninjured. So they remained, but on my last visit children had defaced the exquisite carving, and were offering portions for sale. Not far off is another relic of antiquity, a decorated and inscribed tablet standing on the back of a granite turtle of prodigious size. Outside the west gate, on a plain near the Peking Pass, was a roofed and highly decorated arch of that form known as the *pailow*, and close by it a sort of palace hall, in which every new sovereign of Korea waited for the coming of a special envoy from Peking, whom he joined at the *pailow*, accompanying him to the palace, where he received from him his investiture as sovereign.

On the slope of Nam-San the white wooden buildings, simple and unpretentious, of the Japanese Legation are situated, and below them a Japanese colony of nearly 5,000 persons, equipped with tea-houses, a theatre, and the various arrangements essential to Japanese well-being. There, in acute contrast to everything Korean, are to be seen streets of shops and houses where cleanliness, daintiness, and thrift reign supreme, and unveiled women, and men in girdled dressing-gowns and clogs, move about as freely as in Japan. There also are to be seen minute soldiers or military police, and smart be-sworded officers, who change guard at due intervals ; nor are such precautions needless, for the heredity of hate is strong in Korea, and on two occasions the members of this Legation have had to fight their way down to the sea. The Legation was occupied at the time of my first visit by Mr. Otori, an elderly man with pendulous white whiskers, who went much into the little society which Seoul boasts, talked nothings, and gave no promise of the rough vigor which he showed a few months later. There also are the Japanese bank and post office, both admirably managed.

The Chinese colony was in 1894 nearly as large, and differed in no respect from such a colony anywhere else. The foreigners depend for many things on the Chinese shops, and as the Koreans like the Chinese, they do some trade with them also. The imposing element connected with China was the *yamen* of Yuan, the Minister Resident and representative of Korea's Suzerain, by many people regarded as "the power behind the throne," who is reported to have gone more than once unbidden into the King's presence, and to have reproached him with his conduct of affairs. Great courtyards and lofty gates on which are painted the usual guardian gods, and a brick dragon screen, seclude the palace in which Yuan lived with his guards and large retinue ; and the number of big, supercilious men, dressed in rich brocades and satins, who hung about both this Palace and the Consulate, impressed the Koreans with the power and stateliness within. The Americans were very severe on Yuan, but so far as I could learn his chief fault was that he let things alone, and neglected to use his unquestionably great power in favor of reform and common honesty—but he was a Chinese mandarin ! He possessed the power of life and death over Chinamen, and his punishments were often to our thinking barbarous, but the Chinese feared him so much that they treated the Koreans fairly well, which is more than can be said of the Japanese.

One of the "sights" of Seoul is the stream or drain or watercourse, a wide, walled, open conduit, along which a dark-colored festering stream slowly drags its malodorous length, among manure and refuse heaps which cover up most of what was once its shingly bed. There, tired of crowds masculine solely, one may be refreshed by the sight of women of the poorest class, some ladling into pails the compound which passes for water, and others washing clothes in the fetid pools which pass for a stream. All wear one costume, which is peculiar to the capital, a green silk coat—a man's coat with the "neck" put over the head and clutched below the eyes, and long wide sleeves falling from the ears. It is as well that the Korean woman is concealed, for she is not a houri. Washing is her manifest destiny so long as her lord wears white. She washes in this foul river, in the pond of the Mulberry Palace, in every wet ditch, and outside the walls in the few streams which exist. Clothes are partially unpicked, boiled with ley three times, rolled into hard bundles, and pounded with heavy sticks on stones. After being dried they are beaten with wooden sticks on cylinders, till they attain a polish resembling dull satin. The women are slaves to the laundry, and the only sound which breaks the stillness of a Seoul night is the regular beat of their laundry sticks.

From the beautiful hill Nam-San, from the Lone Tree Hill, and from a hill above the old Mulberry Palace, Seoul is best seen, with its mountainous surroundings, here and there dark with pines, but mostly naked, falling down upon the city in black arid corrugations. These mountains enclose a valley about 5 miles long by 3 broad, into which 200,000 people are crammed and wedged. The city is a sea of low brown roofs, mostly of thatch, and all but monotonous, no trees and no open spaces. Rising out of this brown sea there are the curved double roofs of the gates, and the gray granite walls of the royal palaces, and within them the sweeping roofs of various audience halls. Cutting the city across by running from the east to the west gate is one broad street, another striking off from this runs to the south gate, and a third 60 yards wide runs from the great central artery to the palace. This is the only one which is kept clear of encumbrance at all times, the others being occupied by double rows of booths, leaving only a narrow space for traffic on either side. When I first looked down on Seoul early in March, one street along its whole length appeared to be still encumbered with the drift of the previous winter's snow. It was only by the aid of a glass that I discovered that this is the great promenade, and that the snowdrift was just the garments of the Koreans, whitened by ceaseless labor with the laundry sticks. In these three broad streets the moving crowd of men in white robes and black dress hats seldom flags. They seem destitute of any object. Many of them are of the *yang-ban* or noble class, to whom a rigid etiquette forbids any but official or tutorial occupation, and many of whom exist by hanging on to their more fortunate relatives. Young men of the middle class imitate their nonchalance and swinging gait.

There, too, are to be seen officials, superbly dressed, mounted on very fat but handsome ponies, with profuse manes and tails, the riders sitting uneasily on the tops of saddles with showy caparisonings a foot high, holding on to the saddle bow, two retainers leading the steed, and two more holding the rider in his place; or officials in palanquins, with bearers at a run, amid large retinues. In the more plebeian streets nothing is to be seen but bulls carrying pine brush, strings of ponies loaded with salt or country produce, water-carriers with pails slung on a yoke, splashing their contents, and coolies carrying burdens on wooden pack saddles.

But in the narrower alleys, of which there are hundreds,

further narrowed by the low deep eaves, and the vile ditches outside the houses, only two men can pass each other, and the noble red bull with his load of brushwood is rarely seen. Between these miles of mud walls, deep eaves, green slimy ditches, and blackened smoke holes, few besides the male inhabitants and burden bearers are seen to move. They are the paradise of mangy dogs. Every house has a dog and a square hole through which he can just creep. He yelps furiously at a stranger, and runs away at the shaking of an umbrella. He was the sole scavenger of Seoul, and a very inefficient one. He is neither the friend nor companion of man. He is ignorant of Korean and every other spoken language. His bark at night announces peril from thieves. He is almost wild. When young he is killed and eaten in spring.

I have mentioned the women of the lower classes, who wash clothes and draw water in the daytime. Many of these were domestic slaves, and all are of the lowest class. Korean women are very rigidly secluded, perhaps more absolutely so than the women of any other nation. In the capital a very curious arrangement prevailed. About eight o'clock the great bell tolled a signal for men to retire into their houses, and for women to come out and amuse themselves, and visit their friends. The rule which clears the streets of men occasionally lapses, and then some incident occurs which causes it to be rigorously reënforced. So it was at the time of my arrival, and the pitch dark streets presented the singular spectacle of being tenanted solely by bodies of women with servants carrying lanterns. From its operation were exempted blind men, officials, foreigners' servants, and persons carrying prescriptions to the druggists'. These were often forged for the purpose of escape from durance vile, and a few people got long staffs and personated blind men. At twelve the bell again boomed, women retired, and men were at liberty to go abroad. A lady of high position told me that she had never seen the streets of Seoul by daylight.

The nocturnal silence is very impressive. There is no human hum, throb, or gurgle. The darkness too is absolute, as there are few if any lighted windows to the streets. Upon a silence which may be felt, the deep, penetrating boom of the great bell breaks with a sound which is almost ominous.

TURTLE STONE

CHAPTER III

THE KUR-DONG

BEFORE leaving England letters from Korea had warned me of the difficulty of travelling in the interior, of getting a trustworthy servant, and above all, a trustworthy interpreter. Weeks passed by, and though Bishop Corfe and others exerted themselves on my behalf, these essential requisites were not forthcoming, for to find a reliable English-speaking Korean is well-nigh impossible. There are English-speaking Koreans who have learned English, some in the Government School, and others in the Methodist Episcopal School, and many of these I interviewed. The English of all was infirm, and they were all limp and timid, a set of poor creatures. Some of them seemed very anxious to go with me, and were partially engaged, and the next day came, looking uneasy, and balanc· ing themselves on the edge of their chairs, told me that their mothers said they must not go because there were tigers, or that three months was too long a journey, or that they could not go so far from their families, etc. At last a young man came who really spoke passable English, but on entering the room with a familiar nod, he threw himself down in an easy-chair, swinging his leg over the arm! He asked many questions about the journey, said it was very long to be away from Seoul, and that he should require one horse for his baggage and another for himself. I remarked that, in order to get through the difficulties of the journey, it would be necessary to limit the baggage as much as possible. He said he could not go with fewer than nine suits of clothes.! I remarked that a foreigner would only take two, and that I should reduce my-

49

self to two. "Yes," he replied, "but foreigners are so dirty in their habits." This from a Korean! So once more I had to settle down, and accept the kindly hospitality of my friends, trusting that something would "turn up."

By this delay I came in for the *Kur-dong*,[1] one of the most remarkable spectacles I ever saw, and it had the added interest of being seen in its splendor for probably the last time, as circumstances which have since occurred, and the necessity for economy, must put an end to much of the scenic display. The occasion was a visit of the King in state to sacrifice in one of the ancestral temples of his dynasty, members of which have occupied the Korean throne for five centuries. Living secluded in his palace, guarded by 1,000 men, his subjects forbidden to pronounce his name, which indeed is seldom known, in total ignorance of any other aspect of his kingdom and capital than that furnished by the two streets through which he passes to offer sacrifice, the days on which he performs this pious act offer to his subjects their sole opportunities of gazing on his august countenance. As the Queen's procession passed by on the day of the Duke of York's marriage, I heard a workingman say, "It's we as pays, and we likes to get the valey for our money." The Korean pays in another and heavier sense, and as in tens of thousands he crowds in reverential silence the route of the *Kur-dong*, he is probably glad that the one brilliant spectacle of the year should be as splendid as possible.

The monotony of Seoul is something remarkable. Brown mountains "picked out" in black, brown mud walls, brown roofs, brown roadways, whether mud or dust, while humanity is in black and white. Always the same bundled-up women clutching their green coats under their eyes, always the same surge of *yang-bans* and their familiars swinging along South

---

[1] If an apology be necessary for the following minute description of this unique ceremonial, I offer it on the ground that it was probably the last of its kind, and that full details of it have not been given before.

Street, the same strings of squealing ponies "spoiling for a fight," the same processions of majestic red bulls under towering loads of brushwood, the same coolies in dirty white, forever carrying burdens, the same joyless dirty children getting through life on the gutters' edge, and the same brownish dogs, feebly wrangling over offal. On such monotony and colorlessness, the *Kur-dong* bursts like the sun. Alas for this mean but fascinating capital, that the most recent steps towards civilization should involve the abolition of its one spectacle!

By six in the morning of the looked-for day we were on our way from the English Legation to a position near the Great Bell, all the male population of the alleys taking the same direction, along with children in colors, and some of the poorer class of women with gay handkerchiefs folded Roman fashion on their hair. For the first time I saw the grand proportions of the road called by foreigners South Street. The double rows of booths had been removed the night before, and along the side of the street, at intervals of 20 yards, torches 10 feet high were let into the ground to light the King on his return from sacrificing. It is only by its imposing width that this great street lends itself to such a display, for the houses are low and mean, and on one side at least are only superior hovels. In place of the booths the subjects were massed twelve deep, the regularity of the front row being preserved by a number of *yamen* runners, who brought down their wooden paddles with an unmerciful whack on any one breaking the line. The singular monotony of baggy white coats and black crinoline hats was relieved by boy bridegrooms in yellow hats and rose pink coats, by the green silk coats of women, and the green, pink, heliotrope and Turkey red dresses of children. The crowd had a quietly pleased but very limp look. There was no jollity or excitement, no flags or popular demonstrations, and scarcely a hum from a concourse which must have numbered at least 150,000, half the city, together with numbers from the country who had walked

three and four days to see the spectacle. Squalid and mean
is ordinary Korean life, and the King is a myth for most of
the year. No wonder that the people turn out to see as splendid a spectacle as the world has to show, its splendor centring
round their usually secluded sovereign. It is to the glory of a
dynasty which has occupied the Korean throne for five centuries as well as in honor of the present occupant.

The hour of leaving the palace had been announced as 6 A.
M., but though it was 7.30 before the boom of a heavy gun
announced that the procession was in motion, the interest
never flagged the whole time. Hundreds of coolies sprinkled
red earth for the width of a foot along the middle of the
streets, for hypothetically the King must not pass over soil
which has been trodden by the feet of his subjects. Squad-
rons of cavalry, with coolies leading their shabby ponies, took
up positions along the route, and in a great mass in front of
us. The troopers sat on the ground smoking, till a very *dis-
trait* bugle-call sent them to their saddles. The ponies bit,
kicked, and squealed, and the grotesque and often ineffectual
attempts of the men to mount them provoked the laughter of
the crowd, as one trooper after another, with one foot in the
stirrup and the other on the ground, hopped round at the
pleasure of his steed. After all, with the help of their coolies,
were mounted, whacks secretly administered by men in the
crowd nearly unhorsed many of them, but they clung with
both hands to their saddle bows and eventually formed into a
ragged line.

Among the very curious sights were poles carried at measured distances supporting rectangular frames resembling small
umbrella stands, filled with feathered arrows, and messengers
dashing along as if they had been shot and were escaping from
another shaft, for from the backs of their collars protruded
arrows which had apparently entered obliquely. Either on
the back or breast or both of the superb dresses of officials
were satin squares embroidered in unique designs, representing

birds and beasts, storks indicating civil, and tigers military, rank, while the number of birds or animals on the lozenge denoted the wearer's exact position.

Though there were long stretches of silence, scarcely broken by the hum of a multitude, there were noisy interludes, novel in their nature, produced by men, sometimes fifteen in a row, who carried poles with a number of steel rings loosely strung upon them, which they tossed into the air and allowed to fall against each other with a metallic clink, loud and strident. Likewise the trains of servants in attendance on mandarins emitted peculiar cries, sounding *G* in unison, then raising their note and singing *C* three times, afterwards, with a falling cadence, singing *G* again.

But of the noises which passed for music, the most curious as to method was that made by the drummers, who marched irregularly in open order in lines extending across the broad roadway. These carried bowl-shaped kettledrums slung horizontally, and bass drum sticks mainly hidden by their voluminous sleeves. In time with the marching, the right hand stick rose above the drummer's head, then the left stick in like manner, but both fell again nearly to the drum without emitting a sound! The next act of the performance consisted in lifting both sticks above the head together and again bringing them down silently. Finally the sticks were crossed, and during two marching steps rose feebly, and as feebly fell on the ends of the drum, producing a muffled sound, and this programme was repeated during the duration of the march.

Soldiers in rusty black belted frocks, wide trousers, bandaged into padded socks, and straw shoes, stacked arms in a side street. Closed black and colored chairs went past at a trot. Palace attendants in hundreds in brown glazed cotton sleeved cloaks, blue under robes tied below the knee with bunches of red ribbon, and stiff black hats, with heavy fan-shaped plumes of peacock's feathers, rode ragged ponies on gay saddles of great height, without bridles, the animals being led by coolies. High officials passed in numbers in chairs or on pony back, each with from twenty to thirty gay attendants running beside him, and a row of bannermen extending across the broad street behind him, each man with a silk banner bearing the cognomen of his lord. These officials were superbly dressed, and made a splendid show. They wore black, high-crowned hats, with long crimson tassels behind, and heavy, black ostrich plumes falling over the brim in front, mazarine blue silk robes, split up to the waist behind, with orange silk under robes and most voluminous crimson trousers, loosely tied above the ankles with knots of sky blue ribbon, while streamers of ribbon fell from throats and girdles, and the hats were secured by throat lashes of large amber beads. Each carried over his shoulder a yellow silk banneret with his style in Chinese characters in crimson upon it, and in the same hand his baton of office, with a profusion of streamers of rich ribbons depending from it. The sleeves were orange in the upper part and crimson in the lower, and very full.

The overfed and self-willed ponies, chiefly roan and gray, are very handsome, and showily caparisoned, the heads covered with blue, red, and yellow balls, and surmounted with great crimson silk pompons, the bridles a couple of crimson silk scarves, the saddles a sort of leather-covered padded pack saddle 12 inches above the animal's back, with wide, deep flaps of bright green silver-bossed leather hanging down on either side, the cruppers folded white silk, and the breastplate shields of gold embroidery. The gorgeous rider, lifted by his servants upon this elevation, stands erect in his stirrups with his feet not halfway down his pony's sides, his left hand clutching rather than holding an arch placed for this purpose at the bow of the saddle. These officials made no attempt to hold their own bridles, their ponies were led by servants, retainers supported them by the feet on either side, and as their mounts showed their resentment of the pace and circumstances by twistings and strugglings with their grooms, the faces of the riders expressed "a fearful joy," if "joy" it was.

Waves of color and Korean grandeur rolled by, official processions, palace attendants, bannermen, with large silk banners trailing on the stiff breeze, each flagstaff crested with a tuft of pheasant's feathers, the King's chief cook, with an enormous retinue, more palace servants, smoking long pipes, drummers, fifers, couriers at a gallop, with arrows stuck into the necks of their coats, holding on to their saddles and rope bridles, mixed up with dishevelled ponies with ragged pack saddles, carrying cushions, lacquer boxes, eatables, cooking utensils, and smoking apparatus, led caparisoned ponies, bowmen, soldiers straggling loosely, armed with matchlock guns, till several thousand persons had passed. Yet this was not the procession, though it might well have served for one.

At 7.30, while this "march past" was still going on, a gun was fired, and the great bell, which was very close to us, boomed heavily, and a fanfaronade of trumpets and the shrill scream of fifes announced that Li Hsi had at last left the palace. The cavalry opposite us prepared to receive His Majesty by *turning tail*, a manœuvre not accomplished without much squealing and fighting. There was a general stir among the spectators, men with arrows in their coats galloped frantically, there was an onslaught on the "Derby dog," and an attack by men, armed with the long wooden paddles which are used for beating criminals, on inoffensive portions of the crowd.

It is said that there were 5,000 servants and officials connected with the palace, and there were nominally 6,000 soldiers in Seoul, and the greater part of these took part in the many splendid processions which went to form the Royal procession. It would be impossible for a stranger to give in detail the component parts of such a show, the like of which has no existence elsewhere on earth, passing for more than an hour in the bright sunshine, in detachments, in compact masses, at a stately walk or a rapid run, in the full spendor of a barbaric mediævalism, or to say what dignitaries flashed by in the kaleidoscopic blaze of color.

The procession of the King was led by the "general of the vanguard," superbly dressed, supported by retainers on his led pony, and followed by crowds of dignitaries, each with his train, soldiers, men carrying aloft frames of arrows, reaching nearly across the road, and huge flags of silk brocade surmounted by plumes of pheasant's feathers, servants in rows of a hundred in the most delicate shades of blue, green, or mauve silk gauze over white, halberdiers, grandees, each with a retinue of bannermen, rows of royal bannermen carrying yellow and blue silk flags emblazoned, cavalry men in imitation gold helmets and mediæval armor, and tiger hunters wearing coarse black felt hats with conical crowns and dark blue coats, trailing long guns. With scarcely a pause followed the President of the Foreign Office, high above the crowd on a monocycle, a black wheel supporting on two uprights a black platform, carrying a black chair decorated with a leopard skin, the occupant of which was carried by eight men at a height of 8 feet from the ground. More soldiers, bannermen, and drummers, and then came the chief of the eunuchs, grandly dressed, with an immense retinue, and a large number of his subordinates, most of whom up to that time, by their position in the palace and their capacity for intrigue, had exercised a very baneful influence on Korean affairs.

The procession became more quaint and motley still. Palace attendants appeared in the brilliant garments of the Korean middle ages; cavalry in antique armor were jumbled up with cavalry in loose cotton frocks and baggy trousers, supposed to be dressed and armed in European fashion, but I failed to detect the flattery of imitation. There were cavalry in black Tyrolese hats with pink ribbon round them, black cotton sacks loosely girdled by leather belts with brass clasps never cleaned, white wadded stockings, and hempen shoes. Some had leather saddles, others rode on pack saddles, with the great pad which should go underneath on the top; some held on to their saddles, others to their rope bridles, the ponies of some were led by coolies in dirty white clothes; the officers were all held on their saddles, many tucked their old-fashioned swords under their arms, lest carrying them in regulation fashion should make their animals kick; the feet of some nearly touched the ground, and those of others hung only halfway down their ponies' sides; ponies squealed, neighed, reared, and jibbed, but somehow or other these singular horsemen managed to form ragged lines.

Then came foot soldiers with rusty muskets and innumerable standards, generals, court dignitaries, statesmen, some with crimson hats with heavy black plumes, others with high peaked crinoline hats with projecting wings, others with lofty mitres covered with tinsel gleaming like gold, each with a splendid train. Mediæval costumes blazing with color flashed past, there were more soldiers, and this time they carried Snider rifles, two Gatling guns were dragged by *yamen* runners, who frantically spanked all and sundry with their paddles, drummers beat their drums unmercifully, fifes shrieked, there were more dignitaries with fairylike retinues in blue and green silk gauze, the King's personal attendants in crowds followed in yellow, with bamboo hats trimmed with rosettes, standard-bearers came next, bearing the Royal standard, a winged tiger rampant on a yellow ground, more flags and troops, and then the curious insignia of Korean Royalty, including a monstrous red silk umbrella, and a singular frame of stones. More grandees, more soldiers, more musical instruments, and then come the Royal chairs, the first, which was canopied with red silk, being empty, the theory being that this was the more likely to receive an assassin's blow. A huge trident was carried in front of it. After this, borne high aloft by forty bearers clothed in red, in a superb chair of red lacquer, richly tasselled and canopied, and with wings to keep off the sun, came the King, whose pale, languid face never changed its expression as he passed with all the dignity and splendor of his kingdom through the silent crowd.

More grandees, servants, soldiers, standard-bearers, arrow-men, officials, cavalry, and led horses formed the procession of the Crown Prince, who was also carried in a red palanquin, and looked paler and more impassive than his father. The supply of officials seemed inexhaustible, for behind him came a quarter of a mile of grandees in splendid costumes, with hats decorated with red velvet and peacock's feathers, and throat lashes of great amber beads, with all their splendid trains, foot-men in armor bossed with large nails, drummers, men carrying arrow frames and insignia on poles, then the "general of the rear guard" in a gleaming helmet and a splendid blue, crimson, and gold uniform, propped up by retainers on his handsome pony, more soldiers armed with old matchlock guns, lastly men bearing arrow frames and standards, and with them the barbaric and bizarre splendor of the *Kur-dong* was over, and the white crowd once more overflowed the mean street. Quite late in the evening the Royal pageant returned by the light of stationary torches, with lanterns of blue and crimson silk undulating from the heads of pikes and bayonets.

This truly splendid display was estimated to cost $25,000— a heavy burden on the small resources of the kingdom. It is only thus surrounded that the King ever appears in public, and the splendor accentuates the squalor of the daily life of the masses of the people in the foul alleys which make up most of the city. It must be remembered that the people taking part in the pageant are not men hired and dressed up by a *costumier*, but that they are actual Court officials and noblemen in the dress of to-day, and that the weapons carried by the soldiers are those with which they are supposed to repel attack or put down rebellion.

CHAPTER IV

SEOUL, THE KOREAN MECCA

FURTHER difficulties and delays, while they pushed my journey into the interior into the hot weather, gave me the advantage of learning a little about the people and the country before starting. In one sense Seoul is Korea. Take a mean alley in it with its mud-walled hovels, deep-eaved brown roofs, and malodorous ditches with their foulness and green slime, and it may serve as an example of the street of every village and provincial town. In country places there are few industrial specialties. A Seoul shop of "assorted notions" represents the shop of every country town. The white clothing and the crinoline dress hat are the same everywhere as in Seoul. Whatever of national life there is exists only in the capital. Strong as is the drift towards London in our own agricultural districts, it is stronger in Korea towards Seoul. Seoul is not only the seat of government, but it is the centre of official life, of all official employment, and of the literary examinations which were the only avenues to employment. It is always hoped that something may be "picked up" in Seoul. Hence there is a constant permanent or temporary gravitation towards it, and the larger proportion of the youths who swing and lounge on sunny afternoons along the broad streets, aping the gait of *yang-bans*, are aspirants for official position. Gusts of popular feeling which pass for public opinion in a land where no such thing exists are known only in Seoul. It is in the capital that the Korean feels the first stress of his unsought and altogether undesired contact with Western civilization, and resembles nothing so much as a man awaking from a profound

59

sleep, rubbing his eyes half-dazed and looking dreamily about him, not quite sure where he is.

Seoul is also the commercial centre of a country whose ideas of commerce are limited to huckstering transactions. All business is done there. All country shops are supplied with goods from Seoul. All produce not shipped from the treaty ports converges on Seoul. It is the centre of the great trading guilds, which exercise a practical monopoly in certain sorts of goods, as well as of the guild of porters by whom the traffic of the country is carried on. The heart of every Korean is in Seoul. Officials have town houses in the capital, and trust their business to subordinates for much of the year. Landed proprietors draw their rents and "squeeze" the people on their estates, but are absentees living in the capital. Every man who can pay for food and lodging on the road trudges to the capital once or twice a year, and people who live in it, of whatever degree, can hardly be bribed to leave it even for a few weeks. To the Korean it is the place in which alone life is worth living.

Yet it has no objects of art, very few antiquities, no public gardens, no displays except the rare one of the *Kur-dong*, and no theatres. It lacks every charm possessed by other cities. Antique, it has no ruins, no libraries, no literature, and lastly an indifference to religion without a parallel has left it without temples, while certain superstitions which still retain their hold have left it without a tomb !

Leaving out the temple of Confucius and the homage officially rendered to his tablet in Korea as in China, there are no official temples in Seoul, nor might a priest enter its gates under pain of death, consequently the emphasis which noble religious buildings give even to the meanest city in China or Japan is lacking. There is a small temple to the God of War outside the south gate, with some very curious frescoes, but I seldom saw any worshippers there. The absence of temples is a feature of the other Korean cities. Buddhism, which for

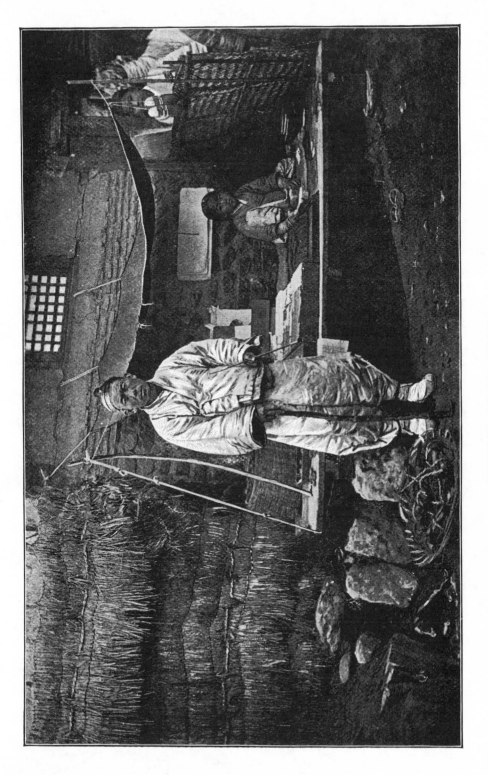

GUTTER SHOP, SEOUL

1,000 years before the founding of the present dynasty was the popular cult, has been "disestablished" and practically proscribed since the sixteenth century, and Koreans account for the severe enactments against priests by saying that in the Japanese invasion three centuries ago Japanese disguised themselves as Buddhist priests and gained admission to cities, putting their garrisons to the sword. Be that true or false, Buddhism in Korea to be found must be sought.

As there are no temples, so there are no other signs of religion, and the hasty observer would be warranted in putting down the Koreans as a people without a religion. Ancestral worship, and a propitiation of dæmons or spirits, the result of a timid and superstitious dread of the forces of Nature, are to the Korean in place of a religion. Both, I am inclined to believe, are the result of fear, the worship of ancestors being dictated far less by filial piety than by the dread that ancestral spirits may do harm to their descendants. This cult prevails from the King to the coolie. It inspires the costly splendors of the *Kur-dong*, as well as the spread of ancestral food in the humblest hovel on New Year's Eve.

The graves within an area of ten miles from the city wall are among the remarkable features of this singular capital. The dead have a monopoly of the fine hill slopes and southern aspects. A man who when alive is content with a mud hovel in a dingy alley, when dead must repose on a breezy hill slope with dignified and carefully tended surroundings. The little fine timber which exists in the denuded neighborhood of Seoul is owed to the Royal and wealthy dead. The amount of good land occupied by the dead is incredible. The grave of a member of the Royal family on a hill creates a solitude for a considerable distance around. In the case of rich and great men as well as of princes, the grave is a lofty grassy mound, often encircled by a massive stone railing, with the hill terraced in front and excavated in a horseshoe shape behind. A stone altar and stone lanterns are placed in front, and the foot of the hill, as at the "Princess's Tomb," is often occupied by a temple-like building containing tablets with the name and rank of the dead.   The Royal tombs are approached by stately avenues of gigantic stone figures, possibly a harmless survival of the practice of offering human and other sacrifices at a burial. These figures represent a priest, a warrior in armor, a servant, a pony, and a sheep (?).   The poorer dead occupy hillsides in numbers, resting under grass mounds on small platforms of grass always neatly kept.   The lucky place for interment is in all cases chosen by the geomancer.   Behind rich men's graves pines are usually planted in a crescent.   The dead population of the hillsides round Seoul is simply enormous.

Funerals usually go out near dusk with a great display of colored lanterns, but I was fortunate enough to see an artisan's corpse carried out by daylight.   First came four drums and a sort of fife perpetrating a lively tune as an accompaniment to a lively song.   These were followed by a hearse, if it may be called so, a domed and gaudily painted construction with a garland of artificial flowers in the centre of the dome, a white Korean coat thrown across the roof, and four flagstaffs with gay flags at the four corners, bamboo poles, flower-wreathed, forming a platform on which the hearse was borne by eight men in peaked yellow hats garlanded with blue and pink flowers.   Bouquets of the same were disposed carelessly on the front and sides of the hearse, the latter being covered with shield-shaped flags of gaudily colored muslin.   The chief mourner followed, completely clothed in sackcloth, wearing an umbrella-shaped hat over 4 feet in diameter, and holding a sackcloth screen before his face by two bamboo handles.   Men in flower-wreathed hats surrounded him, some of them walking backwards and singing.   He looked fittingly grave, but it is a common custom for those who attend the chief mourner to try to make him laugh by comic antics and jocular remarks. There are "burial clubs" in Seoul to which 100,000 *cash* are contributed (then worth about thirty-three dollars, silver).

The first man to die receives 30,000 *cash*, the second 33,000, and the third 37,000. This man had belonged to one of these, which accounts for an artisan having such a handsome funeral.

Mourners dress in straw-colored hempen cloth, and all wear the enormous hats mentioned before, which so nearly conceal the face that the carrying of the grass-cloth screen is almost a work of supererogation. A mourner may not enter the palace grounds, and as mourning for a father lasts for three years, a courtier thus bereaved is for that time withdrawn from Court.

Among the curious customs mainly of Chinese origin connected with death are the dressing the dying person in his best clothes when death is very close at hand. The very poor are buried coffinless in a wrapping of straw, and are carried by two men on a bier, the nature of the burden being concealed by hoops covered with paper.

When Buddhist priests and temples were prohibited in the walled towns three centuries ago, anything like a national faith disappeared from Korea, and it is only through ancestral worship and a form of " Shamanism " practiced by the lower and middle classes that any recognition of the unseen survives, and that is in its most superstitious and rudimentary form. Protestant Christian missionaries, preceded in 1784 by those of the Roman Catholic Church, entered Korea in 1884, almost as soon as the country was opened by treaty, and agents of the American Methodist Episcopal and Northern Presbyterian Churches took up their abode in Seoul. They have been followed by representatives of several of the divisions among Protestants—Southern Presbyterians, Canadian Presbyterians, Australian Presbyterians, and Baptists—and in 1890 the first English mission to Korea was founded under Bishop Corfe. A Roman Catholic Church and a very large Roman Catholic Cathedral with a spire occupy two of the most prominent sites in Seoul. One of the best sites is covered with the buildings belonging to the Methodist Episcopal Mission, schools for girls and boys, a printing press, a Union Church, and hospitals for men and women, with which dispensaries are connected. The girls' school connected with this mission is one of the most admirable in its organization and results that I have seen. The Presbyterians occupy a lowlier position, but have the same class of agencies at work, and lately the King handed over to them a large hospital in the city, known as the "Government Hospital."

Bishop Corfe's mission occupies two modest sites in modest fashion, all its buildings being strictly Korean. On one side of Seoul, at Nak-tong, it has the Community House, where the bishop, clergy, doctor, and printer live and have their private chapel, also the Mission press, and a very efficient hospital for men, admirably nursed by the Sisters of St. Peter's Kilburn. On the slope of the British Legation Hill are the English Church of the Advent, a beautiful Korean building, the Community House of the Sisters of St. Peter, and the Women's Hospital buildings, embracing a dispensary, a new hospital (the Dora Bird Memorial) of eighteen beds, with a room for a private patient, besides an old hospital, to be used only for infectious diseases. These are under the charge of a lady physician, and are also nursed by the Sisters of St. Peter, who in both hospitals do admirable work in a bright and loving spirit which is beyond all praise.

There are about 75 Protestant and 34 Roman missionaries in Korea, mostly in Seoul. The language has the reputation of being very difficult, and few of this large number have acquired facility in the use of it. The idea of a nation destitute of a religion, and gladly accepting one brought by the foreigner, must be dropped. The religion the Korean would accept is one which would show him how to get money without working for it. The indifference is extreme, the religious faculty is absent, there are no religious ideas to appeal to, and the moral teachings of Confucius have little influence with any class.

The Korean has got on so well without a religion, in his own opinion, that he does not want to be troubled with one, specially a religion of restraint and sacrifice which has no worldly good to offer. After nearly twelve years of work, the number of baptized native Protestant Christians in 1897 was 777.[1] The Roman Catholics claim 28,802, and that the average rate of increase is 1,000 a year.[2] Their priests live mostly in the wretched hovels of the people, amidst their foul surroundings, and share their unpalatable food and sordid lives. Doubtless, mission work in Korea will not differ greatly from such work elsewhere among the older civilizations. Barriers of indifference, superstition, and inertness exist, and whatever progress is made will probably be chiefly through medical missions, showing Christianity in action, and native agency, and through such schools as I have already alluded to, which leave every feature of Korean custom, dress, and manner of living untouched, while Christian instruction and training are the first objects, and where the gentle, loving, ennobling influence of the teacher is felt during every hour of the day.

[1] In 1897 the influence of Christianity was much stronger than in 1895, and the prospects of its spread much more encouraging.

[2] For statistics of Missions in February, 1897, see Appendix.

CHAPTER V

THE SAILING OF THE SAMPAN

AT a point when the difficulties in the way of my projected journey had come to be regarded as insurmountable, owing to the impossibility of getting an interpreter, and I had begun to say "*if* I go" instead of "*when* I go," Mr. Miller, a young missionary, offered his services, on condition that he might take his servant to supplement his imperfect knowledge of Korean. Bishop Corfe provided me with a Chinese servant, Wong, a fine, big, cheery fellow, with inexhaustible good-nature and contentment, never a cloud of annoyance on his face, always making the best of everything, ready to help every one, true, honest, plucky, passionately fond of flowers, faithful, manly, always well and hungry, and with a passable knowledge of English ! He was a Chefoo *sampan*-man when Bishop Corfe picked him up, and nothing could make him into a regular servant, but he suited me admirably, and I was grieved indeed when I had to part with him.

The difficulty about money which then beset every traveller in the interior cost a good deal of anxious planning. The Japanese *yen* and its subdivisions were only current in Seoul and the treaty ports, there were no bankers or money-changers anywhere, and the only coin accepted was the *cash*, of which at that time 3,200 nominally went to the dollar. This coin is strung in hundreds on straw strings, and the counting of it, and the carrying of it, and the being without it are all a nuisance. It takes six men or one pony to carry 100 *yen* in *cash*, £10 ! Travellers, through their Consuls, can obtain from the Foreign Office a letter to officials throughout the country called a *kwan-ja*, entitling the bearer to their good

THE AUTHOR'S SAMPAN, HAN RIVER.

offices, and especially to food, transport, and money. But as it usually happens that a magistrate advancing money to a foreigner is not repaid by the Government, however accurately the sum has been paid in Seoul, the arrangement is a very odious one to officials, and I promised our Consul that I would not make use of it for money. Consequently, the boat which I engaged for the earlier part of the journey was ballasted with *cash*, and I took a bag of silver *yen*, and trusted to my usual good fortune, which in this case did not altogether fail.

In addition to this uncouth and heavy burden, I took a saddle, a trestle-bed with bedding and mosquito net, muslin curtains, a folding chair, two changes of clothing, Korean string shoes, and a " regulation " waterproof cloak. Besides, I took green tea, curry powder, and 20 ℔s. of flour. I discarded all superfluities, such as flasks, collapsing cups, hand mirrors, teapots, sandwich tins, lamps, and tinned soups, meats, bouillon, and fruits. The kitchen equipment consisted of a Japanese brazier for charcoal, a shallow Japanese pan and frying-pan, and a small kettle, with charcoal tongs, the whole costing under two dollars ! The " table equipment " was limited : a small mug, two plates and a soup plate, all in enamelled iron, and a knife, fork, and spoon, which folded up, a knife, fork, and spoon of common make being reserved for the " kitchen." Tables, trays, tablecloths, and sheets were from thenceforth unknown luxuries. I mention my outfit, because I know it to be a sufficient one, and that every pound of superfluous weight adds to the difficulty of getting transport in Korea and in many other countries. Besides, I was encumbered for the first time with a tripod camera weighing 16 ℔s., and a hand camera weighing 4 ℔s., with the apparatus belonging to them, and had to reduce other things accordingly. On the whole, it is best to trust to the food of the country. Korea produces eggs, and in some regions chickens. The chestnuts are good, and though the flour, which can be got in a few places, is gritty, and the rice is a bad color, both are eatable, and the foreigner, always an object of suspicion, is less so when he buys and eats native viands, and does not carry about with him a number of (to Koreans) outlandish-looking utensils and commodities.

Regarding much of the region which I purposed to visit no information could be obtained, either from Europeans or Korean officials, and the best map, a reduction of a Japanese map by Sir E. Satow, turned out to be astray. Mr. Warner, of Bishop Corfe's Mission, had ascended the north branch of the Han, but it is still doubtful whether any European has been up the south and much larger branch which I explored on this journey. It was certain only that the country was mountainous, and that the rapids were numerous and severe. It had also been said earnestly, and with an appearance of knowledge, by several people that it would be impossible for a lady to travel in the interior; and certainly much of what I heard, supposing it to be fact, was sufficiently deterring, but from many similar statements in other countries I knew that a deduction of at least fifty per cent. must be made!

On the 14th of April, 1894, when the environs of Seoul were seen through a mist of green, and plum and peach blossom was in the ascendant, and the heliotrope azalea was just beginning to tint the hillsides, and the air was warm and muggy, I left the kind friends who had done much to make my visit to Seoul interesting and agreeable, and went on ponyback through the south gate, passing the temple of the God of War, and over a pine-clothed ridge of Nam-San to Han Kang, four miles from Seoul, a little shipping village, where my boat lay, to avoid a rapid which lies between it and Ma-pu. Up to Ma-pu, 56 miles from Chemulpo, there is a very considerable tidal rise and fall which ceases at the rapid.

A limp, silent crowd of men and boys denoted the whereabouts of the boat, from which Mr. Miller's servant, Che-on-i, emerging with the broad smile with which Orientals announce bad news, informed us that the boat was too small! There were very few to be got, and I had not seen this one, Mr. Wyers, the Legation constable, having engaged her for me; and I went "on board" at once, with much curiosity, as she was to be my home for an indefinite number of weeks. And small she truly was, only 28 feet over all, by 4 feet 10 inches at her widest part, and with her whole cargo, animate and inanimate, on board she only drew 3 inches of water. The roof which was put on at my request was a marvel. A slight framework of a ridge pole and some sticks precariously tied together supported some mats of pheasant grass, with the long blades hanging down outside and over the gunwale, which was only 12 inches high. These mats were tied together over the ridge pole, and let in a streak of daylight all the way along. At its highest part this roof was only 4 feet 6 inches. It was just possible to sit under it without stooping. By putting forked sticks under what by courtesy were called the rafters, they could be lifted a foot from the gunwale to let in light and air. Two or three times in a strong breeze this roof collapsed and fell about our heads!

In the fore part of the boat, 7 feet long, one boatman paddled or poled, and in the hinder part, 4 feet long, the other poled or worked an oar. But the fore part was also our kitchen and poultry yard and the boatmen's kitchen. There also were kept faggots, driftwood, and miscellaneous stores, with the food and water in unappetizing proximity. There, too, Wong and Che-on-i spent their day; and there they all cooked, ate, and washed clothes; and there at night the boatmen curled themselves up and slept in a space 4 feet×4. The rest of the *sampan* divided itself naturally by the thwarts. My part, the centre, was originally 8 feet×4 feet 10 inches, but encroachments by no means gradual constituted it a "free coup" for sacks, rice-bags, clothing, and baskets, till it was reduced to a bare 6 feet, into which space my bed, chair, saddle, and luggage were packed for five weeks. In the hinder division, 7 feet×4 feet 4 inches, Mr. Miller lived and studied, and he, Wong, and Che-on-i slept. It was scarcely possible for six people and their gear to be more closely packed. Mr. Miller, though not an experienced traveller, cheerfully made the best of everything then and afterwards, and preserved the serenity of his temper under all circumstances.

The *sampan's* crew of two consisted of Kim, her owner, a tall wiry, picturesque, aristocratic-looking old man, and his "hired man," who was never heard to speak except on two occasions, when, being very drunk, he developed a remarkable loquacity. On the whole, they were well behaved and quiet. I saw them in close proximity every hour of the day and was never annoyed by anything they did. Kim was paid $30 per month for the boat, and his laziness was wonderful. To dawdle along, to start late and tie up early, to crawl when he tracked, and to pole or paddle with the least expenditure of labor, was his policy. To pole for an hour, then tie up and take a smoke, to spend half a day now and then on buying rice, to work on my sensibilities by feigning exhaustion, and to adopt every dodge of the lazy man, was his practice. The contract stipulated for three men, and he only took one, making some evasive excuse. But I have said the worst I can say when I write that they never made more than 10 miles in a day, and often not more than 7, and that when they came to severe rapids they always wanted to go back.[1]

Mr. Wyers busied himself in putting a mat on the floor and stowing things as neatly as possible, and when curtains had been put up, the quarters, though "cribbed, cabined, and confined," looked quite tolerable. The same limp, silent crowd looked on till we left Han Kang at midday. In a few hours things shook into shape, and after all the discomforts were not great, possibly the greatest being that the smoke and the smell of the boatmen's malodorous food blew through the boat.

[1] I took very careful notes on the Han, but as minute details would be uninteresting to the general reader, and would involve a good deal of apparent repetition, I shall give only the most salient features of a journey which, if it has ever been made, has certainly not been described.

CHAPTER VI

ON THE RIVER OF GOLDEN SAND

DURING the five weeks which I spent on the Han, though the routine of daily life varied little, there was no monotony. The country and the people were new, and we mixed freely, almost too freely, with the latter; the scenery varied hourly, and after the first few days became not only beautiful, but in places magnificent, and full of surprises; the spring was in its early beauty, and the trees in their first vividness of green, red, and gold; the flowers and flowering shrubs were in their glory, the crops at their most attractive stage, birds sang in the thickets, rich fragrant odors were wafted off on the water, red cattle, though rarely, fed knee-deep in abounding grass, and the waters of the Han, nearly at their lowest, were clear as crystal, and their broken sparkle flashed back the sunbeams which passed through a sky as blue as that of Tibet. There was a prosperous look about the country too, and its security was indicated by the frequent occurrence of solitary farms, with high secluding fences, standing under the deep shade of fine walnut and persimmon trees.

Unlike the bare, arid, denuded hillsides between Chemulpo and Seoul, the slopes along much of the route are wooded, and in many cases forested both with coniferæ and deciduous trees, among which there are occasionally picturesque clumps of umbrella pines. The *Pinus Sinensis* and the *Abies Microsperma* abound, and there are two species of oak and three of maple, a *Platanus*, juniper, ash, mountain ash, birch, hazel, *Sophora Japonica*, *Euonymus alatus*, *Thuja Orientalis*, and many others. The heliotrope, pink, and scarlet azaleas were in all their beauty, flushing the hillsides, and white and sul-

71

phur-yellow clematis, actinidia, and a creeping *Euonymus* were abundant. Of the wealth of flowering shrubs, mostly white blossomed, I had never seen one before either in garden or greenhouse, except the familiar syringa and spirea. The beautiful *Ampelopsis Veitchiana* was in its freshest spring green and tender red, concealing tree trunks, depending from branches, and draping every cliff and rock with its exquisite foliage; and roses, red and white, of a free-growing, climbing variety, having possession even of tall trees, hung their fragrant festoons over the roads.

It was all very charming, though a little wanting in life. True, there were butterflies and dragon-flies innumerable, and brilliant green and brown snakes in numbers, and at first the Han was cheery with mallard and mandarin-duck, geese and common teal. In the rice fields the imperial crane, the egret, and the pink ibis with the deep flush of spring on his plumage, were not uncommon, and peregrines, kestrels, falcons, and buzzards were occasionally seen. But the song-birds were few. The forlorn note of the night-jar was heard, and the loud, cheerful call of the gorgeous ringed pheasant to his dowdy mate; but the trilling, warbling, and cooing which are the charm of an English copsewood in springtime are altogether absent, the chatter of the blue magpie and the noisy flight of the warbler being poor substitutes for that entrancing concert. Of beast life, undomesticated, there were no traces, and the domestic animals are few. Sheep do not thrive on the sour natural grasses of Korea, and if goats are kept I never saw any. A small black pig not much larger than a pug is universal, and there are bulls and ponies about the better class of farms. There are big buff dogs, but these are kept only to a limited extent on the Han, in the idea that they attract the nocturnal visits of tigers. The dogs are noisy and voluble, and rush towards a stranger as if bent on attack; but it is mere bravado—they are despicable cowards, and run away howling at the shaking of a stick.

Leopards, antelopes, and several species of deer are found among the mountains bordering the Han, but the beast by pre-ëminence there, as throughout Korea, is the tiger.   At first I was very incredulous regarding his existence and depredations. It was impossible to believe that peaceful agricultural valleys surrounded by hills, thinly clothed with dwarf oak scrub, could be ravaged by him, that dogs, pigs, and cattle are continually carried off by him, and that human beings visiting each other at night or belated on the roads are his frequent prey.   But the constant repetition of tiger stories, the terror of the villagers, the refusal of *mapu* and coolies to travel after dark, the certainty that in several places the loss of life had been recent, and that even in the trim settlement of Wön-san a boy and child had been seized the day before I arrived and had been eaten on the hillside above the town, have made me a believer.   Possibly some of the depredations attributed to tigers may be really the work of leopards, which undoubtedly abound, and have been shot even within the walls of Seoul. High up the Han, in a very lovely lake-like stretch, there is a village recently deserted because of the persistency with which tigers had carried of its inhabitants.   The Korean tiger, judging from its skin, in which the long hair grows out of a thick coat of fine fur, resembles the Manchurian tiger.   I have heard of one which measured 13 feet 4 inches, but never saw a skin more than 11 feet 8 inches in length.

The tiger-hunters form what may be called a brigade or corps, and may be called on for military service.   They were conspicuous objects in the *Kur-dong*, with their long matchlock guns, loose blue uniforms, and conical-crowned, broad-brimmed hats.   The tiger appears on the Royal standard, and tigers' skins are the insignia of high office, the leopard skins, indicating lower rank.   The Chinese give a very high price for tigers' bones as a medicine, considering them a specific for strength and courage.   Tiger-hunting as a business seems confined to the northern provinces.   On the Han, and specially along its northern affluents, are found three if not four species of deer, and the horns, in the velvet, of the large deer (*Cervus Manchuricus*), which fetch from forty to sixty dollars a pair, are the prize most wanted by the hunters. Pheasants are literally without number and are very tame; I constantly saw them feeding among the crops within a few yards of the peasants at their work. They are usually brought down by falcons, which, when well trained, command as high a price as nine dollars. To obtain them three small birds are placed in a cylinder of loosely woven bamboo, mounted horizontally on a pole. On the peregrine alighting on this, a man who has been concealed throws a net over the whole. The bird is kept in a tight sleeve for three days. Then he is daily liberated in a room, and trained to follow a piece of meat pulled over the floor by a string. At the end of a week he is taken out on his master's wrist, and slipped when game is seen. He is not trained to return. The master rushes upon him and secures him before he has time to devour the bird. A man told me that he sometimes got between twenty and thirty pheasants a day, but had to walk or run 100 *li* to do it. The season was nearly over, yet I bought fine pheasants on the Han for threepence and fourpence each. They were cheaper than chickens.

The Han itself, rising in the Diamond Mountain of Kong-wön-Do, and formed by a number of nearly parallel affluents, next to the border river Am-nok, is *the* river of Korea, which it cuts nearly across, its eastern extremity being within 25 miles of the Sea of Japan and its western at Chemulpo. I ascended it to within 40 miles of the Sea of Japan, and estimate the length of its navigable waters for small flat-bottomed craft at about 170 miles. A clear bright stream with a bottom of white sand, golden gravel or rock, chiefly limestone, with an average width of 250 yards well sustained to the head of navigation, narrowed at times by walls of rock or divided by grassy islands in its lower course, full of pebbly shallows, over which it ripples gaily, its upper waters abounding in rocky rapids, many of them severe and dangerous, its most marked features, to my thinking, are its absence of affluents after it emerges from the Diamond Mountain, and its singular alternations of shallow with very deep water. It was a common occurrence to have to drag my boat, drawing only 3 inches, through water too shallow to float her, and at the top of the ripple to come upon a broad, still, lake-like, deep, green expanse, 20 feet deep, continuing for a mile or two.

After passing the forks there are 46 rapids, many of them very severe, before reaching Yöng-Chhun, which for practical purposes may be regarded as the limit of navigable water.

These are a most serious obstacle in the way of navigation, but as there is usually a deep water channel in the middle, sailing junks of 25 tons, taking advantage of strong, favorable winds, get up as far as Tan-Yang. Beyond, boats not twice the size of my *sampan* must be used, which are only poled and dragged, and as they must keep near the shore, among rocks and furious water, their progress is very slow, not more than 7 miles a day. Nevertheless, the Han, with all its difficulties and obstructions, is the great artery of communication for much of Kong-wön-Do and Kyöng-Kivi Do, and for the northeast portion of Chung-Chöng Do; down it all the excess produce of this great region goes to Seoul, and nearly all merchandise, salt, and foreign goods come up it from the sea-board, to pass into the hands of the *posang*, or merchant pedlars, at various points, and through them to reach the market-places of the interior. During the first ten days from Han Kang there were 75 junks a day on an average bound up and down stream. There is a very large floating population on the Han. There is not a bridge along its whole length, but communication is kept up by 47 free ferries, provided by Government.

Not having been able to learn anything about the route or any of its features, I was much surprised to find a very large population, not only along the river, but in the parallel valleys, many of them of great length and extreme fertility, in its neighborhood. It was only necessary to climb a ridge or hill to see numbers of these, given up to rice culture, and thickly sprinkled with farming villages. Along the river banks only, between Han Kang and Yöng-Chhun, there are 176 villages. Much of the soil is rich alluvium, from 5 to 11 feet deep, and most prolific, bearing two heavy crops a year (not rice lands) with little or no manure. There is on the whole an air of greater ease and prosperity about the Han valley than about any other region that I have seen in Korea.[1]

The people are of fine physique and generally robust appearance. Some of them had evidently attained great age. There were a few sore eyes and some mild skin diseases, both produced by dirt, but there were no sickly-looking people; infants abounded.

Except for a monastery and temple, both Buddhist, not far from Seoul, and the Confucian temples at the magistracies, there were no signs of any other cult than that of dæmons. There were two shrines containing *mirioks*, in both cases water-worn boulders chafed into some resemblance to humanity; spirit shrines on heights; and under large trees heaps of stones sacred to dæmons; tall posts, with the tops rudely cut into something suggestive of distorted human faces, painted black and blue, with straw ropes with dependent straw tassels, like those denoting Shinto shrines in Japan, stretched across the road to prevent the ingress of malignant spirits, and trees with many streamers of rag, as well as worn-out straw shoes hanging in their branches, as offerings to these beings.

[1] I am inclined to think that Europeans habitually underestimate the population. The average I obtained is 8 to a house, taking 70 houses at random, and this estimate is borne out by General Greathouse, for some years in Korean Government service, and Mr. Moffett, a resident and traveller in Korea for seven years, both of whom have given some attention to the subject. It must be understood that a Korean household rarely, if ever, consists of a man, wife and children only; there are parents and relationly hangers-on, to say nothing of possible servants.

The dwellings do not vary much, except that the roofs of the better class are tiled. In villages where there is a resident *yang-ban* or squire-noble, his house is usually pretentious, and covers a considerable area, but yields in stateliness to the family tomb, always on a hill slope, a great grass mound on a grass platform backed by horseshoe-shaped grass banks, and usually by a number of fine pines. In front of the mound is invariably a stone altar on two stone drums, stone posts which support the canopy used when sacrifices are offered to the spirit of the deceased, and stone lanterns. A few of the grander tombs are approached by a short avenue of stone fig- ures of warriors, horses, servants, and sheep.[1]

The peasant's houses do not differ from those of the poorer classes in Seoul. The walls are of mud, and the floors, also of mud, are warmed by a number of flues, the most economical of all methods of heating, as the quantity of dried leaves and weeds that a boy of ten can carry keeps two rooms above 70° for twelve hours. Every house is screened by a fence 6 feet high of bamboo or plaited reeds, and is usually surrounded by fruit trees. In one room are *ang-pak*, great earthenware jars big enough to contain a man, in which rice, millet, barley, and water are kept. That is frequently in small houses the women's room. The men's room has little in it but the mat on the floor, pillows of solid wood, and large red and green hat-cases ranging from the rafters, in which the crinoline dress hats are stowed away. Latticed and paper-covered doors and windows denote a position above that of the poorest. A pig- stye, much more substantial than the house, is always along- side of it.

The villages from about 50 *li* up the Han from Seoul may all be described as "farming villages." Lower down they export large quantities of firewood and charcoal for the daily

[1] Such figures where they occur are always spoken of by foreigners as sheep, but I doubt whether this animal appears at any but royal tombs, where it is probably represented as offered in sacrifice by the King.

needs of a capital which has left itself without a stick available for fuel in its immediate neighborhood. No special industries exist. The peasants make their rude wooden ploughs and spades shod with iron, and two villages within 40 *li* of Seoul supply them with their *ang-paks* and culinary utensils of the same coarse ware, which stands fire and serves instead of iron pots. Such iron utensils as are used are imported from Seoul along with salt, and foreign piece goods for dress clothes, and are paid for with rice, grain, and tobacco.

The people are peasant farmers in the strictest sense, most of them holding their lands from the *yang-bans* at their pleasure. The proprietor has the right to turn them out after harvest, but it does not seem to be very oppressively exercised. He provides the seed, and they pay him half the yield. Some men buy land and obtain title-deeds. In 1894 they paid in taxes on one day's ploughing, so much for barley, beans, rice, and cotton, the sum varying; but a new system of collecting tax on the assessed value of the land has come into operation, which renders "squeezing" on the part of the tax collector far more difficult. Money is scarcely current, business transactions are by barter, or the peasant pays with his labor. His chief outlay is on foreign piece cottons for his best clothes. These are 30 *cash* per measure of 20 inches, dearer at Yöng-Wol, the reputed head of navigation, than at Seoul.

The population of the Han valley is not poor, if by poverty is to be understood scarcity of the necessaries of life. The people have enough for themselves and for all and sundry who, according to Korean custom, may claim their hospitality. Probably they are all in debt; it is very rare indeed to find a Korean who has not this millstone round his neck, and they are destitute of money or possessions other than those they absolutely require. They appear lazy. I then thought them so, but they live under a *régime* under which they have no security for the gains of labor, and for a man to be reported to be "making money," or attaining even the luxury of a brass din-

ner service, would be simply to lay himself open to the rapacious attentions of the nearest mandarin and his myrmidons,
or to a demand for a loan from an adjacent *yang-ban*.   Nevertheless, the homesteads of the Han valley have a look of substantial comfort.

Certainly the meals of the *men* are taken in far greater tidi-
ness than is usual among laborers.   The women, as is the
fashion with women, eat " anyhow," and gobble up their
lords' leavings.   All meals for men are served on small, circular, dark wooden tables, a few inches high, one for each person.   Rice is the staple of diet, and is served in a great bowl,
but besides this, there are seldom fewer than five or six glazed
earthenware vessels containing savory, or rather tasty, condi-
ments.[1]   Chop-sticks and small flattish spoons of horn or base
metal are used for eating.

In the villages, as distinguished from the hamlets, on the
Han there are schools, but they are not open to the public.
Families club together and engage a teacher, but the pupils are
only of the scholarly class, and only Chinese learning in
Wenli is taught, this being the stepping-stone to official position, the object of the ambition of every Korean.   *En-mun* is
despised, and is not used as a written language by the educated
class.   I observed, however, that a great many men of the
lower orders on the river were able to read their own script.

With the exception of two small Buddhist establishments
not far from Seoul, priests are non-existent on the Han, nor is
there any Christian propaganda, Protestant or Roman, at
work, though Roman missionaries were formerly stationed at
two points near the forks.   Dæmon worship prevails throughout the whole region.

The river is frozen for from three to four months in the
winter, and tends to inundate the lower lands for two months
in the summer.   The bridle tracks which skirt it and diverge
from it are infamous.   The valley has no mails, and of course

[1] These remarks apply to every part of Korea which I afterwards saw.

no newspapers. The Tong-haks (rebels, or armed reformers) were strong in a region immediately to the south of the great bend, which showed some dissatisfaction with things as they were, and a desire for reform in some minds.

So far as I could learn, the region is not rich in ordinary minerals. I could hear nothing of "the burning earth," though the geological formation renders its existence probable. Copper and iron are worked not far from the north branch to a limited extent. But the Han is the "River of Golden Sand," and though the height of the gold season is after the summer rains, the *auri sacra fames* even then attracted gangs of men to the river banks, and gold in the mountains was a subject on which the Koreans were always voluble.

The attitude of the people was friendly. I never saw a trace of actual hostility, though on the higher waters of the south branch it was very doubtful whether they had seen a European before. Their curiosity was naturally enormous, and whenever the boat tied up for a day it showed itself by crowds sitting on the bank as close to it as they could get, staring apathetically. They were frequently timid, and snatched up their fowls and hid them when we came in sight, but a little friendly explanation of our honesty of purpose, and above all, the sight of a few strings of *cash*, usually set everything straight. A foreigner is absolutely safe. During the ofttimes tedious process of hauling up the rapids, when Mr. Miller and the servants were tugging at the ropes, I constantly strolled for two or three hours by myself along the river bank, and whether the path led through solitary places or through villages, I never met with anything more disagreeable than curiosity shown in a very ill-bred fashion, and that was chiefly on the part of women. When the people understood that they would be paid it was not difficult to procure the little they had to sell at fairly reasonable rates. They were disposed to be communicative, and showed very little suspicion, far less indeed than in parts of Korea where foreigners are common.

My Chinese servant was everywhere an object of most friendly curiosity and a centre of pleasurable interest.

The mercury during April and May ranged from 42° to 72°, and the barometer showed remarkable steadiness. There were two heavy rainfalls, but the weather on the whole was superb, and the atmosphere clear and dry.

KOREAN PEASANTS AT DINNER.

CHAPTER VII

VIEWS AFLOAT

A FEW hours sufficed for settling in our very narrow quarters, and by the end of the second day we had shaken down into an orderly routine. By dint of much driving Kim was induced to start about seven, at which hour I had my flour and water stirabout. The halts for smoking, cooking, and eating were many, and about five o'clock he used to simulate exhaustion, a deception to which his lean form and thin face with its straight straggling white hair lent themselves effectively. Then followed the daily wrangle about the place to tie up, Kim naturally desiring a village and the proximity of junks, with much nocturnal smoking and gossip, while my wish was for solitude, quiet, and a pebbly river bottom, and with Mr. Miller's aid I usually carried my point. Between Kim's laziness and the frequent occurrence of rapids, 10 miles came to be considered a good day's journey! The same rapids made any settled plan of occupation impossible, yet on the early stages of the journey, when there were long quiet stretches of water between them, it was pleasant to elevate the roof and have a quiet morning's work till dinner at twelve.

This, it must be confessed, was a precarious meal. Chickens for curry were not always attainable, and were often so small as to suggest the egg shell, and the river fish which were sometimes got by pouncing on a boy fisherman were very minute and bony. Chestnuts often eked out a very scanty meal. Wong used to hunt along the river banks for wild onions and carrots, after the stock of the cultivated roots was exhausted, and he made paste of flour and water, rolled it with a bamboo on the top of a box, cut it into biscuits with the lid of a tin, and baked them in the frying-pan. Rice fritters too he made morning, noon, and night. Afternoon tea of Burrough's and Wellcome's " tabloids " was never omitted, and after tying up came supper, an impoverished repetition of dinner, the whole a wholesome regimen, invariably eaten with appetite.

Visiting villages and small towns, only to find the first a collection of mud hovels, and the last mud hovels with the addition of ruinous official buildings and a forlorn Confucian temple, climbing to ridges bordering the Han to get a view of fertile and populous valleys, conversing with and interrogating the people through Mr. Miller and his servant, taking geographical notes, temperatures, altitudes, barometric readings, and measurements of the river (nearly all unfortunately lost in a rapid on the downward journey), collecting and drying plants, photographing, and developing negatives under difficulties, all the blankets and waterproofs in the boat being requisitioned for the creation of a " dark room "—all these occupations made up busy and interesting days.

The first two days were spent in turning the flank of the range on which is the so-called fortress of Nam Han, with its priest soldiers, one of the four which are supposed to guard Seoul and offer refuge in times of trouble. On the right bank there are many villages of farmers, woodcutters, and charcoal burners, and on the left an expanse of cultivated sandy soil between the mountains and the river, there a broad rapid stream rippling brightly over white sand or golden gravel. After passing the Yang-kun magistracy, a large village with a long street, where a whole fleet of *sampans* was loading with country produce for the capital, and a number of junks were unloading salt, the Han makes a sharp bend to the south, and after a long rapid expands into a very broad stream. The valley broadens also, and becomes flat, the hills, absolutely denuded even of scrub, are low, and recede from the river; their serrated black ridges of rock, and their deeply scored, corrugated, flushed

sides, which spring had scarcely tinged with green, are forbidding, and though the valley was green with young wheat,
that is quite the most monotonous and uninteresting part of the
journey.

After circumventing the fine fortress summit of Nam Han,
the river enters the mountains. From that time up to the
head of possible navigation, the scenery in its variety, beauty,
and unexpectedness exhausts the vocabulary of admiration.

A short distance above Han Kang is the Buddhist temple,
of Ryeng-an Sa, dedicated to the Dragon, one of the two
Buddhist sanctuaries on the long course of the Han. On the
left bank a low stone wall encloses a spot on which a female
dragon alighted from heaven in the days of the last dynasty,
and where still, in times of flood or drought, sacrifices are
offered and libations poured out to "Heaven." The only
other temple is that of Pyök-chol on the right bank of the Han,
above Yö Ju, four days from Seoul. A steep wooded prom-
ontory projects into the still, deep, green water, crowned
with two brick and stone pagodas. In a wooded dell at the
back there are some picturesque and elaborately carved and
painted temples and monastic buildings, and a fine bell five
centuries old, surmounted by an entanglement of dragons,
which, with some medallions on the sides, are of very bold design and successful workmanship, and the whole is said to have
been cast in Chung-Chöng Do before the Japanese stole the
arts and artists! A pavilion for the temple dramas was occupied for the afternoon by a large picnic of women and children
from Yö Ju. In one of the monastic courts there is a marble
pagoda with some finely executed bas-reliefs on its sides,
claiming a not distant kinship with those of the "marble
pagoda" in Seoul. The establishment consisted of an abbot,
nineteen monks, and four novices. The abbot was the most
refined, intellectual, and aristocratic looking man that I saw in
Korea, with an innate courtesy and refinement of manner rare
anywhere. He carried the weight of seventy years with much

grace and dignity, and made us cordially welcome. This was the last we saw of Buddhism till we reached the Diamond Mountain six weeks later.

At the village of Tomak-na-dali, where we tied up, they make the great purple-black jars and pots which are in universal use. Their method is primitive. They had no objection to be watched, and were quite communicative. The potters pursue their trade in open sheds, digging up the clay close by. The stock-in-trade is a pit in which an uncouth potter's wheel revolves, the base of which is turned by the feet of a man who sits on the edge of the hole. A wooden spatula, a mason's wooden trowel, a curved stick, and a piece of rough rag are the tools, efficient for the purpose. Fifty *li* higher up, a few *li* from the river, are beds of kaolin used in the Government pottery and for the finer kinds of porcelain.

For two days the Han was about 400 yards wide, with a very tortuous course, abounding in rapids, shallows, and green islands, with great expanses of pure white sand on its left bank, and frequent villages of woodcutters and charcoal burners on both. On the 16th we reached the forks at the village of Ma-chai. There the north branch, which was to be afterwards traversed, comes down, and the south branch, in every way more important, arrives from the southward. Between the two there is a pretty wooded island then pink with azalea blossom. Beyond is a fine stretch of alluvium, nearly 6 feet deep, bearing rich crops of barley and wheat, but entirely unprotected from the desolations of the river in its annual rise, which engulfs every year acres of this prolific soil. Ten years ago the Han, altering its course, brought down from the top of a steep bank at some distance a hugh concrete double coffin 9 feet long and 16 inches thick ! The great alluvial expanse was make over to the Buddhists by the King, who receives annually a fixed amount of the produce.

Between Kim's laziness and plausibility, and the rapids, which though not severe were frequent, and the food hunt, which was a necessity, our progress was slow, and it was not till the 19th of April that we reached Yö Ju, the first town of any importance and the birthplace of the late Queen. It is memorable to me as being the first place where the crowd was obstreperous and obnoxious, though not hostile. It is humiliating to be a "show" and to get nothing by it! I went out on a rock in the river in the hope of using the prismatic compass in peace, and was nearly pushed into the water, and when I went up into the gate tower a stamping, curious crowd, climbing on everything that afforded a point of vantage, shook the old fabric so severely that the delicately balanced needle never came to rest. The crowd was dirty, the streets were foul and decayed, and worst of all was the magistrate's *yamen*, to which we had occasion to go, and where I found that a *kwan-ja* was powerless to obtain even common civility.

The *yamen*, though finely situated and enclosing in its grounds a large and much decorated pavilion for Royal use, but used as a children's playground, was in a state of wreck. The woodwork was crumbling, beams and rafters were falling down, lacquer and paint were scaling off, torn paper fluttered from the lattice windows, plaster hung from the grimy walls, the once handsome gate tower was on its last legs, in the courtyard some flagstones had subsided, others were exalted, and audacious ragweed and shepherd's purse grew in their crevices. Poverty, neglect, and melancholy reigned supreme. Within the gates were plenty of those persons who suck the lifeblood of Korea. There were soldiers in Tyrolese hats and coarse cotton uniforms in which blue predominated, *yamen* runners in abundance, writers, officers of *in*justice, messengers pretending to have business on hand, and many small rooms, in which were many more men sitting on the floor smoking long pipes, with writing materials beside them.

One attendant, by no means polite, took my *kwan-ja* to the magistrate, and very roughly led the way to two small rooms, in the inner one of which the official was seated on the floor,

surrounded by a few elderly men. We were directed to stand
at the opening between the two rooms, and behind us pressed
as many of the crowd as could get in. I bowed low. No notice was taken. An attendant handed the magistrate a pipe,
so long that it would have been impossible for him to light it
for himself, and he smoked. Mr. Miller hoped that he was in
good health. No reply, and the eyes were never raised. Mr.
Miller explained the object of the visit, which was to get a little information about the neighborhood. There was only a
very curt reply, and as the great man turned to one of his subordinates and began to talk to him, and rude remarks were circulating, we took leave with the usual Korean phrases of politeness, which were not reciprocated.

We were told that there are many " high *yang-bans* " in
Yö Ju, and it seemed natural that the magistrate of a town of
only 700 houses should not be a man of high rank. The story
goes that when he came they used " low talk " to him and ordered him about as their inferior. So he lives chiefly in Seoul,
and the man who sat in sordid state amidst the ruins of the
spacious and elaborately decorated *yamen* does his work and
divides the spoils, and the *yang-bans* are left to whatever their
devices may be. But this is not an isolated case. Nearly all
the river magistrates are mainly absentees, and spend their time,
salaries, and squeezings in the capital. I had similar interviews with three other magistrates. I asked nothing except
change in *cash* for three *yen*, and on each occasion was told
that the treasury was empty. My *kwan-ja*, a pompous document from the Foreign Office, was of this use only, it procured me a chicken at a high price in a town where the people
were unwilling to sell !

At Yö Ju I saw for the only time either in Korea or China
the interior of an ancestral temple. It is a lofty building, with
a curved tile roof and blackwood ceiling, approached by a
roofed gateway. Opposite the entrance is an ebony stool, on
which are a brass bowl and incense burner. Above this is a

large altar, supporting two candlesticks with candles, and above that again an ebony stand on which rests a polished black marble tablet inscribed with the name of the deceased. Behind that, in a recess in the wall, with elaborate fretwork doors, is his life-sized portrait in Chinese style. The floor is covered with plain matting. In the tablet the third soul of the deceased is supposed to dwell. Food is placed before it three times daily for three years in the case of a parent, and there the relations, after the expiration of that period, meet at stated seasons every year and offer sacrifice and "worship."

At the large and prosperous-looking village of Chön-yaing the people told us that a "circus" was about to perform and impelled us towards it; but finding that it was in the court-yard of a large tiled-roof mansion, in good repair and of much pretension, we were retiring, when we were cordially invited to enter, and I was laid hold of (literally) by the serving-women and dragged through the women's court and into the women's apartments. I was surrounded by fully forty women, old and young, wives, concubines, servants, all in gala dress and much adorned. The principal wife, a very young girl wearing some Indian jewellery, was very pretty and had an exquisite complexion, but one and all were destitute of manners. They investigated my clothing, pulled me about, took off my hat and tried it on, untwisted my hair and absorbed my hairpins, pulled off my gloves and tried them on with shrieks of laughter, and then, but not till they had exhausted all the amusement which could be got out of me, they bethought themselves of entertaining me by taking me through their apartments, crowding upon me to such an extent as they did so that I was nearly carried off my feet. They took me through fourteen communicating rooms, with fine parquet floors, mostly spoiled by being covered in whole or in part with Brussels tapestry carpets of "loud" and vulgar patterns in hideous aniline dyes. Great mirrors in tawdry gilt frames glared from the tender coloring of the walls, and French clocks asserted their expensive vulgarity in every room.

In the outer court a rope was stretched for the rope-dancers, and kettledrums and reed-pipes gave promise of such music as Koreans love. I was escorted across two other courts surrounded by verandas supported on dressed stone, and with iron railings instead of wood, to an elevated reception room, where a foreign table and some tawdry velvet-covered chairs clashed with the tastefulness of the walls and the fine mats bordered with the Greek fret on the floor. French clocks, all keeping different time, were much *en évidence*. The host, a youth of eighteen, eldest son of the governor of one of the most important governorships in Korea, welcomed us, and seemed anxious to receive us courteously. Wine, soup, eggs, and *kimchi*, an elaborate sort of " sour kraut," were produced, and had to be partaken of, our host meanwhile smoking an expensive foreign cigar, which gave him an opportunity for the ostentatious display of a showy diamond ring. He was dressed in sea-green silk, and wore a hat of very fine quality.

He wanted to see the inside of my camera and to be photographed, for which purpose we retired to the back of the house to avoid the enormous crowd which had collected, and which was becoming every moment more impolite and disorderly. I made him exchange the foreign cigar, vulgar in a Korean's mouth, for the national long pipe. At this juncture some friends came up, hangers-on, who were feasting with him to celebrate his having obtained a good place in a recent examination, and made a rudely-worded request for our immediate departure. It was obvious that, after their unmannerly curiosity had been satisfied, our presence, and the courteous treatment extended to us, spoilt their amusement. The ring-leader spoke roughly to our host, who turned his back on us and retired meekly to his own apartments, although he is a son of an official of the highest rank, and a near relative of the late Queen. We could only make a somewhat ignominious exit, having been truly "played out."

This rage for French clocks, German mirrors, foreign cigars, chairs upholstered in velvet, and a general foreign tawdriness is spreading rapidly among the young "swells" who have money to spend, vulgarizing Korean simplicity, and setting the example to those below them of an extravagant and purely selfish expenditure. The house, with its many courtyards, was new and handsome, and money glared from every point. I was glad to return to the simplicity of my boat, hoping that with the "plain living, high thinking" might be combined !

Beyond the mountains east of Yö Ju, the Han passes through a noble stretch of rich alluvium, bearing superb, and fairly clean crops, and bordered by low, serrated, denuded, and much corrugated ranges, faintly tinged with green. On this gently rolling plain are many towns and villages, among the larger of which are Won Ju, Chung Ju, Chöng-phyöng, and Tan-Yang, all on or near the river, by which they conveniently export their surplus produce, chiefly beans, tobacco, and rice, and receive in return their supplies of salt and foreign goods. Even at that season of low water the traffic was considerable.

Higher up, the scenery changes. Lofty limestone bluffs, often caverned, rise abruptly from the river, and wall in the fertile and populous valleys which descend upon it, giving place higher up to grand basaltic formation, range behind range, terraces of columnar basalt occasionally appearing. It was a lovely season, warm days, cold nights, brilliant sunshine, great white masses of sunlit clouds on a sky of heavenly blue, distances idealized in a blue veil which was not a mist, flowers at their freshest, every bird that has a note or a cry vocal, butterflies and red and blue dragon-flies hovering over the grass and water, fish leaping, all nature awake and jubilant. And every rift and bluff had its own beauty of blossoming scarlet azaleas, or syringas, contorted or stately pines, and

Ampelopsis Veitchiana rose-pink in its early leafage. There was a note of gladness in the air.

Eight days above Seoul, on the left bank of the river, there is a ruinous pagoda built of large blocks of hewn stone, standing solitary in the centre of a level plain formed by a bend of the Han. The people, on being asked about it, said, "When Korea was surveyed so long ago that nobody knows when, this was the centre of it." They call it the "Halfway Place." After that the only suggestions of antiquity are some stone foundations, and a few stone tombs among the trees, which, from their shape, may denote the sites of monasteries.

Near that pagoda were a number of men very drunk, and there were few days on which the habit of drinking to excess was not more or less prominent. The junkmen celebrated the evening's rest by hard drinking, and the crowd which nightly assembled on the shore when we tied up was usually enlivened by the noisy antics of one or more intoxicated men. From my observation on the Han journey and afterwards, I should say that drunkenness is an outstanding feature in Korea. And it is not disreputable. If a man drinks rice wine till he loses his reason, no one regards him as a beast. A great dignitary even may roll on the floor drunk at the end of a meal, at which he has eaten to repletion, without losing caste, and on becoming sober receives the congratulations of inferiors on being rich enough to afford such a luxury. Along with the taste for French clocks and German gilding, a love of foreign liquors is becoming somewhat fashionable among the young *yang-bans*, and willing caterers are found who produce potato spirit rich in fusel oil as "old Cognac," and a very effervescent champagne at a shilling a bottle !

The fermented liquors of Korea are probably not unwholesome, but the liking for them is an acquired taste with Europeans. They vary from a smooth white drink resembling buttermilk in appearance, and very mild, to a water-white spirit of strong smell and fiery taste. Between these comes

the ordinary rice wine, slightly yellowish, akin to Japanese
sake and Chinese *samshu*, with a faint, sickly smell and flavor.
They all taste more or less strongly of smoke, oil, and alcohol,
and the fusel oil remains even in the best.   They are manufactured from rice, millet, and barley.   The wine-seller projects a cylindrical basket on a long pole from his roof, resembling the " bush " formerly used in England for a similar purpose.   Probably one reason that the Koreans are a drunken
people is that they scarcely use tea at all even in the cities, and
the luxury of " cold water " is unknown to them.   The
peasants drink hot rice water with their meals, honey water as
a luxury, and on festive occasions an infusion of orange peel
or ginger.   The drying of orange peel is quite a business with
Korean housewives.   There were quantities of it hanging from
the eaves of all the cottages.

Up to a short distance above this pagoda, the rapids for
which the Han is famous, though they made our progress
slow, had not suggested serious difficulty, far less risk, but for
the remaining fortnight they were tortuous rocky channels,
through which the river, compressed in width, rushes with
great violence and tremendous noise and clatter, or they are
successive broken ledges of rock, with a chaos of flurry and
foam, varied by deep pools, presenting formidable, and at
some seasons insuperable, obstacles to navigation.   To all appearance they are far more dangerous than the celebrated
rapids of the Yangtze, and the remains of timber rafts and
junks attest their destructive properties.   They occur at
shorter and shorter intervals as the higher waters are reached,
till eventually the Han becomes an unbroken rapid or
cataract.

Kim, though paid handsomely, was far too stingy to pay for
any help *en route*, his ropes were manifestly bought in " the
cheapest market," and though Wong, my powerful *sampan*-
man, worked with both strength and skill, and Mr. Miller and
his servant toiled at the tow ropes, and in great exigencies I

gave a haul myself, we sometimes made only 7 miles a day, and ofttimes took two hours to ascend a few yards, two poling with might and main in the boat, and three tugging with all their strength on shore. Often the ropes snapped, when the boat went spinning and flying to the foot of the rapid, sometimes with injury to herself and her contents, sometimes escaping. After a few of such risks I habitually landed, either on a boatman's back or wading in waterproof Wellingtons, which caused great wonderment in the lookers on. The worst rapids were always in the most beautiful places, and the strolls and climbs of three or four hours along the river banks, through fields with bounteous crops, through odorous Spanish chestnut groves, through thickets with their fascinating bewilderments of roses, clematis, and honeysuckle, and past farmhouses with their privacy of bamboo screens, and deep shade of blossoming fruit trees, were very delightful.

In ten days from Seoul we reach Chöng-phyöng, a town of some pretensions, where in connection with the *yamen* is a temple pavilion with a high white chair, facing a table with candlesticks upon it, floor, table, and chair deep in dust, though the building is used regularly for offering prayers and sacrifices for the King. Dust is not noteworthy in Korea, but the paintings in this temple are. On the end walls are vivid groups of six noblemen wearing fine horsehair palace hats with wings, each man holding a piece of folded paper in his hand, and listening intently as he bends forward towards the chair. The conception and technique of these paintings are admirable, and the sunset scenes on the back wall, though inferior in execution, are the work of a true artist.

Close by is a Royal pavilion hanging over the edge of a high bluff above the Han, surrounded by superb elms, some of their trunks from 20 to 23 feet in circumference. The view of the fertile valley and of the mountains beyond is very fine, and the decorative woodwork, painted in Korean style, has been very handsome; but the phrase "has been" describes most things Korean, and official squalor and neglect could scarcely go farther.

At Chöng-phyöng and elsewhere the common people, in spite of their overpowering curiosity, were not rude, and usually retired to a respectful distance to watch us eat; but from the class of scholars who hang on round all *yamens* we met with a good deal of underbred impertinence, some of the men going so far as to raise the curtain of my compartment and introduce their heads and shoulders beneath it, brow-beating the boatmen when they politely asked them to desist. On the other hand, men of the non-cultured class showed us various small attentions, sometimes helping with a haul at the ropes at a rapid, only asking in return that their wives might see me, a request with which I always gladly complied. At Chöng-phyöng, so great was female curiosity that a number of women waded waist deep after the boat to peer under the mats of the roof, and one of them, scrambling out to a rock for a final stare, overbalanced herself and fell into deep water. At one point, in the very early morning, some women presented themselves at the boat, having walked several *li* with a present of eggs, the payment for which was to be a sight of me and my poor equipments, they having heard that there was a boat with a foreign woman on board. The old cambric curtains brought from Persia, with a red pattern on a white ground, always attracted them greatly, and the small Japanese cooking utensils.

In thirteen days from Seoul we reached Tan-Yang, a magistracy prettily situated on the left bank of the Han, with a picturesque Confucian temple on the hill above; and a day later entered upon mountainous country of extreme beauty. The paucity of tributaries is very marked. Up to that point, except the north branch, there are but two—one which joins the Han at the village of Hu-nan Chang, on the right bank, and is navigable for 60 *li*, as far as the important town of Wan Ju; and another, which enters 2 *li* above the picturesquely-situated village of So-il, on the left bank. Above Tan-Yang the river forms long and violent rapids, alternating with broad stretches of blue, quiet water from 10 to 20 feet deep, rolling majestically, making sharp and extraordinary bends among lofty limestone precipices. Villages on natural terraces occur constantly, the lower terrace planted with mulberry or weeping willows. Hemp is cultivated in great quantities, and is used for sackcloth for mourners' wear, bags, and rope. In my walks along the river I had several opportunities of seeing the curious method of separating the fibre, rude and primitive, but effectual. At the bottom of a stone paved pit large stones are placed, which are heated from a rough oven at the side. The hemp is pressed down in bundles upon these, and stakes are driven in among them. Piles of coarse Korean grass are placed over the hemp, and earth over all, well beaten down. The stakes are then pulled up and water is poured into the holes left by them. This, falling on the heated stones, produces a dense steam, and in twenty-four hours the hemp fibre is so completely disintegrated as to be easily separated.

A grand gorge, 3 miles long, with lofty cliffs of much-caverned limestone, varied by rock needles draped with *Ampelopsis* and clematis, and giving foothold to azaleas, spirea, syringa, pear, hawthorn, climbing roses, wistaria, cyclamen, lycopodium, yellow vetches, many *Labiatæ*, and much else, contains but one village, piled step above step in a deep wooded fold of the hills, on which millet culture is carried to a great height, on slopes too steep to be ploughed by oxen. This gorge opens out on slopes of rich soil, some of which is still uncultivated. The hamlets are small, and grow much hemp, and each has its hemp pit. They also grow *Urtica Nivea*, from the bleached fibre of which their grass cloth summer clothes are made. All these are surrounded with mulberry groves.

The large village of Cham-su-ki, at the head of two severe rapids, in ascending which our ropes snapped three times, offers a good example of the popular belief in spirits. It is approached under a tasselled straw rope, one end of which is wound round a fine tree with a stone altar below it. On another rope were suspended a few small bags containing offerings of food. If a person dies of the pestilence or by the roadside, or a woman dies in childbirth, the spirit invariably takes up its abode in a tree. To such spirits offerings are made on the stone altar of cake, wine, and pork, but where the tree is the domicile of the spirit of a man who has been killed by a tiger, dog's flesh is offered instead of pork. The Cham-su-ki tree is a fine well-grown elm. Gnarled trees, of which we saw several on hilltops and sides, are occupied by the spirits of persons who have died before reaching a cycle, *i.e.* sixty years of age. A steep cliff above Cham-su-ki is also denoted as the abode of dæmons by a straw rope and a stone altar.

We had some very cold and windy days near the end of April, the mercury falling to 34°, and one night of tempestuous rain. It would be absurd to write of sufferings, but at that temperature in an open boat, with the roof lifting and flapping and threatening to take its departure, it was impossible to sleep. Afterwards the weather was again splendid.

Abrupt turns, long rapids full of jagged rocks, long stretches of deep, still water, abounding in fish, narrow gorges walled in by terraces of basalt, lateral ravines disclosing fine snow-streaked peaks, succeeded each other, the shores becoming less and less peopled, while the parallel valleys abounded in fairly well-to-do villages. Just below a long and dangerous rapid we stopped to dine, and though the place seemed quite solitary, a crowd soon gathered, and sat on the adjacent stones talking noisily, trying to get into the boat, lifting the mats, discussing whether it were polite to watch people at dinner, some taking one side and some another, those who were half tipsy taking the affirmative. Some said that they had got news from several miles below that this great sight was coming up the river, and it was a shame to deprive them of it by keeping the curtains down. After a good deal of obstreperousness, mainly the result of wine, a man overbalanced himself and fell into the river, which raised a laugh, and then they followed us good-naturedly up the rapid, one man helping to track, and asking as his reward that his wife might see me, on which I exhibited myself on the bow of the boat.

At the village of Pang-wha San, built, contrary to Korean practice, on a height of 800 feet, there is a stone platform, on which was nightly lighted one of that chain of beacon-fires terminating at Nam-San in Seoul, which assured the King that his kingdom was at peace.[1]   Another village, Ha-chin, was impressive from the frightful ugliness of its women.   After leaving Tan-Yang the curiosity increased.   People walked great distances to see us, saying they had never seen foreigners, and bringing eggs to pay for the sight, which I paid for, telling the people that we had nothing to show ; but extravagant rumors of what was to be seen in the boat had preceded us, and as the people assembled at daylight and generally waited patiently, I always yielded to their wishes, raised the thatch, and made the most of the red and white curtains.   In one place I gave them some tea to drink.   They had never seen it, and thought it was medicine, and on tasting it said, " It must be very good for indigestion ! "

[1] The telegraph has now superseded this picturesque arrangement.

CHAPTER VIII

NATURAL BEAUTY—THE RAPIDS

IN superb weather, and in the full glory of spring, we continued the exploration of the Han above Tan-Yang, encountering innumerable rapids, some of them very severe and
horrible to look upon. The river valley, continually narrowing into gorges, rarely admits of hamlets, and the population
is relegated to lateral and parallel valleys. On the 30th of
April we tugged and poled the boat up seven long and severe
rapids, with deep still stretches of water between them. The
flora increased in variety, and the shapes of the mountains became very definite. Among other trees there were a large
branching *Acanthopanax ricinifolia*, two species of euonymus,
mistletoe on the walnut and mulberry, the *Rhus semi-alata*
and *Rhus vernicifera*, pines, firs, the *Abies microsperma*, the
Actinidia pueraria, Elæagnus, Spanish chestnuts in great
groves, alders, birches, maples, elms, limes, and a tree infrequently seen which I believe to be a *Zelkawa*. Among the
flowers, there were marigolds, buttercups, scentless white and
purple violets, yellow violas, white aconite, lady's slipper, hawk-
weed, camomile, red and white dandelions, guelder roses, wyge-
lias, mountain peonies, martagon and tiger lilies, gentians, pink
spirea, yellow day lilies, white honeysuckle, the *Iris Rossii*,
and many others.

The day after leaving Tan-Yang we entered on the most
beautiful part of the river. Great limestone cliffs swing open
at times to reveal glorious glimpses, through fantastic gorges,
of peaks and ranges, partly forest-covered, fading in the far
distance into the delicious blue veil of dreamland ; the river,

occasionally compressed by its colossal walls, vents its fury in flurry and foam, or expands into broad reaches 20 and even 30 feet in depth, where pure emerald water laps gently upon crags festooned with roses and honeysuckle, or in fairy bays on pebbly beaches and white sand. The air was full of gladness. The loud call of the fearless ringed pheasant was heard everywhere, bees hummed and butterflies and dragon-flies flashed through the fragrant air. What mattered it that our ropes broke three times, that we stuck on a rock in a rapid and hung there for an hour in a deafening din and a lather of foam, and that we "beat the record" in only making 5 miles in twelve hours!

The limestone cliffs are much caverned, and near the village of To-tam, where they fall back considerably from the river, we explored one cave worthy of notice, with a fine entrance arch 43 feet in height, admitting into a vault considerably higher, with a roof of stalagmites. We ascended this cavern for 315 feet, and then had to return for lack of light. Near the mouth a natural shaft and rock-ladder give access to a fine upper gallery 12 feet high, only 60 feet of which we were able to investigate. Just above To-tam there is another limestone freak on the river bank, a natural bridge or arch, 127 feet in height and 30 feet wide, below which a fair green lawn slopes up to a height above. The bridge is admirably buttressed, and draped with roses, honeysuckle, and clematis, and various fantastic specimens of coniferæ grow out of its rifts.

The beauty of the Han culminates at To-tam in the finest river view I had then ever seen, a broad stretch, with a deep bay and lofty limestone cliffs, between which, on a green slope, the picturesque, deep-eaved, brown-roofed houses of the village are built. The gray cliff is crowned with a goodly group of umbrella pines, in Korea called "Parasol Pines," because they resemble in shape those carried before the King. Guarding the entrance of the bay are three picturesque jagged pyramidal rocks much covered with the *Ampelopsis Veitchiana,* and of course sacred to dæmon worship. These sentinels are from 40 to 83 feet high. To the southwest the Han, dark and deep, rolls out of sight round a pine-clad bluff, among the magnificent ranges of the Sol-rak-San mountains—masses of partially pine-clothed peaks and pinnacles of naked rock. To the northeast the river makes an abrupt bend below superb limestone cliffs, and disappears at the foot of Sölmi-San, a triplet of lofty peaks. To-tam on its park-like slopes embraces this view, and were it not for the rapids and their delays and risks, might be a delightful summer resort from Seoul.

There is fertility as well as grandeur, for the ridge behind the village, abrupt on the riverside, falls gently down on the other to a broad, well-watered level valley, cultivated for rice with extreme neatness and care, and which, after gladdening the eye with its productiveness for several miles, winds out of view among the mountains.

There, and in most parts of the Han valley, I was much surprised with the neatness of the cultivation. It was not what the reports of other travellers had led me to expect, and it gives me the impression that the river passes through one of the most productive and prosperous portions of Korea. The crops of wheat and barley were usually superb, and remarkably free from weeds—in fact, the cleanliness would do credit to "high farming" in the Lothians. It was no uncommon thing to find from 12 to 18 stalks as the product of one grain. At the end of April the barley was in ear, and beginning to change color, and the wheat was 6 inches high. As a general rule the stones were carefully picked off the land and were used for retaining walls for the rice terraces, or piled in heaps. Steep hillsides were being cleared of scrub and stones for cotton planting, and in many instances the cultivation is carried to a height of 1,000 feet, the cultivators always, however, living in the holes. All the parallel valleys are neatly and carefully cultivated. The favorable climate, with its abundant, but not superabundant, rainfall, renders irrigation needless, except in the case of rice.   Every valley has its streamlet, and is barred across by dykes of mud from its head down to the Han, rice, with tobacco, beans, hemp, and cotton, being the great articles of export.   On the whole, I was very agreeably surprised with the agriculture of the Han valley, and doubt not that it is capable of enormous development if the earnings of industry were secure.   The soil is most prolific, heavy crops being raised without the aid of fertilizers.

After leaving beautiful To-tam, the rapids become more and more frequent and exasperating, and when Kim sank down, playing upon my feelings by well-simulated exhaustion, I feared it would soon become real.   The ropes broke frequently, and the constant scraping and bumping over rocks increased the leakiness of the boat so much, that in a lovely reach, where crystal water rippled on the white sand, I pitched my tent, and unloaded and beached the craft for repairs.   In one strong deep rapid that day the rope parted, and the boat swirled down the surges, striking rocks as she spun down with such effect as to spoil a number of photographic negatives and soak my bedding.

At the beautifully situated village of Pa-ka Mi, a post bore the following inscription in large characters—"If any servant of a *yang-ban* passing through Pa-ka Mi is polite and behaves well, all right, but if he behaves badly he will be beaten," an assertion of independence as refreshing as it is rare !

For among the curses of Korea is the existence of this privileged class of *yang-bans* or nobles, who must not work for their own living, though it is no disgrace to be supported by their relations, and who often live on the clandestine industry of their wives in sewing and laundry work.   A *yang-ban* carries nothing for himself, not even his pipe.   *Yang-ban* students do not even carry their books from their studies to the classroom.   Custom insist that when a member of this class travels he shall take with him as many attendants as he can muster.   He is supported on his led horse, and supreme helplessness is the conventional requirement. His servants browbeat and bully the people and take their fowls and eggs without payment, which explains the meaning of the notice at Pa-ka Mi.[1]

There is no doubt that the people, *i. e.* the vast mass of the unprivileged, on whose shoulders rests the burden of taxation, are hard pressed by the *yang-bans*, who not only use their labor without paying for it, but make merciless exactions under the name of loans. As soon as it is rumored or known that a merchant or peasant has laid up a certain amount of *cash*, a *yang-ban* or official seeks a loan. Practically it is a levy, for if it is refused the man is either thrown into prison on a false charge and whipped every morning until he or his relations pay the sum demanded, or he is seized and practically imprisoned on low diet in the *yang-ban's* house until the money is forthcoming. It is the best of the nobles who disguise their exactions under the name of loans, but the lender never sees principal or interest. It is a very common thing for a noble, when he buys a house or field, to dispense with paying for it, and no mandarin will enforce payment. At Paik-kui Mi, where I paid off my boatmen, the *yang-ban's* servants were impressing all the boats for the purpose of taking roofing tiles to Seoul without payment. Kim begged me to give him some trifle to take down the river, with a few *cash* as payment, and a line to say that the boat was in my employment, service with a foreigner being a protection from such an exaction.

There were two days more of most severe toil, in which it was scarcely possible to make any progress. The rapids were frightful, and when we reached a very bad one below the town of Yöng-chhun, Kim, after making several abortive efforts, not, I think, in good faith, to ascend it, collapsed, and said he could not get up any higher. At another season boats of light draught can ascend to Yang-wöl, 20 *li* farther. We had per-

[1] Class privileges are now abolished, on paper at least, but their tradition carries weight.

formed a great feat in getting up to Yŏng-chhun in early May. There were no boats on the higher waters, and for much of the distance my *sampan* could hardly be said to be afloat. At Yŏng-chhun we were within 40 miles of the Sea of Japan.

Wind and heavy rain which raised the river forbade all locomotion until the following evening, when we crossed the Han and reached the Yŏng-chhun ferry by a pretty road through a village and a wood, most attractive country, with many novelties in its flora. At the ferry a still expanse of the Han is over 10 feet deep, but the roar of another rapid is heard immediately above. A double avenue of noble elms with fine turf underneath them leads to the town, a magistracy of 1,500 people, a quiet market-place without shops, situated in a rich farming basin of alluvial soil, covered in May with heavy crops of barley and wheat, among which were fields hillocked for melons.

The magistracy buildings are large and rambling, with what has been a fine entrance gate, with a drum and other instruments of aural torture for making the deafening din with which the *yamen* is closed and opened at sunrise and sunset. There are many stone tablets (not spontaneously erected) to worthy officials, a large enclosure in which sacrifices are offered to " Heaven " (probably to the Spirits of the Land), a Confucian temple, and a king's pavilion, all very squalid and ruinous.

A crowd not altogether polite followed us to the *yamen*, where I hoped that some information regarding an overland route to the Diamond Mountain might be obtained. On entering the *yamen* precincts the underling officials were most insolent, and it was only after enduring their unpleasant behavior for some time that we were conducted to a squalid inner room, where a deputy-mandarin sat on the floor with a smoking apparatus beside him, a man with a scornful and sinister physiognomy, who took not the slightest notice of us, and when he deigned to speak gave curt replies through an underling, while we stood outside the entrance, withstanding with difficulty the pressure of the crowd, which had surged in after us, private interviews being rare in the East. This was my last visit to a Korean *yamen*.

As we walked back to the town, the crowd followed us closely, led by some "swells" of the literary class. One young man came up behind me and kicked me on the ankle, stepping back and then coming forward and repeating the offense. He was about to give me a third kick, when Mr. Miller turned round and very quietly, without anger, dealt him a scientific blow on the chest, which sent him off the road upon his back into a barley field. There was a roar of laughter from the crowd, and the young bully's companions begged Mr. Miller not to punish him any more. The crowd dispersed, the bullies, cowards like all their species, fell far behind, and we had a pleasant walk back to the ferry, where, although we had to wait a long time in the ferry boat, there was no assemblage, and the ferryman and passengers were very civil. Mr. Miller regretted the necessity for inflicting punishment. It was Lynch law no doubt, but it was summary justice, and the perfect coolness with which it was administered would no doubt leave a salutary impression. The ferryman told us that a tiger had carried off a pig from Yöng-chhun the previous night, and said that the walk to our boat through the wood without lanterns was very unsafe. Our boatmen had become alarmed and were hunting for us with torches. The circumstances were eerie, and I was glad to see the lights.

Ferries are free. The Government provides the broad, strong boats which are used for ferrying cattle as well as people, and the villages provide the ferrymen with food. Passengers who are not poor usually give a small *douceur*.

A gale of wind with torrents of rain set in that night, and the rain continued till the next afternoon, giving me an opportunity of seeing more of the detail of the magnificent cliffs of laminated limestone, which occur frequently, and are the most striking geological features of the Han valley, continually presenting the appearance of the leaves of a colossal book. Above the Yöng-chhun rapid, on a steep and almost inaccessible declivity, buttressed by these cliffs, are the remains of a very ancient fortress, the outer wall of which, enclosing the summit of the hill, is 2,500 feet in circumference, 25 feet high on the outside, from 1 to 12 feet on the inside, and from 9 to 12 feet thick. It is so arranged that its two gates, which open on nearly direct descents of 20 feet, and are approached by very narrow pathways, could only admit one man at a time. It was obviously incapable of reduction by any force but starvation. No mortar is used in the walls, which are very efficiently built of small slabs of stone never more than 6 inches thick. The people have no traditions of its construction, but Mr. Miller, who is familiar with the fortresses of Nam-San and Puk Han, thinks that it is of a much earlier date than either. One of the signal fire stations is visible from this point on the river.

On the 3rd of May we began the descent of the Han. The worn-out ropes were used for the cooking fire, the poles were stowed away, and paddles took their place. The heavy rains had raised the river a foot, and changed its bright waters into a turbid flood, down which we often descended in two minutes distances which had taken two laborious hours on the upward journey, flying down the centre of the stream instead of crawling up the sides. Many small disasters occurred. Several times the boat was nearly swamped by heavy surges, or shivered by striking sunken rocks ; or, losing steerage way, spun round and round, progressing downwards with many gyrations, usually stern foremost, amidst billows and foam, but Kim, who was at his best on such occasions, usually contrived to bring her to shore, bow on, at the foot of the rapid. On one occasion, however, in a long rapid, in which the surges were high and strong, by some mismanagement, regarding which the boatmen quarrelled for an hour afterwards, the *sam-pan* shipped such heavy seas from both sides as nearly to

swamp her. I was all but washed off my camp-bed, which
was on a level with the gunwale ; a number of sheets of geographical notes were washed away, some instruments belonging to the R.G.S. were drowned in their box, more than forty
photographic negatives were destroyed, and clothing, bedding,
and flour were all soaked ! The rapids were in fact most exciting, and their risks throw those of the Fu and the Yangtze
from Cheng-tu to Ichang quite into the shade.

In spite of a delay of half a day at Tan-Yang, owing to a
futile attempt to get *cash* for silver, and another half-day spent
in beaching and repairing the boat, which had been badly
bumped on a rock, we did the distance from Nang-chhön to
Ma-chai on the forks in four and a half days, or less than a
third of the time taken by the laborious ascent.

The penniless situation became so serious that one day before reaching Ma-chai I had to decide on returning to Seoul
for *cash !* The treasuries were said to be empty ; no one believed in silver or knew anything about it, and supplies could
not be obtained. Fortunately we arrived at the market-place
of Ma-Kyo, a village of 1,850 people, on the market day, and
the pedlars gladly exchanged *cash* for 35 silver *yen* at the rate
of 3,000, and would willingly have changed 70. It took six
men to carry the coin to the boat, which was once more sub-
stantially ballasted. Ma-Kyo is the river port of Che-chön,
and has an unusually flourishing aspect, boasting of many
good houses with tiled roofs. It exports rice, beans, and grain
from the very rich agricultural country on both sides of the
river, and imports foreign cottons, Korean sackcloth, and salt.
Cotton in 20 *cash* the measure of 20 inches dearer at Ma-Kyo
than in Seoul, and at Nang-chhön 70 *cash* dearer.

When we reached the forks at Ma-chai, the boatmen, who
were tired of the trip, wanted to go back, but eventually they
were induced to fulfil their contract, and we entered the north
branch of the Han on a cool, glorious afternoon, following on
a night and morning of wind and rain. This north branch

also rises in the Keum-kang San or Diamond Mountain in the province of Kong-wön, and after a turbulent course of about 98 miles unites with the southern and larger branch of the Han about two days' journey from Seoul. For a considerable distance the country which it drains is populous and well cultivated, and the hills of its higher reaches provide much of the timber which is used in Seoul, as well as a large proportion of the firewood and charcoal. The timber is made up into very peculiar rafts, which come down at high water, but even then are frequently demolished in the rapids. The river widens out above Ma-chai, and for a considerable distance has an average breadth of 440 yards, but as a rule it is shallow, and its bottom dangerously rocky, and it has incessant rapids full of jagged rocks, some of which are very dangerous, and so " ugly " that as I went up them I was truly glad that I had not to descend them. Many a long, hard tug and broken hawser we had, but succeeded in hauling the *sampan* 7 miles above the limit of low water navigation, which is the same distance from the termination of boat traffic at high water. I estimate the distance from Ma-chai to Ut-Kiri, where further progress was stopped by an insurmountable rapid, at 76 miles, which took nine days, though Kim and his man, anxious to go home, worked much harder than on our earlier trip.

For the first few days there are villages every quarter of a mile, and lateral and parallel valleys, then rich in clean crops of barley and wheat. The river villages are surrounded by groves of Spanish chestnut, mulberry, cherry, persimmons, and weeping willows. There are deep crateriform cavities, now full of trees and abundant vegetation. The hills are covered with oak scrub, affording cover for tigers, which appear to abound. The characteristics of the villages and the agriculture hardly vary from those on the south branch, except that the potato is more extensively grown. The absence of provincial and local peculiarities is a feature of Korea. An alley in Seoul may serve for a village street anywhere else.

Gold in small quantities is found along the river, and rumor says that Ur-röp-so, a conical hill near the dangerous rapid of Chum-yöl, is rich in it, but that the district official prohibits digging. Higher up a number of men were washing for gold. Their apparatus consists of a wooden sieve or gridiron, on which the supposed auriferous earth is placed above a deep wooden tray, and rocked under water till the heavier stuff passes through, to be again rocked in search of the glittering particles. The results are placed on the river bank in pieces of broken pottery, each watched by a man. The earth is obtained by removing the heavy shingle of the river bank and digging up the sand to a depth of about 2 feet, when rock is reached. From 60 to 100 trays are equal to a bushel and a half, and the yield of this quantity averages half a thimbleful of gold in a state of fine subdivision. These gold-washers seldom make more than 16s. per month, and only about 50s. when working in the best goldfields.

Gold ornaments are rarely seen in Korea, gold is scarcely if at all used in the arts (if arts there are), and gold coins do not exist. Nevertheless, as is shown by the Customs Reports, the quantity of gold dust exported, chiefly to Japan, is very far from being despicable, although the reefs which presumably contain the metal, of which the washings are the proof, have not yet been touched. The fees paid by the miners to the Government vary with the locality. Gold-digging without Government authorization is prohibited by law under most severe penalties. Among the richest goldfields in Korea are Phyöng Kang, not far from the Han, and Keum-San in Phyöng-an Do, not far from the Tai-dong. The larger washings collect as elsewhere the scum of the country, and riots often occur among the miners. I know not on which subject the Korean is the more voluble, tigers or gold. He is proud of Korea as a gold-producing country, and speaks as if its dust were golden sand !

The groves of Spanish chestnuts with which the North Han

is fringed gave off an overpowering odor. Their fruit is an important article of diet. Usually the arable land below the villages is little more than a terrace, but on the hillsides above the grain rippled in long yellow waves in the breeze, and the hills constantly swing apart and reveal terraced valleys and brown orchard embowered hamlets; or slightly receding, expose stretches of white sand or heaps of fantastic boulders.

After two days of severe work we reached the beautifully situated town of Ka-phyöng, which straggles along the valley of a small tributary of the Han on slopes backed by high mountains which, following the usual Korean custom, are without names. The bright green of the wheat fields, varied by the darker green of clumps of conifers and chestnuts, arranged as if by a landscape gardener, and the lines of trees along the river bank were enchanting, but Ka-phyöng does not bear close inspection. The telegraph wire from Seoul to Wön-san crosses the river at Sin-gang Kam, and there is actually a telegraph station at Chun-chön, the most important town of that region, at which messages are received and sent about once a month !

Chun-chön is four miles from the Han on its left bank. It is fortified, and has nominally a garrison of 300 men. Having a population of 3,000, and being in the centre of a fine agricultural district, it is a place of some trade, as trade is understood in Korea. Just below it the Han, after running for some distance below a lofty quartz ridge, makes an abrupt turn and penetrates it, the walls of the passage having the regularity of a railway cutting, while the bed of the stream is of pure white quartz.

Beyond this singular gateway the river valley opens out, and the spectacle, rare in Korea, of cattle is to be seen. Indeed, I only once saw cattle feeding elsewhere. The grass is coarse and sour, and hand feeding is customary. It was most pleasant to be awoke in the dewy morning by bellowing of cattle, shouts and laughter of boys and yelping of dogs, as bulls old and young were driven to the river bank to be tethered in the flowery grass. The frolicsome bull calves, which are brought up in the Korean home, and are attended to by the children, who are their natural playmates, develop under such treatment into that maturity of mingled gentleness and stateliness which is characteristic of the Korean bull,—the one grand thing remaining to Korea. When full grown a bull can carry from 350 to 500 lbs. They are fed on boiled beans, cut millet stalks, and cut pea haulm, and the water in which the beans are boiled. They are led by a rope passed round the horns from a bamboo ring in the nose. The prevailing color is a warm red, and the huge animal in build much resembles the shorthorn. The Korean cow, which is to be seen carrying loads in Northern Korea, is a worthy dam of such a splendid progeny.

The scenery, though always pretty, becomes monotonous after a few days, and monotonous too were the adventures in the rapids, which were innumerable, and the ceaseless toiling, dragging, and tugging they involved. Reaching Won-chön, a post station on the road to Wön-san, we halted and engaged horses for a land journey, at a very high rate, but they and their *mapu* or grooms turned out well, and as Wong sententiously remarked, "If you pay well, you will be served well." The agreement, which I caused to be put into writing, and which I made use of in other journeys, with much mutual satisfaction, was duly signed, and we continued the boat journey.

After spending half a day at the prefectural town of Nang-chhön, where I am glad to record that the officials were very courteous, we ascended the Han to a point above the wild hamlet of Ut-Kiri, on a severe rapid full of jagged rocks. Ut-Kiri is above the head of low water navigation, but in two summer months during the rains small boats can reach Ku-mu-nio, "the last village," 20 *li* higher. It was a wild termination of the long boat journey. An abrupt turn of the river, and its monotonous prettiness is left behind, and there is a superb mountain view of saddleback ridges and lofty gray peaks surrounding a dark expanse of water, with a margin of gray boulders and needles of gray rock draped with the *Ampelopsis*, a yellow clematis, and a white honeysuckle. It was somewhat sad not to be able to penetrate the grim austerity to the northward, but the rapids were so severe and the water ofttimes so shallow that it was impossible to drag the *sampan* farther, though at that time she only drew 2 inches of water. From Ma-chai on the forks she had been poled and dragged up forty rapids, making eighty-six on the whole journey.

From the thinly peopled solitudes of these upper waters we descended rapidly, though not without some severe bumps, to the populous river banks, where villages are half hidden among orchards and chestnut and mulberry groves, and the crops are heavy, and that abundance of the necessaries of life which in Korea passes for prosperity is the rule.

Ta-rai, a neat, prosperous place of 240 people, among orchards, and hillsides terraced and bearing superb crops, is an example of the riverine villages. Its houses are built step above step along the sides of a ravine, down which a perennial stream flows, affording water power for an automatic rice hulling machine. For exports and imports the Han at high water is a cheap and convenient highway. The hill slopes above the village, with their rich soil, afford space for agricultural expansion for years to come. And not to dwell altogether on the material, there is a shrine of much repute on a fork-like slope near the river. It contains a group of *mirioks*, in this case stones worn by the action of water into the semblance of human beings. The central figure, larger than life, may even to a dull imagination represent a person carrying an infant, and its eyes, nose, and mouth are touched in with China ink. It is surrounded by Phallic symbols and *mirioks*, which may be supposed to represent children, and women make prayers and offerings in this shrine in the hope of obtaining a much coveted increase in their families, for male children are still regarded as a blessing in Korea, and " happy is the man that hath his quiver full of them."

Ka-phyöng again, a small prefectural town of 400 houses 1½ miles from the river, is a good specimen of the small towns of the Han valley, with a ruinous *yamen*, of course, with its non-producing mob of hangers-on. It is on the verge of an alluvial plain, rolling up to picturesque hills, gashed by valleys, abounding in hamlets surrounded by chestnut groves and care-ful cultivation. The slopes above Ka-phyöng break up into knolls richly wooded with conifers and hard-wood trees, fring-ing off into clumps and groups which would not do discredit to the slopes of Windsor. The people of a large district bring their produce into the town, and barter it for goods in the market. The telegraph wire to Wön-san crosses the affluent on which Ka-phyöng is built, and is carried along a bridle path which for some *li* runs along the river bank. Junks loaded 10 feet above their gunwales, as well as 4 feet outside of them with firewood, and large rafts were waiting for the water to rise. Boats were being built and great quantities of the strong rope used for towing and other purposes, which is made from a "creeper" which grows profusely in Central Korea, were awaiting water carriage. Yet Ka-phyöng, like other small Korean towns, has no life or go. Its "merchants" are but pedlars, its commercial ideas do not rise above those of the huckster, and though poverty, as we understand it, is unknown, prosperity as we understand it is absent. There are no special industries in any of the riverine towns, and if they were all to disappear in some catastrophe it would not cause a ripple on the surface of the general commercial apathy of the country.

Similar remarks apply to the prefectural town of Nang-chhön, where we again wasted some hours, while Kim's rice was first bargained for and then cleaned. At that point there is a fine deep stretch of the river 230 yards broad abounding in fish.   From Nang-chhön we dropped down the Han to a deep and pretty bay on which the small village of Paik-kui Mi is situated, where we halted for Sunday, our last day in the *sampan*, which had been a not altogether comfortless home for five weeks and a half.

CHAPTER IX

KOREAN MARRIAGE CUSTOMS

PAIK-KUI MI was not without a certain degree of life on that
Sunday. A *yang-ban's* steward impressed boats for the
gratuitous carriage of tiles to Seoul, which caused a little feeble excitement among the junkmen. There was a sick person,
and a *mutang* or female exorcist was engaged during the whole
day in the attempt to expel the malevolent dæmon which was
afflicting him, the process being accompanied by the constant
beating of a drum and the loud vibrating sound of large cymbals. Lastly, there was a marriage, and this deserves more
than a passing notice, marriage, burial, and exorcism, with
their ceremonials, being the outstanding features of Korea.[1]

The Korean is nobody until he is married. He is a being
of no account, a "hobbledehoy." The wedding-day is the
entrance on respectability and manhood, and marks a leap upwards on the social ladder. The youth, with long abundant
hair divided in the middle and plaited at the back, wearing a
short, girdled coat, and looking as if he had no place in the
world though he may be quite grown up, and who is always
taken by strangers for a girl, is transformed by the formal reciprocal salutations which constitute the binding ceremony of
marriage. He has received the tonsure, and the long hair surrounding it is drawn into the now celebrated "topknot."
He is invested with the *mangan*, a crownless skullcap or fillet
of horsehair, without which, thereafter, he is never seen. He

[1] The notes on marriage customs which follow were given me by English-speaking Koreans and were taken down at the time. They apply
chiefly to the middle class.

wears a black hat and a long full coat, and his awkward gait is metamorphosed into a dignified swing. His boy companions have become his inferiors. His name takes the equivalent of "Mr." after it; honorifics must be used in addressing him— in short, from being a "nobody" he becomes a "somebody."

A girl by marrying fulfils her "manifest destiny." Spinsterhood in Korea is relegated to the Buddhist nunneries, where it has no reputation for sanctity. Absolutely secluded in the inner court of her father's house from the age of seven, a girl passes about the age of seventeen to the absolute seclusion of the inner rooms of her father-in-law's house. The old ties are broken, and her husband's home is thenceforth her prison. It is "custom." It is only to our thinking that the custom covers a felt hardship. It is needless to add that the young couples do not choose each other. The marriage is arranged by the fathers, and is consented to as a matter of course. A man gains the reputation of being a neglectful father who allows his son to reach the age of twenty unmarried. Seventeen or eighteen is the usual age at which a man marries. A girl may go through the marriage ceremony as a mere child if her parents think an "eligible" may slip through their fingers, but she is not obliged to assume the duties of wifehood till she is sixteen. On the other hand, boys of ten and twelve years of age are constantly married when their parents for any reason wish to see the affair settled and a desirable connection presents itself, and the yellow hats and pink and blue coats and attempted dignity of these boy bridegrooms are among the sights of the cities.

A go-between is generally employed for the preliminary arrangements. No money is given to the bride's father by the bridegroom, nor does the daughter receive a dowry, but she is supplied with a large *trousseau*, which is packed in handsome marriage chests with brass clamps and decorations. There is no betrothal ceremony, and after the arrangement has been made the marriage may be delayed for weeks or even months.

When it is thought desirable that it should take place, but not until the evening before, the bridegroom's father sends a sort of marriage-contract to the bride's father, who receives it without replying, and two pieces of silk are sent to the bride, out of which her outer garments must be made for the marriage day.

A number of men carrying gay silk lanterns bear this present to the bride, and on the way are met by a party of men from her father's house bearing torches, and a fight ensues, which is often more than a make-believe one, for serious blows are exchanged, and on both sides some are hurt. Death has occasionally been known to follow on the wounds received. If the bridegroom's party is worsted in the *melée* it is a sign that he will have bad luck; if the bride's, that she will have misfortunes. The night before the marriage the parents of the bride and groom sacrifice in their respective houses before the ancestral tablets, and acquaint the ancestors with the event which is to occur on the morrow.

The auspicious day having been decided on by the sorcerer, about an hour before noon, the bridegroom on horseback, and in Court dress, leaves his father's house, and on that occasion only a plebeian can pass a *yang-ban* on the road without dismounting. Two men walk before him, one carrying a white umbrella, and the other, who is dressed in red cloth, a goose, which is the emblem of conjugal fidelity. He is also attended by several men carrying unlighted red silk lanterns, by various servants, by a married brother, if he has one, or by his father if he has not. On reaching his destination he takes the goose from the hands of the man in red, goes into the house, and lays it upon a table. *Apropos* of this emblem it must be observed that conjugal fidelity is only required from the wife, and is a feminine virtue only.

Two women who are hired to officiate on such occasions lead the bride on to the veranda, or an estrade, and place her opposite the bridegroom, who stands facing her, but at some little distance from her. The wedding guests fill the court-yard. This is the man's first view of his future wife. She may have seen him through a chink in the lattice or a hole in the wall. A queer object she is to our thinking. Her face is covered with white powder, patched with spots of red, and her eyelids are glued together by an adhesive compound. At the instigation of her attendants she bows twice to her lord, and he bows four times to her. It is this public reciprocal " salu-tation " which alone constitutes a valid marriage. After it, if he repudiates her, he cannot take another wife. The perma-nence of the marriage tie is fully recognized in Korea, though a man can form as many illicit connections as he chooses. A cup of wine is then given to the bridegroom, who drinks a little, after which it is handed to the bride, who merely tastes it.

Afterwards within the house a table with a dainty dinner is set before the husband, who eats sparingly. The bride retires to the women's rooms, and the groom rejoices with his friends in the men's apartments. There is no simultaneous banquet. Each guest on arriving is supplied with a table of food. Such a table, in the case of people of means, costs from five to six *yen* (from 10s. to 12s.), and a very cheap wedding costs seventy-five *yen*, so that several daughters are a misfortune.

During the afternoon the husband returns to his father's house, and after a time the bride, bundled up in a mass of wedding clothes, and with her eyelids still sealed, attended by the two women mentioned before, some hired girls, and men with lanterns, goes thither also, in a rigidly closed chair, in the gay decorations of which red predominates. There she is received by her father and mother-in-law, to whom she bows four times, remaining speechless. She is then carried back to the house of her own parents, her eyelids are unsealed, and the powder is washed from her face. At five her husband ar-rives, but returns to his father's house on the following morn-ing, this process of going and returning being repeated for three days, after which the bride is carried in a plain chair to her future home, under the roof of her parents-in-law, where she is allotted a room or rooms in the seclusion of the women's apartments.

The name bestowed on her by her parents soon after her birth is dropped, and she is known thereafter only as "the wife of so and so," or "the mother of so and so." Her husband addresses her by the word *yabu*, signifying "Look here," which is significant of her relations to him.

Silence is regarded as a wife's first duty. During the whole of the marriage day the bride must be as mute as a statue. If she says a word or even makes a sign she becomes an object of ridicule, and her silence must remain unbroken even in her own room, though her husband may attempt to break it by taunts, jeers, or coaxing, for the female servants are all on the *qui vive* for such a breach of etiquette as speech, hanging about the doors and chinks to catch up and gossip even a single utterance, which would cause her to lose caste for ever in her circle. This custom of silence is observed with the greatest rigidity in the higher classes. It may be a week or several months before the husband knows the sound of his wife's voice, and even after that for a length of time she only opens her mouth for necessary speech. With the father-in-law the law of silence is even more rigid. The daughter-in-law often passes years without raising her eyes to his, or addressing a word to him.

The wife has recognized duties to her husband, but he has few, if any, to her. It is correct for a man to treat his wife with external marks of respect, but he would be an object for scorn and ridicule if he showed her affection or treated her as a companion. Among the upper classes a bridegroom, after passing three or four days with his wife, leaves her for a considerable time to show his indifference. To act otherwise would be "bad form." My impression is that the community of interests and occupations which poverty gives, and the embargo which it lays on other connections, in Korea as in some other Oriental countries, produces happier marriages among the lower orders than among the higher. Korean women have always borne the yoke. They accept inferiority as their natural lot; they do not look for affection in marriage, and probably the idea of breaking custom never occurs to them. Usually they submit quietly to the rule of the *belle-mère*, and those who are insubordinate and provoke scenes of anger and scandal are reduced to order by a severe beating, when they are women of the people. But in the noble class custom forbids a husband to strike his wife, and as his only remedy is a divorce, and remarriage is difficult, he usually resigns himself to his fate. But if, in addition to tormenting him and destroying the peace of his house, the wife is unfaithful, he can take her to a mandarin, who, after giving her a severe beating, may bestow her on a satellite.

The seclusion of girls in the parental home is carried on after marriage, and in the case of women of the upper and middle classes is as complete as is possible. They never go out by daylight except in completely closed chairs. At night, attended by a woman and a servant with a lantern, and with a mantle over her head, a wife may stir abroad and visit her female friends, but never without her husband's permission, who requires, or may require, proof that the visit has been actually paid. Shopping is done by servants, or goods are brought to the veranda, the vendors discreetly retiring. Time, which among the leisured classes hangs heavily on the hands, is spent in spasmodic cooking, sewing, embroidering, reading very light literature in *En-mun*, and in the never-failing resources of gossip and the interminable discussion of babies. If a wife is very dull indeed, she can, with her husband's permission, send for actors, or rather posturing reciters, to the compound, and look at them through the chinks of the bamboo blinds. Through these also many Korean ladies have seen the splendors of the *Kur-dong*.

When the Korean wife becomes a mother her position is improved. Girls, as being unable to support their parents in old age or to perform the ancestral rites, are not prized as boys are, yet they are neither superfluous nor unwelcome as in some Eastern countries. The birth of a girl is not made an occasion for rejoicing, but that of the firstborn son is, and after the name has been bestowed on him, the mother is known as "the mother of so and so." The first step alone of the first boy is an occasion for family jubilation. Korean babies have no cradles, and are put to sleep by being tapped lightly on the stomach.

A KOREAN LADY.

CHAPTER X

THE KOREAN PONY—KOREAN ROADS AND INNS

A GRAY and murky morning darkening into drizzle, which thickened into a day's pouring rain, was an inauspicious beginning of a long land journey, but the crawling up the north Han had become monotonous and change and action were desirable. Being an experienced muleteer, I had arranged the loads for each pony so equitably as to obviate the usual quarrel among the *mapu* or grooms at starting! The men were not regular *mapu*, and were going chiefly to see the Diamond Mountain. One was well educated and gentlemanly, and the bystanders jeered at them for "loading like scholars." They were a family party, and there were no disputes.

My first experience of the redoubtable Korean pony was not reassuring. The men had never seen a foreign saddle and were half an hour in getting it "fixed." Though a pony's saddle, it was far too large for the creature's minute body, the girths were half a yard and the crupper nearly a foot too long. The animal bit, squealed, struck with his fore and hind feet, and performed the singular feat of bending his back into such an inward curve that his small body came quite near the ground. The men were afraid of him, and it was only in the brief intervals of fighting that they dared to make a dash at the buckles. It was "tight-lacing" that he objected to.

The Korean pony is among the most salient features of Korea. The breed is peculiar to it. The animals used for burdens are all stallions, from 10 to 12 hands high, well formed, and singularly strong, carrying from 160 to 200 lbs. 30 miles a day, week after week, on sorry food. They are

most desperate fighters, squealing and trumpeting on all occasions, attacking every pony they meet on the road, never
becoming reconciled to each other even on a long journey, and
in their fury ignoring their loads, which are often smashed to
pieces.   Their savagery makes it necessary to have a *mapu* for
every pony, instead of, as in Persia, one to five.   At the inn
stables they are not only chained down to the troughs by
chains short enough to prevent them from raising their heads,
but are partially slung at night to the heavy beams of the roof.
Even under these restricted circumstances their cordial hatred
finds vent in hyena-like yells, abortive snaps, and attempts to
swing their hind legs round.   They are never allowed to lie
down, and very rarely to drink water, and then only when
freely salted.   Their nostrils are all slit in an attempt to im-
prove upon Nature and give them better wind.   They are fed
three times a day on brown slush as hot as they can drink it,
composed of beans, chopped millet stalks, rice husks, and
bran, with the water in which they have been boiled.   The
mapu are rough to them, but I never saw them either ill-used
or petted.   Dearly as I love horses, I was not able on two
journeys to make a friend of mine.   On this journey I rode
a handsome chestnut, only 10 hands high.   He walked 4
miles an hour, and in a month of travelling, for much of it
over infamous mountain roads, never stumbled, but he resented
every attempt at friendliness both with teeth and heels.   They
are worth from 50s. upwards, and cost little to keep.

Their attendants, the *mapu*, who are by no means always
their owners, or even part owners, are very anxious about them
and take very great care of them, seeing to what passes as their
comfort before their own.   The pack saddle is removed at once
on halting, the animals are well rubbed, and afterwards thick
straw mats are bound round their bodies.   Great care is given
to the cooking of their food.   I know not whether the partial
slinging of them to the crossbeams is to relieve their legs or
to make fighting more difficult.   On many a night I have been

kept awake by the screams of some fractious animal, kicking and biting his neighbors as well as he was able, till there was a general plunging and squealing, which lasted till blows and execrations restored some degree of order.

After I mounted my steed, he trudged along very steadily, unless any of his fellows came near him, when, with an evil glare in his eyes and a hyena-like yell, he rushed upon them teeth and hoof, entirely oblivious of bit and rider.

A torrent of rain fell, and the day's journey consisted in splashing through deep mud, fording swollen streams, because the bridges which crossed them were rotten, getting wet to the skin, and getting partially dry by sitting on the hot floor of a hovel called an inn at the noonday halt, along with a steaming crowd of all sorts and conditions of men in clean and dirty white clothes.

The road by which we travelled is the main one from Seoul to the eastern treaty port of Wön-san. It passes through rice valleys with abundant irrigation, and along the sides of bare hills. Goods and travellers were not to be looked for in such weather, but there were a few strings of coolies loaded with tobacco, and a few more taking dried fish and dried seaweed, the latter a great article of diet, from Wön-san to the capital. *Pangas*, or water pestles for hulling rice, under rude thatched sheds, were numerous. These work automatically, and their solemn thud has a tone of mystery. The machine consists of a heavy log centred on a pivot, with a box at one end and a pestle at the other. Water from a stream with some feet of fall is led into the box, which when full tips over its contents and bears down one end of the log, when the sudden rise, acting on the pestle at the other end, brings it down with a heavy thud on the rice in the hollowed stone, which serves as a mortar. Where this simple machine does not exist the work is performed by women.

Denuded hillsides gave place to wooded valleys with torrents much resembling parts of Japan, the rain fell in sheets, and

quite in the early afternoon, on reaching the hamlet of Sar-
pang Kori, the *mapu* declined to proceed farther, and there I
had my first experience of a Korean inn.   Many weeks on that
and subsequent journeys showed me that this abominable shelter, as I then thought it, may be taken as a fair average specimen, and many a hearty meal and good sound sleep may be
enjoyed under such apparently unpropitious circumstances.

There are regular and irregular inns in Korea.   The irregular inn differs in nothing from the ordinary hovel of the village roadway, unless it can boast of a yard with troughs, and
can provide entertainment for beast as well as for man.   The
regular inn of the towns and large villages consists chiefly of a
filthy courtyard full of holes and heaps, entered from the road
by a tumble-down gateway.   A gaunt black pig or two tethered
by the ears, big yellow dogs routing in the garbage, and fowls,
boys, bulls, ponies, *mapu*, hangers-on, and travellers' loads
make up a busy scene.

On one or two sides are ramshackle sheds, with rude, hollowed trunks in front, out of which the ponies suck the hot
brown slush which sustains their strength and pugnacity.   On
the other is the furnace-shed with the oats where the slush is
cooked, the same fire usually heating the flues of the *kang* floor
of the common room, while smaller fires in the same shed cook
for the guests.   Low lattice doors filled in with torn and dirty
paper give access to a room the mud floor of which is concealed
by reed mats, usually dilapidated, sprinkled with wooden blocks
which serve as pillows.   Farming gear and hat boxes often find
a place on the low heavy crossbeams.   Into this room are
crowded *mapu*, travellers, and servants, the low *residuum* of
Korean travel, for officials and *yang-bans* receive the hospital-
ities of the nearest magistracy, and the peasants open their
houses to anybody with whom they have a passing acquaintance.   There is in all inns of pretensions, however, another
room, known as "the clean room," 8 feet by 6, which, if it
existed, I obtained, and if not I had a room in the women's

quarters at the back, remarkable only for its heat and vermin, and the amount of *ang-paks*, bundles of dirty clothes, beans rotting for soy, and other plenishings which it contained, and which reduced its habitable portion to a minimum. At night a ragged lantern in the yard and a glim of oil in the room made groping for one's effects possible.

The room was always overheated from the ponies' fire. From 80° to 85° was the usual temperature, but it was frequently over 92°, and I spent one terrible night sitting at my door because it was 105° within. In this furnace, which heats the floor and the spine comfortably, the Korean wayfarer revels.

On arriving at an inn, the master or servant rushes at the mud, or sometimes matted, floor with a whisk, raising a great dust, which he sweeps into a corner. The disgusted traveller soon perceives that the heap is animate as well as inanimate, and the groans, sighs, scratchings, and restlessness from the public room show the extent of the insect pest. But I never suffered from vermin in a Korean inn, nor is it necessary. After the landlord had disturbed the dust, Wong put down either two heavy sheets of oiled paper or a large sheet of cotton dressed with boiled linseed oil on the floor, and on these arranged my camp-bed, chair, and baggage. This arrangement (and I write from twenty months' experience in Korea and China) is a perfect preventative.

In most inns rice, eggs, vegetables, and a few Korean dainties, such as soup, vermicelli, dried seaweed, and a paste made of flour, sugar, and oil, can be procured, but tea never, and the position of the well, which frequently receives the soakage of the courtyard, precludes a careful traveller from drinking aught but boiled water. At the proper seasons chickens can be purchased for about 4d. each, and pheasants for less. Dog meat is for sale frequently in the spring, and pork occasionally.

The charges at Korean inns are ridiculously low. Nothing is charged for the room with its glim and hot floor, but as I took nothing for " the good of the house," I paid 100 *cash* per night, and the same for my room at the midday halt, which gave complete satisfaction. Travellers who eat three meals a day spend, including the trifling gratuities, from 200 to 300 *cash* per diem. Millet takes the place of rice in the northern inns.

The Korean inn is not noisy unless wine is flowing freely, and even then the noise subsides early. The fighting of the ponies, and the shouts and execrations with which the *mapu* pacify them, are the chief disturbances till daylight comes and the wayfarers move on. Travelling after dark is contrary to Korean custom.

From this slight sketch, the shadows of which will bear frequent and much intensifying, it will be seen that Korean travelling has a very seamy side, that it is entirely unsuited to the "globe trotter," and that even the specialist may do well to count the cost before embarking upon it.

To me the curse of the Korean inn is the ill-bred and un-manageable curiosity of the people, specially of the women. A European woman had not been seen on any part of the journey, and I suffered accordingly. Sar-pang Kori may serve as a specimen.

My quarters were opposite to the ponies, on the other side of the foul and crowded courtyard. There were two rooms, with a space under the roof as large as either between them, on which the dripping baggage was deposited, and Wong established himself with his cooking stove and utensils, though there was nothing to cook except two eggs obtained with difficulty, and a little rice left over from the boat stores. My room had three paper doors. The unwalled space at once filled up with a crowd of men, women, and children. All the paper was torn off the doors, and a crowd of dirty Mongolian faces took its place. I hung up cambric curtains, but long sticks were produced and my curtains were poked into the middle of the room. The crowd broke in the doors, and filled the small space not occupied by myself and my gear.

The women and children sat on my bed in heaps, examined my clothing, took out my hairpins and pulled down my hair, took off my slippers, drew my sleeves up to the elbow and pinched my arms to see if they were of the same flesh and blood as their own; they investigated my few possessions minutely, trying on my hat and gloves, and after being turned out by Wong three times, returned in fuller force, accompanied by unmarried youths, the only good-looking "girls" ever seen in Korea, with abundant hair divided in the middle, and hanging in long plaits down their backs. The pushing and crushing, the odious familiarity, the babel of voices, and the odors òf dirty clothing in a temperature of 80°, were intolerable. Wong cleared the room a fourth time, and suggested that when they forced their way in again, they should find me sitting on the bed cleaning my revolver, a suggestion I accepted. He had hardly retired when they broke in again, but there was an immediate stampede, and for the remainder of the evening I was free from annoyance. Similar displays of aggressive and intolerable curiosity occurred three times daily, and it was hard to be always amiable under such circumstances.

The Koreans travel enormously, considering that they seldom make pilgrimages. The pedlars, who solely supply the markets, are always on the move, and thousands travel for other reasons, such as the gatherings at ancestral tablets, restlessness, *ennui*, *ku-kyong* or sightseeing, visits to tombs, place-hunting, literary examinations, place-keeping and attempting to deprive others of place, litigation, and business. The fear of tigers and dæmons prevents people from journeying by night, which is as well, as the bearers of official passports have the right to demand an escort of torchbearers from each village. If necessity compells nocturnal travel, the wayfarers associate themselves in bands, swinging lanterns, waving torches, yelling, and beating gongs. The dread of the tiger is so universal as to warrant the Chinese proverbial saying, "The Korean hunts the tiger one half of the year, and the

tiger hunts the Korean the other half." As I have before remarked, the mandarins and *yang-bans*, with their trains,
quarter themselves on the magistracies, and eat the fat of the
land. Should they be compelled to have recourse to the discomforts of an inn and the food of a village, they appropriate
the best of everything without paying for it. Hence the visit
of a foreigner armed with a *kwan-ja* is such an object of dread,
that on this land journey I never let it be known that I had
one, and on my second journey discarded it altogether, trusting in both to the reputation for scrupulous honesty which I at
once established with my men to overcome the repugnance
which the innkeepers felt to receiving me.

The roads along which the traveller rides or trudges, at a
pace, in either case, of 3 miles an hour, are simply infamous.
There are few made roads, and those which exist are deep in
dust in summer and in mud in winter, where they are not
polished tracks over irregular surfaces and ledges of rock. In
most cases they are merely paths worn by the passage of
animals and men into some degree of legibility. Many of the
streams are unbridged, and most of the bridges, the roadways
of which are only of twigs and sod, are carried away by the
rains of early July, and are not restored till the middle of
October. In some regions traffic has to betake itself to fords
or ferries when it reaches a stream, with their necessary risks
and detentions. Even on the "Six Great Roads" which
centre in the capital, the bridges are apt to be in such a rotten condition that a *mapu* usually goes over in advance of his
horses to ascertain if they will bear their weight. Among the
mountains, roads are frequently nothing else than boulder-
strewn torrent beds, and on the best, that between Seoul and
Chemulpo, during the winter, there are tracts on which the
mud is from one to three feet deep. These infamous bridle
tracks, of which I have had extensive experience, are one of
the great hindrances to the development of Korea.

Among the worst of these is that part of the main road from

Seoul to Wön-san which we followed from Sar-pang Kori for two days to Sang-nang Dang, where we branched off for the region known as Keum-Kang San, or the Diamond Mountain. The earlier part of this route was through wooded valleys, where lilies of the valley carpeted the ground, and over the very pretty pass of Chyu-pha (1,,300 feet), on the top of which is a large spirit shrine, containing some coarsely painted pictures of men who look like Chinese generals, the usual offerings of old shoes, rags, and infinitesimal portions of rice, and a tablet inscribed, "I, the spirit Söng-an-chi, dwell in this place." There, as at the various trees hung with rags, and the heaps of stones on the tops of passes, the *mapu* bowed and expectorated, as is customary at the abodes of dæmons.

More than once we passed not far from houses outside of which the *mutang* or sorceress, with much feasting, beating of drums, and clashing of cymbals, was exercising the dæmon which had caused the sickness of some person within. Portions of the expensive feast prepared on these occasions are offered to the evil spirit, and after the exorcism part of the food so offered is given to the patient, in the belief that it is a curative medicine, often seriously aggravating the disease, as when a patient suffering from typhoid fever or dysentery is stuffed with pork or *kimshi!* Recently a case came under the notice of Dr. Jaisohn (*So Chai pil*) in Seoul, in which a man, suffering from the latter malady, died immediately after eating raw turnips, given him by the *mutang* after being offered to the dæmons at the usual feast at the ceremony of exorcism.

There is much wet rice along the route, as well as dry rice, with a double line of beans between every two rows, and in the rice revel and croak large frogs of extreme beauty, vivid green with black velvet spots, the under side of the legs and bodies being cardinal red. These appeared to be the prey of the graceful white and pink ibis, the latter in the intensified flush of his spring coloring.

A descent from a second pass leads to the Keum-San Kang,

a largish river in a rich agricultural region, and to the village of Pan-pyöng, where they were making in the rudest fashion the great cast-iron pots used for boiling horse food, from iron obtained and smelted 33 *li* farther north.

On two successive days there were tremendous thunderstorms, the second succeeded, just as we were at the head of a wild glen, by a brief tornado, which nearly blew over the ponies, and snapped trees of some size as though they had been matchwood. Then came a profound calm. The clouds lay banked in pink illuminated masses on a sky of tender green, cleft by gray mountain peaks. Mountain torrents boomed, crashed, sparkled, and foamed, the silent woods rejoiced the eye by the vividness of their greenery and their masses of white and yellow blossom, and sweet heavy odors enriched the evening air. On that and several other occasions, I recognized that Korea has its own special beauties, which fix themselves in the memory; but they must be sought for in spring and autumn, and off the beaten track. Dirty and squalid as the villages are, at a little distance their deep-eaved brown roofs, massed among orchards, on gentle slopes, or on the banks of sparkling streams, add color and life to the scenery, and men in their queer white clothes and dress hats, with their firm tread, and bundled-up women, with a shoggling walk and long staffs, brought round with a semicircular swing at every step, are adjuncts which one would not willingly dispense with.

Before reaching the Paik-yang Kang, a broad, full river, an affluent of the northern Han, with singularly abrupt turns and perpendicular cliffs of a formation resembling that of the Palisades on the Hudson River, we crossed one of the great lava fields described by Consul Carles.[1]

This, which we crossed in a northeasterly direction, is a rough oval about 40 miles by 30, a tableland, in fact, sur-

[1] "Recent Journeys in Korea," *Proceedings of the Royal Geographical Society*, May, 1896.

rounded by a deep chasm where the torrents which encircle it meet the mountains.   Its plateaux are from 60 to 100 feet above these streams, which are all affluents of the Han, and are supported on palisades of basalt, exhibiting the prismatic columnar formation in a very striking manner.   In some places the lava, which is often covered either with conglomerate or a stiffish clay, is very near the surface, and large blocks of it lie along the streams.   It is a most fertile tract, and could support a large population, but not being suited for rice, is very little cultivated, and grows chiefly oats, millet, and beans, which are not affected by the strong winds.

There are two Dolmens, not far from the Paik-yang Kang. In one the upper stone is from 7 to 10 feet long, by 7 feet wide, and 17 inches deep, resting on three stones 4 feet 2 inches high.   The other is somewhat smaller.   The openings of both face due north.

After crossing the Paik-yang Kang, there 162 yards wide and 16 feet deep, by a ferry boat of remarkably ingenious construction, rendered necessary by the fact that the long bridge over the broad stream was in ruins, and that the appropriation for its reconstruction had been diverted by the local officials to their own enrichment, we entered the spurs or ribs of the great mountain chain which, running north and south, divides Korea into two very unequal longitudinal portions at the village of Tong-ku.

The scenery became very varied and pretty.   Forests clothed many of the hills with a fair blossoming undergrowth untouched by the fuel gatherers' remorseless hook; torrents flashed in foam through dark, dense leafage, or bubbled and gurgled out of sight; the little patches of cultivation were boulder-strewn; there were few inhabitants, and the tracks called roads were little better than the stony beds of streams. As they became less and less obvious, and the valleys more solitary, our tergiversations were more frequent and prolonged, the *mapu* drove the ponies as fast as they could walk, the fords were many and deep, and two of the party were unhorsed in them, still we hurried on faster and faster. Not a word was spoken, but I knew that the men had *tiger on the brain !*

Blundering through the twilight, it was dark when we reached the lower village of Ma-ri Kei, where we were to halt for the night, two miles from the Pass of Tan-pa-Ryöng, which was to be crossed the next day. There the villagers could not or would not take us in. They said they had neither rice nor beans, which may have been true so late in the spring. However, it is, or then was, Korean law that if a village could not entertain travellers it must convoy them to the next halt-ing-place.

The *mapu* were frantic. They yelled and stormed and banged at the hovels, and succeeded in turning out four sleepy peasants, who were reinforced by four more a little farther on ; but the torches were too short, and after sputtering and flaring, went out one by one, and the fresh ones lighted slowly. The *mapu* lost their reason. They thrashed the torchbearers with their heavy sticks ; I lashed my *mapu* with my light whip for doing it ; they yelled, they danced. Then things improved. Gloriously glared the pine knots on the leaping crystal torrents that we forded, reddening the white clothes of the men and the stony track and the warm-tinted stems of the pines, and so with shouts and yells and waving torches we passed up the wooded glen in the frosty night air, under a firmament of stars, to the mountain hamlet of upper Ma-ri Kei, consisting of five hovels, only three of which were inhabited.

It is a very forlorn place and very poor, and it was an hour before my party of eight human beings and four ponies were established in its miserable shelter, though even that was wel-come after being eleven hours in the saddle.

CHAPTER XI

DIAMOND MOUNTAIN MONASTERIES

IT was a glorious day for the Pass of Tan-pa-Ryöng (1,320 feet above Ma-ri Kei), the western barrier of the Keum-Kang San region. Mr. Campbell, of H.B.M.'s Consular Service, one of the few Europeans who has crossed it, in his charming narrative mentions that it is impassable for laden animals, and engaged porters for the ascent, but though the track is nothing better than a torrent bed abounding in great boulders, angular and shelving rocks, and slippery corrugations of entangled tree roots, I rode over the worst part, and my ponies made nothing of carrying the baggage up the rock ladders. The mountain-side is covered with luxuriant and odorous vegetation, specially oak, chestnut, hawthorn, varieties of maple, pale pink azalea, and yellow clematis, interspersed with a few distorted pines, primulas and lilies of the valley covering the mossy ground.

From the spirit shrine on the summit a lovely panorama unfolds itself, billows of hilly woodland, gleams of water, wavy outlines of hills, backed by a jagged mountain wall, attaining an altitude of over 6,000 feet in the loftiest pinnacle of the Keum-Kang San. A fair land of promise, truly! But this pass is a rubicon to him who seeks the Diamond Mountain with the intention of immuring himself for life in one of its many monasteries. For its name, Tan-pa, "crop-hair," was bestowed on it early in the history of Korean Buddhism for a reason which remains. There those who have chosen the cloister emphasize their abandonment of the world by cutting off the "topknot" of married dignity, or the heavy braid of bachelorhood.

The eastern descent of the Tan-pa-Ryöng is by a series of zigzags, through woods and a profusion of varied and magnificent ferns. A long day followed of ascents and descents, deep fords of turbulent streams, valley villages with terrace cultivation of buckwheat, and glimpses of gray rock needles through pine and persimmon groves, and in the late afternoon, after struggling through a rough ford in which the water was halfway up the sides of the ponies, we entered a gorge and struck a smooth, broad, well-made road, the work of the monks, which traverses a fine forest of pines and firs above a booming torrent.

Towards evening "The hills swung open to the light"; through the parting branches there were glimpses of granite walls and peaks reddening into glory; red stems, glowing in the slant sunbeams, lighted up the blue gloom of the coniferæ; there were glints of foam from the loud-tongued torrent below; the dew fell heavily, laden with aromatic odors of pines, and as the valley narrowed again and the blue shadows fell the picture was as fair as one could hope to see. The monks, though road-makers, are not bridge-builders, and there were difficult fords to cross, through which the ponies were left to struggle by themselves, the *mapu* crossing on single logs. In the deep water I discovered that its temperature was almost icy. The worst ford is at the point where the first view of Chang-an Sa, the Temple of Eternal Rest, the oldest of the Keum-Kang San monasteries, is obtained, a great pile of temple buildings with deep curved roofs, in a glorious situation, crowded upon a small grassy plateau in one of the narrowest parts of the gorge, where the mountains fall back a little and afford Buddhism a peaceful shelter, secluded from the outer world by snow for four months of the year.

Crossing the torrent and passing under a lofty *Hong-Sal-Mun*, or "red arrow gate," significant in Korea of the patronage of royalty, we were at once among the Chang-an Sa buildings, which consist of temples large and small, a stage for religious dramas, bell and tablet houses, stables for the ponies of wayfarers, cells, dormitories, and a refectory for the abbot and monks, quarters for servants and neophytes, huge kitchens, a large guest hall, and a nunnery. Besides these there are quarters devoted to the lame, halt, blind, infirm, and solitary; to widows, orphans, and the destitute.

These guests, numbering 100, seemed well treated. Between monks, servants, and boys preparing for the priesthood there may be 100 more, and 20 nuns of all ages, from girlhood up to eighty-seven years. This large number of persons is supported by the rent and produce of Church lands outside the mountains, the contributions of pilgrims and guests, the moneys collected by the monks, who all go on mendicant expeditions, even up to the gates of Seoul, which at that time it was death for any priest to enter, and benefactions from the late Queen, which had become increasingly liberal.

The first impression of the plateau was that it was a wood-yard on a large scale. Great logs and piles of planks were heaped under the stately pines and under a superb *Salisburia adiantifolia*, 17 feet in girth; 40 carpenters were sawing, planing, and hammering, and 40 or 50 laborers were hauling in logs to the music of a wild chant, for mendicant effort had been resorted to energetically, with the result that the great temple was undergoing repairs, almost amounting to a reconstruction.

Of the forty-five monasteries and monastic shrines which exist in the Diamond Mountain, enhancing its picturesqueness and supplying it with a religious and human interest, Chang-an Sa may be taken as a fair specimen of the three largest, as it is undoubtedly the oldest, assuming the correctness of a historical record quoted by Mr. Campbell, which gives the date of its restoration by two monks, Yul-sa and Chin-h'yo, as A.D. 515, in the reign of Pöp-heung, a king of Silla, then the most important of the kingdoms, afterwards amalgamated as Korea.

The large temple is a fine old building of the type adapted

from Chinese Buddhist architecture, oblong, with a heavy tiled roof 48 feet in height, with wings, deep eaves protecting masses of richly-colored wood-carving. The lofty reticulated roof is internally supported on an arrangement of heavy beams, elaborately carved and painted in rich colors. The panels of the doors, which serve as windows, and let in a "dim religious light," are bold fretwork, decorated in colors enriched with gold.

The roofs of the actual shrines are supported on wooden pillars 3 feet in diameter, formed of single trees, and the panelled ceilings are embellished with intricate designs in colors and gold. In one Sakyamuni's image, with a distinctly Hindu cast of countenance, and a look of ineffable abstraction, sits under a highly decorative reticulated wooden canopy, with an altar before it, on which are brass incense burners, books of prayer, and lists of those deceased persons for whose souls masses have been duly paid for. Much rich brocade, soiled and dusty, and many gonfalons, hang round this shrine.

The "Hall of the Four Sages" contains three Buddhas in different attitudes of abstraction or meditation, a picture, wonderfully worked in gold and silks in Chinese embroidery, of Buddha and his disciples, for which the monks claim an antiquity of fourteen centuries, and sixteen Lohans, with their attendants. Along the side walls are a host of dæmons and animals. Another striking shrine is that dedicated to the Lord of the Buddhistic Hell and his ten princes. The monks call it the "Temple of the Ten Judges." This is a shrine of great resort, and is much blackened by the smoke of incense and candles, but the infernal torments depicted in the pictures at the back of each judge are only too conspicuous. They are horrible beyond conception, and show a diabolical genius in hellish art, akin to that which inspired the creation of the groups in the Inferno of the temple of Kwan-yin at Ting-hai on Chusan, familiar to some of my readers.

Besides the ecclesiastical buildings and the common guest-room, there are Government buildings marked with the Korean national emblem, for the use of officials who go up to Chang-an Sa for pleasure.

It was difficult for me to find accommodation, but eventually a very pleasing young priest of high rank gave up his cell to me. Unfortunately, it was next the guests' kitchen, and the flues from the fires passing under it, I was baked in a temperature of 91°, although, in spite of warnings about tigers, the dangers from which are by no means imaginary, I kept both door and window open all night. The cell had for its furniture a shrine of Gautama and an image of Kwan-yin on a shelf, and a few books, which I learned were Buddhist classics, not volumes, as in a cell which I occupied later, full of pictures by no means inculcating holiness. In the next room, equally hot, and without a chink open for ventilation, thirty guests moaned and tossed all night, a single candle dimly lighting a picture of Buddha and the dusty and hideous ornaments on the altar below.

A 9 P.M., midnight, and again at 4 A.M., which is the hour at which the monks rise, bells were rung, cymbals and gongs were beaten, and the praises of Buddha were chanted in an unknown tongue. A feature at once cheerful and cheerless is the presence at Chang-an Sa of a number of bright, active, orphan boys from ten to thirteen years old, who are at present servitors, but who will one day become priests.

It is an exercise of forbearance to abstain from writing much about the beauties of Chang-an Sa as seen in two days of perfect heavenliness. It is a calm retreat, that small, green, semicircular plateau which the receding hills have left, walling in the back and sides with rocky precipices half clothed with forest, while the bridgeless torrent in front, raging and thundering among huge boulders of pink granite, secludes it from all but the adventurous. Alike in the rose of sunrise, in the red and gold of sunset, or gleaming steely blue in the prosaic glare of midday, the great rock peak on the left bank, one of the highest in the range, compels ceaseless admiration. The appearance of its huge vertical topmost ribs has been well compared to that of the " pipes of an organ," this organ-pipe formation being common in the range ; seams and ledges half-way down give roothold to a few fantastic conifers and azaleas, and lower still all suggestion of form is lost among dense masses of magnificent forest.

As I proposed to take a somewhat different route from Yu-chöm Sa (the first temple on the eastern slope) from that traversed by my predecessors, the Hon. G. W. Curzon and Mr. Campbell, I left the ponies and baggage at Chang-an Sa, the *mapu*, who were bent on *ku-kyöng*, accompanying me for part of the distance, and took a five days' journey in the glorious Keum-Kang San in unrivalled weather, in air which was elixir, crossing the range to Yu-chöm Sa by the An-mun-chai (Goose-Gate Terrace), 4,215 feet in altitude, and recrossing it by the Ki-cho, 3,570 feet.

Taking two coolies to carry essentials, and a *na-myö* or mountain chair with two bearers, for the whole journey, all supplied by the monks, I walked the first stage to the monasteries of P'yo-un Sa and Chyang-yang Sa, the latter at an elevation of about 2,760 feet. From it the view, which passes for the grandest in Korea, is obtained of the " Twelve Thousand Peaks." There is assuredly no single view that I have seen in Japan or even in Western China which equals it for beauty and grandeur. Across the grand gorge through which the Chang-an Sa torrent thunders, and above primæval tiger-haunted forests with their infinity of green, rises the central ridge of the Keum-Kang San, jagged all along its summit, each yellow granite pinnacle being counted as a peak.

On that enchanting May evening, when odors of paradise, the fragrant breath of a million flowering shrubs and trailers, of bursting buds, and unfolding ferns, rose into the cool dewy air, and the silence could be felt, I was not inclined to enter a protest against Korean exaggeration on the ground that the

number of peaks is probably nearer 1,200 than 12,000. Their
yellow granite pinnacles, weathered into silver gray, rose up
cold, stern, and steely blue from the glorious forests which
drape their lower heights—winter above and summer below—
then purpled into red as the sun sank, and gleamed above the
twilight, till each glowing summit died out as lamps which are
extinguished one by one, and the whole took on the ashy hue
of death.

The situation of P'yo-un Sa is romantic, on the right bank
of the torrent, and is approached by a bridge, and by passing
under several roofed gateways. The monastery had been
newly rebuilt, and is one mass of fretwork, carving, gilding,
and color, the whole decoration being the work of the monks.

The front of the "Temple of the Believing Mind" is a
magnificent piece of bold wood-carving, the *motif* being the
peony. Every part of the building which is not stone or tile
is carved, and decorated in blue, red, white, green, and gold.
It may be barbaric, but it is barbaric splendor. There too is
a "Temple of Judgment," with hideous representations of the
Buddhist hells, one scene being the opening of the books in
which the deeds of men's mortal lives are written.

The fifty monks of P'yo-un Sa were very friendly, and not
impecunious. One gave up to me his oven-like cell, but repaid
himself for the sacrifice by indulging in ceaseless staring. The
wind bells of the establishment and the big bell have a melody
in their tones such as I have rarely heard, and when at 4 A. M.
bells of all sizes and tones announced that "prayer is better
than sleep," there was nothing about the sounds to jar on the
pure freshness of morning. The monks are well dressed and
jolly, and have a well-to-do air which clashes with any pretensions to asceticism. The rule of these monasteries is a
strict vegetarianism which allows neither milk nor eggs, and
in the whole region there are neither fowls nor domestic animals. Not to wound the prejudices of my hosts, I lived on
tea, rice, honey water, edible pine nuts, and a most satisfying

combination of pine nuts and honey.   After a light breakfast
on these delicacies, the sub-abbot, took me to see his grandmother, a very bright pleasing woman of eighty, who came
from Seoul thirteen years ago and built a house within the
monastery grounds, in order to die in its quiet blessedness.
There I had to eat a second ethereal meal, and the hospitable
hostess forced on me a pot of exquisite honey and a bag of pine
nuts.   These, the product of the *Pinus pinea*, which grows
profusely throughout the range, furnish an important and nu-
tritious article of monkish diet, and are exported in quantities
as a luxury.   They are rich and very oily, and turn rancid
soon after being shelled.   The honey is also locally produced.
The beehives, which usually stand two together in cavities in
the rocks, are hollow logs with clay covers mounted on blocks
of wood or stone.   Leaving this friendly hostess and the seven
nuns of the nunnery behind, the sub-abbot showed me the
direction in which to climb, for road there is none, and at
parting presented me with a fan.

A visit to the Keum-Kang San elevates a Korean into the
distinguished position of a traveller, and many a young resident of Seoul gains this fashionable reputation.   It is not as
containing shrines of pilgrimage, for most Koreans despise
Buddhism and its shaven mendicant priests, that these mountains are famous in Korea, but for their picturesque beauties,
much celebrated in Korean poetry.   The broad backbone of
the peninsula which has trended near to the east coast from
Puk-chöng southwards has degenerated into tameness, when
suddenly Keum-Kang San, or the Diamond Mountain, with its
elongated mass of serrated, jagged, and inaccessible peaks,
and magnificent primæval forest, occupying an area of about
32 miles in length by 22 in breadth, starts off from it near the
39th parallel of latitude in the province of Kang-wön.
Buddhism, which, as in Japan, possesses itself of the fairest
spots in Nature, fixed itself in this romantic seclusion as early
as the sixth century A. D., and the venerable relics of the time

THE DIAMOND MOUNTAINS.

when for 1,000 years it was the official as well as the popular cult of the country are chiefly to be found in the recesses of this mountain region, where the same faith, though now discredited, disestablished, and despised, still attracts a certain number of votaries, and a far larger number of visitors and so-called pilgrims, who resort to the shrines to indulge in *ku-kyöng*, a Korean term which covers pleasure-seeking, sight-seeing, the indulgence of curiosity, and much else.

So far as I have been able to learn, there are only two routes by which the Keum-Kang San can be penetrated, the one which, after following the bed of a singularly rough torrent, crosses the watershed at An-mun-chai, and on or near which the principal monasteries and shrines are situated, and the Ki-cho, a lower and less interesting pass. Both routes start from Chang-an Sa. The forty-two shrines are the headquarters of about 400 monks and about 50 nuns, who add to their religious exercises the weaving of cotton and hempen cloth. The lay servitors possibly number 1,000. The four great monasteries, two on the eastern and two on the western slope, absorb more than 300 of the whole number. All except the high monastic officials beg through the country, alms-bowl in hand, the only distinctive features of their dress being a very peculiar hat and the rosary. They chant the litanies of Buddha from house to house, and there are few who deny them food and lodging and a few *cash* or a little rice.

The monasteries are presided over by what we should call "abbots," superiors of the first or second class according to the importance of the establishment. These *Chong-söp* and *Sön-tong* are nominally elected annually, but actually continue in office for years, unless their conduct gives rise to dissatisfaction. Beyond the confirmation of the election of the *Chong-söp* of those monasteries which possess a "Red Arrow Gate" by the Board of Rites at Seoul, the disestablished Church appears to be quite free from State interference. In the case of restoring and rebuilding shrines, large sums are collected in Seoul and the southern provinces, though faith in Buddhism as a creed rarely exists.

On making inquiries through Mr. Miller as to the way in which the number of monks is kept up, I learned that the majority are either orphans or children whose parents have given them to the monasteries at a very early age owing to poverty. These are more or less educated and trained by the monks. It must be supposed that among the number there are a few who escape from the weariness and friction of secular life into a region in which seclusion and devotion are possible. Of this type was the pale and interesting young priest who gave up his room to me at Chang-an Sa, and two who accompanied us to Yu-chöm Sa, one of whom chanted *Na Mu Ami Tabu* nearly the whole day as he journeyed, telling a bead on his rosary for each ten repetitions. Mr. Miller asked him what the words meant. "Just letters," he replied; "they have no meaning, but if you say them many times you will get to heaven better." Then he gave Mr. Miller the rosary, and taught him the mystic syllables, saying, "Now, you keep the beads, say the words, and you will go to heaven." Among the younger priests several seemed in earnest. Others make the monasteries (as is largely the case with the celebrated shrines of Kwan-yin on the Chinese island of Pu-tu) a refuge from justice or creditors, some remain desiring peaceful indolence, and not a few are vowed and tonsured who came simply to view the scenery of the Keum-Kang San and were too much enchanted to leave it.

As to the moribund Buddhism which has found its most secluded retreat in these mountains, it is overlaid with dæmonolatry, and like that of China is smothered under a host of semi-deified heroes. Of the lofty aims and aspirations after righteousness which distinguish the great reforming sects of Japan, such as the Monto, it knows nothing.

The monks are grossly ignorant and superstitious. They know nearly nothing of the history and tenets of their own creed, or of the purport of their liturgies, which to most of them are just "letters," the ceaseless repetition of which constitutes "merit." Though some of them know Chinese, and this knowledge means "education" in Korea, worship consists in the mumbling or loud intoning of Sanscrit or Tibetan phrases, of the meaning of which they have no conception. My impression of most of the monks was that their religious performances are absolutely without meaning to them, and that belief, except among a few, does not exist. The Koreans universally attribute to them gross profligacy, of the existence of which at one of the large monasteries it was impossible not to become aware, but between their romantic and venerable surroundings, the order and quietness of their lives, their benevolence to the old and destitute, who find a peaceful asylum with them, and in the main their courtesy and hospitality, I am compelled to admit that they exercise a certain fascination, and that I prefer to remember their virtues rather than their faults. My sympathies go out to them for their appreciation of the beautiful, and for the way in which religious art has assisted Nature by the exceeding picturesqueness of the positions and decoration of their shrines.

The route from Chang-an Sa to Yu-chöm Sa, about 11 miles, is mainly the rough beds of two great mountain torrents. Along this, in romantic positions, are three large monasteries P'yo-un Sa, Ma-ha-ly-an Sa, and Yu-chöm Sa, besides a number of smaller shrines, with from two to five attendants each, one especially, Po-tok-am sa, dedicated to Kwan-yin, picturesque beyond description—a fantastic temple built out from the face of a cliff, at a height of 100 feet, and supported below the centre by a pillar, round which a blossoming white clematis, and an *Ampelopsis Veitchiana*, in the rose flush of its spring leafage, had entwined their lavish growth.

No quadruped can travel this route farther than Chang-an Sa. Coolies, very lightly laden, and chair-bearers carrying a *na-myö*, two long poles with a slight seat in the middle, a noose of rope for the feet, and light uprights bound together with a wistaria rope to support the back, can be used, but the occupant of the chair has to walk much of the way.

The torrent bed contracts above Chang-an Sa, opens out here and there, and above P'yo-un Sa narrows into a gash, only opening out again at the foot of the An-mun-chai. Surely the beauty of that 11 miles is not much exceeded anywhere on earth. Colossal cliffs, upbearing mountains, forests, and gray gleaming peaks, rifted to give roothold to pines and maples, ofttimes contracting till the blue heaven above is narrowed to a strip, boulders of pink granite 40 and 50 feet high, pines on their crests and ferns and lilies in their crevices, round which the clear waters swirl, before sliding down over smooth surfaces of pink granite to rest awhile in deep pink pools where they take a more brilliant than an emerald green with the flashing lustre of a diamond—rocks and ledges over which the crystal stream dashes in drifts of foam, shelving rock surfaces on which the decorative Chinese characters, the laborious work of pilgrims, afford the only foothold, slides, steeper still, made passable for determined climbers by holes, drilled by the monks, and fitted with pegs and rails, rocks with bas-reliefs, or small shrines of Buddha draped with flowering trailers, a cliff with a bas-relief of Buddha, 45 feet high on a pedestal 30 feet broad, rocks carved into lanterns and altars, whose harsh outlines are softened by mosses and lichens, and above, huge timber and fantastic peaks rising into

The summer heaven's delicious blue.

A description can be only a catalogue. The actuality was intoxicating, a canyon on the grandest scale, with every element of beauty present.

This route cannot be traversed in European shoes. In Korean string foot-gear, however, I never slipped once. There was much jumping from boulder to boulder, much winding round rocky projections, clinging to their irregularities with scarcely foothold, and one's back to the torrent far below, and much leaping over deep crevices and "walking tight-rope fashion" over rails. Wherever the traveller has to leave the difficulties of the torrent bed he encounters those of slippery sloping rocks, which he has to traverse by hanging on to tree trunks.

Our two priestly companions were most polite to me, giving me a hand at the dangerous places, and beguiling the way by legends, chiefly Buddhistic, concerning every fantastic and abnormal rock and pool, such as the Myo-kil Sang, the colossal figure of Buddha referred to before, a pothole in the granite bed of the stream, the wash-basin of some mythical Bodhisattva, the Fire Dragon Pool, and the bathing-places of dragons in the fantastic Man-pok-Tong (Grotto of Myriad Cascades), and the Lion Stone which repelled the advance of the Japanese invaders in 1592.

Beyond the third monastery the gorge becomes wider and less fantastic, the forest thinner, allowing scattered glimpses of the sky, and finally some long zigzags take the traveller up to the open grassy summit of the An-mun-chai, on which plums, pears, cherries, blush azaleas, and pink rhododendrons, which had long ceased blooming below, were in their first flush of beauty. To the west the difficult country of the previous week's journey, gray granite, deep valleys, and tiger-haunted forest faded into a veil of blue, and in the east, over diminishing forest-covered ranges, gleamed the blue Sea of Japan, more than 4,000 feet below.

On the eastern descent there are gigantic pines and firs, some of them ruthlessly barked, and the long dependent streamers of the gray-green *Lycopodium Sieboldii* with which they are festooned, give the forest a funereal aspect. Of this the peculiar fringed hats are made which are worn on occasion by both monks and nuns. After many downward zigzags, the track enters another rocky gorge with a fine torrent, in the bed of which are huge "potholes," shown as the bathing-places of dragons, whose habits must have been much cleanlier than those of the present inhabitants of the land.

The great monastery of Yu-chöm Sa, with its many curved roofs and general look of newness and wealth, is approached by crossing a very tolerable bridge. The road, which passes through a well-kept burial-ground, where the ashes of the pious and learned abbots of several centuries repose under more or less stately monuments, was much encumbered near the monastery by great pine logs newly hewn for its restoration, which was being carried out on a very expensive scale.

The monks made a difficulty about receiving us, and it was not till after some delay, and the production of my *kwan-ja*, that we were allotted rooms in the Government buildings for the two days of our halt. After this small difficulty, they were unusually kind and friendly, and one of the young priests, who came over the An-mun-chai with us, offered Mr. Miller the use of his cell on Sunday, saying that "it would be a quieter place than the great room to study his belief"!

I had hoped for rest and quiet on the following day, having had rather a hard week, but these were unattainable. Besides 70 monks and 20 nuns, there were nearly 200 lay servitors and carpenters, and all were bent upon *ku-kyöng*, the first European woman to visit the Keum-Kang San being regarded as a great sight, and from early morning till late at night there was no rest. The *kang* floor of my room being heated from the kitchen, it was too hot to exist with the paper front closed, and the crowds of monks, nuns, and servitors, finishing with the carpenters, who crowded in whenever it was opened, and hung there hour after hour, nearly suffocated me, the day being very warm. The abbot and several senior monks discussed with Mr. Miller the merits of rival creeds, saying that the only difference between Buddhists and ourselves is that they don't kill even the smallest insect, while we disregard what we call "animal life," and that we don't look upon monasticism and other forms of asceticism as means of salvation. They admitted that among their priests there are more who live in known sin than strivers after righteousness.

TOMBSTONES OF ABBOTS, YU-CHÖM SA.

There are many bright busy boys about Yu-chŏm Sa, most of whom had already had their heads shaved. To one who had not, Che on-i gave a piece of chicken, but he refused it because he was a Buddhist, on which an objectionable-looking old sneak of a priest told him that it was all right to eat it so long as no one saw him, but the boy persisted in his refusal.

At midnight, being awakened by the boom of the great bell and the disorderly and jarring clang of innumerable small ones, I went, at the request of the friendly young priest, our fellow-traveller, to see him perform the devotions, which are taken in turn by the monks.

The great bronze bell, an elaborate piece of casting of the fourteenth century, stands in a rude, wooden, clay-floored tower by itself. A dim paper lantern on a dusty rafter barely lighted up the white-robed figure of the devotee, as he circled the bell, chanting in a most musical voice a Sanscrit litany, of whose meaning he was ignorant, striking the bosses of the bell with a knot of wood as he did so. Half an hour passed thus. Then taking a heavy mallet, and passing to another chant, he circled the bell with a greater and ever-increasing passion of devotion, beating its bosses heavily and rhythmically, faster and faster, louder and louder, ending by producing a burst of frenzied sound, which left him for a moment exhausted. Then, seizing the swinging beam, the three full tones which end the worship, and which are produced by striking the bell on the rim, which is 8 inches thick, and on the middle, which is very thin, made the tower and the ground vibrate, and boomed up and down the valley with their unforgettable music. Of that young monk's sincerity, I have not one doubt.

He led us to the great temple, a vast "chamber of imagery," where a solitary monk chanted before an altar in the light from a solitary lamp in an alabaster bowl, accompanying his chant by striking a small bell with a deer horn. The dim light left cavernous depths of shadow in the temple, from which eyes and teeth, weapons, and arms and legs of other-

wise invisible gods and devils showed uncannily.   Behind the
altar is a rude and monstrous piece of wood-carving representing the upturned roots of a tree, among which fifty-three idols
are sitting and standing.   As well by daylight as in the dimness of midnight, there are an uncouthness and power about
this gigantic representation which are very impressive.   Below
the carving are three frightful dragons, on whose faces the artist
has contrived to impress an expression of torture and defeat.

The legend of the altar-piece runs thus.   When fifty-three
priests come to Korea from India to introduce Buddhism, they
reached this place, and being weary, sat down by a well under
a spreading tree.   Presently three dragons came up from the
well and began a combat with the Buddhists, in the course of
which they called up a great wind which tore up the tree.
Not to be out-manœuvred, each priest placed an image of Buddha on a root of the tree, turning it into an altar.   Finally,
the priests overcome the dragons, forced them into the well,
and piled great rocks on the top of it to keep them there,
founded the monastery, and built this temple over the dragons'
grave.   On either side of this unique altar-piece is a bouquet
of peonies 4 feet wide by 10 feet high.

The " private apartments " of this and the other monasteries
consist of a living room, and very small single cells, each with
the shrine of its occupant, and all very clean.   It must be remembered, however, that this easy, peaceful, luxurious life
only lasts for a part of the year, and that all but a few of the
monks must make an annual tramp, wallet and begging-bowl
in hand, over rough, miry, or dusty Korean roads, put up
with vile and dirty accommodation, beg for their living from
those who scorn their tonsure and their creed, and receive
"low talk " from the lowest in the land.

Just before we left, the old abbot invited us into his very
charming suite of rooms, and with graceful hospitality prepared a repast for us with his own hands—square cakes of rich
oily pine nuts glued together with honey, thin cakes of

"popped" rice and honey, sweet cake, Chinese sweatmeat, honey, and bowls of honey water with pine nuts floating on its surface. The oil of these nuts certainly supplied the place of animal food during my enforced abstinence from it, but rich vegetable oil and honey soon pall on the palate, and the abbot was concerned that we did not do justice to our entertainment. The general culture produced by Buddhism at these monasteries, and the hospitality, consideration, and gentleness of deportment, contrast very favorably with the arrogance, superciliousness, insolence, and conceit which I have seen elsewhere in Korea among the so-called followers of Confucius.

When we departed all the monks and laborers bade us a courteous farewell, some of the older priests accompanying us for a short distance.

After descending the slope by the well-made road which leads down to the large monastery of Sin-kyei Sa, at the northeast foot of the Keum-Kang San, we left it for a rough and difficult westerly track, which, after affording some bright gleams of the Sea of Japan, enters dense forest full of great boulders and magnificent specimens of the *Filix mas* and *Osmumda regalis*. A severe climb up and down an irregular, broken staircase of rock took us over the Ki-cho Pass, 3,700 feet in altitude, after which there is a tedious march of some hours along bare and unpicturesque mountain-sides before reaching the well-made path which leads through pine woods to the beautiful plateau of Chang-an Sa. The young priest had kept our baggage carefully, but the heat of his floor had melted the candles in the boxes and had turned candy into molasses, making havoc among photographic materials at the same time!

CHAPTER XII

ALONG THE COAST

ON leaving Chang-an Sa for Wön-san we retraced our route as far as Kal-rön-gi, and afterwards crossed the Mak-pai Pass, from which there is a grand view of the Keum-Kang San. Much of a somewhat tedious day was spent in crossing a rolling elevated plateau bordered by high denuded hills, on which the potatoe flourishes at a height of 2,500 feet. The soil is very fertile, but not being suited to rice, is very little occupied. Crossing the Sai-kal-chai, 2,200 feet in altitude, the infamous road descends on a beautiful alluvial valley, a rich farming country, sprinkled with hamlets and surrounded by pretty hills wooded with scrub oak, which in the spring is very largely used for fertilizing rice fields. The branches are laid on the inundated surface till the leaves rot off, and they are then removed for fuel. In this innocent-looking valley the tiger scare was in full force. A tiger, the people said, had carried off a woman the previous week, and a dog and pig the previous night. It seemed incredible, yet there was a consensus of evidence. Tigers are occasionally trapped in that region by baiting a pit with a dog or pig, and the ensnared animal is destroyed by poison or hunger to avoid injury to the skin, which, if it is that of a fine animal, is very valuable.

A man is not the least ashamed of saying that he has not nerve or pluck for tiger-hunting, which in Korea is a dangerous game, for the hunters are stationed at the head of a gorge, usually behind brushwood, and sometimes behind rocks, the big game, tigers and leopards, being driven up towards them by large bodies of men. When one realizes that the arms used are matchlocks lighted by slow matches from cords wound round the arm, and that the charge consists of three imperfectly rounded balls the size of a pea, and that, owing to the thickness of the screen behind which the hunters are posted, the game is only sighted when quite close upon them, one ceases to wonder at the reluctance of the village peasants to turn out in pursuit of a man-eater, even though the bones bring a very high price as Chinese medicine.

We put up at the only inn in the region. It had no "clean room," but the landlord's wife gave up hers to me on condition that I would not keep the door open for fear of a tiger. The temperature was 93°, and to secure a little ventilation and yet keep my promise, I tore the paper off the lattice-work of the door. Mr. Miller described his circumstances thus. "I wanted to sleep in the yard, but the host would not let me for fear of tigers, so I had to sleep in a room 8 feet by 10" (with a hot floor), "with seven other men, a cat, and a bird. By tearing the paper off a window near my head I saved myself from death by suffocation, and could have had a good night's rest had not the four horses been crowded into two stalls in the kitchen. They found their quarters so close that they squealed, kicked, bit, and fought all night, and their drivers helped them to make night hideous by their yelling." Nobody slept, and I had my full share of the unrest and disturbance, a bad preparation for an eleven hours' ride on the next day, which was fiercely hot, as were the remaining six days of the journey.

The road from this lofty tiger-haunted valley to the sea level at Chyung-Tai is for the most part through valleys very sparsely peopled. Much forest land, however, was being cleared for the planting of cotton, and the peasant farmers are energetic enough to carry their cultivation to a height of 2,000 feet. [On nearly the whole of this journey I estimated that the land is capable of supporting double its present population.] At Hoa-chung, a prettily situated market-place, a student who had successfully passed the literary examination at the *Kwagga* in Seoul, surrounded by a crowd in bright colored festive clothing, was celebrating his return by sacrificing at his father's grave. On the various roads there were many processions escorting village students home from the great competition in the Royal presence at the capital, the student in colored clothes, on a gaily-caparisoned horse or ass, with music and flags in front of him, and friends, gaily dressed, walking beside him. On approaching his village he was met with flags and music, the headman and villagers, even the women in gay apparel, going out to welcome him. After this success he was entitled to erect a tall pole, with a painted dragon upon it, in front of his house. Success was, however, very costly, and often hung the millstone of debt round a man's neck for the remainder of his life. After "passing" the student became eligible for official position, the sole object of ambition to an "educated" Korean.

At Hoa-chung we turned eastwards, and took the main road to the coast, attaining an altitude (uncorrected) of 3,117 feet by continued ascents over rounded hills, which, when not absolutely bare except for coarse, unlovely grasses, only produced stunted hazel bush. After this an easy ascent among absolutely denuded hills leads up to a spirit shrine of more than usual importance, crowded with the customary worthless *ex votos*, rags and old straw shoes. At that point the road makes an altogether unexpected and surprising plunge over the bare shoulders of a bare hill into Paradise !

This pass of the "Ninety-nine Turns," Tchyu-Chi-chang, deserves its name, the number of sharp zigzags not being exaggerated, as in the case of the "Twelve Thousand Peaks." It is so absolutely rocky, and so difficult in consequence, that it is more passable in snow than in summer. Its abrupt turns lead down a forest-clothed mountain ridge into a magnificent gorge, densely wooded with oak, Spanish chestnut, weeping lime, *Abies excelsa*, and magnolia, looped together with the white *mille-fleur* rose. On the northern side rises Hoang-chyöng San, a noble mountain and conspicuous landmark, much broken up into needles and precipices, and clothed nearly to its summit with forests, of which the *Pinus sylvestris* is the monarch. The descent of the pass takes one hour and a half, the road coming down upon a torrent 50 feet wide, only visible in glints of foam here and there, amid its smothering overgrowth of blossoming magnolia, syringa, and roses.

The filthy, miserable hamlet of Chyung-Tai, composed of five hovels, all inns, was rather a comfortless close to a fatiguing day. These houses are roofed, as in some other villages, with thick slabs of wood heaped on each other, kept on, so far as they are kept on, by big stones. The forest above on the mountains is a Royal reservation, made so by the first king of this dynasty, who built stone walls round the larger trees.

I had occasion to notice at Chyung-Tai, and in many other places, the extreme voracity of the Koreans. They eat not to satisfy hunger, but to enjoy the sensation of repletion. The training for this enjoyment begins at a very early age, as I had several opportunities of observing. A mother feeds her young child with rice, and when it can eat no more in an upright position, lays it on its back on her lap and feeds it again, tapping its stomach from time to time with a flat spoon to ascertain if further cramming is possible. "The child is father to the man," and the adult Korean shows that he has reached the desirable stage of repletion by eructations, splutterings, slapping his stomach, and groans of satisfaction, looking round with a satisfied air. A quart of rice, which when cooked is of great bulk, is a laborer's meal, but besides there are other dishes, which render its insipidity palatable. Among them are pounded capsicum, soy, various native sauces of abominable odors, *kimshi*, a species of sour kraut, seaweed, salt fish, and salted seaweed fried in batter. The very poor only take two meals a day, but those who can afford it take three and four.

In this respect of voracity all classes are alike.   The great
merit of a meal is not so much quality as quantity, and from
infancy onwards one object in life is to give the stomach as
much capacity and elasticity as is possible, so that four pounds
of rice daily may not incommode it.   People in easy circumstances drink wine and eat great quantities of fruit, nuts, and
confectionery in the intervals between meals, yet are as ready
to tackle the next food as though they had been starving for a
week.   In well-to-do houses beef and dog are served on large
trenchers, and as each guest has his separate table, a host can
show generosity to this or that special friend without helping
others to more than is necessary.   I have seen Koreans eat
more than three pounds of solid meat at one meal.   Large as
a "portion" is, it is not unusual to see a Korean eat three and
even four, and where people abstain from these excesses it
may generally be assumed that they are too poor to indulge in
them.   It is quite common to see from twenty to twenty-five
peaches or small melons disappear at a single sitting, and without being peeled.   There can be no doubt that the enormous
consumption of red pepper, which is supplied even to infants,
helps this gluttonous style of eating.   It is not surprising
that dyspepsia and kindred evils are very common among
Koreans.

The Korean is omnivorous.   Dog meat is in great request at
certain seasons, and dogs are extensively bred for the table.
Pork, beef, fish, raw, dried, and salted, the intestines of
animals, all birds and game, no part being rejected, are eaten
—a baked fowl, with its head, claws, and interior intact, being
the equivalent of "the fatted calf."   Cooking is not always
essential.   On the Han I saw men taking fish off the hook,
and after plunging them into a pot of red pepper sauce, eating
them at once with their bones.   Wheat, barley, maize, millet,
the Irish and sweet potato, oats, peas, beans, rice, radishes,
turnips, herbs, and wild leaves and roots innumerable, seaweed, shrimps, pastry made of flour, sugar, and oil, *kimshi,*

on the making of which the whole female population of the
middle and lower classes is engaged in November, a home-
made vermicelli of buckwheat flour and white of egg, largely
made up into a broth, soups, dried persimmons, sponge-cakes,
cakes of the edible pine nut and honey, of flour, sugar, and
sesamum seeds, onions, garlic, lily bulbs, chestnuts, and very
much else are eaten. Oil of sesamum is largely used in cooking, as well as vinegar, soy, and other sauces of pungent and
objectionable odors, the basis of most of them being capsicums
and fermented rotten beans !

The magistracy of Thong-chhön, where we halted the next
day at noon, and where the curiosity of the people was absolutely *suffocating*, is a town sheltered from the sea, which is
within 2 miles, by a high ridge, and is situated prettily in a
double fold of hills remarkable for the artistic natural grouping of very grand pines.

At this point a spell of the most severe heat of the year set
in, and the remainder of the journey was accomplished in a
temperature ranging from 89° to 100° in the shade, and seldom falling below 80° at night, phenomenal heat for the first
days of June. Taking advantage of it, the whole male population was in the fields rice planting. Rice valleys, reaching
the unusual magnitude for Korea of from 3 to 7 miles in
breadth, and from 6 to 14 miles in length, sloping gently to
the sea, with innumerable villages on the slopes of the hills
which surround them, were numerous. Among them I saw,
for the only time, reservoirs for the storage of water for irrigation. The pink ibis and the spotted green frog were abundant
everywhere. The country there has a look of passable prosperity, but the people are kept at a low level by official exactions.

On this coast of Kong-wön-Do are the P'al-kyöng or " Eight
Views," which are of much repute in Korea. We passed two
of them. Su-chung Dai (The Place Between the Waters) is a
narrow strip of elevated white sand with the long roll of the

Pacific on the east, and the gentle plash of a lovely fresh-water lake on the west. This lake of Ma-cha Töng, the only body of fresh water which I saw in Korea, about 6 miles in length by 2 in breadth, has mountainous shores much broken by bays and inlets, at the head of each of which is a village half hidden among trees in the folds of the hills, while wooded conical islets break the mirror of the surface. On the white barrier of sand there are some fine specimens of the red-stemmed *Pinus sylvestris*, with a carpet of dwarf crimson roses and pink lilies. Among the mountain forests are leopards, tigers, and deer, and the call of the pheasant and the cooing of the wild dove floated sweetly from the lake shore. It was an idyll of peace and beauty. The other of the " Eight Views " is rather a curiosity than a beauty, miles of cream-colored sand blown up in wavy billows as high as the plumy tops of thousands of fir trees which are helplessly embedded in it.

During the long hot ride of eleven hours, visions of the evening halt at a peaceful village on the seashore filled my mind, and hope made the toilsome climb over several promontories of black basalt tolerable, even though the descents were so steep that the *mapu* held the ponies up by their tails! In the early twilight, when the fierce sun blaze was over, in the smoky redness of a heated evening atmosphere, when every rock was giving forth the heat it had absorbed in the day, across the stream which is at once the outlet of the lake and the boundary between the provinces of Kang-wön and Ham-gyöng, appeared a large, straggling, gray-roofed village, above high-water mark, on a beach of white sand. Several fishing junks were lying in shelter at the mouth of the stream. Women were beating clothes and drawing water, and children and dogs were rolling over each other on the sand, all more or less idealized by being silhouetted in purple against the hot, lurid sky.

As the enchantment of distance faded and Ma-cha Töng revealed itself in plain prose, fading from purple into sober

gray, the ideal of a romantic halt by the pure sea vanished.
A long, crooked, tumble-down narrow street, with narrower
off-shoots, heaps of fish offal and rubbish, in which swine,
mangy, blear-eyed dogs, and children, much afflicted with
skin disease, were indiscriminately routing and rolling, pools
covered with a thick brown scum, a stream which had degenerated into an open sewer, down which thick green slime
flowed tardily, a beach of white sand, the upper part of which
was blackened with fish laid out to dry, frames for drying fish
everywhere, men, women, children, all as dirty in person and
clothing as it was possible to be, thronging the roadway as we
approached, air laden with insupportable odors, and the vilest
accommodation I ever had in Korea, have fixed this night in
my memory.

The inn, if inn it was, gave me a room 8 feet by 6, and 5
feet 2 inches high. *Ang-paks*, for it was the family granary,
iron shoes of ploughs and spades, bundles of foul rags, seaweed, ears of millet hanging in bunches from the roof, pack
saddles, and worse than all else, rotten beans fermenting for
soy, and malodorous half-salted fish, just left room for my
camp-bed. This den opened on a vile yard, partly dunghill
and partly pigpen, in which is the well from which the women
of the house, with sublime *sang-froid*, draw the drinking
water ! Outside is a swamp, which throughout the night gave
off sickening odors. Every few minutes something was wanted
from my room, and as there was not room for two, I had every
time to go out into the yard. Wong's good-night was, "I
hope you won't die." When I entered, the mercury was $87°$.
After that, cooking for man and beast and the *kang* floor
raised it to $107°$, at which point it stood till morning, vivify-
ing into revoltingly active life myriads of cockroaches and
vermin which revel in heat, not to speak of rats, which ran
over my bed, ate my candle, gnawed my straps, and would
have left me without boots, had I not long before learned to
hang them from the tripod of my camera. From nine years

of travelling, some of it very severe and comfortless, that night stands out as hideously memorable.

The *raison d'être* of Ma-cha Töng, and the numerous coast villages which exist wherever a convenient shore and a protection for boats occur together, is the coast fishing. The fact that a floating population of over 8,000 Japanese fishermen make a living by fishing on the coast near Fusan shows that there is a redundant harvest to be reaped. The Korean fisherman is credited with utter want of enterprise, and Mr. Oiesen, in the Customs' report for Wön-san for 1891, accuses him of "remaining content with such fish as will run into crudely and easily constructed traps, set out along the shore, which only require attention for an hour or so each day." I must, however, say that each village that I passed possessed from seven to twelve fishing junks, which were kept at sea. They are unseaworthy boats, and it is not surprising that they hug the shore. I believe that the fishing industry, with every other, is paralyzed by the complete insecurity of the earnings of labor and by the exactions of officials, and that the Korean fisherman does not care to earn money of which he will surely be deprived on any or no pretence, and that, along with the members of the industrial classes generally, he seeks the protection of poverty.

The fish taken on this coast, when salted and dried, find their way by boat to Wön-san, and from thence over central Korea, but in winter pedlars carry them directly inland from the fishing villages. Salterns on the plan of those often seen in China occur frequently near the villages. The operation of making salt from sea water is absolutely primitive, and so rough and dirty that the whiteness of the coarse product which results is an astonishment. In spite of heavy losses and heavier "squeezings," this industry, which is carried on from May to October, is a profitable one.

The road beyond that noisome halting-place traverses picturesque country for many miles, being cut out of the sides of noble cliffs, or crosses basaltic spurs by arrangements resembling rock ladders, keeping perforce always close to the sea, now on dizzy precipices, then descending to firm hard stretches of golden sand, or winding just above high-water mark among colossal boulders which are completely covered with the *Ampelopsis Veitchiana*, the creeper *par excellence* of Korea. The sea was green and violet near the shore and a vivid blue in the distance, and on its rippleless surface fishing boats with gray hulls and brown sails lay motionless, for the rush and swirl of tides, rising and falling as they do on the west coast from 25 to 38 feet, are unknown on the east coast, the variation between high and low water being within 18 inches.

It was the hottest day of the year, and it was fortunate that the prettily situated market-place of Syo-im had a new and clean inn, in which it was possible to prolong the noonday halt, and to get a good dinner of fresh and salt fish, vegetables, herbs, sauces, and rice, for the sum of two cents gold. There also, being the market-day, Mr. Miller succeeded in obtaining *cash* for four silver *yen* from the pedlars.

After passing over a tedious sandy plain with a reserve of fine firs, under which the countless dead of ages lie under great sand mounds held together by nets or branches of trees, we reached at sunset my ideal, a clean, exquisitely situated village of nine houses, of which one was an inn where, contrary to the general rule, we were made cordially welcome.[1] The nine families at Chin-pul possessed seven good-sized fishing boats.

That inn is of unusual construction. There is a broad mud

---

[1] A *kwan-ja*, being an official passport, lays a traveller open to the suspicion that, like officials, he will take the best of everything he can get without paying for it, and this dread, added to a natural distrust of foreigners, led to more or less unwillingness to receive us in many places, the *mapu* having to console the people by asseverating that I paid the full price for all I got, and that even when I tore a sheet of paper from the window I paid for it!

platform of which fireplaces and utensils for cooking for man
and beast occupy one half, and the other is matted for sleeping
and eating.   My room, which had no window, but was clean
and plastered, opened on this, and as the mercury was at 111°
until 3 A. M. owing to the heated floor, I sat at the door nearly
all night, so the dawn and an early start, and the coolness of
the green and violet shades of the almost rippleless ocean,
which laved its varied shore of bays, promontories, and lofty
cliffs, were very welcome.

A valley opening on the sea which it took five hours to skirt
and cross, covered with grain and newly planted rice, is literally fringed with villages, which look comfortably prosperous
in spite of exactions.   A smaller valley contains about 3,000
acres of rice land only, and on the slopes surrounding all these
are rich lands, bearing heavy crops of wheat, millet, barley,
cotton, tobacco, castor oil, sesamum, oats, turnips, peas, beans,
and potatoes.   The ponies are larger and better kept in that
region, and the red bulls are of immense size.   The black pig,
however, is as small and mean as ever.   The crops were clean,
and the rice dykes and irrigation channels well kept.   Good
and honest government would create as happy and prosperous
a people as the traveller finds in Japan, the soil being very
similar, while Korea has a far better climate.

During the land journey from Chang-an Sa to Wön-san I
had better opportunities of seeing the agricultural methods of
the Koreans than in the valleys of the Han.   As compared
with the exquisite neatness of the Japanese and the diligent
thriftiness of the Chinese, Korean agriculture is to some extent
wasteful and untidy.   Weeds are not kept down in the summer
as they ought to be, stones are often left on the ground, and
there is a raggedness about the margins of fields and dykes
and a dilapidation about stone walls which is unpleasing to the
eye.   The paths through the fields are apt to be much worn
and fringed with weeds, and the furrows are not so straight as
they might be.   Yet on the whole the cultivation is much bet-

ter and the majority of the crops far cleaner than I had been
led to expect. Domestic animals are very few, and very little
fertilizing material is applied to the ground except in the neighborhood of Seoul and other cities, a fact which makes its exceeding fertility very noteworthy.

The rainfall is abundant but not excessive, and the desolat-
ing floods which afflict Korea's opposite neighbor, Japan, are
as unknown as earthquakes. Irrigation is only necessary for
rice, which is the staple of Korea. Except on certain rice
lands, two crops a year are raised throughout central and southern Korea, the rice being planted in June, or rather transplanted from the nurseries in which it is sown in May, and is
harvested early in October, when the ground is ploughed and
barley or rye is sown, which ripens in May or early June of
the next year, after which water is let in, the field is again
ploughed while flooded, and the rice plants are set out in rows
of "clumps," two or four or even six plants in a "clump."
Where only one crop is raised, the rice field lies fallow from
the end of October till the following May. In wheat, barley,
or rye fields the sowing is in October, and the harvest in May
or June, after which beans, peas, and other vegetables are sown.
Along the "great roads," as the crops approach ripeness, elevated watch-sheds are erected in the fields as safeguards against
depredations. The crops, on the whole, are very fine, and
would be immense were it not for the paucity of fertilizing
material.

Agricultural implements are rude and few. A wooden
ploughshare with a removable iron shoe is used which turns
the furrows the reverse way to ours. A wooden spade, also
shod with iron, is largely used for heavy work. This, which
excites the ridicule of foreigners as a gratuitous waste of man
power, is furnished with several ropes attached to the blade,
each of which is jerked by a man while another man guides
the blade into the ground by its long handle. The other implements are the same sort of sharp-pointed sharp hoe which is

in use in China, and which in the hands of the eastern peasant fills the place of shovel, hoe, and spade, a reaping hook, a short knife, a barrow, and a bamboo rake which is largely used in the denudation of the hills.

Grain, peas, and beans are threshed out with flails as often as not in the roadway of a village, while the grinding of flour and the hulling of rice are accomplished by the stone quern, and the stone or wooden mortar, with an iron pestle worked by hand or foot, the "*pang-a*," or, as has been previously described, by a "*mul*," or water "*pang-a*." Rice is threshed by beating the ears over a board, and all grain is winnowed by being thrown up in the wind.

The pony is not used in agriculture. Ploughing is done by the powerful, noble, tractable, Korean bull, a cane ring placed in his nostrils when young rendering him manageable even by a young child. He is four years in attaining maturity, and is now worth from £3 to £4, his value having been enhanced by the late war and the prevalence of rinderpest in recent years. Milk is not an article of diet. In some districts ox-sleds of very simple construction are used for bringing down fuel from the hills and produce from the fields, and at Seoul and a few other cities rude carts are to be seen; but ponies, men, and bulls are the means of transport for produce and goods, the loads being adjusted evenly on wooden pack saddles, or in the case of small articles in panniers of plaited straw or netted rope. In the latter, ingeniously made to open at the bottom and discharge their contents, manure is carried to the fields. Both bulls and ponies are shod with iron. The pony carries from 160 to 200 lbs. Sore backs are lamentably common.

The breed of pigs is very small. Pigs are always black and loathsome. Their bristles stand up along their backs, and they are lean, active, and of specially revolting habits. The dogs are big, usually buff, long-haired, and cowardly, and caricature the Scotch collie in their aspect. The fowls are plebeian, and for wildness, activity, and powers of flight are unequalled in my experience. Ducks are not very common, and geese are kept chiefly as guards, and for presentation at weddings as emblems of fidelity. The few sheep bred in Korea are reserved for Royal sacrifices. I have occasionally seen mutton on tables in Seoul, but it has been imported from Chefoo. The villages which make their living altogether by agriculture are usually off the high roads, those which the hasty traveller passes through depending as much on the entertaining of wayfarers as on the cultivation of the land. In these, nearly every house has a covered shelf in front at which food can be obtained, but lodging is not provided, and the villages which can feed and lodge beasts as well as men are few. The fact that the large farming villages are off the road gives an incorrect notion of the population of Korea.

On the slope of a hillside above a pleasant valley lies the town of An-byöng, once, judging from the extent of its decaying walls and fortifications, and the height of its canopied but ruinous gate-towers, a large city. The *yamen* and other Government buildings are well kept, and being in good repair, are in striking contrast to those previously seen on the route. The " main street " is, however, nothing but a dirty alley. The town has a diminishing population, and though it makes some paper from the *Brousonettia Papyrifera*, and has several schools, and exchanges rice and beans for foreign cottons at Wön-san, it has a singularly decaying look, and is altogether unworthy of its position as being one of the chief places in the province of Ham-gyöng. Outside of it the road crosses a remarkably broad river bed by a bridge 720 feet long, so dilapidated that the ponies put their feet through its rotten sods several times.

From An-byöng to Ta-ri-mak, a short distance from Nam-San on the main road from Seoul to Wön-san, is a long and tedious ride through thinly peopled country and pine woods full of graves. We spent two nights there at a very noisy and disagreeable inn, in which privacy was unattainable and the vermin were appalling. There the host was specially unwilling to take in foreigners, on the ground that we should not pay, a suspicion which irritated our friendly *mapu*, who vociferated at the top of their voices that we paid "even for the smallest things we got." The swinging season was at hand, each amusement having its definite date for beginning and ending, and in every village swings were being erected on tall straight poles. Wong could never resist the temptation of taking a swing, which always amused the people.

At this inn there were some musical performers who made both night and day wearisome to me, but gave great pleasure to others. I have not previously mentioned my sufferings on the Han from the sounds produced by itinerant musicians, and by the *mutang* or sorceress and her coadjutors; but, as has been forcibly brought out in a paper on Korean music by Mr. Hulbert in the *Korean Repository*,[1] the sounds are peculiar and unpleasing, because we neither know nor feel what they are intended to express, and we bring to Korean music not the Korean temperament and training but the Western, which demands "time" as an essential. It may be added that the Koreans, like their neighbors the Japanese, love our music as little as we love theirs, and for the same reason, that the ideas we express by it are unfamiliar to them.

One reason of the afflictive and discordant sounds is that the gamut of Korea differs from the musical scale of European countries, with the result that whenever music seems to be trembling on the verge of a harmony, a discord assails the ear. The musical instruments are many, but they are not carefully finished. Among instruments of percussion are drums, cymbals, gongs, and a species of castanet. For wind instruments there are unkeyed bugles, flutes, and long and short trumpets; and the stringed instruments are a large guitar, a twenty-five stringed guitar, a mandolin, and a five-stringed violin. The

[1] February, 1896.

discord produced by a concert of several of these instruments
is heard in perfection at the opening and closing of the gates
of cities.

There are three classes of Korean vocal music, the first being
the *Si-jo* or "classical" style, *andante tremuloso*, and "punc-
tuated with drums," the drum accompaniment consisting mainly
of a drum beat from time to time as an indication to the vo-
calist that she has quavered long enough upon one note. The
Si-jo is a slow process, and is said by the Koreans to require
such long and patient practise that only the dancing girls can
excel in it, as they alone have leisure to cultivate it. One
branch of it deals with convivial songs, of one of which I
give a translation from the gifted pen of the Rev. H. B. Hulbert of Seoul.[1]

The Korean, prisoned during the winter in his small, dark,
dirty, and malodorous rooms, with neither a glowing fireside

[1] I

'Twas years ago that Kim and I
Struck hands and swore, however dry
The lip might be or sad the heart,
The merry wine should have no part
In mitigating sorrow's blow
Or quenching thirst. 'Twas long ago.

II

And now I've reached the flood-tide mark
Of life; the ebb begins, and dark
The future lowers. The tide of wine
Will never ebb. 'Twill aye be mine
To mourn the desecrated fane
Where that lost pledge of youth lies slain.

III

Nay, nay, begone! The jocund bowl
Again shall bolster up my soul
Against itself. What, good-man, hold!
Canst tell me where red wine is sold?
Nay, just beyond that peach tree there?
Good luck be thine, I'll thither fare.

nor brilliant lamp to mitigate the gloom, welcomes spring with lively excitement, and demands music and song as its natural accompaniment—song that shall express the emancipation, breathing space, and unalloyed physical pleasure which have no counterpart in our English feelings. Thus a classical song runs:—

> The willow catkin bears the vernal blush of summer's dawn
> When winter's night is done;
> The oriole, who preens herself aloft on swaying bough,
> Is summer's harbinger;
> The butterfly, with noiseless *ful-ful* of her pulsing wing,
> Marks off the summer hour.
> Quick, boy, thy zither! Do its strings accord? 'Tis well.
> Strike up! *I must have song.*

The second style of Korean vocal music is the *Ha Ch'i* or popular. The most conspicuous song in this class is the *A-ra-rüng*, of 782 verses. It is said that the *A-ra-rüng* holds to the Korean in music the same place that rice does in his food—all else being a mere appendage. The tune, but with the trills and quavers, of which there are one or two to each note, left out, is given here, though Mr. Hulbert, to whom I am greatly indebted, calls it "a very weak attempt to score it."

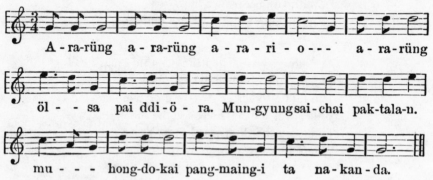

A - ra-rüng   a - ra-rüng   a - ra - ri - o - - -   a - ra - rüng

öl - - sa   pai ddi - ö - ra. Mun-gyung sai - chai pak-tala-n.

mu - - - hong-do-kai pang-maing-i   ta   na - kan - da.

The chorus of *A-ra-rüng* is invariable, but the verses which are sung in connection with it take a wide range through the fields of lyrics, epics, and didactics.

There is a third style, which is between the classical and the popular, but which hardly deserves mention.

To my thinking, the melancholy which seems the *motif* of most Oriental music becomes an extreme plaintiveness in that of Korea, partly due probably to the unlimited quavering on one note. While what may be called concerted music is torture to a Western ear, solos on the flute ofttimes combine a singular sweetness with their mournfulness and suggest "Far-off Melodies." Love songs are popular, and there is a tender grace about some of them, as well as an occasional glint of humor, as indicated by the last line of the third stanza of one translated by Mr. Gale.[1] The allusions to Nature generally

[1] LOVE SONG

Farewell's a fire that burns one's heart,
And tears are rains that quench in part,
But then the winds blow in one's sighs,
And cause the flames again to rise.

My soul I've mixed up with the wine,
And now my love is drinking,
Into his orifices nine
Deep down its spirit's sinking.
To keep him true to me and mine,
A potent mixture is the wine.

Silvery moon and frosty air,
Eve and dawn are meeting;
Widowed wild goose flying there,
Hear my words of greeting!
On your journey should you see
Him I love so broken-hearted,
Kindly say this word for me,
That it's death when we are parted.
Flapping off the wild goose clambers,
Says she will if she remembers.

Fill the ink-stone, bring the water,
To my love I'll write a letter;
Ink and paper soon will see
The one that's all the world to me,
While the pen and I together,
Left behind, condole each other.

show a quick and sympathetic insight into her beauties, and occasional stanzas, of which the one cited is among several translated by Mr. Hulbert, have a delicacy of touch not unworthy of an Elizabethan poet.[1] The *Korean Repository* is doing a good work in making Korean poetry accessible to English readers.

There was not, however, any flute music at Ta-ri-mak. There were classical songs, with a direful drum accompaniment, and a wearisome repetition of the *A-ra-rüng*, continuing all day and late into the hot night.

A few pedlars passed by, selling tobacco, necessaries, and children's toys, the latter rudely made, and only attractive in a country in which artistic feeling appears dead. There are shops in Seoul, Phyöng-yang, and other cities devoted to the sale of such toys, painted in staring colors, and illustrative chiefly of adult life. There are also monkeys, puppies, and tigers on wheels, all for boys, and soldiers in European uniforms have appeared during the recent military craze, and boys are very early taught to look forward to official life by representations of mandarins' chairs, red-tasselled umbrellas, and fringed hats. Girls being of comparatively small account, toys specially suited to them are not many.

Japanese lucifer matches, which, when of the cheap sort, seem only slightly inflammable, as I have several times used a whole box without igniting one, were in the stock of the pedlars, and are making rapid headway in the towns, but even so near Wön-san as Ta-ri-mak is, the people were still using flint and steel to light chips of wood dipped in sulphur, though the cheap and smoky kerosene lamp has displaced the tall, upright candlestick and the old-fashioned dish lamps there and in very many other country places.

[1] I asked the spotted butterfly
   To take me on his wing and fly
   To yonder mountain's breezy side.
   The trixy tiger moth I'll ride
      As home I come.

From the high road from Seoul to Wŏn-san we diverged at Nam-San to visit the large monastery of Sŏk-wang Sa, famous as being the place where, in the palmy days of Korean Buddhism, Atai-jo, the first king of the present dynasty, was educated and lived. The monastery itself, with its temples, was erected by this king to mark the spot where, 504 years ago, he received that supernatural message to rule in virtue of which his descendant occupies the Korean throne to-day. In this singularly beautiful spot Atai-jo's early years were spent in religious exercises, study, and preparation, and many of the superb trees which adorn the grand mountain clefts in which Sŏk-wang Sa is situated are said to have been planted by his hands. His regalia and robes of state are preserved in a building by themselves, which no one is allowed to enter except the duly appointed attendant. A bridle track alongside of a clear mountain stream leads through very pretty and prosperous-looking country, and over wooded foothills for some miles to the base of a fine mountain range. We passed for a length of time through rich and heavily-timbered monastic property, then the beautiful valley narrowed, and by a " Red Arrow Gate " we entered on a smooth broad road, on which the sun glinted here and there through the heavy foliage of an avenue of noble pines, a gap now and then giving entrancing glimpses of the deep delicious blue of the summer sky, of a grand gorge dark with pines, firs, and the exotic *Cleyera Japonica* and zelkawa, brightened by the tender green of maples and other deciduous trees, and by flashes of foam from a torrent booming among great moss-covered boulders.

Then came bridges with decorative roofs, abbots' tombstones under carved and painted canopies, inscribed stone tablets, glorious views of a peaked, forest-clothed mountain barring the gorge, and as the pines of the avenue fell into groups at its close, and magnificent zelkawas, from whose spreading branches white roses hung in graceful festoons, overarched the road, a long irregular line of temples and monastic buildings appeared, clinging in singular picturesqueness to the sides of the ravine, which there ascends somewhat rapidly towards the mountain, which closes it.

An abbot, framed in the doorway of a quaint building, and looking like a picture of a portly, jolly, mediæval friar, welcomed us, and he and his monks regaled us with honey water in the large guest-hall, but simultaneously produced a visitors' book and asked us how much we were going to pay, the sum being duly recorded. The grasping ways of these monks, who fleeced the *mapu* so badly as to make them say they " had fallen among thieves," contrast with the friendly hospitality of their brethren of the Diamond Mountain, and can only be accounted for by the contaminating influences of a treaty port, from which they are distant only a long day's journey!

" See the sights first and then pay," they said, the glorious views and the quaint picturesqueness of the monastic buildings clustering on the crags above the cataracts being the sight *par excellence*. It was refreshing to turn from the contemplation of the sensual, acquisitive, greedy faces of most of the monks to Nature at her freshest and fairest, on one of the loveliest days of early June.

The interiors of the temples are shabby and dirty, the paint is scaling off the roofs, and the floors and even the altars were hidden under layers of herbs drying for kitchen use. Besides the tablet to the first king of the present dynasty in a handsome tablet-house, the noteworthy " sight " to be seen is a small temple dedicated to the " Five Hundred Disciples." Sök-wang Sa is not a holy place, and the artist who caricatured the devout and ascetic followers of the ascetic Sakymuni has bequeathed a legacy of unhallowed suggestion to its inmates !

The " Five Hundred " are stone images not a foot in height, arranged round the dusty temple in several tiers, each one with a silk cap on, worn with more or less of a jaunty air on one side of the head or falling over the brow. The variety of features and expression is wonderful; all Eastern nationalities are represented, and there are not two faces or attitudes alike. The whole display shows genius, though not of a high order.

Among the infinite variety, one figure has deeply set eyes, an aquiline nose, and thin lips; another a pug nose, squinting eyes, and a broad grinning mouth; one is Mongolian, another Caucasian, and another approximates to the Negro type. Here is a stout, jolly fellow, with a leer and a broad grin suggestive of casks of porter and the archaic London drayman; there is an idiot with drooping head, receding brow and chin, and a vacant stare; here again is a dark stage villain, with red cheeks and a cap drawn low over his forehead; then .Mr. Pecksniff confronts one with an air of sanctimoniousness obviously difficult to retain; Falstaff outdoes his legendary jollity; and priests and monks of all nations leer at the beholders from under their jaunty caps. It is an exhibition of unsanctified genius. Nearly all the figures look worse for drink, and fatuous smiles, drunken leers, and farcical grins are the rule, the effect of all being aggravated by the varied and absurd arrangements of the caps. The grotesqueness is indescribable, and altogether " unedifying."

It was a great change to get on the broad main road to Wön-san, and to see telegraph poles once more. There was plenty of goods and passenger traffic across the fine plain covered with rice and grain, margined by bluffs, and dotted with what have obviously once been islands, near which Wön-san is situated.

Where the road is broad, a high heap of hardened mud runs along the centre, with hardened mud corrugations on either side; where narrow, it is merely the top of a rice dyke. The bridges are specially infamous; in fact, they were so rotten that the *mapu* would not trust their ponies upon them, and we forded all the streams. Yet this road, which I found

equally bad at the three points at which I touched it, is one of
the leading thoroughfares by which goods pass from the east to
the west coast and *vice versa*,—tobacco, copper, salt fish, seaweed, galena, and hides from the east, and foreign shirtings,
watches, and miscellaneous native and foreign articles from the
west.

The heat of the sun was but poorly indicated by a shade
temperature of 84°, and it was in his full noontide fierceness
that we reached the huddle of foul and narrow alleys and irregular rows of thatched shops along the high road which
make up the busy and growing Korean town of Wön-san,
which, with an estimated population of 15,000 people, lies
along a strip of beach below a pine-clothed bluff and ranges
of mountains, then green to their summits, but which I saw in
December of the same year in the majesty of the snow which
covers them from November to May.   The smells were fearful,
the dirt abominable, and the quantity of wretched dogs and of
pieces of bleeding meat blackening in the sun perfectly sickening.   This aspect of meat, produced by the mode of killing
it, has made foreigners entirely dependent on the Japanese
butchers in Seoul and elsewhere.   The Koreans cut the throat
of the animal and insert a peg in the opening.   Then the
butcher takes a hatchet and beats the animal on the rump until
it dies.   The process takes about an hour, and the beast suffers
agonies of terror and pain before it loses consciousness.   Very
little blood is lost during the operation ; the beef is full of it,
and its heavier weight in consequence is to the advantage of
the vendor.

Then came a level stretch of about a mile, much planted
with potatoes, glimpses of American Protestant mission-houses
in conspicuous and eligible positions (eligible, that is, for
everything but mission work), and the uneven Korean road
glided imperceptibly into a broad gravel road, fringed on both
sides with neat wooden houses standing in gardens, which
gradually thickened into the neatest, trimmest, and most at-

tractive town in all Korea, the Japanese settlement of the treaty port of Wön-san, opened to Japanese trade in 1880 and to foreign trade generally in 1883.

Broad and well-kept streets, neat wharves, trim and fairly substantial houses, showing the interior dollishness and daintiness characteristic of Japan, a large and very prominent Japanese Consulate in Anglo-Japanese style, the offices of the " N.Y.K.," the Japan Mail Steamship Company (an abbreviation as familiar to residents in the Far East as " P. & O."), a Japanese Bank of solid reputation, Customs' buildings, of which a neat reading-room forms a part, neat Japanese shops where European articles can be bought at moderate prices, a large schoolhouse, with a teacher in European dress, and active manikins and hobbling but graceful women, neither veiled nor muffled up, are the features of this pleasant Japanese colony, which is so fortunate as to have no history, its progress, though not rapid, having been placid and peaceful, not marred by friction either with Koreans or foreigners of other nationalities ; and even the recent war, though it led to the removal of the Chinese consul and his countrymen, an insignificant fraction of the population, had left no special traces, except that the enormous wages paid to transport coolies by the Japanese had enabled them to gamble with *yen* instead of *cash !*

I was most hospitably received by Mr. and Mrs. Gale of the American Presbyterian Mission. Mr. Gale's work was the important one of the preparation of a dictionary of the Korean language in Korean, Chinese, and English, which was published in 1897.

During the twelve days which I spent at Wön-san I made a junk excursion in Yung-hing or Broughton Bay, in the southwest corner of which the port is situated. It is a superb bay, with an area of fully 40 square miles, a depth of from 6 to 12 fathoms, with good holding ground, never freezes in winter, is sheltered by promontories and mountains from the winds of every quarter, and its entrance is protected by islands. To English readers it is probable that the sole interest of this fine bay lies in the fact that its northern arm, Port Lazareff, which was the object of my cruise, is the harbor which Russia is credited with desiring to gain possession of for the terminus of her Trans-Siberian Railway. Whether this be so or no, or whether Port Shestakoff, on the same coast, but 60 miles farther north, is more defensible and better adapted for a naval as well as a terminal port, the time has gone by for grudging to Russia an outlet on the Pacific, and I for one should prefer it on the coast of eastern Korea than on the northern shore of the Yellow Sea.

The head of Port Lazareff is about 16 miles from Wön-san, and is formed by the swampy outlets of the river Dun-gan, among the many branches of which lie inhabited, low-lying islands. There are rude but extensive salt works at the shallows in which this noble inlet terminates, after receiving several streams besides the Dun-gan. Port Lazareff has, in addition, abundant supplies of water from natural springs. The high hills which surround the bay are grassy to their summits, but there is very little wood, and the villages are small and far between. Game is singularly abundant. Pheasants are nearly as plentiful as sparrows are with us, the wary turkey bustard abounds, there are snipe in the late summer, and pigeons, plover, and water-hen are common. In spring and autumn wild fowl innumerable crowd the waters of every stream and inlet, swans, teal, geese, and ducks darkening the air, which they rend with their clamor as the sportsman invades their haunts.

A Korean junk does not impress one by its seaworthiness, and it is not surprising that the junkmen hug the shore and seek shelter whenever a good sailing breeze comes on. She is built without nails, iron, or preservative paint, and looks rather like a temporary and fortuitous aggregation of beams and planks than a deliberate construction. Two tall, heavy masts fixed by wedges among the timbers at the bottom of the boat require frequent attention, as they are always swaying and threatening to come down. The sails are of matting, with a number of bamboos running transversely, with a cord attached to each, united into one sheet, by means of which tacking is effected, or rather might be. Practically, navigation consists in running before a light breeze, and dropping the mass of mats and bamboos on the confusion below whenever it freshens, varying the process by an easy pull at the sweeps, one at the stern and two working on pins in transverse beams amidships, which project 3 feet on each side. The junk is fitted with a rudder of enormous size, which from its position acts as a keel board. The price is from 60 to 80 dollars. This singular craft sails well before the wind, but under other circumstances is apt to become unmanageable.

Wŏn-san has telegraphic communication with Seoul, and chiefly through the enterprise of the N.Y.K., it is connected by most comfortable steamers with Korean ports and with Wladivostok, Kobe, and Nagasaki, Hong-Kong, Shanghai, Chefoo, Newchwang, and Tientsin. Steamers of a Russian line call there at intervals during the summer season. There are no Western merchants or Western residents except the missionaries and the Customs staff, and foreign trade is chiefly in the hands of the Japanese.

About 60 *li* from Wŏn-san are some large grass-covered mounds, of which the Koreans do not care to speak, as they regard them as associated with an ancient Korean custom, now looked upon as barbarous. During the last dynasty, and more than five centuries ago, it was customary, when people from age and infirmity became burdensome to their relations, to incarcerate them in the stone cells which these mounds contain, with a little food and water, and leave them there to die. In similar mounds, elsewhere in Korea, bowls and jars of coarse pottery have been found, as well as a few specimens of gray *celadon.*

There is nothing sensational about Wön-san.[1] It has no "booms" in trade or land, but "keeps the even tenor of its way." It is to me far the most attractive of the treaty ports. Its trim Japanese settlement, from which green hills rise abruptly, backed by fine mountain forms, dignified by snow for seven months of the year, and above all, the exquisite caves to the northwest, where the sea murmurs in cool grottos, and beats the pure white sand into ripples at the feet of cliffs hidden by flowers, ferns, and grass, and its air of dreamy repose—"a land where it is always afternoon"—point to its future as that of a salubrious and popular sanitarium.

[1] In January of 1897, the population of Wön-san was as follows:—

Japanese	.	.	1,299	French	.	.	.	2
Chinese	.	.	39	Russian	.	.	.	2
American	.	.	8	Danish	.	.	.	1
German	.	.	3	Norwegian	.	.	.	1
British	.	.	2					

1,357

Estimated Korean population, 15,000.

CHAPTER XIII

IMPENDING WAR—EXCITEMENT AT CHEMULPO

HAVING heard nothing at all of public events during my long inland journey, and only a few rumors of unlocalized collisions between the Tong-haks (rebels) and the Royal troops, the atmosphere of *canards* at Wŏn-san was somewhat stimulating, though I had already been long enough in Korea not to attach much importance to the stories with which the air was thick. One day it was said that the Tong-haks had gained great successes and had taken Gatling guns from the Royal army, another that they had been crushed and their mysterious and ubiquitous leader beheaded, while the latest rumor before my departure was that they were marching in great force on Fusan. Judging from the proclamation which they circulated, and which, while stating that they rose against corrupt officials and traitorous advisers, professed unswerving loyalty to the throne, it seemed credible that, if there were a throb of patriotism anywhere in Korea, it was in the breasts of these peasants. Their risings appeared to be free from excesses and useless bloodshed, and they confined themselves to the attempt to carry out their programme of reform. Some foreign sympathy was bestowed upon them, because it was thought that the iniquities of misrule could go no further, and that the time was ripe for an armed protest on a larger scale than the ordinary peasant risings against intolerable exactions.

But at the very moment when these matters were being discussed in Wŏn-san with not more than a languid interest, a formidable menace to the established order of things was taking shape, destined in a few days to cast the Tong-haks into the shade, and concentrate the attention of the world on this insignificant peninsula.

Leaving Wön-san by steamer on 17th June, and arriving at Fusan on the 19th, I was not surprised to find a Japanese gunboat in the harbor, and that 220 Japanese soldiers had been landed from the *Higo Maru* that morning and were quartered in the Buddhist temples on the hill, and that the rebels had cut the telegraph wires between Fusan and Seoul.

Among the few Europeans at Fusan there was no uneasiness. The Japanese, with their large mercantile colony there, have considerable interests to safeguard, and nothing seemed more natural than the course they took. A rumor that Japanese troops had been landed at Chemulpo was quite disregarded.

On arriving at Chemulpo, however, early on the morning of the 21st, a very exciting state of matters revealed itself. A large fleet, six Japanese ships of war, the American flag ship, two French, one Russian, and two Chinese, were lying in the outer harbor. The limited accommodation of the inner harbor was taxed to its utmost capacity. Japanese transports were landing troops, horses, and war material in steam launches, junks were discharging rice and other stores for the commissariat department, coolies were stacking it on the beach, and the movement by sea and land was ceaseless. Visitors from the shore, excited and agitated, brought a budget of astounding rumors, but confessed to being mainly in the dark.

On landing, I found the deadly dull port transformed: the streets resounded to the tread of Japanese troops in heavy marching order, trains of mat and forage carts blocked the road. Every house in the main street of the Japanese settlement was turned into a barrack and crowded with troops, rifles and accoutrements gleamed in the balconies, crowds of Koreans, limp and dazed, lounged in the streets or sat on the knolls, gazing vacantly at the transformation of their port into a foreign camp. Only two hours had passed since the first of the troops landed, and when I visited the camp with a young

Russian officer there were 1,200 men under canvas in well-ventilated bell tents, holding 20 each, with matted floors and drainage trenches, and dinner was being served in lacquer boxes. Stables had been run up, and the cavalry and mountain guns were in the centre. The horses of the mountain battery train, serviceable animals, fourteen hands high, were in excellent condition, and were equipped with pack saddles of the latest Indian pattern. They were removing shot and shell for Seoul from the Japanese Consulate with 200 men and 100 horses, and it was done almost soundlessly. The camp, with its neat streets, was orderly, trim, and quiet. In the town sentries challenged passers-by. Every man looked as if he knew his duty and meant to do it. There was no swagger. The manikins, well armed and serviceably dressed, were obviously in Korea for a purpose which they meant to accomplish.

What that purpose was, was well concealed under color of giving efficient protection to Japanese subjects in Korea, who were said to be imperilled by the successes of the Tonghaks.

The rebellion in southern Korea was exciting much alarm in the capital. Such movements, though on a smaller scale, are annual spring events in the peninsula, when in one or other of the provinces the peasantry, driven to exasperation by official extortions, rise, and, with more or less violence (occasionally fatal), drive out the offending mandarin. Punishment rarely ensues. The King sends a new official, who squeezes and extorts in his turn with more or less vigor, until, if he also passes bearable limits, he is forcibly expelled, and things settle down once more. This Tong-hak ("Oriental" or "National") movement, though lost sight of in presence of more important issues, was of greater moment, as being organized on a broader basis, so as to include a great number of adherents in Seoul and the other cities, and with such definite and reasonable objects that at first I was inclined to

call its leaders "armed reformers" rather than "rebels." At
that time there was no question as to the Royal authority.

The Tong-hak proclamation began by declaring in respectful language loyal allegiance to the King, and went on to
state the grievances in very moderate terms.   The Tong-haks
asserted, and with undoubted truth, that officials in Korea, for
their own purposes, closed the eyes and ears of the King to all
news and reports of the wrongs inflicted on his people.   That
ministers of State, governors, and magistrates were all indiffer-
ent to the welfare of their country, and were bent only on
enriching themselves, and that there were no checks on their
rapacity.   That examinations (the only avenues to official life)
were nothing more than scenes of bribery, barter, and sale,
and were no longer tests of fitness for civil appointment.
That officials cared not for the debt into which the country
was fast sinking.   That "they were proud, vainglorious,
adulterous, avaricious."   That many officials receiving appointments in the country lived in Seoul.   That "they flatter
and fawn in peace, and desert and betray in times of trouble."

The necessity for reform was strongly urged.   There were
no expressions of hostility to foreigners, and the manifesto did
not appear to take any account of them.   The leader, whose
individuality was never definitely ascertained, was credited
with ubiquity and supernatural powers by the common people,
as well as with the ability to speak both Japanese and Chinese,
and it was evident from his measures, forethought, the disposition of his forces, and some touches of Western strategic
skill, that he had some acquaintance with the modern art of
war.   His followers, armed at first with only old swords and
halberds, had come to possess rifles, taken from the official
armories and the defeated Royal troops.   For in the midst of
the thousand wild rumors which were afloat, it appeared certain
that the King sent several hundred soldiers against the Tong-
haks under a general who, on his way to attack their camp,
raised and armed 300 levies, who, in the engagement which

followed, joined the "rebels" and turned upon the King's
troops, that 300 of the latter were killed, and that the general
was missing.   This, following other successes, the deposition
of several important officials, and the rumored march on Seoul,
had created great alarm, and the King was supposed to be prepared for flight.

But the events of the two or three days before I landed at
Chemulpo threw the local disturbance into the shade, and it
is only with the object of showing with what an excellent
pretext for interference the Tong-haks had furnished the Japanese, that I recall this petty chapter of what is now ancient
history.

The questions vital to Korea and of paramount diplomatic
importance were, "What is the object of Japan?   Is this an
invasion?   Is she here as an enemy or a friend?"   Six thousand troops provisioned for three months had been landed.
Fifteen of the *Nippon Yusen Kaisha's* steamers had been withdrawn from their routes to act as transports, the Japanese had
occupied the Gap, a pass on the Seoul road, and Ma-pu, the
river port of the capital, and with guns, and in considerable
force, had established themselves on Nam Han, a wooded
hill above Seoul, from which position they commanded both
the palace and capital.   All these movements were carried out
with a suddenness, celerity, and freedom from hitch which in
their military aspects were worthy of the highest praise.

To any student of Far Eastern politics it must have been apparent that this skilful and extraordinary move on the part of
Japan was not made for the protection of her colonies in
Chemulpo and Seoul, nor yet against Korea.   It has been said
in various quarters, and believed, that the Japanese ministry
was shaky, and had to choose between its own downfall and a
foreign war.   This is a complete sophism.   There can be no
question that Japan had been planning such a movement for
years.   She had made accurate maps of Korea, and had
secured reports of forage and provisions, measurements of the

width of rivers and the depth of fords, and had been buying up rice in Korea for three months previously, while even as far as the Tibetan frontier, Japanese officers in disguise had gauged the strength and weakness of China, reporting on her armies on paper and, in fact, on her dummy guns, and antique, honeycombed carronades, and knew better than the Chinese themselves how many men each province could put into the field, how drilled and how armed, and they were acquainted with the infinite corruption and dishonesty, combined with a total lack of patriotism, which nullified even such commissariat arrangements as existed on paper, and rendered it absolutely impossible for China to send an army efficiently into the field, far less sustain it during a campaign.

To all appearance Japan had completely outwitted China in Korea, and a panic prevailed among the Chinese. Thirty ladies of the households of the Chinese Resident and Consul embarked for China on the appearance of the Japanese in Seoul, and 800 Chinamen left Chemulpo the day I arrived, the consternation in the Chinese colony being so great that even the market gardeners, who have a monopoly of a most thriving trade, fled.

I never before saw the Chinaman otherwise than aggravatingly cool, collected, and master of the situation, but on that June day he lost his head, and, frenzied by race hatred and pecuniary loss, was transformed into a shouting barbarian, not knowing what he would be at. The Chinese inn where I spent the day was one centre of the excitement, and each time that I came in from a walk or received a European visitor, a number of the *employés*, usually most quiet and reticent, huddled into my room with faces distorted by anxiety, asking what I had heard, what was going to be, whether the Chinese army would be there that night, whether the British fleet was coming to help them, etc., and even my Chinese servant, a most excellent fellow, was beside himself, muttering in English through clenched teeth, "I must kill, kill, kill!"

Meanwhile the dwarf battalions, a miracle of rigid discipline and good behavior, were steadily tramping to Seoul, where matters then and for some time afterwards stood thus. The King was in his secluded palace, and that which still posed as a Government had really collapsed. Mr. Hillier, the English Consul-General, was in England on leave, and the acting Consul-General, Mr. Gardner, C.M.G., had only been in Korea for three months. The American Minister was a newer man still. The French and German Consuls need hardly be taken into account, as they had few, if any, interests to safeguard. Mr. Waeber, the able and cautious diplomatist who had represented Russia for nine years, and had the confidence of the whole foreign community, had been appointed *chargé d'affaires* at Peking, and had left Seoul in the previous week. There remained, therefore, facing each other, Otori San, the Japanese ambassador to Peking, who was in Korea on a temporary mission, and Yuan, a military mandarin who had been for some years Chinese Resident in Seoul, a man entrusted by the Chinese Emperor with large powers, who was credited by foreigners with great force, tact, and ability, and who was generally regarded as "the power behind the throne."

I had frequently seen Otori San in the early months of the year, a Japanese of average height, speaking English well, wearing European dress as though born to it, and sporting white "shoulder-of-mutton" whiskers. He lounged in drawing-rooms, making trivial remarks to ladies, and was remarkable only for his insignificance. I believe he made the same impression, or want of impression, at Peking. But circumstances or stringent orders from Tokyo had transformed Mr. Otori. Whether he had worn a mask previously I know not, but he showed himself rough, vigorous, capable, a man of action, unscrupulous, and not only clever enough to outwit Yuan in a difficult and hazardous game, but everybody else.

In the afternoon of that memorable day at Chemulpo the

Vice-Consul called on me and warned me that I must leave Korea that night, and the urgency and seriousness of his manner left me no doubt that he was acting on information which he was not at liberty to divulge. I had left my travelling gear at Wön san in readiness for an autumn journey, and was going to Seoul that night for a week to get my money and civilized luggage before going for the summer to Japan. It was a serious blow. Other Europeans advised me not to be "deported," but it is one of my travelling rules never to be a source of embarrassment to British officials, and supposing the crisis to be an acute one, I reluctantly yielded, and that night, with two English fellow-sufferers, left Chemulpo in the Japanese steamer *Higo Maru*, bound for ports in the Gulf of Pechili, which *cul-de-sac* would have proved a veritable "lion's mouth" to her had hostilities been as imminent as the Vice-Consul believed them to be. I had nothing but the clothing I wore, a heavy tweed suit, and the mercury was 80°, and after paying my passage to Chefoo, the first port of call, I had only four cents left. It was four months before I obtained either my clothes or my money!

CHAPTER XIV

DEPORTED TO MANCHURIA

THOUGH I landed at Chefoo in heavy tweed clothing, I was obliged to walk up the steep hill to the British Consulate, though the mercury was 84° in the shade, because I had no money with which to pay for a *jinriksha!* My reflections were anything but pleasant. My passport and letters of introduction, both private and official, were in Seoul, my travelling dress was distinctly shabby, and I feared that an impecunious person without introductions, and unable to prove her identity, might meet with a very cool reception. I experienced something of the anxiety and timidity which are the everyday lot of thousands, and I have felt a far tenderer sympathy with the penniless, specially the educated penniless, ever since. I was so extremely uncomfortable that I hung about the gate of the British Consulate for some minutes before I could summon up courage to go to the door and send in a torn address of a letter which was my only visiting card! I thought, but it may have been fancy, that the Chinese who took it eyed me suspiciously and contemptuously.

The sudden revulsion of feeling which followed I cannot easily forget. Mr. Clement Allen, our justly popular Consul, met me with a warm welcome. I needed no proof of identity or anything else, he only desired to know what he could do for me. My anxiety was not quite over, for I had to make the humiliating confession that I needed money, and immediately he took me to Messrs. Ferguson and Co., who transact banking business, and asked them to let me have as much as I wanted. An invitation to tiffin followed, and Lady O'Conor, and the wife of the Spanish minister at Peking, who were staying at the Consulate, made up a bundle of summer clothing for me, and my "deportation" enriched me with valued friendships.

Returning in a very different frame of mind to the *Higo Maru*, I went on in her in severe heat to the mouth of the Peiho River in sight of the Taku forts, and after rolling on its muddy surges for two days, proceeded to Newchwang in Manchuria, reaching the mouth of the Liau River in five days from Chemulpo. Rain was falling, and a more hideous and disastrous-looking country than the voyage of two hours up to the port revealed, I never saw. The Liau, which has a tremendous tide and strong current, and is thick with yellow mud, is at high water nearly on a level with the adjacent flats, of which one sees little, except some mud forts on the left bank of the river, which are said to be heavily armed with Krupp guns, and an expanse of mud and reeds.

Of the mud-built Chinese city of Ying-tzŭ (Military Camp), known as Newchwang, though the real Newchwang is a derelict port 30 miles up the Liau, nothing can be seen above the mud bank but the curved, tiled roofs of *yamens* and temples, though it is a city of 60,000 souls, the growth of its population having kept pace with its rapid advance in commercial importance since it was opened to foreign trade in 1860. Several British steamers with big Chinese characters on their sides were at anchor in the tideway, and the river sides were closely fringed with up-river boats and sea-going junks, of various picturesque builds and colors, from Southern China, steamers and junks alike waiting not only for cargoes of the small beans for which Manchuria is famous, but for the pressed bean cake which is exported in enormous quantities to fertilize the sugar plantations and hungry fields of South China.

There is a Bund, and along and behind it is the foreign settlement, occupied by about forty Europeans. The white buildings of the Chinese Imperial Maritime Customs, the houses of the staff, the *hongs* of two or three foreign merchants, and the British Consular buildings, may be said to constitute the settlement. It has the reputation of being one of the kindliest and friendliest in the Far East, and the fact that the river closes annually about the 20th of November for about four months, and that the residents are thrown entirely on their own resources and on each other, only serves to increase that interdependence which binds this and similarly isolated communities so strongly together.

I was most kindly welcomed at the English Consulate then and on my return, and have most pleasant remembrances of Newchwang, its cordial kindness, and cheerful Bund, and breezy blue skies, but at first sight it is a dreary, solitary-looking place of mud, and muddy waters for ever swallowing large slices of the land, and threatening to engulf it altogether.

" Peas," really beans,[1] are its chief *raison d'être*, and their ups and downs in price its mild sensations. " Pea-boats," long and narrow, with matting roofs and one huge sail, bring down the beans from the interior, and mills working night and day express their oil, which is as good for cooking as for burning.

The viceroyalty of Manchuria, in which I spent the next two months, is interesting as in some ways distinct from China, besides having a prospective interest in connection with Russia. Lying outside of the Great Wall, it has a population of several distinct and mixed races, Manchus (Tartars), Gilyaks, Tungusi, Solons, Daurs, and Chinese. Along with these must be mentioned about 30,000 Korean families, the majority of whom have left Korea since 1868, in consequence of political disturbance and official exactions.[2]

The facts that the dynasty which has ruled China by right of conquest since 1644 is a Manchu dynasty, and that it im-

---

[1] *Glycene hispides* (Dr. Morrison).

[2] According to information obtained by the Russian Diplomatic Mission in Peking.

posed the shaven forehead and the pigtail on all Chinese men successfully, while it absolutely failed to prevent the women from crippling their feet, though up to this day no woman with "Golden Lilies" (crushed feet) is allowed to enter the Imperial palace, naturally turn attention to this viceroyalty, which, in point of its area of 380,000 square miles, is larger than Austria and Great Britain and Ireland put together, while its population is estimated at from 18,000,000 to 20,000,000 only. Thus it offers a vast field for emigration from the congested provinces of Northern China, and Chinese immigrants are steadily flocking in from Shan-tung, Chi-li, and Shen-si, so that Southern Manchuria at this time is little behind the inner provinces of China in density of population.

It is different in the northern province, where a cold climate and vast stretches of forest render agriculture more difficult. If it had not been for the war and its attendant complications, I had purposed to travel through it from Northern Korea. But it is unsettled at all times. The majority of its immigrants consists of convicts, fugitive criminals, soldiers who have left the colors, and gold and ginseng hunters. There is something almost comical about some of the doings of this unpromising community.

It comprises large organized bands of mounted brigands, well led and armed, who do not hesitate to come into collision with the Imperial troops, frequently coming off victors, and at times, as when I was in Mudken, wresting forts from their hands. During the Taiping rebellion, when the Chinese troops were withdrawn from Manchuria, these bands carried havoc and terror everywhere, and seizing upon towns and villages, ruled them by right of conquest![1] In recent years the Government has decided to let voluntary colonists settle in the northern provinces, and has even furnished them with material assistance.

Still, things are bad, and the brigands have come to be re-

[1] Information received by the Russian Diplomatic Mission in Peking.

garded as a necessary evil, and are "arranged with." They are not scrupulous as to human life, and when they catch a rich merchant from the south, they send an envoy to his guild with a claim for ransom, strengthened by the threat that if it is not forthcoming in so many days, the captive's head will be cut off. Winter, when the mud is frozen hard, is the only time for the transit of goods by land, and long trains of mule carts may then be seen, a hundred or more together, starting from Newchwang, Mukden, and other southern cities, each carrying a small flag, which denotes that a suitable blackmail has been paid to an agent of the brigand chiefs, and that they will not be robbed on the journey! Later, when I was on the Siberian frontier of Manchuria, the brigands were in great force, and having been joined by half-starved deserters from the Chinese army, were harrying the country, and the peasants were flying in terror from their farms.

Among the curious features of Manchurian brigandage, is that its virulence rises or falls with good or bad harvests, inundations, etc. For many of the usually respectable peasant farmers, in times of floods and scanty crops, join the robber bands, returning to their honest avocations the next season!

In spite, however, of this terrorism in the northeast, Manchuria is one of the most prosperous of the Chinese viceroyalties, and its foreign trade is assuming annually increasing importance.[1]

I was disappointed to find that the Manchus (or Tartars)

[1] Taking the port of Newchwang, through which, with certain exceptions, all exports of native produce and imports of foreign merchandise and Chinese productions pass, in 1871 16 steamers and 203 sailing vessels entered the port, with a total tonnage of 65,933 tons; in 1881, 114 steamers and 218 sailing vessels, with a tonnage of 159,098 tons; and in 1891, 372 steamers and 61 sailing vessels, with a total tonnage of 334,709 tons. In the same period, British tonnage had increased from 38.6 of the whole to 58 per cent. of the whole. In 1871 German tonnage nearly equalled British, being 37.6 of the whole, but it had declined in 1891 to 28 per cent. of the whole.

differ little in appearance from the race which they have subdued.   The women, however, are taller, comlier, and more
robust in appearance, as may be expected from their retaining
the natural size and shape of their feet, and not only their
coiffure but their costume is different, the Manchu women
wearing sleeveless dresses from the throat to the feet, over
under dresses with wide embroidered sleeves.   With some exceptions, they are less secluded than their Chinese sisters, and
have an air of far greater freedom.

Most of the Manchu customs have disappeared along with
the language, which is only spoken in a few remote valleys,
and is apparently only artificially preserved because the ruling
dynasty is Manchu.   It is only those students who are aspirants for literary degrees and high office in the viceroyalty who
are obliged to learn it.

People of pure Manchu race are chiefly met with in the
north.   Manchus, as kinsmen of the present Imperial dynasty,
enjoy various privileges.   Every male adult, as soon as he can
string a short and remarkably inflexible bow (no easy task),
becomes a " Bannerman," *i.e.* he is enrolled in one of eight
bodies of irregulars, called " Banners " from their distinctive
flags, and from that time receives one *tael* (now about three
shillings) per month, increased to from five to seven *taels* a
month when on active service.   These " Bannermen," as a
rule, are not specially reputable characters.   They gamble,
hang about *yamens* for odd bits of work, in hope of permanent
official employment, and generally sublet to the Chinese the
lands which they receive from the Government.

It is a singular anomaly that bows and arrows are relied
upon as a means of defence in an empire which buys rifles and
Krupp guns.   Later, in Peking, which was supposed to be
threatened by the Japanese armies, it was intended to post
Bannermen with bows and arrows at the embrasures of the
wall, and on the Peking and Tungchow road I met twenty
carts carrying up loads of these primitive weapons for the de-

fence of the capital ! Bow and arrow drill is one of the most amusing of the many military mediæval sights of China. The Chinese Bannermen are descendants of those Chinese who, in the seventeenth century, espoused the cause of the Manchu conquerors of China. The whole military force of the three provinces of the viceroyalty is 280,000 men. Tartar garrisons and " Tartar cities " exist in many of the great provincial cities of China, and as the interests of these troops are closely bound up with those of the present Tartar dynasty, their faithfulness is relied upon as the backbone of Imperial security.

From its history and its audacious and permanent conquest of its gigantic neighbor, its mixed population and numerous aboriginal tribes, its mineral and agricultural wealth, and a certain freedom and breeziness which constitute a distinctive feature, Manchuria is a very interesting viceroyalty, and the two months which I spent in it gave it a strong hold upon me.

Mud is a great feature of Newchwang, perhaps the leading feature for some months of the year, during which no traffic by road is possible, and the Bund is the only practicable walk. The night I arrived rain began, and continued with one hour's cessation for five days and nights, for much of the time coming down like a continuous thundershower. The atmosphere was steamy and hazy, and the mercury by day and night was pretty stationary at 78°. About 8.46 inches of rain fell on those days. The barometer varied from 29° to 29.3°. Afterwards, when the rain ceased for a day, the heat was nearly unbearable. Of course, no boat's crew would start under such circumstances. Rumors of an extensive inundation came down the river, but these and all others of purely local interest gave place to an intense anxiety as to whether war would be declared, and what the effect of war would be on the great trading port of Newchwang.

CHAPTER XV

A MANCHURIAN DELUGE—A PASSENGER CART—AN ACCIDENT

IT surprised me much to find that only one foreign resident had visited Mukden, which is only 120 miles distant by a road which is traversable in winter, and is accessible by river during the summer and autumn in from eight to ten days. I left Newchwang on the 3rd of July, and though various circumstances were unpropitious, reached Mukden in eight days, being able to avoid many of the windings of the Liau by sailing over an inundation.

The kindly foreign community lent me necessaries for the journey, but even with these the hold of a " pea-boat " was not luxurious. My camp-bed took up the greater part of it, and the roof was not much above my head. The descent into the hold and the ascent were difficult, and when wind and rain obliged me to close the front, it was quite dark, cockroaches swarmed, and the smell of the bilge water was horrible. I was very far from well when I started, and in two days was really ill, yet I would not have missed the special interest of that journey for anything, or its solitude, for Wong's limited English counted for nothing and involved no conversational effort.

For some distance above Newchwang or Ying-tzŭ, as far as the real Newchwang, there is a complication of muddy rivers hurrying through vast reed beds, the resort of wild fowl, with here and there a mud bank with a mud hovel or two upon it. At that time reed beds and partially inundated swamps stretched away nearly to the horizon, which is limited in the far distance by the wavy blue outline of some low hills.

We ran up the river till the evening of the second day before a fair wind, and then were becalmed on a reedy expanse swarming with mosquitos. The mercury was at 89° in the hold that night. I had severe fever, with racking pains in my head, back, and limbs, and in the morning the stamping of the junkmen to and fro, along the narrow strip of deck outside the roof, was hardly bearable. Wong had used up the ample supply of water, and there was nothing wherewith to quench thirst but the brown, thick water of the Liau, the tea made with which resembled peasoup.

On the morning of the third day it began to rain and blow, and for the next awful four days the wind and rain never ceased. The oiled paper which had been tacked over the roof of the boat was torn into strips by the violence of the winds, which forced the rain through every chink. I lay down that night with the mercury at 80°, woke feeling very cold, but, though surprised, fell asleep again. Woke again much colder, feeling as if my feet were bandaged together, extricated myself with difficulty, struck a light, and got up into 6 inches of a mixture of bilge water and rain water, with an overpowering stench, in or on which all things were sunk or floating. Wondered again at being so very cold, found the temperature at 84°, and that I had been sleeping under a wringing sheet in soaked clothing and on soaked sacking, under a soaked mosquito net, and that there was not a dry article in the hold. For the next three days and nights things remained in the same condition, and though I was really ill I had to live in wet clothing and drink the " liquid cholera " of the flood, all the wells being submerged.

Telegrams later in the English papers announced " Great floods in Manchuria," but of the magnitude of the inundation which destroyed for that season the magnificent crops of the great fertile plain of the Liau, and swept away many of its countless farming villages, only the experience of sailing over it could give any idea.

In that miserable night there were barkings of dogs, shouts of men, mewings of cats, and general noises of unrest, and in the morning, of the village of Piengdo opposite to which we had moored the evening before, only one house and a barn remained, which were shortly carried away.   Many of the people had escaped in boats, and the remainder, with their fowls, dogs, and cats, were in the spreading branches of a large tree. Although the mast of my boat was considerably in the way, and it was difficult to make fast, I succeeded in rescuing the whole menagerie and in transferring it in two trips to a village on the other side, which was then 5 feet above the water.

We had reached the most prosperous region of Manchuria, a plain 60 miles in length, of deep, rich alluvial soil, bearing splendid crops, the most lucrative of which are the bean, the oil from which is the staple export of the country, the opium poppy, and tobacco.   The great and small millet, wheat, barley, melons, and cucumbers cover the ground, mulberry trees for the silkworm surround the farmhouses, and the great plain is an idyll of bounteousness and fertility.   Of all this not a trace remained, except in a few instances the tops of the 8-feet millet, which supplies the people not only with food, but with fuel, and fodder for their animals.

The river bank burst during the night, and the waters were raging into the plain, from which I missed many a brown-roofed village, which the evening before stood among its willow and poplar trees.   At 11 a fair wind sprang up, junks began to move, and my boatmen, who had talked of returning, untied and moved too.   After an exciting scene at a bend, where the river, leaping like a rapid, thumped the junks against the opposite shore, we passed one wrecked village after another, bits of walls of houses alone standing.   The people and their fowls were in the trees.   The women clung to their fowls as much as to their babies.   Dugouts, scows, and a few junks, mine among them, were busy saving life, and we took three families and their fowls to Sho-wa Ku, a large junk port, where a number of houses were still standing. These families had lost all their household goods and gods, as well as mules, pigs, and dogs. On our way we sailed into a farmyard to try to get some eggs, and the junk not replying to her helm, thumped one of the undermined walls down. It was a large farmhouse and full of refugees. The water was 3 feet deep in the rooms, naked children were floating about in tubs, and the women, looking resigned, sat on the tables. The men said that it was the last of four houses, and that they might as well be dead, for they had lost all their crops and their beasts.

A fearful sight presented itself at Sho-wa Ku. There the river, indefinite as it had previously been, disappeared altogether, and the whole country was a turbulent muddy sea, bounded on the east by a range of hills, and to the north and south limitless. Under it lay all the fruits of the tireless industry and garden cultivation of a large and prosperous population, and the remorseless waters under the influence of a gale were rolling in muddy surges, " crested with tawny foam," over the fast dissolving homes.

On this vast flood we embarked to shorten the distance, and sailed with three reefs in the sail for 13 miles over it, till we were brought up by an insurmountable obstacle in the shape of a tremendous rush of water where a bank had given way. There we were compelled to let go two anchors in the early afternoon. The wind had become foul, and the rain, which fell in torrents, was driven almost horizontally. Nothing that suggested human life was in sight. It might have been " the Deluge," for the windows of heaven were opened. There were a muddy, rolling sea, and a black sky, dark with tremendous rain, and the foliage of trees with submerged trunks was alone suggestive of even vegetable life and of the villages which had been destroyed by the devouring waters.

In 13 miles just one habitation remained standing, a large, handsome brick house with entrance arch, quadrangle, curved roofs, large farm buildings, and many servants' houses, some of which were toppling, and others were submerged up to their roofs. There was a lookout on the principal roof and he hailed us, but as there were several scows about, enough to save life, I disregarded him, and we sailed on into the tempestuous solitude where we anchored.

The day darkened slowly into night, the junk rolled with short plunging rolls, the rain fell more tremendously than ever, and the strong wind, sweeping through the rigging with a desolate screech, only just overpowered the clatter on the roof. I was ill. The seas we shipped drowned the charcoal, and it was impossible to make tea or arrowroot. The rain dripped everywhere through the roof. My lamp spluttered and went out and could not be relighted, bedding and clothing were soaked, my bed stood in the water, the noise was deafening.

Never in all my journeys have I felt so solitary. I realized that no other foreigner was travelling in Manchuria, that there was no help in illness, and that there was nothing to be done but lie there in saturated clothes till things took a turn for the better.

And so they did. By eight the next morning the scene was changed. The sky was blue and cloudless, there was a cool north wind, and the waste of water dimpled and glittered, the broken sparkle of its mimic waves suggesting the ocean after a destructive storm has become a calm. After sailing over broad blue water all day, and passing "islands" on which the luckier villages were still standing, towards evening we sailed into a village of large farmhouses and made fast to the window-bars of one of them, which, being of brick, had not suffered greatly. Eleven of the farms had disappeared, and others were in process of disappearing. The gardens, farmyards, and open spaces were under 5 feet of water, the surface of which was covered by a bubbly scum. The horses and cattle were in the rooms of the brick houses where many human beings had taken refuge. A raft made of farming implements ferried the people among the few remaining dwellings.

At that farm the skipper brought a quantity of rice for his family, and by a lovely moonlight we sailed over the drowned country to his village. The flood currents were strong, and when we got there we were driven against two undermined houses and knocked them down, afterwards drifting into a road with fine trees which entangled the mast and sail, and our stern bumped down the wall of the road, and the current carried us into a square of semi-submerged houses, and eventually we got into the skipper's garden, and saw his family mounted on tables and chairs on the top of the *kang*.

Two uneventful days followed. The boatmen were in ceaseless dread of pirates, and I was so ill that I felt I would rather die than make another effort.

Arriving within 3 miles of Mukden, Wong engaged a passenger cart, a conveyance of the roughest description, which is only rendered tolerable by having its back, sides, and bottom padded with mattresses, and I was destitute of everything ! Nothing can exaggerate the horrors of an unameliorated Chinese cart on an infamous road. Down into ruts 2 feet deep, out of which three fine mules could scarcely extricate us, over hillocks and big gnarled roots of trees, through quagmires and banked ditches, where, in dread of the awful jerk produced by the mules making a non-simultaneous jump up the farther side, I said to myself, " This is my last hour," getting a blow on my head which made me see a shower of sparks—so I entered the gate of the outer wall of beaten clay 11½ miles in circuit which surrounds the second city of the empire. Then, through a quagmire out of which we were dragged by seven mules, I bruised, breathless, and in great pain, and up a bank where the cart turned over, pulled the mules over with it, and rolled down a slight declivity, I found myself in the roof with the cameras on the top of me and my right arm twisted under me, a Chinese crowd curious to see the "foreign devil," a vague impress of disaster in my somewhat dazed brain, and Wong raging at large! Then followed a shady compound ablaze with flowers, a hearty welcome at the house of Dr. Ross, the senior missionary of the Scotch U.P. Church, sweet homelike rooms in a metamorphosed Chinese house, a large shady bedroom replete with comforts, the immediate arrival of Dr. Christie, the medical missionary, who pronounced my arm-bone "splintered" and the tendons severely torn, and placed the limb in splints, and a time of kind and skilled nursing by Mrs. Ross, and of dreamy restfulness, in which the horrors of the hold of the "pea-boat" and of the dark and wind-driven flood only served to emphasize the comfort and propitiousness of my surroundings.

PASSENGER CART, MUKDEN.

CHAPTER XVI

MUKDEN AND ITS MISSIONS

MUKDEN stands at an altitude of 160 feet above the sea, in Lat. 41° 51′ N. and Long. 123° 37′ E., in the centre of an immense alluvial plain, bearing superb crops and liberally sprinkled with farming villages embowered in wood, a wavy line of low blue hills at a great distance limiting the horizon. It is 3 miles from the Hun-ho, a tributary of the Liau, and within its outer wall idles along the silvery Siao-ho or "small river," with a long Bund affording a delightful promenade and an airy position for a number of handsome houses, the residences of missionaries and mandarins, with stately outer and inner gates, through which glimpses are obtained of gardens and flowering plants and pots. This city of 260,000 inhabitants, owing to its connection with the reigning dynasty, is the second city officially in the empire, and the Peking "boards" with one exception are nominally duplicated there. Hence it not only has an army of Chinese and Tartar officials of all grades, but a large resident population of retired and expectant mandarins, living in handsome houses and making a great display in the streets. There is an incessant movement of mule carts, the cabs of Mukden, with their superb animals and their blue canopies covering both mule and driver, official mule carts driven at a trot, with four or more outriders with white hats and red plumes, private carts belonging to young mandarin swells, who give daily entertainments at a restaurant on the Bund, mandarins on horseback with runners clearing the way, carts waiting for "lotus viewers," tall, "big-footed" women promenading with their

children, their hair arranged in loops on silver frames and
decorated with flowers, hospital patients on stretchers and in
chairs, men selling melons and candies, and beggars who by
blowing through a leaf imitate the cry of nearly every bird.
Then in the summer evenings, when the mercury has fallen to
80°, the servants of rich men bring out splendid ponies and
mules and walk them on the Bund, and there come the crowds
to stare at the foreigners and hang round their gates.   The
presence of well-dressed women is a feature rare in the East.
Up to the war people were polite and friendly, but progress was
difficult and the smell of garlic strong.   At night the dogs bark,
guns are fired, drums and gongs are beaten, and the clappers
of the watchmen rival each other in making night hideous.

All this life lies between the outer wall and the lofty quad-
rangular inner wall, 3 miles in circuit, built of brick, flanked
by lofty towers, and pierced by eight gates protected by lofty
brick bastions.   This wall, on which three carriages could
drive abreast, protects the commercial and official part of the
city, which is densely crowded, Mukden, besides being a great
grain emporium, being the centre of the Chinese fur trade,
which attracts buyers from all parts of the world.   Fine streets,
though full of humps and quagmires, divide the city into nine
wards or quarters, the central quarter being Imperial property,
and containing a fine palace with much decorative yellow
tiling, the examination hall, and a number of palaces and
yamens, all solidly built.   To my thinking no Chinese city is
so agreeable as Mukden.   The Tartar capital is free from that
atmosphere of decay which broods over Peking.   Its wide
streets are comparatively clean.   It is regularly built, and its
fine residences are well kept up.   It is a busy place, and does
a large and lucrative trade, specially in grain, beans, and furs.
It has various industries, which include the tanning and dressing of furs and the weaving of silk stuffs; its bankers and
merchants are rich, and it has great commercial as well as
some political importance.

TEMPLE OF GOD OF LITERATURE, MUKDEN.

As the old capital of Manchuria and the abode of the Prince ancestors of the family which was placed on the Chinese throne in 1644, it has special privileges, among which are " Ministres de Parade," nominally holding the same rank as the actual ministers in Peking. Near it are the superb tombs of the ancestors of the present Emperor, on which grand avenues of trees converge, bordered by colossal stone animals after the fashion of those at the Ming tombs near Peking. Formerly the Manchu Emperors made pilgrimages to these tombs and the sacred city of their dynasty, but since the second decade of this century the Chinese Emperor's portrait only has been sent at intervals in solemn procession, the Peking road being in the meantime closed to ordinary traffic.

The Governor-General of Manchuria resides in Mukden, as well as the military Governor, who is assisted by a civil administrator and by the Presidents of five Boards. The great offices of State are filled in duplicate by Chinese and Manchus, and criminals of the two races are tried in separate courts.

The favorable reception given to Christianity is one of the features of Mukden. The fine pagoda of the Christian Church is *en évidence* everywhere. The Scotch U. P. missionaries, who have been established there for twenty-five years, are on friendly terms with the people, and specially with many of the mandarins and high officials, who show them tokens of regard publicly and privately on all occasions. Dr. Christie, the medical missionary, is the trusted friend as well as the medical adviser of many of the leading officials and their wives, who, with every circumstance of ceremonial pomp, have presented complimentary tablets to the hospital, and altogether the relations between the Chinese and the missionaries are unique. I attribute these special relations with the upper classes partly to the fact that Dr. Ross, the senior missionary, and Dr. Christie, and those who have joined them subsequently, have studied Chinese custom and etiquette very closely, and are careful to conform to both as far as is possible, while they are not only keen-sighted for the good that is in the Chinese, but bring the best out of them.

Thus Christianity, divested of the nonchalant or contemptuous insularity by which it is often rendered repulsive, has made considerable progress not only in the capital but in the province, and until the roads became unsafe there was scarcely a day during my long visit in which there were not deputations from distant villages asking for Christian workers, representing numerous bands of rural worshippers, who, having received some knowledge of Christianity from converts, colporteurs, or catechists, had renounced many idolatrous practices, and desired further instruction. Of the "professing Christians," Dr. Ross said that it was only a very small percentage who had heard the Gospel from Europeans! Four thousand were already baptized, and nearly as many again were "inquirers" with a view to baptism. It was most curious to see men coming daily from remote regions asking for some one to go and instruct them in the "Jesus doctrine," for "they had learned as much as they could without a teacher." In many parts of Manchuria there are now Christian communities carrying on their own worship and discipline, and it is noteworthy that very many of the converts are members of those Secret Societies whose strongest bond of union is the search after righteousness.

The Mission Hospital is one of the largest and best equipped in the Far East, and besides doing a great medical and surgical work, is a medical school in which students pass through a four years' curriculum. There also Dr. Christie gives illustrated popular scientific lectures in the winter, which are attended among others by a number of sons of mandarins. Donations, both of money and food, are contributed to this hospital both by officials and merchants; and General Tso, a most charitable man and beloved by the poor, only the night before he started for Korea, sent a bag of tickets for ice, so that the hospital might not suffer for the lack of it during his absence. Only a few months before he presented it with a handsome tablet and subscription.[1]

Even in so civilized a city as Mukden, with its schools and literary examinations, its thousands of literary aspirants to official position, its streets full of a busy and splendid officialism, its enormous trade, its banks and *yamens*, its 20,000 Mussulmans, with their many mosques, and hatred of the pig, and the slow interpenetration of enlightened Western ideas, Chinese superstitions of the usual order, well known by every reader, prevail.

The system of medicine, though it contains the knowledge and use of some valuable native drugs among the sixty which are exported, is in many respects extremely barbarous. The doctors have no operative surgery and cannot even tie an artery ! They use cupping, the cautery, and acupuncture hot or cold, with long coarse uncleanly needles, with which they pierce the liver, joints, and stomach for pains, sprains, and rheumatism. They close all abscesses, wounds, and ulcers with a black impervious plaster. Witch doctors are resorted to in cases of hysteria or mental derangement. Vaccination is now to some extent adopted with calf or transferred lymph, the puncture being made in the nostrils. In order to ascertain whether a sick person is likely to live, they plunge long

---

[1] General Tso's cavalry brigade was perhaps the best disciplined in the Chinese army, and he was a severe disciplinarian, but he was also an earnest philanthropist, and though a strict Mussulman, always showed himself friendly to the Christian religion, specially in its benevolent aspects. His soup kitchens saved many a family from starvation. He established and was the chief support of a foundling hospital. During the terrible inundation of 1888 he distributed food among the famishing with his own hands. His friendly help could always be relied on by the missionaries, who joined in the sorrow with which Manchuria mourned for his premature death at Phyöng-yang in Korea. The benevolence of rich Chinese ought not to be overlooked. The charities of China are on a gigantic scale, and many of them are admirably administered by men who expend much self-sacrificing effort on their administration.

needles into the body, and give up the case as hopeless if blood does not flow. When death is near the friends dress the patient in the best clothes they can afford and remove him from the *kang* (the usual elevated sleeping place) to the floor, or lay him on ashes. As the spirit departs they cry loudly in the ear. In connection with death, it may be mentioned that some of the most striking shops in Mukden, after the coffin shops, are those in which are manufactured and sold admirable lifesize representations of horses, men, asses, elephants, carts, and all the articles of luxury of this life, which are carried in procession and are burned at the grave, sometimes to the value of $1,000.

Few children under nine years old are buried, and those only among the richest class. When death occurs, the mother, wailing bitterly, wraps the body in matting, and throws it away, *i.e.* she places it where the dogs can get at it. This ghastly burden must not be carried out of a door or window, but through a new or disused opening, in order that the evil spirit which causes the disease may not enter. The belief is that the Heavenly Dog which eats the sun at the time of an eclipse demands the bodies of children, and that if they are denied to him he will bring certain calamity on the household.

I have mentioned the *kang*, which is a marked feature of the houses and inns of Manchuria, which for its latitude has the coldest winter in the world, the mercury often reaching 17° F. below zero. The *kang* is a brick platform covered with matting and heated economically by flues, and is at once sleeping and sitting place. The stalks of the *Holcus Sorghum* are used for fuel. In winter, when the external temperature may be a little above and much below zero for a month at a time, the Chinaman, unable to heat his whole room, drops his shoes, mounts his *kang*, sits crosslegged on the warm mat, covers his padded socks with his padded robe, and there takes his meals and receives his friends in comfort. When I was invited to climb the *kang* I felt myself a *persona grata*.

The pawnshops of Mukden, with their high outer walls, lofty gateways, two or three well-kept courts, fine buildings, and tall stone columns at the outer gate, with the sign of the business upon them, their scrupulous cleanliness, and their armies of polite, intelligent clerks, are as respectable as banks with us. They demand for every sum borrowed movable property to double its amount. If the pledge be not redeemed within two years, it falls to the pawnbroker. Government fixes the interest. The proprietor takes the same position as a capitalist owning a bank in the West, and a *samshu* distiller takes an equal place in local esteem.

The prevalence of suicide is a feature of Mukden as of most Chinese cities. Certain peculiarities of Chinese justice render it a favorite way of wreaking spite upon an employer or neighbor, who is haunted besides by the spirit of the self-murderer. Hence servants angry with their masters, shopmen with their employers, wives with their husbands, and above all, daughters-in-law with their mothers-in-law, show their spite by dying on their premises, usually by opium, or eating the tops of lucifer matches! It is quite a common thing for a person who has a grudge against another to go and poison himself in his court-yard, securing revenge first by the mandarin's inquiry and next by the haunting terrors of his malevolent spirit. Young girls were daily poisoning themselves with lucifer matches to escape from the tyranny of mothers-in-law and leave unpleasantness behind them.

But it is not the seamy side which is uppermost in Mukden.

CHAPTER XVII

CHINESE TROOPS ON THE MARCH

THE weeks which I spent in Mukden were full of rumors and excitement. A few words on the origin of the war with Japan may make the situation intelligible.

The Tong-haks, as was mentioned in chapter xiii., had on several occasions defeated the Royal Korean troops, and after much hesitation the Korean King invoked the help of China. China replied promptly by giving Japan notice of her intention to send troops to Korea on 7th June, 1894, both countries, under the treaty of Tientsin, having equal rights to do so under such circumstances as had then arisen. On the same day Japan announced to China a similar intention. The Chinese General, Yi, landed at A-san with 3,000 men, and the Japanese occupied Chemulpo and Seoul in force.

In the Chinese despatch Korea was twice referred to as " our tributary state." Japan replied that the Imperial Government had never recognized Korea as a tributary state of China.

Then came three proposals from Japan for the administration of Korea, to be carried out jointly by herself and China. These were—(1) Examination of the financial administration ; (2) Selection of the central and local officials ; (3) The establishment of a disciplined army for national defence and the preservation of the peace of the land.

To these proposals China replied that Korea must be left to reform herself, and that the withdrawal of the Japanese troops must precede any negotiations, a suggestion rejected by Japan, who informed China on 14th July, that she should regard the dispatch of any more troops to Japan as a belligerent act. On

20th July Japan demanded that the King of Korea should order the Chinese troops to leave the country, threatening "decisive measures" if this course were not adopted.

Meanwhile, at the request of the King, the representatives of the Treaty Powers were endeavoring to maintain peace, suggesting the simultaneous withdrawal of the troops of both countries. To this China agreed, but Japan demanded delay, and on 23rd July took the "decisive measure" she had threatened, assaulted and captured the Palace, and practically made the King a prisoner, his father, the Tai-Won-Kun, at his request, but undoubtedly at Japanese instigation, taking nominally the helm of affairs.

After this events marched with great rapidity. On 25th July the transport *Kowshing*, flying the British flag and carrying 1,200 Chinese troops, was sunk with great loss of life by the Japanese cruiser *Naniwa*, and four days later the Japanese won the battle of A-san and dispersed the Chinese army. Before 30th July Korea gave notice of the renunciation of the Conventions between herself and China, which was equivalent to renouncing Chinese sovereignty. On 1st August war was declared. Of the sequence of these events, and even of the events themselves, we knew little or nothing, and up to the middle of July Mukden kept "the even tenor of its way."

Manchuria is far less hostile to foreigners than the rest of China, and the name "devil" may even be used as a polite address with the prefix of "honorable"! No European women had previously passed through the gate of the inner wall and through the city on foot, but I not only was able to do so without molestation, though several times only attended by my servant, but actually was able to photograph in the quieter streets, the curiosity of the crowd being quite friendly. The Scotch missionaries had then been established in Mukden for twenty-two years, were on very friendly terms with the people, there was much social intercourse, and altogether their relations with the Chinese were unique.

Before the end of July, however, the many wild rumors which were afloat, and the continual passage of troops on their way to Korea (war being a foregone conclusion before it was declared), produced a general ferment. I had to abandon peregrinations in the city, and also photography, a hostile crowd having mobbed me as I was " taking " the Gate of Victory, in the belief that I kept a black devil in the camera, with such a baleful Cyclopean eye that whatever living thing it looked on would die within a year, and any building or wall would crumble away !

After war was declared on 1st August, 1894, things grew worse rapidly. As Japan had full command of the sea, all Chinese troops sent to Korea were compelled to march through Manchuria, and undisciplined hordes of Manchu soldiers from Kirin, Tsitsihar, and othern northern cities poured through Mukden at the rate of 1,000 a day, having distinguished themselves on the southern march by seizing on whatever they could get hold of, riotously occupying inns without payment, beating the innkeepers, and wrecking Christian chapels, not from anti-Christian but from anti foreign feeling. Their hatred of foreigners culminated at Liau-yang, 40 miles from Mukden, when Manchu soldiers, after wrecking the Christian chapel, beat Mr. Wylie, a Scotch missionary, to death, and attacked the chief magistrate for his friendliness to the " foreign devils."

Anti-foreign feeling rose rapidly in Mukden. The servants of foreigners, and even the hospital assistants, were insulted in the town, and the wildest rumors concerning foreigners were spread and believed. The friendly authorities, who took the safety of the three mission families into serious consideration, requested them to give up their usual journeys into the interior, and to avoid going into the city or outside the walls. Next the " street chapels " were closed, the native Christians, a large body, being very apprehensive for their own safety, being regarded as " one with the foreigners," who, unfortunately, were generally supposed to be " the same as the Japanese."

GATE OF VICTORY. MUKDEN.

The perils of the roads increased.   Not a cart or animal was to be seen near them.   ·The great inns were closed or had their shutters wrecked, and the villages and farms were deserted. All tracks converging on Mukden were thronged with troops, not marching, but straggling along anyhow, every tenth man carrying a great silk banner, but few were armed with modern weapons.   I saw several regiments of fine physique without a rifle among them !   In some, gingalls were carried by two men each, others were armed with antique muzzle-loading muskets, very rusty, or with long matchlocks, and some carried only spears, or bayonets fixed on red poles.   All were equipped with such umbrellas and fans as I saw some time later in the ditches of the bloody field of Phyŏng-yang.   It was nothing but murder to send thousands of men so armed to meet the Japanese with their deadly Murata rifles, and the men knew it, for when they happened to see a foreigner they made such remarks as, " This is one of the devils for whom we are going to be shot," and when a large party of them, in attempting to make a forcible entry into the Governor-General's palace, were threatened by the guard with being shot, the reply was, " We are going to be shot in Korea, we may as well be shot here."

The nominal pay of soldiers is higher than that of laborers, and it was only after the defeat and the great slaughter at A-san that there was any unwillingness to enter the ranks.   The uniform is easy, but unfit for hard wear, and very stagey—a short, loose, sleeved red cloak, bordered with black velvet, loose blue, black, or apricot trousers, and long boots of black cotton cloth with thick soles of quilted rag.   The discipline may be inferred from the fact that some regiments of fine physique straggled through Mukden for the seat of war carrying rusty muskets in one hand, and in the other poles with perches, on which singing birds were loosely tethered !   The men fell out of the ranks as they pleased, to buy fruit or tobacco or to speak to friends.   Yet they made a goodly scenic display in their brilliant coloring, with their countless long banners of crimson silk undulating in the breezy sunshine, and their officers with sable-tailed hats and yellow jackets riding beside them.

Those who had rifles and modern weapons at all had them of all makes; so cartridges of twenty different sorts and sizes were huddled together without any attempt at classification, and in one open space all sorts were heaped on the ground, and the soldiers were fitting them to their arms, sometimes trying eight or ten before finding one to suit the weapon, and throwing them back on the heap! There were neither medical arrangements nor an ambulance corps, Chinese custom being to strip the wounded and leave them, "wounded men being of no use." The commissariat was not only totally inefficient but grossly dishonest, and where stores had accumulated the contractors sold them for their own benefit. Thus there was little provision of food or fodder in advance, and in a very short time the soldiers were robbing at large, and eating the horses and transport mules. The Chinese soldiers, bad as their drill and discipline are, are regarded by European officers as "excellent material," but the Manchus of the North (Tartars) are a shambling, disorderly, insubordinate horde, dreaded by peaceable citizens, presuming on their Imperial relationship, and in disturbed times little better than licensed brigands.

Among the first troops to leave the city was the Fengtien Chinese brigade of cavalry 5,000 strong, under General Tso, a brave and experienced officer, who was at once feared and trusted, so that when he fell with his face to the foe at Phyöng-yang, his loss demoralized the army, and the Japanese showed their appreciation of him by erecting an obelisk to his memory. His brigade was in a state of strict discipline, admirably drilled, and on the whole well armed. The troopers were mounted on active, well-built ponies, a little over 13 hands high, up to great weight. After leaving Mukden they were entangled in a quagmire which extended for 100 miles, and

CHINESE SOLDIERS

the telegrams of disaster were ominous.   On the first day their
commander beheaded six men for taking melons without payment, and on the second fourteen were decapitated for desertion.

After General Tso's departure with his disciplined force the
disorder increased, and the high officials, being left with few
reliable soldiers, became alarmed for their own positions, the
hatred and jealousy between the Chinese and Manchu troops
not only constituting one of the great difficulties of the war,
but threatening official safety.

Rumors of disaster soon began to circulate, and with each
one the ferment increased, and an Imperial proclamation sent
by courier from Peking in the interests of foreigners, declaring that the Emperor was only at war with the " rebel *wojen* "
(dwarfs), and was at peace with all other nations, did little to
allay it.   The able-bodied beggars and unemployed coolies in
the city were swept into the army, and were sent off after three
weeks' drill.   The mule-carts of Mukden and the neighborhood
were requisitioned for transport, paralyzing much of the trade
of the city.   Later, many of these carts were burned as fuel
to cook the mules for the starving troops.   As Manchu soldiers
continued to pour in, the shops were closed and the streets
deserted at their approach, and many of the merchants fled to
the hills.   A Japanese occupation, ensuring security and order,
came to be hoped for by many sufferers.   The price of provisions rose, because the country people had either been robbed
of all or did not dare to bring them in, and even the hospital
and dispensary for the same reason began to be scantily attended.   After Mr. Wylie's murder, things became increasingly serious, and by the end of August it became apparent to
the authorities that the safety of foreigners would be jeopard-
ized by remaining much longer in Mukden.   Somewhat later
they left, Dr. Ross and Dr. Christie remaining behind for a
short time at the special request of the Governor.   I left on
20th August, and though my friends were very anxious about

my safety, I reached Newchwang five days later, having encountered no worse risk than that of an attack by pirates, who
captured some junks with some loss of life, after I had eluded
them by travelling at night.

CHAPTER XVIII

NAGASAKI—WLADIVOSTOK

AFTER the collapse of the rumor regarding the landing of the Japanese in force on the shores of the Gulf of Pechili, which obtained credence for nearly a fortnight in the Far East, fluttered every Cabinet in Europe, forced even so cool and well-informed a man as Sir Robert Hart into hasty action, and produced a hurried exodus of Europeans from Peking and a scare generally among the foreign residents in North China, I returned from Peking to Chefoo to await the course of events.

The war, its requirements, and its uncertainties disarranged the means of ocean transit so effectually that, after hanging on for some weeks, in the midst of daily rumors of great naval engagements, for a steamer for Wladivostok, I only succeeded in getting a passage in a small German boat which reluctantly carried one passenger, and in which I spent a very comfortless five days, in stormy weather, varied by the pleasant interlude of a day at Nagasaki, then in the full glory of the chrysanthemum season, and aflame with scarlet maples. Lighted, cleaned, and policed to perfection, without a hole or a heap, this trim city of dwarfs and dolls contrasts agreeably with the filth, squalor, loathsomeness, and general abominableness which are found in nearly all Chinese cities outside the foreign settlements.

Chinese moved about the streets with an air as of a ruling race, and worked at their trades and pursued the important calling of *compradores* with perfect freedom from annoyance, the only formality required of them being registration ; while from China all the Japanese had fled by the desire of their consuls, not always unmolested in person and property, and any stray "dwarf" then found in a Chinese city would have been all but certain to lose his life.

The enthusiasm for the war was still at a white heat. Gifts in money and kind fell in a continual shower on the Nagasaki authorities, nothing was talked of but military successes, and a theatre holding 3,000 was giving the profits of two daily performances to crowded audiences in aid of the War Fund. The fact that ships were only allowed to enter the port by daylight, and were then piloted by a Government steam-launch in charge of a "torpedo pilot," was the only indication in the harbor of an exceptional state of things.

It was warm autumn weather at Nagasaki, but when I reached Wladivostok the hills which surround its superb harbor were powdered with the first snows of winter, and a snowstorm two days later covered the country to a depth of 18 inches. Wooded islands, wooded bays, wooded hills, deep sheltered channels and inlets, wooded to the water's edge, bewilder a stranger, then comes Fort Godobin, and by a sharp turn the harbor is entered, one of the finest in the world, two and a half miles long by nearly one wide, with deep water everywhere, so deep that ships drawing 25 feet lie within a stone's throw of the wharves, and moor at the Government pier.

The first view of Wladivostok ("Possession of the East") is very striking, although the vandalism of its builders has deprived it of its naturally artistic background of wood. Otherwise the purple tone of the land and the blue crystal of the water reminded me of some of our Nova Scotian harbors. There is nothing Asiatic about the aspect of this Pacific capital, and indeed it is rather Transatlantic than European. Seated on a deeply embayed and apparently landlocked harbor, along the shores of which it straggles for more than 3 miles, climbing audaciously up the barren sides of denuded hills, irregular, treeless—lofty buildings with bold fronts,

WLADIVOSTOK.

Government House, "Kuntz and Albers," the glittering domes of a Greek cathedral, a Lutheran church, Government Administrative Offices, the Admiralty, the Arsenal, the Cadet School, the Naval Club, an Emigrant Home, and the grand and solid terminus and offices of the Siberian Railway, rising out of an irregularity which is not picturesque, attract and hold the voyager's attention.

Requesting to be taken at once to the Customs, the bewildered air of astonishment with which my request was met informed me that Wladivostok had up to that time been a free port, and that I was at liberty to land unquestioned. After thumping about for some time among a number of stout *sampans* in the midst of an unspeakable Babel, I was hauled on shore by a number of laughing, shouting, dirty Korean youths, who, after exchanging pretty hard blows with each other for my coveted possessions, shouldered them and ran off with them in different directions, leaving me stranded with the tripod of my camera, to which I had clung desperately in the *mêlée*. There were droskies not far off, and four or five Koreans got hold of me, one dragging me towards one vehicle, others to another, yelling Korean into my ears, till a Cossack policeman came and thumped them into order. There were hundreds of them on the wharf, and except that they were noisier and more aggressive, it was like landing at Chemulpo. Getting into a drosky, I said, "Golden Horn Hotel," in my most distinct English, then "Hôtel Corne d'or," in my most distinct French. The *moujik* nodded and grinned out of his fur hood, and started at a gallop in the opposite direction ! I clutched him, and made emphatic signs, speech being useless, and he turned and galloped in a right direction, but stopped at the disreputable doorway of one of the lowest of the many drinking saloons with which Wladivostok is infested.

There all my Koreans reappeared, vociferating and excited. I started the *moujik* off again at a gallop, the drosky jumping ruts and bounding out of holes with an energy of elasticity which took my breath away, the Koreans racing. More gallops, more stoppages at pothouses, and in this fashion I reached at last the Golded Horn Hotel—a long, rambling, "disjaskit" building, with a shady air of disreputableness hanging about it,—the escort of Koreans still good-natured and vociferous. The landlady emerged. I tried her in English and French, but she knew neither. The *moujik* shouted at us both in Russian, a little crowd assembled, each man trying to put matters straight, and when every moment made them more entangled, and the *moujik* was gathering up his reins to gallop off on a further quest, a Russian officer came up, and in excellent English asked if he could help me, interpreted my needs to the lady, lent me some *kopecks* with which to appease the Koreans and the *moujik*, and gave me the enjoyment of listening to my own blessed tongue, which I had not heard for five days.

By a long flight of stairs, past a great bar and dining-room, where *vodka* was much *en évidence*, even in the forenoon, past a billiard-room, occupied even at that early hour, and through a large, dark, and dusty theatre, I attained my rooms, a "parlor" and bedroom *en suite*, opening on and looking out upon a yard with pigsties. There were five doors, not one of which would lock. The rooms were furnished in Louis Quatorze style, much gilding and velvet, all ancient and dusty. They looked as if they had known tragedies, and might know them again. The barrier of language was impassable, and I must be unskilled in the use of signs, for I quite failed to make any one understand that I wanted food.

I went out, cashed a circular note at the great German house of Kuntz and Albers, the "Whiteleys" of Eastern Siberia, where all the information that I then needed was given in the most polite way, found it impossible anywhere else to make myself understood in English or French, failed in an attempt to buy postage stamps or to get food, delivered the single letter of introduction which I had somewhat ungraciously accepted, and returned to my melodramatic domicile to consider the possibilities of travel, which at that moment were not encouraging.

Before long Mr. Charles Smith, the oldest foreign resident in Wladivostok, to whom my letter was addressed, called, a kindly and genial presence, and, as I afterwards found, full of good deeds and benevolence. He took me at once to call on General Unterberger, the Governor of the Maratime Province. I think I never saw so gigantic a man—military, too, from his spurs to his coat collar. As he rose to receive me he looked as if his head might eventually touch the lofty ceiling.

Mr. Smith is a *persona grata* in Wladivostok, and very much so with the Governor, who consequently received me with much friendliness, and asked me to let him know my plans. I explained what I wanted to do, subject to his approval, and presented my credentials, which were of the best. He said that he quite approved of my project, and would do anything he could to help me, and wrote on the spot a letter to the Frontier Commissioner, but he added that the disorganized and undisciplined state of the Chinese army near the frontier might render some modification of my plan necessary, as I afterwards found. The Governor and his wife speak excellent English, and the social intercourse which I had with them afterwards was most agreeable and instructive.

During the afternoon Mr. Smith returned, and saying that he and his wife could not endure my staying in that hotel, took me away to his home high up on a steep hillside, with a glorious view of the city and harbor, and of which it is difficult to say whether the sunshine were brighter within or without. Under such propitious circumstances my two visits became full of sunny memories, and I may be pardoned if I see Wladivostok a little *couleur de rose ;* for the extraordinary kindness which dogs and shadows the traveller in the Far East were met with there in perfection, and where I was received by strangers I left highly valued friends.

After a snowstorm splendid weather set in. The snow prevented dust blasts, the ordinary drawback of an Eastern Siberian winter, the skies were brilliant and unclouded, the sunsets carnivals of color, the air exhilarating, the mercury at night averaging 20°, there was light without heat, the main road was full of sleighs going at a gallop, their bells making low music, all that is unsightly was hidden, and this weather continued for five weeks!

"The Possession of the East" is nothing if not military and naval. Forts, earthworks, at which it is prudent not to look too long or intently, great military hospitals, huge red brick barracks in every direction, offices of military administration, squads of soldiers in brown ulsters and peaked *pashaliks*, carrying pickaxes or spades on their shoulders,[1] sappers with their tools, in small parties, officers, mostly with portfolios or despatch boxes under their arms, dashing about in sleighs, and the prohibition of photography, all indicate its fortress character. Certainly two out of every three people in the streets are in uniform, and the Cossack police, who abound, are practically soldiers.

Naval it is also. There are ships of war in and out of commission, a brand-new admiralty, a navy yard, a floating dock, a magnificent dry dock, only just completed, and a naval clubhouse, which is one of the finest buildings in Wladivostok. No matter that Nature closes the harbor from Christmas to the end of March! Science has won the victory, and the

---

[1] The Russian soldier does a great amount of day labor. Far from disporting himself in brilliant uniform before the admiring eyes of boys and "servant girls," he digs, builds, carpenters, makes shoes and harness, and does a good civil day's work in addition to his military duties, and is paid for this as "piecework" on a fixed scale, his daily earnings being duly entered in a book. When he has served his time these are handed over to him, and a steady, industrious man makes enough to set himself up in a small business or on a farm. *Vodka* and *schnaps* are the Russian soldier's great enemies.

port has been kept open for the last two winters by means of a powerful ice-breaker and the services of the troops in towing the blocks of ice out to sea. Large steamers of the "Volunteer Fleet" leave Odessa and Wladivostok monthly or fortnightly. As the eastern terminus of the Trans-Siberian Railway, Wladivostok aspires to be what she surely will be—at once the Gibraltar and Odessa of the Far East, one of the most important of commercial emporiums, as the "distributing point" for the commerce of that vast area of prolific country which lies south of the Amur. Possibly a branch line to Port Shestakoff in Ham-gyöng Do may enable the Government to dispense with the services of the ice-breaker!

The progress of the city is remarkable. The site, then a forest, was only surveyed in 1860. In 1863 many of the trees were felled and some shanties were erected. Later than that a tiger was shot on the site of the new Government House, and a man leaving two horses to be shod outside the smithy had them both devoured by tigers. Gradually the big oaks and pines were cleared away, and wooden houses were slowly added, until 1872, when the removal of the naval establishment of 60 men from Nicolaeffk on the Amur to the new settlement gave it a decided start. In 1878 it had a population of 1,400. In 1897 its estimated civil population was 25,000, including 3,000 Koreans, who have their own settlement a mile from the city, and are its draymen and porters, and 2,000 Chinese. The latter keep most of the shops, and have obtained a monopoly of the business in meat, fish, game, fruit, vegetables, and other perishable commodities, their guild being strong enough to squeeze the Russians out of the trade in these articles, which are sold in four large wooden buildings by the harbor known as the "Bazar." There are some good Japanese shops, but the Japanese are usually domestic servants at high wages, and after a few years return to enjoy their savings in their own country. A naturalized German is the only British subject, and my host and his family are the only Americans.

The capital has two subsidized and two independent lines of steamers, 700 families of Russian assisted emigrants enter Primorsk annually, each head of a household being required to be the possessor of 600 roubles (£60), and from 8,000 to 10,000 Chinese from the Shan-tung province arrive every spring to fulfil labor contracts, returning to China in December, carrying out of the country from 25 to 50 dollars each, convict labor from the penal settlement of Saghalien having been abandoned as impracticable.

The Chinese shops, which are a feature of Wladivostok, undersell both Russians and Germans, and have an increasing trade. Kuntz and Albers, a Hamburg firm of importers, bankers, shipping agents, and Whiteleyism in general, with sixty clerks, mostly German, with a few Russians, Danes, and Koreans, conduct an enormous wholesale and retail business in a "palatial" pile of brick and stone buildings, and has sixteen branch houses in Eastern Siberia, and the German firm of Langalutje runs them very closely.

The railway station and offices are solid and handsome ; an admirably built railroad, open to the Ussuri Bridge, 186 miles, and progressing towards the Amur with great rapidity, points to a new commercial future ; streets of shops and dwelling-houses, in which brick and stone are fast replacing wood, are extending to the north, east, and west, and along the Gulf of Peter the Great, for fully three miles ; and new and handsome official and private edifices of much pretension were being rapidly completed. One broad road, with houses sometimes on one, sometimes on both sides, running along the hillside for 2 miles at a considerable height, is the "Main Street" or "High Street" of Wladivostok. Along it are built most of the public buildings, and the great shops and mercantile offices. It is crossed by painfully steep roads climbing up the hill and descending with equal steepness to the sea. There are two or three parallel roads of small importance.

The builder was at work in all quarters, and the clink of

the mason's trowel and the ring of the carpenter's hammer were only silent for a few hours during the night. Several of Government buildings were barely finished, and were occupied before they were painted and stuccoed. Building up and pulling down were going on simultaneously. Roads were being graded, culverts and retaining walls built, and wooden houses showed signs of disappearing from the principal thoroughfare. There was a " boom " in real property. The value of land has risen fabulously. " Lots " which were bought in 1864 for 600 and 3,000 roubles are now worth 12,- 000 and 20,000, and in the centre of the town land is not to be bought at any price.

Newness, progress, hopefulness are characteristics of civil Wladivostok. It has the aspect of a growing city in the American Far West. Few things are finished and all are going ahead. The sidewalks are mostly narrow, and composed of rough planks, with a tendency to tip up or down, but here and there is a fine piece of granite flagging 10 feet wide. The hotels have more of the shady character of " saloons " or barrooms than of anything reputable or established. Handsome houses of brick and stone shoulder wooden shanties. Fashionable carriages or sleighs bounce over ungraded streets. The antediluvian ox-cart with its Korean driver bumps and creaks through the streets alongside of the *troika*, with its three galloping horses in showy harness, and its occupants in the latest and daintiest of Parisian costumes.

But the all-pervading flavor of militarism overpowers the suggestion of the American Far West. The first buildings on the barren coast are military hospitals and barracks, and barracks thicken as the city is approached. The female element is in a remarkable minority. The dull roll of artillery and commissariat wagons, the tramp, morning and night, of brown battalions, and the continual throb of drum and blare of trumpet and bugle, recall one to the fact that this is the capital of Russia's vast, growing, aspiring, Pacific Empire.

Theatricals, concerts, and balls fill up the winter season. Except on the few days on which snow falls, the skies are cloudless, the temperature is not seriously below zero, and the dryness of the air is very invigorating. In winters, happily somewhat exceptional, in which there is no snowfall, and the strong winds create dust-storms, the climate is less agreeable. Spring is abrupt and pleasant, and autumn is a fine season, but summer is hot, damp, and misty.

A fine Greek cathedral, with many domes and lofty gilded crosses, which gleam mysteriously in the sunset when the gloom of twilight has wrapped all else, a prominent Lutheran church, and a Chinese joss-house, provide for the religious needs of the population. The Governor of the Maritime Province, several of the leading, and many of the lower officials are of German origin from the Baltic provinces, Lutherans, and possibly imbued with a few liberal ideas. But among the kindly, cultured, and agreeable people whose acquaintance I made in Wladivostok one peculiarity impressed me forcibly —the absolute stagnation of thought, or the expression of it, on politics and all matters connected with them, the administration of government, religion, the orthodox church, dissent, home and foreign policy, etc. It is true that certain subjects, and these among the most interesting, are carefully eliminated from conversation, and that to introduce any one of them might subject the offender to social ostracism.

CHAPTER XIX

KOREAN SETTLERS IN SIBERIA

THE chief object of my visit to Russian Manchuria was to settle for myself by personal investigation the vexed question of the condition of those Koreans who have found shelter under the Russian flag, a number estimated in Seoul at 20,000. It was there persistently said that Russia was banishing them in large numbers, and that several thousands of them had already recrossed the Tumen, and were in such poverty that the King of Korea had sent agents to the north who were to settle them on lands in Ham-gyöng Do.

But in Wladivostok the servant-interpreter difficulty was absolutely insurmountable. No efforts on the part of my friends could obtain what did not exist, and I was on the verge of giving up what proved a very interesting journey, when the Director of the Siberian Telegraph Lines very kindly liberated the senior official in his department, who had not had a holiday for many years, to go with me. Mr. Heidemann, a German from the Baltic provinces, spoke German, Russian, and English with nearly equal ease, and as a Russian official was able to make things smoother than they might otherwise have been in a very rough part of Primorsk. He was tall, good-looking, and verging on middle age, very gentlemanly, never failed in any courtesy, understood how to manage *moujiks*, and was a capable and willing interpreter ; but he was official, reticent, and uninterested, and gave me the impression of being frozen into his uniform !

Fortified as to my project by the cordial approval of the

Governor, the courtesy of the Telegraph Department, and the singular splendor of the weather, I left Wladivostok by a red sunrise in a small steamer, which accomplished the 60 miles to Possiet Bay in seven hours, landing us in a deep inlet of clear water and white sand, soon to be closed by ice, at the foot of low and absolutely barren hills fringing off into sandy knolls, where Koreans with their ox-carts awaited the steamer. A well spread tea-table at the house of the Russian postmaster was very welcome. Such a strong-looking family I had seldom seen, but afterwards I found that size and strength are characteristic of the Russian settlers in Primorsk.

Possiet Bay is a large military station of fine barracks and storehouses. It scarcely seemed to possess a civil population, but there are Korean settlements at no great distance, from which much of the beef supply of Wladivostok is derived. We met a number of strong, thriving-looking Koreans driving 60 fine fat cattle down to the steamer.

The post wagon, in which we were cramped up among and under the mail-bags, took us at a two hours' gallop along frozen inlets of the sea and across frozen rivers, over grassy, hilly country, scarcely enlivened by Korean farms in the valleys, to Nowo Kiewsk, which we reached after nightfall, and were hospitably received by the representative of Messrs. Kuntz and Albers, whose large brick and stone establishment is the prominent object in the settlement.

Nowo Kiewsk is a great military post, to which 1,000 civilians, chiefly Koreans and Chinese, have been attracted by the prospect of gain. Koreans indeed form the bulk of this population, and do all the hauling of goods and fuel with their ox-teams. The centre of the town is a great dusty slope intersected by dusty and glaring roads, which resound at intervals from early morning till sunset with the steady tramp of brown-ulstered battalions. Between Possiet Bay and Nowo Kiewsk there were 10,000 infantry and artillery, and at the latter post 8 pieces of field artillery and 24 two-wheeled ammunition wagons.   Barracks for 10,000 more men were in course of rapid construction.   Long wooden sheds shelter the artillery ponies, and villages of low mud houses of two rooms each, with windows consisting of a single small pane of glass, the families of soldiers.   There are great drill and parade grounds and an imposing Greek church of the usual pattern.

With its great open spaces and wide streets, Nowo Kiewsk looks laid out for futurity, straggling along a treeless and bushless hill slope for 2 miles.   In addition to Kuntz and Albers, with their polyglot staff of clerks, among whom a young Korean in European dress was conspicuous for his gentlemanliness and alacrity, there is another German house, and there are forty small shops, chiefly kept by Chinese, at all of which *schnaps* and *vodka* are sold.

I was detained there for three days while arrangements for my southern journey were being made, and during that time the Chief of Police, who spoke French, took me to several Korean villages.   So far as I saw and heard, the whole agricultural population of the neighborhood is Korean, and is in a very prosperous condition.   There, and down to the Korean frontier, most of these settlers are doing well, and some of them are growing rich as contractors for the supply of meat and grain to the Russian forces.   At this they have beaten their Chinese neighbors, and they actually go into Chinese Manchuria, buy up lean cattle, and fatten them for beef.   To those who have only seen the Koreans in Korea, such a statement will be hardly credible.   Yet it does not stand alone, for I have it on the best authority that the Korean settlers near Khabaroffka have competed so successfully with the Chinese in market gardening that the supplying that city with vegetables is now entirely in their hands !

The Russian *tarantass* is one of the most uncouth of civilized vehicles—all that can be said of it is that it suits the roads, which in that region are execrable.   On two sets of stout wheels and axles, attached to each other by long solid timbers, a long shallow box is secured, with one, two, or even three boards, cushioned or not, "roped" across it for seats. It may be drawn by either two or three horses abreast, one in the shafts and one or two outside, each with the most slender attachment to the vehicle, and his head held down and inwards by a tight strap. This outer animal is trained to a showy gallop, which never slackens even though the shaft horse may keep up a decorous trot. The *tarantass* has no springs, and, going at a gallop, bumps and bounces over all obstacles, holes, hillocks, ruts and streams being alike to it.

The *tarantass* of the Chief of Police made nothing of the obstacles on the road to Yantchihe, where we were to hear of a Korean interpreter. The level country, narrowing into a valley bordered by fine mountains, is of deep, rich black soil, and grows almost all cereals and roots. All the crops were gathered in and the land was neatly ploughed. Korean hamlets with houses of a very superior class to those in Korea were sprinkled over the country. At one of the largest villages, where 140 families were settled on 750 acres of rich land, we called at several of the peasant farmers' houses, and were made very welcome, even the women coming out to welcome the official with an air of decided pleasure. The farmers had changed the timid, suspicious, or cringing manner which is characteristic of them to a great extent at home, for an air of frankness and manly independence which was most pleasing.

The Chief of Police was a welcome visitor. The Koreans had nothing to fear, unless his quick scent discerned an insanitary odor or his eye an anwarrantable garbage heap! The farmyards were clean and well swept, and the domestic animals were lodged in neat sheds. The houses, of strictly Korean architecture, were large, with five or six rooms, carefully thatched, and very neat within, abounding in such comforts and plenishings as would only be dreamed of by mandarins at home. It is insisted on, however, that, instead of the flues which heat the floors vomiting forth their smoke through many blackened apertures in the walls, they shall unite in sending it heavenwards through a hollow tree trunk placed at a short distance from the house. This, and cleanly surroundings in the interests of sanitation, are the only restrictions on their Korean habits. The clothing and dwellings are the same as in Korea, and the " topknot " flourishes.

A little farther on there is the large village of Yantchihe, with a neat schoolhouse, in which Russian and Korean pupils sit side by side at their lessons, a Greek church, singularly rich in internal decorations, and a priest's house adjoining. This is a very prosperous village. In the neat police station a Korean sergeant wrote down my requirements and sent off a smart Korean policeman in search of an interpreter. Four hundred Koreans in this neighborhood have conformed to the Greek Church and have received baptism. On asking the priest, who was more picturesque than cultivated, and whose large young family seemed oppressively large for the house, what sort of Christians they made, he replied suggestively that they had " a great deal to learn," and that there would be " more hope for the next generation."

I am not clear in my own mind as to the cause of the success which has attended " missionary effort " at Yantchihe and elsewhere. The statements I received on the subject differed widely, and in most cases were made hesitatingly, as if my informants were not sure of their ground. My impression is that while Russia is tolerant of devil-worship, or any other worship which is not subversive of the externals of morality, " conformity " is required to obtain for the Korean alien those blessings which belong to naturalization as a Russian subject.

Preparations being completed for travelling to the Korean frontier, and into Korea as far as Kyöng-heung, a town which a Trade Convention in 1888 opened to the residence of Russian subjects in the hope of creating a market there after the style of Kiachta, I had an interview with Mr. Matunin, the

Frontier Commissioner, who gave me a very unpleasant account of insecurity on the frontier owing to the lawlessness of the Chinese troops, and an introduction to the Governor of Kyöng-heung.

A large *tarantass* with three ponies and a driver, a Korean on another pony, and the Korean headman of a neighboring village, who spoke Russian well, and our saddles were our modest outfit. The details of the two days' journey to the Tumen are too monotonous for infliction on the reader. The road was infamous, and at times disappeared altogether on a hillside or in a swamp, and swamps are frequent for the first 40 *versts*. The *tarantass*, always attempting a gallop, bounced, bumped, and thumped, till breathing became a series of gasps. Occasionally we stuck fast in swampy streams where the ice was broken, being extricated by a tremendous, united, and apparently trained, jump on the part of the ponies, which compelled a strong grip of the vehicle with hands and feet, and would have dislocated any other. Mr. Heidemann smoked cigarettes unceasingly, and made no remarks.

We crossed the head of Possiet Bay and other inlets at a gallop on thin ice, forded several streams in the aforesaid fashion, and passed through several Korean coast villages given up to the making of salt by a rude process, the finished product being carted away to Hun-chun in China in baskets of finely woven reeds. These Chinese carts are drawn by seven mules each, constantly driven at a gallop.

After 30 *versts* the country became very hilly, with rugged mountains in the distance, all without a tree or bush, and covered with coarse and fine grasses mixed up with myriads of withered flower stalks of *Compositæ* and *Umbelliferæ*, and here and there a lonely, belated purple aster shivered in the strong keen wind, which made an atmosphere at zero somewhat hard to face. The valleys are flat and broad, and their rich black soil, the product of ages of decaying vegetation, is absolutely stoneless. Almost all crops can be raised upon it. Besides being a rich agricultural country, the region is well suited for cattle breeding. There were large herds on the hills, and hay-stacks thickly scattered over the landscape indicated abundance of winter keep. The potato, which flourishes and is free from the disease, is largely cultivated, and is now with the Koreans an article of ordinary diet.

The whole of this fine country is settled by Koreans, for the few hamlets of wretched, tumble-down Chinese houses are of no account. Whether as squatters or purchasers, they are making the best of the land. The number of their domestic animals enables them to fertilize it abundantly; they plough deep, and rotate their crops, and get a splendid yield from their lands. We halted at Saretchje, a village of 120 families, admirably housed, and with all material comforts abounding about them. Out of its 600 inhabitants, 450 have " conformed." The Koreans, having no religion, are apparently not unwilling to secure the possible advantages of conversion, and though none of the Greek priests who conversed with me were enthusiastic about their " consistency," it is at least more satisfactory to see an " *Ecce Homo* " on the wall than the family dæmon.

At distances of 3 and 4 miles there are Korean villages, of which prosperity in greater or less degree is a characteristic. The houses are large and well built, and the farmyards are well stocked with domestic animals, the people and children are well clothed, and the village lands carefully cultivated.

A long ascent, during which the road, which for some time had been intermittent, gradually disappeared, leads to the summit of a high hill, from which the mountainous frontiers of Russia, China, and Korea are seen to converge. After losing our way and our time, and crossing several ranges of hills without a road, just as the winter sun was setting in a flood of red gold, glorifying the mountains on the Chinese frontier, a turn round a bluff revealed what is geographically and politically a striking view.

The whole of the Russo-Korean frontier, 11 miles in length, and a broad river full of sandbanks, passing through a desert of sandhills to the steely blue ocean, lay crimson in the sunset. On a steep bluff above the river a tall granite slab marks the spot where the Russian and Chinese frontiers meet. Across the Tumen, the barren mountains of Korea loomed purple through a haze of gold. Three empires are seen at a glance. A small and poor Korean village is situated in a valley below. Close to the Boundary Stone, on the high steep bluff above the Tumen, there is a large mud hut from which most of the whitewash had scaled off, with thatch held on by straw ropes, weighted with stones.

It was a very lonely scene. A Korean told us that it was absolutely impossible for us to sleep at the village. A Cossack came out of the hut, took a long look at us, and returned. Then a forlorn-looking corporal appeared, who also took a long look, and having hospitable instincts, came up and told us that the village was impossible except for the drivers and horses, but that he could put us up roughly in the hut, which consisted of one fair sized room, another very small one, and a lean-to.

The latest English papers had stated that "Russia has lately massed 5,000 men on the Korean frontier, and 4,000 at Hunchun." It is not desirable to make any inquiries about the positions and numbers of Russian troops, and I had prudently abstained from asking questions, and had looked forward with interest to seeing a great display of military force. This hut is the military post of Krasnoye Celo, and the "army" of Russia "massed on her Korean frontier" consisted of 15 men and a corporal, the officer being required to endure the isolation of the position for six months, and the privates for one. The roars of laughter which greeted the English statement were not complimentary to newspaper accuracy.

The corporal's small room was of no particular shape, and was furnished with only a deal chair and small table, and a

big earthen jar of water, but it was well warmed, and had an
iron camp-bed in a recess with a wire-wove mattress, much
broken and "sagging," the sharp points of the broken wires
sticking up in several places through the one rug with which I
attempted to mollify their asperities. This recess, which just
contained the bed, was curtained off for me, and the corporal,
Mr. Heidemann, and three Korean headmen lay closely packed
on the floor. The corporal, glad to have people to talk with,
talked more than half the night, and began again before daybreak. We supped on barrack fare—black bread, barley
brose, and tea, with the addition of a little *kwass*, a very
slightly fermented drink, made from black bread, raisins,
sugar, and a little *vodka*, *schnaps* and *vodka* containing 40 per
cent. of alcohol. At 9 P.M. I was surprised and delighted with
the noble strains of a Greek Litany, chanted in well-balanced
parts from the barrack-room, the evening worship of the Cossacks.

My last sunset view of the Tumen was of a sheet of ice.
The headmen of the Korean villages of Sajorni and Krasnoe,
who were in council till near midnight, thought it was impossible to get across, and they said that the ferryboat was drawn
ashore and was frozen in for the winter, and that two Russian
Commissioners and a General, after waiting for three days,
had left the day before, having failed. However, yielding to
my urgency, they set all the able-bodied men of Sajorni to
work at 2 A.M. to dig the boat out, and by 7 she had moved
some yards towards the river, which, however, was still a sheet
of ice. Later, the corporal sent 14 of his men to help the
Koreans, laughingly saying that I had the "whole Russian
frontier army to get me across." At 9 word came that the
boat was nearly afloat, and we started, on horseback, with two
baggage ponies, and rode a mile over the hills and through
the prosperous Korean village of Sajorni, down to a dazzling
expanse of sand through which the Tumen flows to the sea,
there 10 miles off.

The river ice was breaking up into large masses under the morning sun, and between Russia and Korea there was much open water about 600 feet broad. The experts said if we could get over at all it would be between noon and 2, after which the ice would pack and freeze together again. Koreans and Cossacks worked with a will, breaking the ice, digging under the boat, and moving her with levers, but it was noon before the unwieldy craft, used for the ferriage of oxen, moved into the water, accompanied by a hearty cheer. She leaked badly, two men were required to bale her, and the stern platform, by which animals enter her, was carried away. The baggage was carried in by men wading much over their knees, and then came the turn of the ponies, but not the whole Russian army by force or persuasion could get those wretched animals embarked.

After a whole hour's work and any amount of kicking, plunging, and injuries, from getting one or two legs over the bulwarks, and struggling back, and rolling backwards into the river, two were apparently safe in the ferryboat, when suddenly they knocked over the man who held them and jumped into the water, one blind animal being rescued with difficulty, and the other cutting his legs considerably. The ice was then fast forming, but the soldiers made one more attempt, which failed, owing to what Americans would not inaptly call the "cussedness" of the Siberian ponies. For the first time on any journey I had to confess myself baffled, for it was impossible to swim the contumacious animals across, owing to the heavy ice floes and the low temperature of the water. I had sat on my pony watching these proceedings for nearly four hours, watching too the grand Korean mountains as they swept down to the icy river in every shade of cobalt blue, varied by indigo shadows of the white cloud masses which sailed slowly across the heavenly sky. At that point from which I most reluctantly turned back, the Tumen has a large volume of water, but above and below sandbanks render the navigation so diffi-

RUSSIAN "ARMY," KRASNOYE CELO.

cult that it is only in the rainy season that flat-bottomed boats make the attempt, and not always with success, to reach the Korean town of K'wan, 80 *versts*, or something over 50 miles, above Krasnoye Celo. The Chinese, in the insane notion that Japan was about to land a large force on the south bank of the Tumen, had seized all the boats above the Russian post.

I photographed the " Russian army " and the barracks as well as the Boundary Stone, and the corporal slouching against the scaly forlorn quarters on the desolate height in an attitude of extreme dejection, as we drove away leaving him to his usual dulness.

The days of the return journey gave me a good opportunity of learning something of the condition of the Koreans under another Government than their own. So long ago as 1863, 13 families from Ham-gyöng Do crossed the frontier and settled on the river Tyzen Ho, a little to the north of Possiet Bay. By 1866 there were 100 families there, very poor, among which the Russian Government distributed cattle and seed for cultivation.

During 1869, a year of very great scarcity in Northern Korea, 4,500 Koreans migrated, hunger-driven, into Primorsk, some 3,800 of them being absolutely destitute. These had to be supported, no easy thing, as the territory, only ceded to Russia a few years before, was but a thinly peopled wilderness, and was also suffering from a bad harvest.

In 1897 there were in Primorsk 32 village districts, *i.e.* villages with outlying hamlets, divided into 5 administrative districts. Besides these, one village belongs to the city of Khabaroffka on the Amur, and there are large Korean settlements adjacent to Wladivostok and Nikolskoye. The total number of Korean immigrants is estimated at from 16,000 to 18,000. It must be remembered that several thousands of these were literally paupers, and that they subsisted for nearly a year on the charity of the Russian authorities, and after that were indebted to them for seed corn. They settled on the rich lands of the

Siberian valleys mostly as squatters, but have been unmolested for many years. Many have purchased the lands they occupy, and in other cases villages have acquired community rights to their adjacent lands. It is the intention of Government that squatting shall gradually be replaced by purchase, the purchasers receiving legal title-deeds.

These alien settlers practically enjoy autonomy. At the head of each district is an Elder or Headman, with from one to three assistants according to its size. The police and their officers are Korean. In each district there are two or three judges with their clerks, who try minor offences. The headmen, who are responsible for order and the collection of taxes, are paid salaries, or receive various allowances. All these officials are Koreans, and are elected by the people themselves from among themselves. The Government taxation is 10 roubles (about £1) on each farm per annum. The local taxation, settled by the villagers in council for their own purposes, such as roads, ditches, bridges, and schools, is limited to 3 roubles per farm per annum. Men who are not landholders pay from 1 to 2 roubles per annum.

Koreans settled in Siberia prior to 1884 can claim rights as Russian subjects, and at this time those who can prove that they have been settled on purchased lands for ten years can do so, as well as certain others, well reported of as being of settled lives and good conduct. Owing to the steady influx of settlers from Southern Russia, the rich lands near the railroad are required for colonization, and further immigration from Korea has been prohibited. The sending of Koreans who are either squatters or of unsettled lives to the Amur Province is under discussion.

The villages between Krasnoye Celo and Nowo Kiewsk are fair average specimens of Russo-Korean settlements. The roads are fairly good, and the ditches which border them well kept. Sanitary rules are strictly enforced, the headman being made responsible for village cleanliness. Unlike the poor, ragged, filthy villages of the peninsula, these are well built in Korean style, of whitewashed mud and laths, trimly thatched, the compounds or farmyards are enclosed by whitewashed walls, or high fences of neatly woven reeds, and look as if they were swept every morning, and the farm buildings are substantial and well kept. Even the pigsties testify to the Argus eyes of the district chiefs of police.

Most of the dwellings have four, five, and even six rooms, with papered walls and ceilings, fretwork doors and windows, "glazed" with white translucent paper, finely matted floors, and an amount of plenishings rarely to be found even in a mandarin's house in Korea. Cabinets, bureaus, and rice chests of ornamental wood with handsome brass decorations, low tables, stools, cushions, brass samovars, dressers displaying brass dinner services, brass bowls, china, tea-glasses, brass candlesticks, brass kerosene lamps, and a host of other things, illustrate the capacity to secure comfort. Pictures of the Tsar and Tsaritza, of the Christ, and of Greek saints, and framed cards of twelve Christian prayers, replace the coarse daubs of the family dæmons in very many houses. Out of doors full granaries, ponies, mares with foals, black pigs of an improved breed, draught oxen, and fat oxen for the Wladivostok market, with ox-carts and agricultural implements, attest solid material prosperity. It would be impossible for a traveller to meet with more cordial hospitality and more cleanly and comfortable accommodation than I did in these Korean homes.

But there is more than this. The air of the men has undergone a subtle but real change, and the women, though they nominally keep up their habit of seclusion, have lost the hang-dog air which distinguishes them at home. The suspiciousness and indolent conceit, and the servility to his betters, which characterize the home-bred Korean have very generally given place to an independence and manliness of manner rather British than Asiatic. The alacrity of movement is a change also, and has replaced the conceited swing of the *yang-*

ban and the heartless lounge of the peasant.   There are many chances for making money, and there is neither mandarin nor *yang-ban* to squeeze it out of the people when made, and comforts and a certain appearance of wealth no longer attract the repacious attentions of officials, but are rather a credit to a man than a source of insecurity.   All who work can be comfortable, and many of the farmers are rich and engage in trade, making and keeping extensive contracts.

Those Koreans who are not settled on lands chiefly in the direction of the Chinese frontier, and who subsist by wood cutting and hauling, are less well off, and their hamlets have something of squalor about them.

In Korea I had learned to think of Koreans as the dregs of a race, and to regard their condition as hopeless, but in Primorsk I saw reason for considerably modifying my opinion. It must be borne in mind that these people, who have raised themselves into a prosperous farming class, and who get an excellent character for industry and good conduct alike from Russian police officials, Russian settlers, and military officers, were not exceptionally industrious and thrifty men.   They were mostly starving folk who fled from famine, and their prosperity and general demeanor give me the hope that their countrymen in Korea, if they ever have an honest administration and protection for their earnings, may slowly develop into *men*.

In parts of Western Asia I have had occasion to note the success of Russian administration in conquered or acquired provinces, and with subject races, specially her creation of an orderly, peaceful, and settled agricultural population out of the nomadic and predatory tribes of Turkestan.   Her success with the Korean immigrants is in its way as remarkable, for the material is inferior.   She is firm where firmness is necessary, but outside that limit allows extreme latitude, avoids harassing aliens by petty prohibitions and irksome rules, encourages those forms of local self government which suit the genius and habits of different peoples, and trusts to time, education, and contact with other forms of civilization to amend what is reprehensible in customs, religion, and costume.

A few days later I went to Hun-chun on the frontier of Chinese Manchuria, from its position an important military post, and was most hospitably received by the Commandant and his married *aide-de-camp*. There, as everywhere in Primorsk, and from the civil as well as the military authorities, I not only received the utmost kindness, courtesy, and hospitality, but information was frankly given on the various topics I was interested in, and help towards the attainment of my objects. Hun-chun is in the midst of mountainous country, denuded of wood in recent years, and abounding in rich, well-watered valleys inhabited only by Koreans. A wilder, drearier, and more wind-swept situation it would be hard to find.

Instead of "4,000 troops" there were only 200 Cossacks, housed in a good brick barrack, one-half of which is a much decorated chapel, besides which there are only open thatched sheds for their hardy, active Baikal horses, a small, well-arranged hospital, a wooden house for the Colonel Commandant, and some terra-cotta mud-houses for the officers and married troopers. The whole Russian military force from Hun-chun to the Amur consisted of 1,500 Cossacks, distributed among thirty frontier posts. The Commandant told me that their chief duty at that time was the "daily" arresting of Chinese brigands who crossed the frontier to harry the Korean villages, and who, on being marched back and handed over to the mandarins, were at once liberated to repeat their forays.

The Chinese had "massed" several thousand of their Manchu troops at Hun-chun, and they had created such a reign of terror that the peasant farmers had deserted their homes over a large area of country. The soldiers, robbed by their officers of their nominal pay, and only half fed, relied on unlimited pillage for making up the deficiency, and neither women nor property were safe from their brutality and violence.

So desperately undisciplined were they that only a few days before the Secretary and Interpreter of the Russian frontier Commissioner at Nowo Kiewsk, visiting Hun-chun on official business, narrowly escaped actual violence at their hands, and the Chinese Governor told them that he had no control at all over the troops. It was only the rigid discipline of the Cossacks which prevented scrimmages which might have produced a serious conflagration.

KOREAN SETTLERS' HOUSE.

CHAPTER XX

AFTER returning to Wladivostok, accompanied by a young Danish gentleman who was kindly lent to me by Messrs. Kuntz and Albers, and who spoke English and Russian, I spent a week on the Ussuri Railway, the eastern section of the Trans-Siberian Railway, going as far as the hamlet of Ussuri on the Ussuri River at the great Ussuri Bridge, beyond which the line, though completed for 50 *versts*, was not open for traffic. Indeed, up to that point from Nikolskoye trains were run twice daily rather to "settle the line" than for profit, and their average speed was only twelve miles an hour. The weather was brilliant, varied by a heavy snowstorm.

The present Tsar is understood to be enthusiastic about this railroad. During his visit to Wladivostok in 1891, when Tsarevitch, he inaugurated the undertaking by wheeling away the first barrowful of earth and placing the first stone in position, after which, work was begun simultaneously at both ends.

The eastern terminus of this great railroad undertaking is close to the sea and the Government deep-water pier, at which the fine steamers from Odessa of the Russian "Volunteer Fleet" discharge their cargoes. The station is large and very handsome, and both it and the noble administrative offices are built of gray stone, with the architraves of the doors and windows in red brick. Buffets and all else were in efficient working order. In the winter of 1895–96 only third and fourth class cars were running, the latter chiefly patronized by Koreans and Chinese. Each third class carriage is divided into three compartments with a corridor, and has a lavatory and steam-heating apparatus. The backs of the seats are hooked up to form upper berths for sleeping, and as the cars are eight feet high they admit of broad luggage shelves above these. The engines which ran the traffic were old American locomotives, but those which are to be introduced, as well as all the rolling stock, are being manufactured in the Baltic provinces. So also are the rails, the iron and steel bridges, the water tanks, the iron work required for stations, and all else.

Large railway workshops with rows of substantial houses for artisans have been erected at Nikolskoye, 102 *versts* from Wladivostok, for the repairs of rolling stock on the Ussuri section, and were already in full activity.

There is nothing about this Ussuri Railway of the newness and provisional aspect of the Western American lines, or even of parts of the Canadian Pacific Railroad. The track was already ballasted as far as Ussuri (327 *versts*), steel bridges spanned the minor streams, and substantial stations either of stone or decorated wood, with buffets at fixed distances, successfully compare both in stability and appearance with those of our English branch lines. The tank houses are of hewn stone. Houses for the employés, standing in neatly fenced gardens, are both decorative and substantial, being built of cement and logs protected by five coats of paint, and contain four rooms each. The crossings are well laid and protected. Culverts and retaining walls are of solid masonry, and telegraph wires accompany the road, which is worked strictly on the block system. The aspect of solidity and permanence is remarkable. Even the temporary bridge over the Ussuri, 1,050 feet in length, a trestle bridge of heavy timber to resist the impact of the ice, is so massive as to make the great steel bridge, the handsome abutments of which were already built, appear as if it would be a work of supererogation.

Up to that point there are no serious embankments or cuttings, and the gradients are easy. The cost of construction of the Ussuri section is 50,000 roubles per *verst*, a rouble at this time being worth about 2s. 2d. This includes rolling stock, stations, and all bridges except that over the Amur, which was to cost 3,000,000 roubles, but may now be dispensed with owing to the diversion of the route through Manchuria. Convict labor was abandoned in 1894, and the line in Primorsk is being constructed by Chinese " navvies," who earn about 80 cents per day, and who were bearing the rigor of a Siberian winter in well-warmed, semi-subterranean huts, the line being pushed on as much as possible during the cold season. For the first 102 *versts*, it passes along prettily wooded shores of inlets and banks of streams, and the country is fairly well peopled, judging from the number of sleighs and the bustle at the six stations *en route*. The line as far as Nikolskoye was opened in early November, 1893, and in a year had earned 280,000 roubles. The last section had only been open for eight weeks when I travelled upon it.

Nikolskoye, where I spent two pleasant days at the hospitable establishment of Messrs. Kuntz and Albers, is the only place between Wladivostok and Ussuri of any present importance. It is a *village* of 8,000 inhabitants on a rich rolling prairie, watered by the Siphun. It has six streets of grotesque width, a *verst* and a half long each. There is no poverty. It is a place of rapid growth and prosperity, the centre of a great trade in grain, and has a large flour mill owned by Mr. Lindholm, a Government contractor. It has a spacious market-place and bazaar, and two churches. It reminds me of parts of Salt Lake City, and the houses are of wood, plastered and whitewashed, with corrugated iron roofs mainly. A few are thatched. All stand in plots of garden ground. Utilitarianism is supreme. I drove for 20 miles in the region round the settlement, and everywhere saw prosperous farms and farming villages on the prairie, Russian and Korean, and found the settlers kindly and hospitable, and surrounded by material comfort. Nikolskoye is a great military station. There were infantry and artillery to the number of 9,000, and there, as elsewhere, large new barracks were being pushed to completion. An area of 50 acres was covered with brick barracks, magazines, stables, drill and parade grounds, and officers' quarters, and the military club is a really fine building.   Newness, progress, and confidence in the future are as characteristic of Nikolskoye as of any rising town in the Far West of America.

The farther journey, occupying the greater part of two days and a night, except when near the swamps of the Hanka Lake, is through a superb farming region.   Large villages with windmills are met with along the line for the first 30 *versts*, as far as the buffet station of Spasskoje.   The stoneless soil, a rich loam 6 feet and more in depth, produces heavy crops of oats, wheat, barley, maize, rye, potatoes, and tobacco.   Beyond Spasskoje and east of the Hanka Lake up to the Amur a magnificent region waits to be peopled.

Well may Eastern Siberia receive the name of Russia's "Pacific Empire," including as it does the Amur and Maritime provinces, with their area of 880,000 square miles,[1] rich in gold, copper, iron, lead, and coal, and with a soil which for a vast extent is of unbounded fertility.   When China ceded to Russia in 1860 the region which we call Russian Manchuria, she probably did so in ignorance of its vast agricultural capacities and mineral wealth.

The noble Amur, with its forest-covered shores, is navigable for 1,000 miles, and already 50 merchant steamers ply upon it, and its great tributary the Ussuri can be navigated to within 120 miles of Wladivostok.   The great basin of the Ussuri, it is estimated, could support five million people, and from Khabaroffka to the Tumen, it is considered by experts that the land could sustain from 20 to 40 to the square mile, while at present the population of the Amur and Ussuri provinces is only $\frac{4}{5}$ths of a man to the square mile !

[1] The area of France is 204,000, and that of the British Isles 120,000 square miles.

Grass, timber, water, coal, minerals, a soil as rich as the prairies of Illinois, and a climate not only favorable to agriculture but to human health, all await the settler, and the broad, unoccupied, and fertile lands which Russian Manchuria offers are clamoring for inhabitants. To set against these advantages there are the frozen waterways and the ice-bound harbor. It is utterly impossible that an increasing population will content itself without an outlet for its produce. A port on the Pacific open all the year is fast becoming as much a commercial as a political necessity, and doubtless the opening of the Trans-Siberian Railroad four years hence will settle the question (if it has not been settled before) and doom the policy which has shut Russia up in regions of " thick ribbed ice " to utter extinction.

In the Maritime Province, Russia is steadily and solidly laying the foundations of a new empire which she purposes to make as nearly as possible a homogeneous one. " No foreigner need apply " ! The emigrants, who are going out at the rate of from 700 to 1,000 families a year, are of a good class. Emigration is fostered in two ways. By the first, the Government grants assisted passages to heads of families who are possessed of 600 roubles (about £60 at present), which are deposited with a Government official at Odessa, and are repaid to the emigrant on landing at Wladivostok. The industry and thrift represented by this sum indicate a large proportion of the best class of settlers. Under the second arrangement, families possessed of little capital or none receive free passages. On arriving, emigrants of both classes are lodged in excellent emigrant barracks, and can buy the necessary agricultural implements at cost price from a Government depôt, advice as to the purchase being thrown in. Each family receives a free allotment of from 200 to 300 acres of arable land, and a loan of 600 roubles, to be repaid without interest in thirty-two years, the young male colonists being exempted from military service for the same period. Already much of the land along the line as far as the Ussuri has been allotted, and houses are rapidly springing up, and there is nothing to prevent this fine country from being peopled up to the Amur, the rivers Sungacha and Ussuri, which form the boundary of Russia from the Hanka Lake to Khabaroffka, giving a natural protection from Chinese brigandage. In addition to direct emigration, large numbers of time-expired men, chiefly Cossacks, are encouraged to settle on lands and do so.

It would be shortsighted to minimize the importance of the present drift of population to Eastern Siberia, which is likely to assume immense proportions on the opening of the railway, or the commercial value of that colossal undertaking, which is greatly enhanced by the treaty under which Russia has taken powers to run the Trans-Siberian line through Chinese Manchuria. The creation of a new route which will bring the Far East within 6,000 miles and 16 days of London, and cheapen the cost of the transit of passengers very considerably, cannot be overlooked either. The railroad is being built for futurity, and is an enterprize worthy of the great nation which undertakes it.[1]

[1] I am very glad to be able to fortify my opinion of the solid and careful construction of this line by that of Colonel Waters, military attaché to the British Embassy at St. Petersburg, who has recently crossed Siberia, and desires to give emphatic testimony to "the magnificent character of the great railway crossing Siberia," as well as by that of another recent traveller, Mr. J. Y. Simpson, who, in *Blackwood's Magazine* for January, 1897, in an article "The Great Siberian Iron Road," after a long description of the laborious carefulness with which the line is being built, writes thus: "Lastly, one is impressed with the *extremely finished* nature of the work."

CHAPTER XXI

THE KING'S OATH—AN AUDIENCE

LEAVING Wladivostok by the last Japanese steamer of the season, I spent two days at Wŏn-san, little changed, except that its background of mountains was snow-covered, that the Koreans were enriched by the extravagant sums paid for labor by the Japanese during the war, that business was active, and that Japanese sentries in wooden sentry-boxes guarded the peaceful streets. Twelve thousand Japanese troops had passed through Wŏn-san on their way to Phyŏng-yang. At Fusan, my next point, there were 200 Japanese soldiers, new waterworks, and a military cemetery on a height, in which the number of graves showed an enormous Japanese mortality.

Reaching Chemulpo on 5th January, 1895, *via* Nagaski, I found a singular contrast to the crowd, bustle, and excitement of the previous June. In the outer harbor there were two foreign warships only, in the inner three Japanese merchant steamers. The former predominant military element was represented by a few soldiers, ten large hospital sheds, and a crowded cemetery, in which the Japanese military dead lie in rows of 60, each grave marked by a wooden obelisk. The solid and crowded Chinese quarter, with its roaring trade, large shops, and noise of drums, gongs, and crackers, by day and night, was silent and deserted, and not a single Chinese was in the street as I went up to I-tai's inn. One shop had ventured to reopen. At night, instead of throngs, noise, lights, and jollification, there was a solitary glimmer from behind a closed shutter. The Japanese occupation had been as destructive of that quarter of Chemulpo as a mediæval pestilence.

In the Japanese quarter and all along the shore the utmost activity prevailed. The beach was stacked with incoming and outgoing cargo. The streets were only just passable, not alone from the enormous traffic on bulls' and coolies' backs, but from the piles of beans and rice which were being measured and packed on the roadway. Prices were high, wages had more than doubled, "squeezing" was diminished, and the Koreans were working with a will.

I went up to Seoul on horseback, snow falling the whole time. So safe was the country that no escort was needed, and I rode as far as Oricol without even a *mapu*. The halfway house of my first visit was a Japanese post, and going to it in ignorance of the change, I was very kindly received by the Japanese soldiers, who gave me tea and a brazier of charcoal. The Seoul road, pegged out by Japanese surveyors for a railroad, was thickly sprinkled for the whole distance with laden men and bulls.

At Seoul I was the guest of Mr. Hillier, the British Consul-General, for five weeks. The weather was glorious, and the mercury sank on two occasions to 7° below zero, the lowest temperature on record. I received the warmest welcome from the kindly foreign community, and was steeped in Seoul life, the political and other interests growing upon me daily; and having a pony and a soldier at my disposal, I saw the city in all its turnings and windings, and the charming country outside the gates, and several of the Royal tombs with their fine trees, and avenues of stately stone figures.

The stagnation of the previous winter was at an end. Japan was in the ascendant. She had a large garrison in the capital, some of the leading men in the Cabinet were her nominees, her officers were drilling the Korean army, changes, if not improvements, were everywhere, and the air was thick with rumors of more to come. The King, whose Royal authority was nominally restored to him, accepted the situation, the Queen was credited with intriguing against the Japanese, but

Count Inouye was acting as Japanese minister, and his firmness and tact kept everything smooth on the surface.

On the 8th of January, 1895, I witnessed a singular ceremony, which may have far-reaching results in Korean history. The Japanese having presented Korea with the gift of Independence, demanded that the King should formally and publicly renounce the suzerainty of China, and having resolved to cleanse the Augean stable of official corruption, they compelled him to inaugurate the task by proceeding in semi-state to the Altar of the Spirits of the Land, and there proclaiming Korean independence, and swearing before the spirits of his ancestors to the proposed reforms. His Majesty, by exaggerating a trivial ailment, had for some time delayed a step which was very repulsive to him, and even the day before the ceremony, a dream in which an Ancestral Spirit had appeared to him adjuring him not to depart from ancestral ways, terrified him from taking the proposed pledge.

But the spirit of Count Inouye proved more masterful than the Ancestral Spirit, and the oath was taken in circumstances of great solemnity in a dark pine wood, under the shadow of Puk Han, at the most sacred altar in Korea, in presence of the Court and the dignitaries of the kingdom. Old and serious men had fasted and mourned for two previous days, and in the vast crowd of white-robed and black-hatted men which looked down upon the striking scene from a hill in the grounds of the Mulberry Palace, there was not a smile or a spoken word. The sky was dark and grim, and a bitter east wind was blowing—ominous signs in Korean estimation.

The Royal procession, which had something of the aspect of the *kur-dong*, was shorn of the barbaric splendor which made that ceremonial one of the most imposing in the Eastern world. It was, in fact, barbaric with the splendor left out; and there were suggestions of a new era and a forthcoming swamping wave of Western civilization, in the presence within the Palace gates and in the procession or a few trim, dapper, blue-ulstered Japanese policemen, as the special protectors of the Home Minister Pak-Yŏng-Ho, one of the revolutionaries of 1884, against whom there was a vow of vengeance, though the King had been compelled to pardon him, to reinstate his ancestors who had been degraded, to recall him from exile, and to confer upon him high office.

The long road outside the Palace was lined with Korean cavalry, who turned their faces to the wall and their backs and their ponies' tails to the King. Great numbers of Korean soldiers carrying various makes of muskets, dressed in rusty black, brown, and blue cotton uniforms, trousers sometimes a foot too short, at others a foot too long, white wadded socks, string shoes, and black felt hats of Tyrolese style, with pink ribbon round the crowns, stood in awkward huddles, mixed up with the newly-created Seoul police in blue European-uniforms, and a number of handsome overfed ponies of Court officials, with saddles over a foot high, gorgeous barbaric trappings, red pompons on their heads, and a flow of red manes. The populace stood without speech or movement.

After a long delay and much speculation as to whether the King at the last moment would resist the foreign pressure, the procession emerged from the Palace gate—huge flags on trident-headed poles, purple bundles carried aloft, a stand of stones conveyed with much ceremony[1]—groups of scarlet- and blue-robed men in hats of the same colors, shaped like fools' caps, the King's personal servants in yellow robes and yellow bamboo hats, and men carrying bannerets. Then came the red silk umbrella, followed not by the magnificent State chair with its forty bearers, but by a plain wooden chair with glass sides, in which sat the sovereign, pale and dejected, borne by only four men. The Crown Prince followed in a similar chair. Mandarins, ministers, and military officers were then assisted to mount their caparisoned ponies, and each, with two attend-

---

[1] These are ancient musical instruments called by the Chinese *ch'ing*, and were in use at courts in the days of Confucius.

KOREAN THRONE.

ants holding his stirrups and two more leading his pony, fell in behind the Home Minister, riding a dark donkey, and rendered conspicuous by his foreign saddle and foreign guard. When the procession reached the sacred enclosure, the military escort and the greater part of the cavalcade remained outside the wall, only the King, dignitaries, and principal attendants proceeding to the altar. The grouping of the scarlet-robed men under the dark pines was most effective from an artistic point of view, and from a political standpoint the taking of the following oath by the Korean King was one of the most significant acts in the tedious drama of the late war.

THE KING'S OATH.

On this 12th day of the 12th moon of the 503rd year of the founding of the Dynasty, we presume to announce clearly to the Spirits of all our Sacred Imperial Ancestors that we, their lowly descendant, received in early childhood, now thirty and one years ago, the mighty heritage of our ancestors, and that in reverent awe towards Heaven, and following in the rule and pattern of our ancestors, we, though we have encountered many troubles, have not loosed hold of the thread. How dare we, your lowly descendant, aver that we are acceptable to the heart of Heaven? It is only that our ancestors have graciously looked down upon us and benignly protected us. Splendidly did our ancestor lay the foundation of our Royal House, opening a way for us his descendants through five hundred years and three. Now, in our generation, the times are mightily changed, and men and matters are expanding. A friendly Power, designing to prove faithful, and the deliberations of our Council aiding thereto, show that only as an independent ruler can we make our country strong. How can we, your lowly descendant, not conform to the spirit of the time and thus guard the domain bequeathed by our ancestors? How venture not to strenuously exert ourselves and stiffen and anneal us in order to add lustre to the virtues of our predecessors. For all time from now no other State will we lean upon, but will make broad the steps of our country towards prosperity, building up the happiness of our people in order to strengthen the foundations of our independence. When we ponder on this course, let there be no sticking in the old ways, no practice of ease or of dalliance; but docilely let us carry out the great designs of our ancestors, watching and observing sublunary conditions, reforming our internal administration, remedying there accumulated abuses.

We, your lowly descendant, do now take the fourteen clauses of the Great Charter and swear before the Spirits of our Ancestors in Heaven that we, reverently trusting in the merits bequeathed by our ancestors, will bring these to a successful issue, nor will we dare to go back on our word. Do you, bright Spirits, descend and behold!

1. All thoughts of dependence on China shall be cut away, and a firm foundation for independence secured.

2. A rule and ordinance for the Royal House shall be established, in order to make clear the line of succession and precedence among the Royal family.

3. The King shall attend at the Great Hall for the inspection of affairs, where, after personally interrogating his Ministers, he shall decide upon matters of State. The Queen and the Royal family are not allowed to interfere.

4. Palace matters and the government of the country must be kept separate, and may not be mixed up together.

5. The duties and powers of the Cabinet and of the various Ministers shall be clearly defined.

6. The payment of taxes by the people shall be regulated by law. Wrongful additions may not be made to the list, and no excess collected.

7. The assessment and collection of the land tax, and the disbursement of expenditure, shall be under the charge and control of the Finance Department.

8. The expenses of the Royal household shall be the first to be reduced, by way of setting an example to the various Ministries and local officials.

9. An estimate shall be drawn up in advance each year of the expenditure of the Royal household and the various official establishments, putting on a firm foundation the management of the revenue.

10. The regulations of the local officers must be revised in order to discriminate the functions of the local officials.

11. Young men of intelligence in the country shall be sent abroad in order to study foreign science and industries.

12. The instruction of army officers, and the practice of the methods of enlistment, to secure the foundation of a military system.

13. Civil law and criminal law must be strictly and clearly laid down; none must be imprisoned or fined in excess, so that security of life and property may be ensured for all alike.

14. Men shall be employed without regard to their origin, and in seeking for officials recourse shall be had to capital and country alike in order to widen the avenues for ability.

> Official translation of the text of the oath taken by His Majesty the King of Korea, at the Altar of Heaven, Seoul, on January 8, 1895.

Though at this date Korea is being reformed under other than Japanese auspices, it is noteworthy that nearly every step in advance is on the lines laid down by Japan.

Count Inouye is reported by the *Nichi Nichi Shimbun* to have said regarding Korea, "In my eyes there were only the Royal Family and the nation." Such a conclusion was legitimate in the early part of 1895, and in arriving at it as I did I am glad to be sheltered by such an unexceptionable authority.

Hence it was with real pleasure that I received an invitation from the Queen to a private audience, to which I was accompanied by Mrs. Underwood, an American medical missionary and the Queen's physician and valued friend. Mr. Hillier sent me to the Kyeng-pok Palace in an eight-bearer official chair, escorted by the Korean Legation Guard. I have been altogether six times at this palace, and always with increased wonder at its intricacy, and admiration of its quaintness and beauty.

Entering by a grand three-arched gateway with its stone-balustraded stone staircase, and stone lions on stone pedestals below, one is bewildered by the number of large flagged court-yards, huge audience-halls, pavilions, buildings of all descriptions more or less decorated, stone bridges, narrow passages, and gateways with double tiered carved roofs through and among which one passes. A Japanese policeman was at the grand gate. At each of the interior gates, and there are many, there were six Korean sentries lounging, who pulled themselves together as we approached and presented arms! What with 800 troops, 1,500 attendants and officials of all descriptions, courtiers and ministers and their attendants, secretaries, messengers, and hangers-on, the vast enclosure of the Palace seemed as crowded and populated as the city itself. We had nearly half a mile of buildings to pass through before we reached a very pretty artificial lake with a decorative island pavilion in the centre, near which are a foreign palace, built not long before, and the simple Korean buildings then occupied by the King and Queen. Alighting at the gateway of the courtyard which led to the Queen's house, we were received by the Court interpreter, a number of eunuchs, two of the Queen's ladies-in-waiting, and her nurse, who was at the head of the Palace ladies—a very privileged person, middle-aged, with decidedly fine features.

In a simple room hung with yellow silk we were entertained in courteous fashion with coffee and cake on arriving, and afterwards at dinner, the nurse, "supported" by the Court interpreter, taking the head of the very prettily decorated table. The dinner was admirably cooked in " foreign style," and included soup, fish, quails, wild duck, pheasant, stuffed and rolled beef, vegetables, creams, glacé walnuts, fruit, claret, and coffee. Several of the Court ladies and others sat at table with us. After this long delay we were ushered, accompanied only by the interpreter, into a small audience-room, upon the dais at one end of which stood the King, the Crown Prince, and the Queen in front of three crimson velvet chairs, which, after Mrs. Underwood had presented me, they resumed and asked us to be seated on two chairs which were provided.

Her Majesty, who was then past forty, was a very nice-looking slender woman, with glossy raven-black hair and a very pale skin, the pallor enhanced by the use of pearl powder. The eyes were cold and keen, and the general expression one of brilliant intelligence. She wore a very handsome, very full, and very long skirt of mazarine blue brocade, heavily pleated, with the waist under the arms, and a full sleeved bodice of crimson and blue brocade, clasped at the throat by a coral rosette, and girdled by six crimson and blue cords, each one clasped with a coral rosette, with a crimson silk tassel hanging from it.   Her headdress was a crownless black silk cap edged with fur, pointed over the brow, with a coral rose and full red tassel in front, and jewelled aigrettes on either side.   Her shoes were of the same brocade as her dress.   As soon as she began to speak, and especially when she became interested in conversation, her face lighted up into something very like beauty.

The King is short and sallow, certainly a plain man, wearing a thin moustache and a tuft on the chin.   He is nervous and twitches his hands, but his pose and manner are not without dignity.   His face is pleasing, and his kindliness of nature is well known.   In conversation the Queen prompted him a good deal.   He and the Crown Prince were dressed alike in white leather shoes, wadded silk socks, and voluminous wadded white trousers.   Over these they wore first, white silk tunics, next pale green ones, and over all sleeveless dresses of mazarine blue brocade.   The whole costume, being exquisitively fresh, was pleasing.   On their heads they wore hats and *mang-huns* of very fine horsehair gauze, with black silk hoods bordered with fur, for the mercury stood at 5° below zero. The Crown Prince is fat and flabby, and though unfortunately very near-sighted, etiquette forbids him to wear spectacles, and at that time he produced on every one as on me the impression of being completely an invalid.   He was the only son and the idol of his mother, who lived in ceaseless anxiety about his health, and in dread lest the son of a concubine should be declared heir to the throne.   To this cause must be attributed several of her unscrupulous acts, her invoking the continual aid of sorcerers, and her always increasing benefactions to the Buddhist monks.   During much of the audience mother and son sat with clasped hands.

After the Queen had said many kind things to me personally, showing herself quick-witted as well as courteous, she said something to the King, who immediately took up the conversation and continued it for another half-hour. At the close of the audience I asked leave to photograph the Lake Pavilion, and the King said, "Why that alone? come many days and photograph many things," mentioning several; and he added, "I should like you to be suitably attended." We then curtseyed ourselves out, after a very agreeable and interesting hour, and as it was dusk, the King sent soldiers with us, and a number of lantern-bearers, with floating drapery of red and green silk gauze.

Two days later the "suitable attendance" turned out to be an unwieldy and embarrassing crowd, consisting of five military officers, half a regiment of soldiers, and a number of Palace attendants! I was greatly impressed by a certain grandeur and stateliness in the buildings, the vast Hall of Audience resting on a much elevated terrace ascended by a triple flight of granite stairs, the noble proportions of the building, the richly carved ceiling with its manifold reticulations, painted red, blue, and green, the colossal circular pillars, red with white bases, and in the dimness of the vast area fronting the entrance, the shadowy splendor of the Korean throne. Grand, too, in its simplicity and solidity, is the Summer Palace or "Hall of Congratulations," on a stone platform approached by three granite bridges, in a lotus lake of oblong form beautified conventionally with two stone-faced islands, and by a broad flagged promenade carried the whole way round it on a stone-faced embankment. This palace is a noble building. The upper hall, with its vast sweeping roof, is supported on forty-eight granite pillars 16 feet in height and 3 feet square at the base—all monoliths. The situation and the views are beautiful.

During the next three weeks I had three more audiences, on the second being accompanied as before by Mrs. Underwood, the third being a formal reception, and the fourth a strictly private interview, lasting over an hour. On each occasion I

SUMMER PAVILION, OR "HALL OF CONGRATULATIONS."

was impressed with the grace and charming manner of the Queen, her thoughtful kindness, her singular intelligence and force, and her remarkable conversational power even through the medium of an interpreter. I was not surprised at her singular political influence, or her sway over the King and many others. She was surrounded by enemies, chief among them being the Tai-Won-Kun, the King's father, all embittered against her because by her talent and force she had succeeded in placing members of her family in nearly all the chief offices of State. Her life was a battle. She fought with all her charm, shrewdness, and sagacity for power, for the dignity and safety of her husband and son, and for the downfall of the Tai-Won-Kun. She had cut short many lives, but in doing so she had not violated Korean tradition and custom, and some excuse for her lies in the fact that soon after the King's accession his father sent to the house of Her Majesty's brother an infernal machine in the shape of a beautiful box, which on being opened exploded, killing her mother, brother, and nephew, as well as some others. Since then he plotted against her own life, and the feud between them was usually at fever heat.

The dynasty is worn out, and the King, with all his amiability and kindness of heart, is weak in character and is at the mercy of designing men, as has appeared increasingly since the strong sway of the Queen was withdrawn. I believe him to be at heart, according to his lights, a patriotic sovereign. Far from standing in the way of reform, he has accepted most of the suggestions offered to him. But unfortunately for a man whose edicts become the law of the land, and more unfortunately for the land, he is persuadable by the last person who gets his ear, he lacks backbone and tenacity of purpose, and many of the best projects of reform become abortive through his weakness of will. To substitute constitutional restraints for absolutism would greatly mend matters, but *cela va sans dire* this could only be successful under foreign initiative.

The King was forty-three, the Queen a little older. During

his minority, and while he was receiving the usual Chinese education, his father, the Tai-Won-Kun, who is described by a Korean writer as having " bowels of iron and a heart of stone," ruled as Regent with excessive vigor for ten years, and in 1866 put 2,000 Korean Catholics slaughtered. Able, rapacious, and unscrupulous, his footsteps have always been blood-stained. He even put to death one of his own sons. From the time when his Regency ceased until the murder of the Queen, Korean political history is mainly the story of the deadly feud between the Queen and her clan and the Tai-Won-Kun. I was presented to him at the Palace, and was much impressed by the vitality and energy of his expression, his keen glance, and the vigor of his movements, though he is an old man.

The King's expression is gentle. He has a wonderful memory, and is said to know Korean history so well that when any question as to fact or former custom arises he can give full particulars, with a precise reference to the reign in which any historic event occurred and to the date. The office of Royal Reader is not a sinecure, and the Royal Library, which is contained in one of the most beautiful buildings of the Kyeng-pok Palace, is a very extensive one in Chinese literature. He has no anti-foreign feeling. His friendliness to foreigners is marked, and in his manifold perils he has frankly relied upon their aid. At the time of my second visit, when Japan was in the ascendant, the King and Queen showed special attention and kindness to Europeans, and even invited the whole foreign community to a skating party on the lake. The King's attitude towards Christian Missions is very friendly, and toleration is a reality. The American medical attendants of both the King and Queen, as well as other foreigners, with whom they were in constant contact, were warmly attached to them, and I think that the general feeling among Koreans is one of affectionate loyalty, the blame for oppressive and mistaken actions being laid on the ministers.

ROYAL LIBRARY, KYENG-POK PALACE.

I have dwelt so long on the King's personality because he is *de facto* the Korean Government, and not a mere figure-head, as there is no constitution, written or unwritten, no representative assembly, and it may be said no law except his published Edicts.   He is extremely industrious as a ruler, acquaints himself with all the work of departments, receives and attends to an infinity of reports and memorials, and concerns himself with all that is done in the name of Government.   It is often said that in close attention to detail he undertakes more than any one man could perform.   At the same time he has not the capacity for getting a general grip of affairs.   He has so much goodness of heart and so much sympathy with progressive ideas, that if he had more force of character and intellect, and were less easily swayed by unworthy men, he might make a good sovereign, but his weakness of character is fatal.

The subjects of conversation introduced at three of my audiences not only showed an intelligent desire for such information as might be serviceable, but reflected the reforms which the Japanese were pressing on the King.   I was very closely questioned as to what I had seen of China and Siberia, as to the Siberian and Japanese railroads, cost of construction per *li*, as to the popular feeling in Japan concerning the war, etc. Again I was catechised as to the avenues to official employment in England, the possibility of men "not of the noble class" reaching high positions in the Government, the position of the English nobility with regard to "privileges," and their attitude to inferiors.   On one day the whole attention of the King and Queen was concentrated on the relations between the English Crown and the Cabinet, specially with regard to the Civil List, on which the King's questions were so numerous and persistent as very nearly to pose me.   He was specially anxious to know if the "Finance Minister" (the Chancellor of the Exchequer, I suppose) exercised any control over the personal expenditure of Her Majesty, and if the Queen's personal accounts were paid by herself or through the Treasury. The affairs under the control of each Secretary of State were the subject of another series of questions.

Many queries were about the duties of the Home Minister, the position of the Premier, and his relations with the other Ministers and the Crown. He was very anxious to know if the Queen could dismiss her Ministers if they failed to carry out her wishes, and it was impossible to explain to him through an interpreter, to whom the ideas were unfamiliar, the constitutional checks on the English Crown, and that the sovereign only nominally possesses the right of choosing her Ministers.

Just before I left Korea, I was summoned to a farewell audience, and asked to take the Legation interpreter with me. I went in an eight-bearer chair, and was received with the usual honors, soldiers presenting arms, etc ! There was no crowd of attendants and no delay. As I was being escorted down a closed veranda by several eunuchs and military officers, a sliding window was opened by the King, who beckoned to me to enter, and then closed it. I found myself in the raised alcove in which the Royal Family usually sat, but the sliding panels between it and the audience-chamber were closed, and as it is not more than 6 feet wide, it was impossible to make the customary profound curtseys. Instead of the usual throng of attendants, eunuchs, ladies-in-waiting in silk gowns a yard too long for them, and heavy coils and pillows of artificial hair on their heads, and privileged persons standing behind the King and Queen and crowding the many doorways, there were present only the Queen's nurse and my interpreter, who stood at a chink between the panels where he could not see the Queen, bent into an attitude of abject reverence, never lifting his eyes from the ground or raising his voice above a whisper. The precautions, however, failed to secure the privacy which the King and Queen desired. I was certain that through the chink I saw the shadow of a man in the audience-room, and the interpreter's subsequent remark, "It was very hard for me to interpret for His Majesty to-day" was intelligible when I heard that the "shadow" belonged to one of the Ministers of State specially distrusted by the King, and who later had to fly from Korea. It was understood that this person carried the substance of what the King and Queen said to a foreign legation.

I cannot here allude to the matter on which the King spoke, but the audience, which lasted for an hour, was an extremely interesting one. On one point the King expressed himself very strongly, as he has done to many others. He considers that now that Korea is formally independent of China, she is entitled to a Resident Minister accredited solely to the Korean Court. He expressed great regard and esteem for Mr. Hillier, and said that nothing would be more acceptable to him than his appointment as the first Minister to Korea.

The Queen spoke of Queen Victoria, and said, "She has everything that she can wish—greatness, wealth, and power. Her sons and grandsons are kings and emperors, and her daughters empresses. Does she ever in her glory think of poor Korea? She does so much good in the world, her life is a good. We wish her long life and prosperity"; to which the King added, "England is our best friend." It was really touching to hear the occupants of that ancient but shaky throne speaking in this fashion.

On this occasion the Queen was dressed in a bodice of brocaded amber satin, a mazarine blue brocaded trained skirt, a crimson girdle with five clasps and tassels of coral, and a coral clasp at the throat. Her head was uncovered, and her abundant black hair gathered into a knot at the back. She wore no ornament except a pearl and coral jewel on the top of the head. The King and Queen rose when I took leave, and the Queen shook hands. They both spoke most kindly, and expressed the wish that I should return and see more of Korea. When I did return nine months later, the Queen had been barbarously murdered, and the King was practically a prisoner in his own palace.

Travellers received by the Korean King have often ridiculed the audience, the surroundings, and the Palace. I must say that I saw nothing to ridicule, unless national customs and etiquette varying from our own are necessarily ridiculous. On the contrary, there were a simplicity, dignity, kindliness, courtesy, and propriety which have left a very agreeable impression on me, and my four audiences at Palace were the great feature of my second visit to Korea.

KOREAN GENTLEMAN IN COURT DRESS.

CHAPTER XXII

A TRANSITION STAGE

DURING January, 1895, Seoul was in a curious condition. The "old order" was changing, but the new had not taken its place. The Japanese, victorious by land and sea, were in a position to enforce the reforms in which before the war they had asked China to coöperate. The King, since the capture of the Palace by the Japanese in July, 1894, had become little more than a "salaried automaton," and the once powerful members of the Min clan had been expelled from their offices. The Japanese were prepared to accept the responsibility of the supervision of all departments, and to . enforce honesty on a corrupt executive. The victory over the Chinese at Phyöng-yang on 17th September, 1894, had set them free to carry out their purposes. Count Inouye, one of the foremost of the statesmen who created the new Japan, arrived as "Resident" on October 20, 1894, and practically administered the Government in the King's name. There were Japanese controllers in all the departments, the army was drilled by Japanese drill instructors, a police force was organized and clothed in badly fitting Japanese uniforms, a Council of Koreans was appointed to draft a scheme of reform, and form the nucleus of a possible Korean Parliament, and Count Inouye as Japanese adviser had the right of continual access to the King, and with an interpreter and stenographer sat at the meetings of the Cabinet. Every day Japanese ascendency was apparent in new appointments, regulations, abolitions, and reforms. The Japanese claimed that their purpose was to reform the administration of Korea as we had done that of Egypt, and I believe they would have done it had they been allowed a free hand. It was apparent, however, that Count Inouye found the task of reformation a far harder one than he expected, and that the difficulties in his way were nearly insurmountable. He said himself that there were " no tools to work with," and in the hope of manufacturing them a large number of youths of the upper class were sent for two years to Japan, one year to be spent in education and another in learning accuracy and " the first principles of honor " in certain Government departments.

Sundry Japanese demands, though conceded at the time by the King, had been allowed to drop, and it was not till December, 1894, that Count Inouye obtained a formal covenant that five of them should be at once carried out. (1) A full pardon for all the conspirators of 1884 ; (2) That the Tai-Won-Kun and the Queen should interfere no more in public affairs ; (3) That no relatives of the Royal Family should be employed in any official capacity ; (4) That the number of eunuchs and " Palace ladies " should at once be reduced to a minimum ; (5) That caste distinctions—patrician and plebeian —should no longer be recognized.

Edicts on some of the foregoing subjects appeared in the *Gazette*, and large numbers of the eunuchs packed up their clothes and left the Palace quietly in the night, along with the " Palace ladies " ; but the King in his vast dwelling was so lonely without them that the next morning he sent an order commanding their immediate return under serious penalties, and it was obeyed at once !

The attitude of the Korean official class, with the exception of a small number who were personally interested in the success of Japan, was altogether unfavorable to the new *régime*, and every change was regarded with indignation. Though destitute of true patriotism, the common people looked upon the King as a sacred person, and they were furious at the indignities to which he had been subjected. The official class saw that reform meant the end of "squeezing" and ill-gotten gains, and they, with the whole army of parasites and hangers-on of *yamens*, were all pledged by the strongest personal interest to oppose it by active opposition or passive resistance. Though corruption has its stronghold in Seoul, every provincial government repeats on a smaller scale the iniquities of the capital, and has its own army of dishonest and lazy officials fattening on the earnings of the industrious classes.

The cleansing of the Augean stable of the Korean official system, which the Japanese had undertaken, was indeed an Herculean labor. Traditions of honor and honesty, if they ever existed, had been forgotten for centuries. Standards of official rectitude were unknown. In Korea when the Japanese undertook the work of reform there were but two classes, the robbers and the robbed, and the robbers included the vast army which constituted officialdom. "Squeezing" and peculation were the rule from the highest to the lowest, and every position was bought and sold.

The transition stage, down to 12th February, 1895, when I left Korea, was a remarkable one. The *Official Gazette* curiously reflected that singular period. One day a decree abolished the 3 feet long tobacco pipes which were the delight of the Koreans of the capital; another, there was an enlightened statute ordering the planting of pines to remedy the denudation of the hills around Seoul, the same *Gazette* directing that duly appointed geomancers should find "an auspicious day" on which the King might worship at the ancestral tablets! One day barbarous and brutalizing punishments were wisely abolished; another, there appeared a string of vexatious and petty regulations calculated to harass the Chinese out of the kingdom, and appointing as a punishment for the breach of them a fine of 100 dollars or 100 blows!

Failure in tact was one great fault of the Japanese. The seizure of the Palace and the King's person in July, 1894, even if a dubious political necessity, did not excuse the indignities to which the sovereign was exposed. The forcing of former conspirators into high office was a grave error, and tactless proceedings, such as the abolition of long pipes, alterations in Court and other dress, many interferences with social customs, and petty and harassing restrictions and regulations, embittered the people against the new *régime*.

The Tong-haks, who had respectfully thrown off allegiance to the King on the ground that he was in the hands of foreigners, and had appointed another sovereign, had been vanquished early in January, and their king's head had been sent to Seoul by a loyal governor. There I saw it in the busiest part of the Peking Road, a bustling market outside the "little West Gate," hanging from a rude arrangement of three sticks like a camp-kettle stand, with another head below it. Both faces wore a calm, almost dignified, expression. Not far off two more heads had been exposed in a similar frame, but it had given way, and they lay in the dust of the roadway, much gnawed by dogs at the back. The last agony was stiffened on their features. A turnip lay beside them, and some small children cut pieces from it and presented them mockingly to the blackened mouths. This brutalizing spectacle had existed for a week.

Three days later, in the stillness of the Korean New Year's Day, I rode with a friend along a lonely road passing through a fair agricultural valley among pine-clothed knolls outside the South and East Gates of Seoul. Snow lay on the ground and the grim sky threatened a further storm. It was cold, and we observed with surprise three coolies in summer cotton clothing lying by the roadside asleep; but it was the last sleep, for on approaching them we found that, though their attitudes were those of easy repose, the bodies were without heads, nor had the headsman's axe been merciful or sharp. In the middle of the road were great, frozen, crimson splashes where the Tong-hak leaders had expiated their treason, criminals in Korea, as in old Jerusalem, suffering "without the gate."

A few days later an order appeared in the *Gazette* abolishing beheading and "slicing to death," and substituting death by strangulation for civil, and by shooting for military capital crimes. This order practically made an end of the prerogative of life and death heretofore possessed by the Korean sovereigns.

So the "old order" was daily changing under the pressure of the Japanese advisers, and on the whole changing most decidedly for the better, though, owing to the number of reforms decreed and in contemplation, everything was in a tentative and chaotic state. Korea was "swithering" between China and Japan, afraid to go in heartily for the reforms initiated by Japan lest China should regain position and be "down" upon her, and afraid to oppose them actively lest Japan should be permanently successful.

On that same New Year's Day there was more to be seen than headless trunks. Through the length of Seoul, towards twilight, an odor of burning hair overpowered the aromatic scent of the pine brush, and all down every street, outside every door, there were red glimmers of light. It is the custom in every family on that day to carry out the carefully preserved clippings and combings of the family hair and burn them in potsherds, a practice which it is hoped will prevent the entrance of certain dæmons into the house during the year. Rude straw dolls stuffed with a few *cash* were also thrown into the street. This effigy is believed to take away troubles and foist them on whoever picks it up. To prevent such a vicarious calamity, more than one mother on that evening pounced upon a child who childlike had picked up the doll and threw it far from him.

On that night round pieces of red or white paper placed in cleft sticks are put upon the roofs of houses, and those persons who have been warned by the sorcerers of troubles to come, pray (?) to the moon to remove them.

A common Korean custom on the same day is for people to paint images on paper, and to write against them their troubles of body or mind, afterwards giving the paper to a boy who burns it.

A more singular New Year custom in Seoul is "Walking the Bridges." Up to midnight, men, women, and children cross a bridge or bridges as many times as they are years old. This is believed to prevent pains in the feet and legs during the year.

This day, the "Great Fifteenth Day," concludes the kite-flying and stone fights which enliven Seoul for the previous fortnight, and every Korean insists on keeping it as a holiday. Graves are formally visited, and gathered families spread food before the ancestral tablets. Curious customs prevail at this time. A few days before, the Palace eunuchs chant invocations, swinging burning torches as they do so. This is supposed to ensure bountiful crops for the next season. People buy quantities of nuts, which they crack, hold the kernels in the mouth, and then throw them away. This is to prevent summer sores and boils. Also on the Great Fifteenth Day men try to find out the probable rainfall for each month by splitting a small piece of bamboo, and laying twelve beans side by side in one of the halves, after which it is closed, and after being bound tightly with cord, is lowered into a well for the night. Each bean represents a month. In the morning, when they are examined in rotation, they are variously enlarged, and the enlargement indicates the proportion of rain in that special moon. If, on the contrary, one or more are wizened, it causes great alarm, as indicating complete or partial drought in one or more months. Dogs do not get their usual meal on the morning of the "Great Fifteenth," in the belief that the deprivation will keep them from being pestered with flies during the long summer.

If a boy has been born during the year, poles bearing paper fish by day and lanterns by night project from the house of the parents. The people at night watch the burning of candles. If they are entirely burned, the life of the child will be long; if only partially burned, it will be proportionately shorter.

I left Seoul very regretfully on 5th February. The Japanese had introduced *jinrikshas*, but the runners were unskilled, and I met with so severe an accident in going down to Chemulpo that I did not recover for a year. The line of steamers to Japan was totally disorganized by the war, and in the week that I waited for the *Higo Maru* war was uppermost in people's thoughts. There were some who even then could not bring themselves to believe in the eventual success of the Japanese. The fall of Wei-hai-wei and the capture of the Chinese fleet opened many eyes. I was in the office of the "N.Y.K." when the news came, and the clerks were too wild with excitement to attend to me, apologizing by saying, "It's another victory!" Chemulpo was decorated, illuminated, and processioned for victories, Li Hung Chang was burned in effigy, and unlimited *sake* for all comers was supplied from tubs at the street corners.

There were indications of the cost of victory, however. The great military hospitals were full, the cemetery was filling fast, military funerals with military pomp and Shinto priests passed down the bannered street, and 600 transport coolies tramping from Manchuria arrived in rags and tatters, some clothed in raw hides and raw skins of sheep, their feet, hands, and lips frost-bitten, and with blackened stumps of fingers and toes protruding from filthy bandages. The Japanese schools teach that Japan has a right to demand all that a man has, and that life itself is not too costly a sacrifice for him to lay on the altar of his country. Undoubtedly the teaching bears fruit. Not long before at Osaka I saw the wharves piled high with voluntary contributions for the troops, and the Third Army leave the city amidst an outburst of popular enthusiasm such as I never saw equalled. Most of these coolies, when they received new clothing, volunteered for further service, and dying soldiers on battlefields and in hospitals uttered "*Dai Nippon Banzai!*" (Great Japan forever!) with their last faltering breath.

When I left Korea the condition of things may be summarized thus.   Japan was thoroughly in earnest as to reforming the Korean administration through Koreans, and very
many reforms were decreed or in contemplation, while some
evils and abuses were already swept away.   The King, deprived of his absolute sovereignty, was practically a salaried
registrar of decrees.   Count Inouye occupied the position of
"Resident," and the Government was administered in the
King's name by a Cabinet consisting of the heads of ten departments, in some measure the nominees of the "Resident."[1]

[1] I repeat this statement in this form for the benefit of the reader, and
ask him to compare it with a summary of Korean affairs early in 1897,
given in the 36th chapter of this volume.

PLACE OF THE QUEEN'S CREMATION.

CHAPTER XXIII

THE ASSASSINATION OF THE QUEEN

IN May, 1895, a treaty of peace between China and Japan was signed at Shimonoseki, a heavy indemnity, the island of Formosa, and a great accession of prestige, being the gains of Japan. From thenceforward no power having interests in the Far East could afford to regard her as a *quantité négligéable*.

After travelling for some months in South and Mid China, and spending the summer in Japan, I arrived in Nagasaki in October, 1895, to hear a rumor of the assassination of the Korean Queen, afterwards confirmed on board the *Suruga Maru* by Mr. Sill, the American Minister, who was hurrying back to his post in Seoul in consequence of the disturbed state of affairs. I went up immediately from Chemulpo to the capital, where I was Mr. Hillier's guest at the English Legation for two exciting months.

The native and foreign communities were naturally much excited by the tragedy at the Palace, and the treatment which the King was receiving. Count Inouye, whose presence in Seoul always produced confidence, had left a month before, and had been succeeded by General Viscount Miura, a capable soldier, without diplomatic experience.

In an interview which Count Inouye had with the Queen shortly before his departure, speaking of the ascendency of the Tai-Won-Kun, after the capture of the Palace by Mr. Otori in the previous July, Her Majesty said, " It is a matter of regret to me that the overtures made by me towards Japan were rejected. The Tai-Won-Kun, on the other hand, who showed his unfriendliness towards Japan, was assisted by the Japanese Minister to rise in power."

In the despatch in which Count Inouye reported this interview to his Government he wrote :—

I gave as far as I could an explanation of these things to the Queen, and after so allaying her suspicions, I further explained that it was the true and sincere desire of the Emperor and Government of Japan to place the independence of Korea on a firm basis, and in the meantime to strengthen the Royal House of Korea. *In the event of any member of the Royal Family, or indeed any Korean, therefore attempting treason against the Royal House, I gave the assurance that the Japanese Government would not fail to protect the Royal House even by force of arms, and so secure the safety of the kingdom.* These remarks of mine seemed to have moved the King and Queen, and their anxiety for the future appeared to be much relieved.

The Korean sovereigns would naturally think themselves justified in relying on the promise so frankly given by one of the most distinguished of Japanese statesmen, whom they had learned to regard with confidence and respect, and it is clear to myself that when the fateful night came, a month later, their reliance on this assurance led them to omit certain possible precautions, and caused the Queen to neglect to make her escape at the first hint of danger.

When the well-known arrangement between Viscount Miura and the Tai-Won-Kun was ripe for execution, the Japanese Minister directed the Commandant of the Japanese battalion quartered in the barracks just outside the Palace gate to facilitate the Tai-Won-Kun's entry into the Palace by arranging the disposition of the *Kun-ren-tai* (Korean troops drilled by Japanese), and by calling out the Imperial force to support them. Miura also called upon two Japanese to collect their friends, go to Riong San on the Han, where the intriguing Prince was then living, and act as his bodyguard on his journey to the Palace. The Minister told them that on the success of the enterprise depended the eradication of the evils which had afflicted the kingdom for twenty years, and INSTI-GATED THEM TO DISPATCH THE QUEEN WHEN THEY ENTERED THE PALACE. One of Miura's agents then ordered the Japanese policemen who were off duty to put on civilian dress, provide themselves with swords, and accompany the conspirators to the Tai-Won-Kun's house.

At 3 A.M. on the morning of the 8th of October they left Riong San, escorting the Prince's palanquin, Mr. Okamoto, to whom much had been entrusted, assembling the whole party when on the point of departure, and declaring to them that on entering the Palace the "Fox" should be dealt with according "as exigency might require." Then this procession, including ten Japanese who had dressed themselves in uniforms taken from ten captured Korean police, started for Seoul, more than three miles distant. Outside the "Gate of Staunch Loyalty" they were met by the *Kun-ren-tai*, and then waited for the arrival of the Japanese troops, after which they proceeded at a rapid pace to the Palace, entering it by the front gate, and after killing some of the Palace Guard, proceeded a quarter of a mile to the buildings occupied by the King and Queen, which have a narrow courtyard in front.

So far I have followed the Hiroshima judgment in its statement of the facts of that morning, but when it has conducted the combined force to "the inner chambers" it concludes abruptly with a "not proven" in the case of all the accused! For the rest of the story, so far as it may interest my readers, I follow the statements of General Dye and Mr. Sabatin of the King's Guard, and of certain official documents.

It is necessary here to go back upon various events which preceded the murder of Her Majesty. Trouble arose in October between the *Kun-ren-tai* and the Seoul police, resulting in the total defeat of the latter. The *Kun-ren-tai*, numbering 1,000, were commanded by Colonel Hong, who in 1882 had rescued the Queen from imminent danger, and was trusted by the Royal Family. The Palace was in the hands of the Old

Guard under Colonel Hyön, who had saved Her Majesty's life in 1884. In the first week of October the strength of this Guard was greatly reduced, useful weapons were quietly withdrawn, and the ammunition was removed.

On the night of the 7th the *Kun-ren-tai*, with their Japanese instructors, marched and countermarched till they were found on all sides of the Palace, causing some uneasiness within. The alarm was given to General Dye and Mr. Sabatin early on the morning of the 8th.[1] These officers, looking through a chink of the gate, saw a number of Japanese soldiers with fixed bayonets standing there, who, on being asked what they were doing, filed right and left out of the moonlight under the shadow of the wall. Skulking under another part of the wall were over 200 of the *Kun-ren-tai*. The two foreigners were consulting as to the steps to be taken when heavy sounds of battering came from the grand entrance gate, followed by firing.

General Dye attempted to rally the Guard, but after five or six volleys from the assailants they broke with such a rush as to sweep the two foreigners past the King's house to the gateway of the Queen's. No clear account has ever been given of the events which followed. Colonel Hong, the commander of the *Kun-ren-tai*, was cut down by a Japanese officer at the great gate, and was afterwards mortally wounded by eight bullets. The *Kun-ren-tai* swarmed into the Palace from all directions, along with Japanese civilians armed with swords, who frantically demanded the whereabouts of the Queen, hauling the Palace ladies about by the hair to compel them to point out Her Majesty, rushing in and out of windows, throwing the ladies-in-waiting from the 7 feet high veranda into the compound, cutting and kicking them, and brutally murdering four in the hope that they had thus secured their victim.

[1] General Dye, late of the U. S. army, was instructor of the Old Guard. Mr. Sabatin, a Russian subject, was temporarily employed as a watchman to see that the sentries were at their posts.

Japanese troops also entered the Palace, and formed in military order under the command of their officers round the small courtyard of the King's house and at its gate, protecting the assassins in their murderous work. Before this force of Japanese regulars arrived there was a flying rout of servants, runners, and Palace Guards rushing from every point of the vast enclosure in mad haste to get out of the gates. As the Japanese entered the building, the unfortunate King, hoping to divert their attention and give the Queen time to escape, came into a front room where he could be distinctly seen. Some of the Japanese assassins rushed in brandishing their swords, pulled His Majesty about, and beat and dragged about some of the Palace ladies by the hair in his presence. The Crown Prince, who was in an inner room, was seized, his hat torn off and broken, and he was pulled about by the hair and threatened with swords to make him show the way to the Queen, but he managed to reach the King, and they have never been separated since.

The whole affair did not occupy much more than an hour. The Crown Prince saw his mother rush down a passage followed by a Japanese with a sword, and there was a general rush of assassins for her sleeping apartments. In the upper story the Crown Princess was found with several ladies, and she was dragged by the hair, cut with a sword, beaten, and thrown downstairs. Yi Kyöng-jik, Minister of the Royal Household, seems to have given the alarm, for the Queen was dressed and was preparing to run and hide herself. When the murderers rushed in, he stood with outstretched arms in front of Her Majesty, trying to protect her, furnishing them with the clue they wanted. They slashed off both his hands and inflicted other wounds, but he contrived to drag himself along the veranda into the King's presence, where he bled to death.

The Queen, flying from the assassins, was overtaken and stabbed, falling down as if dead, but one account says that, recovering a little, she asked if the Crown Prince, her idol, was safe, on which a Japanese jumped on her breast and stabbed her through and through with his sword. Even then, though the nurse whom I formerly saw in attendance on her covered her face, it is not certain that she was dead, but the Japanese laid her on a plank, wrapped a silk quilt round her, and she was carried to a grove of pines in the adjacent deer park, where kerosene oil was poured over the body, which was surrounded by faggots and burned, only a few small bones escaping destruction.

Thus perished, at the age of forty-four, by the hands of foreign assassins, instigated to their bloody work by the Minister of a friendly power, the clever, ambitious, intriguing, fascinating, and in many respects lovable Queen of Korea. In her lifetime Count Inouye, whose verdict for many reasons may be accepted, said, "Her Majesty has few equals among her countrymen for shrewdness and sagacity. In the art of conciliating her enemies and winning the confidence of her servants she has no equals."

A short time after daylight the Tai-Won-Kun issued two proclamations, of which the following sentences are specimens :—

1st, "The hearts of the people dissolve through the presence in the Palace of a crowd of base fellows. So the National Grand Duke is returned to power to inaugurate changes, expel the base fellows, restore former laws, and vindicate the dignity of His Majesty."

2nd, "I have now entered the Palace to aid His Majesty, expel the low fellows, perfect that which will be a benefit, save the country, and introduce peace."

The Palace gates were guarded by the mutinous *Kun-ren-tai* with fixed bayonets, who allowed a constant stream of Koreans to pass out, the remnants of the Old Palace Guard, who had thrown off their uniforms and hidden their arms, each man being seized and searched before his exit was permitted. Near the gate was a crimson pool marking the spot where Colonel Hong fell. Three of the Ministers were at once dismissed from their posts, some escaped, and many of the high officials sought safety in flight. Nearly every one who was trusted by the King was removed, and several of the chief offices of State were filled by the nominees of the officers of the *Kun-ren-tai*, who, later, when they did not find the Cabinet, which was chiefly of their own creation, sufficiently subservient, used to threaten it with drawn swords.

Viscount Miura arrived at the Palace at daylight, with Mr. Sugimura, Secretary of the Japanese Legation (who had arranged the details of the plot), and a certain Japanese who had been seen by the King apparently leading the assassins, and actively participating in the bloody work, and had an audience of His Majesty, who was profoundly agitated. He signed three documents at their bidding, after which the Japanese troops were withdrawn from the Palace, and the armed forces, and even the King's personal attendants, were placed under the orders of those who had been concerned in attack. The Tai-Won-Kun was present at this audience.

During the day all the Foreign Representatives had audiences of the King, who was much agitated, sobbed at intervals, and, believing the Queen to have escaped, was very solicitous about his own safety, as he was environed by assassins, the most unscrupulous of all being his own father. In violation of custom, he grasped the hands of the Representatives, and asked them to use their friendly offices to prevent further outrage and violence. He was anxious that the *Kun-ren-tai* should be replaced by Japanese troops. On the same afternoon the Foreign Representatives met at the Japanese Legation to hear Viscount Miura's explanation of circumstances in which his countrymen were so seriously implicated.

Three days after the events in the Palace, and while the King and the general public believed the Queen to be alive, a so-called Royal Edict, a more infamous outrage on the Queen even than her brutal assassination, was published in the *Official Gazette*. The King on being asked to sign it refused, and said he would have his hands cut off rather, but it appeared as his decree, and bore the signatures of the Minister of the Household, the Prime Minister, and six other members of the Cabinet.

ROYAL EDICT.

It is now thirty-two years since We ascended the throne, but Our ruling influence has not extended wide. The Queen Min introduced her relatives to the Court and placed them about Our person, whereby she made dull Our senses, exposed the people to extortion, put Our Government in disorder, selling offices and titles. Hence tyranny prevailed all over the country and robbers arose in all quarters. Under these circumstances the foundation of Our dynasty was in imminent peril. We knew the extreme of her wickedness, but could not dismiss and punish her because of helplessness and fear of her party.

We desire to stop and suppress her influence. In the twelfth moon of last year we took an oath at Our Ancestral Shrine that the Queen and her relatives and Ours should never again be allowed to interfere in State affairs. We hoped this would lead the Min faction to mend their ways. But the Queen did not give up her wickedness, but with her party aided a crowd of low fellows to rise up about Us and so managed as to prevent the Ministers of State from consulting Us. Moreover, they have forged Our signature to a decree to disband Our loyal soldiers, thereby instigating and raising a disturbance, and when it occurred she escaped as in the Im O year. We have endeavored to discover her whereabouts, but as she does not come forth and appear We are convinced that she is not only unfitted and unworthy of the Queen's rank, but also that her guilt is excessive and brimful. Therefore with her We may not succeed to the glory of the Royal Ancestry. So We hereby depose her from the rank of Queen and reduce her to the level of the lowest class.

Signed by
       YI CHAI-MYON, Minister of the Royal Household.
       KIM HONG-CHIP, Prime Minister.
       KIM YUN-SIK, Minister of Foreign Affairs.
       PAK CHONG-YANG, Minister of Home Affairs.
       SHIM SANG-HUN, Minister of Finance.
       CHO HEUI-YON, Minister of War.
       SO KWANG-POM, Minister of Justice.
       SO KWANG-POM, Minister of Education.
       CHONG PYONG-HA, Vice-Minister of Agriculture and Commerce.

On the day following the issue of this fraudulent and infamous edict, another appeared in which Her Majesty, out of pity for the Crown Prince and as a reward for his deep devotion to his father, was "raised" by the King to the rank of "Concubine of the First Order"!

The diplomats were harassed and anxious, and met constantly to discuss the situation. Of course the state of extreme tension was not caused solely by "happenings" in Korea and their local consequences. For behind this well-executed plot, and the diabolical murder of a defenceless woman, lay a terrible suspicion, which gained in strength every hour during the first few days after the tragedy till it intensified into a certainty, of which people spoke as in cipher, by hints alone, that other brains than Korean planned the plot, that other than Korean hands took the lives that were taken, that the sentries who guarded the King's apartments while the deed of blood was being perpetrated wore other than Korean uniforms, and that other than Korean bayonets gleamed in the shadow of the Palace wall.

People spoke their suspicions cautiously, though the evidence of General Dye and of Mr. Sabatin pointed unmistakably in one direction. So early as the day after the affair, the question which emerged was, "Is Viscount General Miura criminally implicated or not?" It is needless to go into particulars on this subject. Ten days after the tragedy at the Palace, the Japanese Government, which was soon proved innocent of any complicity in the affair, recalled and arrested Viscount Miura, Sugimura, and Okamoto, Adviser to the Korean War Department, who, some months later, along with forty-five others, were placed on their trial before the Japanese Court of First Instance at Hiroshima, and were acquitted on the technical ground that there was "no sufficient evidence to prove that any of the accused actually committed the crime originally meditated by them," this crime, according to the judgment, being that two of the accused, "AT THE INSTIGATION OF

MIURA, DECIDED TO MURDER THE QUEEN, and took steps by collecting accomplices . . . more than ten others were directed by these two persons to do away with the Queen."

Viscount Miura was replaced by Mr. Komura, an able diplomatist, and shortly afterwards Count Inouye arrived, bearing the condolences of the Emperor of Japan to the unfortunate Korean King. A heavier blow to Japanese prestige and position as the leader of civilization in the East could not have been struck, and the Government continues to deserve our sympathy on the occasion. For when the disavowal is forgotten, it will be always remembered that the murderous plot was arranged in the Japanese Legation, and that of the Japanese dressed as civilians and armed with swords and pistols, who were directly engaged in the outrages committed in the Palace, some were advisers to the Korean Government and in its pay, and others were Japanese policemen connected with the Japanese Legation—sixty persons in all, including those known as *Soshi*, and exclusive of the Japanese troops.

The Foreign Representatives with one exception informed the Cabinet that until steps were taken to bring the assassins to justice, till the *Kun-ren-tai* Guard was removed from the Palace, and till the recently introduced members of the Cabinet who were responsible for the outrages had been arraigned or at least removed from office, they declined to recognize any act of the Government, or to accept as authentic any order issued by it in the King's name. The prudence of this course became apparent later.

On 15th October, in an extra issue of the *Official Gazette*, it was announced "By Royal Command" that, as the position of Queen must not remain vacant for a day, proceedings for the choice of a bride were to begin at once! This was only one among the many insults which were heaped upon the Royal prisoner.

During the remainder of October and November there was no improvement in affairs. The gloom was profound. Instead of Royal receptions and entertainments, the King, shaken by terror and in hourly dread of poison or assassination, was a close prisoner in a poor part of his own palace, in the hands of a Cabinet chiefly composed of men who were the tools of the mutinous soldiers who were practically his jailers, compelled to put his seal to edicts which he loathed, the tool of men on whose hands the blood of his murdered Queen was hardly dry. Nothing could be more pitiable than the condition of the King and Crown Prince, each dreading that the other would be slain before his eyes, not daring to eat of any food prepared in the Palace, dreading to be separated, even for a few minutes, without an adherent whom they could trust, and with recent memories of infinite horror as food for contemplation.

General Dye, the American military adviser, an old and feeble man, slept near the Palace Library, and the American missionaries in twos took it in turns to watch with him. This was the only protection which the unfortunate sovereign possessed. He was also visited daily by the Foreign Representatives in turns, with the double object of ascertaining that he was alive and assuring him of their sympathy and interest. Food was supplied to him in a locked box from the Russian or U. S. Legations, but so closely was he watched, that it was difficult to pass the key into his hand, and a hasty and very occasional whisper was the only communication he could succeed in making to these foreigners, who were his sole reliance. Undoubtedly from the first he hoped to escape either to the English or Russian Legation. At times he sobbed piteously and shook the hands of the foreigners, who made no attempt to conceal the sympathy they felt for the always courteous and kindly sovereign.

Entertainments among the foreigners ceased. The dismay was too profound and the mourning too real to permit even of the mild gaieties of a Seoul winter. Every foreign lady, and specially Mrs. Underwood, Her Majesty's medical attendant, and Mme. Waeber, who had been an intimate friend, felt her death as a personal loss. Her Oriental unscrupulousness in politics was forgotten in the horror excited by the story of her end. Yet then and for some time afterwards people clung to the hope that she had escaped as on a former occasion, and was in hiding. Among Koreans opinion was greatly concealed, for there were innumerable arrests, and no one knew when his turn might come, but it was believed that there was an earnest desire to liberate the King. A number of foreign warships lay at Chemulpo, and the British, Russian, and American Legations were guarded by marines.

Nearly a month after the assassination of the Queen, and when all hope of her escape had been abandoned, the condition of things was so serious under the rule of the new Cabinet, that an attempt was made by the Foreign Representatives to terminate it by urging on Count Inouye to disarm the *Kun-ren-tai*, and occupy the Palace with Japanese troops until the loyal soldiers had been drilled into an efficiency on which the King might rely for his personal safety. It will be seen from this proposal how completely the Japanese Government was exonerated from blame by the diplomatic agents of the Great Powers. This proposal was not received with cordial alacrity by Count Inouye, who felt that the step of an armed reoccupation of the Palace by the Japanese, though with the object of securing the King's safety, would be liable to serious misconstruction, and might bring about very grave complications. Such an idea was only to be entertained if Japan received a distinct mandate from the Powers. The telegraph was set to work, a due amount of consent to the arrangement was obtained, and when I left Seoul on a northern journey on November 7th, it was in the full belief that on reaching Phyöng-yang I should find a telegram announcing that this serious *coup d'état* had been successfully accomplished in the presence of the Foreign Representatives. Japan, however, did not undertake the task, though urged to do so both by Count Inouye and Mr. Komura, the new Representative, and the *Kun-ren-tai* remained in power, and the King a prisoner. Had the recommendation of the Foreign Representatives, among whom the Russian Representatives was the most emphatic in urging the interference of Japan, been adopted, it is more than probable that the present predominance of Russian influence in Korea would have been avoided. It is only fair to the Russian Government to state that it gave a distinct mandate to the Japanese to disarm the *Kun-ren-tai* and take charge of the King. The Japanese Government declined, and therefore is alone responsible for Russia's subsequent intervention.

During November the dissatisfaction throughout Korea with the measures which were taken and proposed increased, and the position became so strained, owing to the demand of the Foreign Representatives and of all classes of Koreans that the occurrences of the 8th of October must be investigated, and that the fiction of the Queen being in hiding should be abandoned, that the Cabinet unwillingly recognized that something must be done. So on 26th November the Foreign Representatives were invited by the King to the Palace, and the Prime Minister, in presence of His Majesty, who was profoundly agitated, produced a decree bearing the King's signature, dismissing the special nominees of the mutineers, the Ministers of War and Police, declaring that the so-called Edict degrading the Queen was set aside and treated as void from the beginning, and that she was reinstated in her former honors ; that the occurrences of the 8th October were to be investigated by the Department of Justice, and that the guilty persons were to be tried and punished. The death of Her Majesty was announced at the same time.

At the conclusion of this audience, Mr. Sill, the United States Minister, expressed to the King " his profound satisfac-with the announcement." Mr. Hillier followed by " congratulating His Majesty on these satisfactory steps, and hoped it would be the beginning of a time of peace and tranquillity,

and relieve His Majesty from much anxiety." These good
wishes were cordially endorsed by his colleagues.

The measures proposed by the King to reassert his lost
authority and punish the conspirators promised very well, but
were rendered abortive by a "loyal plot," which was formed
by the Old Palace Guard and a number of Koreans, some of
them by no means insignificant men. It had for its object
the liberation of the sovereign and the substitution of loyal
troops for the *Kun-ren-tai*. Though it ended in a fiasco two
nights after this hopeful interview, its execution having been
frustrated by premature disclosures, its results were disastrous,
for it involved a number of prominent men, created grave suspicions, raised up a feeling of antagonism to foreigners, some
of whom (American missionaries) were believed to be cogni-
zant of the plot, if not actually accessories, and brought about
a general confusion, from which, when I left Korea five weeks
later, there was no prospect of escape. The King was a closer
prisoner than ever; those surrounding him grew familiar and
insolent; he lived in dread of assassination; and he had no
more intercourse with foreigners, except with those who had an
official right to enter the Palace, which they became increasingly unwilling to exercise.

It was with much regret that I left Seoul for a journey in the
interior at this most exciting time, when every day brought
fresh events and rumors, and a *coup d'état* of great importance was believed to be impending; but I had very little
time at my disposal before proceeding to Western China on a
long-planned journey.

CHAPTER XXIV

AFTER the interpreter difficulty had appeared as before insurmountable, I was provided with one who acquitted himself to perfection, and through whose good offices I came much nearer to the people than if I had been accompanied by a foreigner. He spoke English remarkably well, was always bright, courteous, intelligent, and good-natured; he had a keen sense of the ludicrous, and I owe much of the pleasure, as well as the interest, of my journey to his companionship. Mr. Hillier equipped me with Im, a soldier of the Legation Guard, as my servant. He had attended me on photographing expeditions on a former visit, and on the journey I found him capable, faithful, quick, and full of "go,"—so valuable and efficient, indeed, as to "take the shine" out of any subsequent attendant. With these, a passport, and a *kwan-ja* or letter from the Korean Foreign Office commending me to official help (never used), my journey was made under the best possible auspices.

The day before I left was spent in making acquaintance with Mr. Yi Hak In, receiving farewell visits from many kind and helpful friends, looking over the backs and tackle of the ponies I had engaged for the journey, and in arranging a photographic outfit. Im was taught to make curry, an accomplishment in which he soon excelled, and I had no other cooking done on the journey. For the benefit of future travellers I will mention that my equipment consisted of a camp-bed and bedding, candles, a large, strong, doubly oiled sheet, a folding chair, a kettle, two pots, a cup and two plates of enamelled iron, some tea which turned out musty, some flour, curry powder, and a tin of Edward's "dessicated soup," which came back unopened ! To the oft-repeated question, " Did you eat Korean food ? " I reply certainly—pheasants, fowls, potatoes, and eggs. Warm winter clothing, a Japanese *kurumaya's* hat (the best of all travelling hats), and Korean string shoes completed my outfit, and I never needed anything I had not got !

The start on 7th November was managed in good time, without any of the usual delays, and I may say at once that the *mapu*, the bugbear and torment of travellers usually, never gave the slightest trouble. Though engaged by the day, they were ready to make long day's journeys, were always willing and helpful, and a month later we parted excellent friends. As this is my second favorable experience, I am inclined to think that Korean *mapu* are a maligned class. For each pony and man, the food of both being included, I paid $1, about 2s., per day when travelling, and half that sum when halting. Mr. Yi had two ponies, I two baggage animals, on one of which Im rode, and a saddle pony, *i.e.* a pack pony equipped with my sidesaddle for the occasion.

Starting from the English Legation and the Customs' buildings, we left the city by the West Gate, and passing the stone stumps which up till lately supported the carved and colored roof under which generations of Korean kings after their accession met the Chinese envoys, who came in great state to invest them with Korean sovereignty, and through the narrow and rugged defile known as the Peking Pass, we left the unique capital and its lofty clambering wall out of sight. The day was splendid even for a Korean autumn, and the frightful black pinnacles, serrated ridges, and flaming corrugations of Puk Han on the right of the road were atmospherically idealized into perfect beauty. For several miles the road was thronged with bulls loaded with faggots, rice, and pine brush, for the supply of the daily necessities of the city ; then, except when passing through the villages, it became solitary enough, except for an occasional group of long-sworded Japanese travellers, or baggage ponies in charge of Japanese soldiers.

The road as far as Pa Ju lies through pretty country, small valleys either terraced for rice, which was lying out to dry on the dykes, or growing barley, wheat, millet, and cotton, surrounded by low but shapely hills, denuded of everything but oak and pine scrub, but with folds in which the *Pinus sinensis* grew in dark clumps, lighted up by the vanishing scarlet of the maple and the glowing crimson of the *Ampelopsis Veitchii*.

On the lower slopes, and usually in close proximity to the timber, are numerous villages, their groups of deep-eaved, brown-thatched roofs, on which scarlet capsicums were laid out to dry, looking pretty enough as adjuncts to landscapes which on the whole lack life and emphasis. The villages through which the road passes were seen at their best, for the roadway, serving for the village threshing floor, was daily swept for the threshing of rice and millet, the passage of travellers being a secondary consideration; everything was dry, and the white clothes of the people were consequently at their cleanliest.

At noon we reached Ko-yang, a poor place of 300 hovels, with ruinous official buildings of some size, once handsome. At this, and every other magistracy up to Phyöng-yang, from 20 to 30 Japanese soldiers were quartered in the *yamens*. The people hated them with a hatred which is the legacy of three centuries, but could not allege anything against them, admitting that they paid for all they got, molested no one, and were seldom seen outside the *yamen* gates. There the *mapu* halted for two hours to give their ponies and themselves a feed. This midday halt is one bone of contention between travellers and themselves. No amount of hunting and worrying them shortens the halt by more than ten minutes, and I preferred peace of spirit, only insisting that when the road admitted of it, as it frequently did, they should travel 12 *li*, or about three and three-quarter miles, an hour. At Ko-yang I began the custom of giving the landlord of the inn at which I halted 100 *cash* for the room in which I rested, which gave great satisfaction. I had my mattress laid upon the hot floor, and as Im, by instinct, secured privacy for me by fastening up mats and curtains over the paper walls and doors, these midday halts were very pleasant. Almost every house in these roadside villages and small towns has a low table of such food as Koreans love laid out under the eaves.

Beyond Ko-yang, standing out in endless solemnity above a pine wood on the side of a steep hill, are two of the strangely few antiquities of which Korea can boast. These are two *mirioks*, colossal busts, about 35 feet in height, carved out of the solid rock. They are supposed to be relics of the very early days of Korean Buddhism, when men were religious enough to toil at such stupendous works, and to represent the male and female elements in nature. They are side by side. One wears a round and the other a square hat. The Buddhistic calm, or rather I should say apathy, rests on their huge faces, which have looked stolidly on many a change in Korea, but on none greater than the last year had witnessed.

During the day we saw three funerals, and I observed that a Japanese detachment which occupied the whole road filed to the right and left to let one of the processions pass, the men raising their caps to the corpse as they did so. These funerals gave an impression of gaiety rather than grief. Two men walked first, carrying silk bannerets which designated the woman about to be interred as the wife of so and so, a married woman having no name. Next came a man walking backwards with many streamers of colored ribbon floating from his hat, ringing a large bell, and accompanying its clang with a dissonance supposed to be singing. The coffin, under a four-posted domed cover and concealed by gay curtains, was borne on a platform by twelve men, and was followed by a large party of male mourners, a man with a musical instrument, a table, and a box of food. None of the faces were composed to a look of grief. On the dome were two mythical birds resembling the phœnix. The dome and curtains were brilliantly colored, and decorated with ribbon streamers. Two corpses, each extended on a board and covered with white paper pasted over small hoops, lay in the roadway at different places. These were bodies of persons who had died far from home and were being conveyed to their friends for burial. Later we met another funeral, the corpse carried as before on a platform by twelve bearers, who moved to a rhythmic chant of the most cheerful description, the whole party being as jolly as if they were going to a marriage. There was a cross in front of the gay hearse with an extended dragon on each arm, and four large gaily painted birds resembling pheasants were on the dome.

Korean customs as to death and burial deserve a brief notice. When a man or woman falls ill, the *mu-tang* or sorceress is called in to exorcise the spirit which has caused the illness. When this fails and death becomes imminent, in the case of a man no women are allowed to remain in the room but his nearest female relations, and in that of a woman all men must withdraw except her husband, father, and brother. After death the body, specially at the joints, is shampooed, and when it has been made flexible it is covered with a clean sheet and laid for three days on a board, on which seven stars are painted. This board is eventually burned at the grave. The "Star Board," as it is called, is a euphemism for death, and is spoken of as we speak of "the grave." During these days the grave-clothes, which are of good materials in red, blue, and yellow coloring, are prepared. Korean custom enjoins that burial shall be delayed in the case of a poor man three days only, in that of a middle-class man nine days, of a nobleman or high official three months, and in that of one of the Royal Family nine months, but this period may be abridged or extended at the pleasure of the King.

Man is supposed to have three souls. After death one occupies the tablet, one the grave, and one the Unknown. During the passing of the spirit there is complete silence. The under garments of the dead are taken out by a servant, who waves them in the air and calls him by name, the relations and friends meantime wailing loudly. After a time the clothes are thrown upon the roof. When the corpse has been temporarily dressed, it is bound so tightly round the chest as sometimes to break the shoulder blades, which is interpreted as a sign of gook luck. After these last offices a table is placed outside the door, on which are three bowls of rice and a squash. Beside it are three pair of straw sandals. The rice and sandals are for the three *sajas*, or official servants, who come to conduct one of the souls to the "Ten Judges." The squash is broken, the shoes burned, and the rice thrown away within half an hour after death. Pictures of the *Siptai-wong* or "Ten Judges" are to be seen in Buddhist temples in Korea. On a man's death one of his souls is seized by their servants and carried to the Unknown, where these Judges, who through their spies are kept well informed as to human deeds, sentence it accordingly, either to "a good place" or to one of the manifold hells. The influence of Buddhism doubtless maintains the observance of this singular custom, even where the idea of its significance is lost or discredited.

The coffin is oblong. Where interment is delayed, it is hermetically sealed with several coats of lacquer. Until the funeral there is wailing daily in the dead man's house at the three hours of meals. Next the geomancer is consulted about the site for the grave, and receives a fee heavy in proportion to the means of the family. He is believed from long study to have become acquainted with all the good and bad influences which are said to reside in the ground. A fortunate site brings rank, wealth, and many sons to the sons and grandsons of the deceased, and should be, if possible, on the southerly slope of a hill. He also chooses an auspicious day for the burial.

In the case of a rich man, the grave with a stone altar in

front of it is prepared beforehand, in that of a poor man not till the procession arrives. The coffin is placed in a gaily decorated hearse, and with wailing, music, singing, wine, food, and if in the evening, with many colored lanterns, the *cortège* proceeds to the grave. A widow may accompany her husband's corpse in a closed chair, though this appears unusual, but the mourners are all men in immense hats, which conceal their faces, and sackcloth clothing.

After the burial and the making of the circular mound over the coffin, a libation of wine is poured out and the company proceeds to sacrifice and to feast. Offerings of wine and dried fish are placed on the stone altar in front of the grave if it has been erected, or on small tables. The relatives, facing these and the grave, make five prostrations, and a formula wishing peace to the spirit which is to dwell there is repeated. Behind the grave similar offerings and prostrations are made to the mountain spirit, who presides over it, and who is the host of the soul committed to his care. The wine is thrown away, and the fish bestowed upon the servants. It will be observed that no priest has any part in the ceremonies connected with death and burial, and that two souls have now been disposed of—one to the judgment of the Unknown, and the other to the keeping of the mountain spirit.

A chair is invariably carried in a funeral procession containing the memorial, or, as we say, the "ancestral tablet" of the deceased, a strip of white wood, bearing the family name, set in a socket. A part of the inscription on this is written at the house, and it is completed at the grave. It is carried back with exactly the same style and attendance that the dead man would have had had he been living, for the third soul is supposed to return to the house with the mourners, and to take up its abode in the tablet, which is placed in a vacant room and raised on a black lacquer chair with a black lacquer table before it, on which renewed offerings are made of bread, wine, cooked meat, and vermicelli soup, the spirit being sup-

posed to regale itself with their odors. The mourners again
prostrate themselves five times, after which they eat the offerings in an adjoining room. It is customary for friends to
strew the rout of the procession with paper money.

In the period between the death and the interment silence
is observed in the house of mourning, and only those visitors
are received who come to condole with the family and speak of
the virtues of the departed. It is believed that conversation on
any ordinary topic will cause the corpse to shake in the coffin
and show other symptoms of unrest. For the same reason the
servants are very particular in watching the cats of the household if there are any, but cats are not in favor in Korea. It
is terribly unlucky for a cat to jump over a corpse. It may
even cause it to stand upright. After the deceased has
been carried out of the house, two or three *mu-tangs* or
sorceresses enter it with musical instruments and the other
paraphernalia of their profession. After a time one becomes
"inspired" by the spirit of the dead man, and accurately im-
personates him, even to his small tricks of manner, movement,
and speech. She gives a narrative of his life in the first person singular, if he were a bad man confessing his misdeeds,
which may have been unsuspected by his neighbors, and if he
were a good man, narrating his virtues with becoming modesty.
At the end she bows, takes a solemn farewell of those present,
and retires.

After the tablet has been removed to the ancestral temple,
and the period of mourning is over, meals are offered in the
shrine once every month, and also on the anniversary of each
death, all the descendants assembling, and these observances
extend backwards to the ancestors of five generations. Thus
it is a very costly thing to have many near relations and a
number of ancestors, the expense falling on the eldest son and
his heirs. A Korean gentleman told me that his nephew,
upon whom this duty falls, spends more upon it than upon his
household expenses.

It is not till the three years' mourning for a father has expired that his tablet is removed to the ancestral temple which rich men have near their houses. During the period of mourning it is kept in a vacant room, usually in the women's apartments. A poor man puts it in a box on one side of his room, and when he worships his other ancestors, strips of paper with their names upon them are pasted on the mud wall. I have slept in rooms in which the tablet lay smothered in dust on one of the crossbeams. Common people only worship for their ancestors of three generations. The anniversary of a father's death is kept with much ceremony for three years. On the previous night sacrifice is offered before the tablet, and on the following day the friends pay visits of condolence to the family, and eat varieties of food. During the day they visit the grave and offer sacrifices to the soul and the mountain spirit.

A widow wears mourning all her life. If she has no son she acts the part of a son in performing the ancestral rites for her husband. It has not been correct for widows to remarry. If, however, a widow inherits property she occasionally marries to rid herself of importunities, in which case she is usually robbed and deserted.

The custom of tolerating the remarriage of widows has, however, lately been changed into the *right* of remarriage.

CHAPTER XXV

SONG-DO: A ROYAL CITY

IT grew dark before we reached Pa Ju, and the *mapu* were in great terror of tigers and robbers. It is unpleasant to reach a Korean inn after nightfall, for there are no lights by which to unload the baggage, and noise and confusion prevail.

When the traveller arrives a man rushes in with a brush, stirs up the dust and vermin, and sometimes puts down a coarse mat. Experience has taught me that an oiled sheet is a better protection against vermin than a pony-load of insect powder. I made much use of the tripod of my camera. It served as a candle-stand, a barometer suspender, and an arrangement on which to hang my clothes at night out of harm's way. In two hours after arrival my food was ready, after which Mr. Yi came in to talk over the day, to plan the morrow, to enlighten me on Korean customs, and to interpret my orders to the faithful Im, and by 8.30 I was asleep!

After leaving Pa Ju the country is extremely pretty, and one of the most picturesque views in Korea is from the height overlooking the romantically situated village of Im-jin, clustering along both sides of a ravine, which terminates on the broad Im-jin Gang, a tributary of the Han, in two steep rocky bluffs, sprinkled with the *Pinus sinensis*, the two being connected by a fine, double-roofed granite Chinese gateway, inscribed "Gate for the tranquillization of the West." The road passing down the village street reaches the water's edge through this relic, one of three or four similar barriers on this high-road to China. The Im-jin Gang, there 343 yards broad, has shallow water and a flat sandy shore on its north side, but a range of high bluffs, crowned with extensive old defensive works, lines the south side, the gateway being the only break for many miles. Below these the river is a deep green stream, navigable for craft of 14 tons for 40 miles from its mouth. There was a still, faintly blue atmosphere, and the sails of boats passing dreamily into the mountains over the silver water had a most artistic effect.

There are two Chinese bridges on that road, curved slabs of stone, supported on four-sided blocks of granite, giving one a feeling of security, even though they have no parapets. Korean bridges are poles laid over a river, with matting or brushwood covered with earth upon them, and are usually full of holes. These precarious structures had just been replaced after the summer rains. A *mapu* usually goes ahead to test their solidity. The region is extremely fertile, producing fine crops of rice, wheat, barley, millet, buckwheat, cotton, sesamum, castor oil, beans, maize, tobacco, capsicums, egg plant, peas, etc. But Russian and American kerosene is fast displacing the vegetable oils for burning, and is producing the same revolution in village evening life which it has effected in the Western Islands of Scotland. I never saw a Korean hamlet south of Phyöng-yang, however far from the main road, into which kerosene had not penetrated.

I was obliged to halt for the night when only 10 *li* from Song-do, all the more regretfully, because the people were unwilling to receive a foreigner, and the family room which I occupied, only 8 feet 6 inches by 6 feet, was heated up to 85°, was poisoned with the smell of cakes of rotting beans, and was so alive with vermin of every description that I was obliged to suspend a curtain over my bed to prevent them from falling upon it.

The next morning, in an atmosphere which idealized everything, we reached Song-do, or Kai-söng, now the second city in the kingdom, once the capital of Hon-jö, one of the three kingdoms which united to form Korea, and the capital of

Korea five centuries ago. A city of 60,000 people, lying to the south of Sang-dan San, with a wall ten miles in circumference running irregularly over heights, and pierced by double-roofed gateways, with a peaked and splintered ridge extending from Sang-dan San to the northeast, its higher summits attaining altitudes of from 2,000 to 3,000 feet, it has a striking resemblance to Seoul.

The great gate is approached by an avenue of trees, and the road is lined with *seun-tjeung-pi*, monuments to good governors and magistrates, faithful widows, and pious sons. A wide street, its apparent width narrowed by two rows of thatched booths, divides the city. It was a scene of bustle, activity, and petty trade, something like a fair. The women wear white sheets gathered round their heads and nearly reaching their feet. The street was thronged with men in huge hats and very white clothing, with boy bridegrooms in pink garments and the quaint yellow hats which custom enjoins for several months after marriage, and with mourners dressed in sackcloth from head to foot, the head and shoulders concealed by peaked and scalloped hats, the identity being further disguised by two-handled sackcloth screens, held up to their eyes. In thatched stalls on low stands and on mats on the ground were all Korean necessaries and luxuries, among which were large quantities of English piece goods, and hacked pieces of beef with the blood in it, Korean killed meat being enough to make any one a vegetarian. Goats are killed by pulling them to and fro in a narrow stream, which method is said to destroy the rank taste of the flesh; dogs by twirling them in a noose until they are unconscious, after which they are bled. I have already inflicted on my readers an account of the fate of a bullock at Korean hands. It was a busy, dirty, poor, mean scene under the hot sun.

The Song-do inns are bad, and a friend of Mr. Yi kindly lent me a house, partly in ruins, but with two rooms which sheltered Im and myself, and in this I spent two pleasant days in lovely weather, Mr. Yi, who was visiting friends, escorting me to the Song-do sights, which may be seen in one morning, and to pay visits in some of the better-class houses. My quarters, though by comparison very comfortable, would not at home be considered fit for the housing of a better-class cow! But Korea has a heavenly climate for much of the year. The squalor, dust, and rubbish in my compound and everywhere were inconceivable, though the city is rather a "well-to-do" one. The water supply is atrocious, offal and refuse of all kinds lying up to the mouths of the wells. It says something for the security of Korea that a foreign lady could safely live in a dwelling up a lonely alley in the heart of a big city, with no attendant but a Korean soldier knowing not a word of English, who, had he been so minded, might have cut my throat and decamped with my money, of which he knew the whereabouts, neither my door nor the compound having any fastening!

Points of interest in a Korean city are few, and the ancient capital is no exception to the rule. There is a fine bronze bell with curiously involved dragons in one of the gate towers, cast five centuries ago, an archery ground with official pavilions on a height with a superb view, the Governor's *yamen*, once handsome, now ruinous, with Japanese sentries, a dismal temple to Confucius, and a showy one to the God of War. Outside the crowd and bustle of the city, reached by a narrow path among prosperous ginseng farms and persimmon-embowered hamlets, are the lonely remains of the palace of the Kings who reigned in Korea prior to the dynasty of which the present sovereign is the representative, and even in their forlornness they give the impression that the Korean Kings were much statelier monarchs then than now.

The remains consist of an approach to the main platform on which the palace stood, by two subsidiary platforms, the first reached by a nearly obliterated set of steps. Four staircases 15 feet wide, of thirty steps each, lead to a lofty artificial platform, faced with hewn stone in great blocks, 14 feet high, and by rough measurement 846 feet in length. On the east side there are massive abutments. On the west the platform broadens irregularly. At the entrance, 80 feet wide, at the top of the steps, there are the bases of columns suggestive of a very stately approach. The palace platform is intersected by massive stone foundations of halls and rooms, some of large area. It is backed by a pine-clothed knoll, and is prettily situated in an amphitheatre of hills.

Song-do as a royal city, and as one of the so-called fortresses for the protection of the capital, still retains many ancient privileges. It is a bustling business town, and a great centre of the grain trade. It has various mercantile guilds with their places of business, small shops built round compounds with entrance gates. It makes wooden shoes, coarse pottery and fine matting, and imports paper, which it manufactures with sesamum oil into the oil paper for which Korea is famous, and which is made into cloaks, umbrellas, tobacco-pouches, and sheets for walls and floors. In answer to many inquiries, I learned that trade had improved considerably since the war, but the native traders now have to compete with fourteen Japanese shops, and to suffer the presence of forty Japanese residents.

I have left until the last the commodity for which Song-do is famous, and which is the chief source of its prosperity—ginseng. *Panax Ginseng* or *quinquefolia* (?) is, as its name imports, a "panacea." No one can be in the Far East for many days without hearing of this root and its virtues. No drug in the British Pharmacopœia rivals with us the estimation in which this is held by the Chinese. It is a tonic, a febrifuge, a stomachic, the very elixir of life, taken spasmodically or regularly in Chinese wine by most Chinese who can afford it. It is one of the most valuable articles which Korea exports, and one great source of its revenue. In the steamer in which I left Chemulpo there was a consignment of it worth

$140,000. But valuable as the cultivated root is, it is nothing to the value of the wild, which grows in Northern Korea, a single specimen of which has been sold for £40! It is chiefly found in the Kang-ge Mountains; but it is rare, and the search so often ends in failure, that the common people credit it with magical properties, and believe that only men of pure lives can find it.

The ginseng season was at its height. People talked, thought, and dreamed ginseng, for the risks of its six or seven years' growth were over, and the root was actually in the factory. I went to several ginseng farms, and also saw the different stages of the manufacturing process, and received the same impression as in Siberia, that if industry were lucrative, and the Korean were sure of his earnings, he would be an industrious and even a thrifty person.

All round Song-do are carefully fenced farms on which ginseng is grown with great care and exquisite neatness on beds 18 inches wide, 2 feet high, and neatly bordered with slates. It is sown in April, transplanted in the following spring, and again in three years into specially prepared ground, not recently cultivated, and which has not been used for ginseng culture for seven years. Up to the second year the plant has only two leaves. In the fourth year it is six inches high with four leaves, standing out at right angles from the stalk. It reaches maturity in the sixth or seventh year. During its growth it is sheltered from both wind and sun by well-made reed roofs with blinds, which are raised or lowered as may be required. When the root is taken up it is known as "white ginseng," and is bought by merchants, who get it "manufactured," about 3¼ *catties* of the fresh root making one *cattie* of "red" or commercial ginseng. The grower pays a tax of 20 cents per *cattie*, and the merchant 16 dollars a *cattie* for the root as received from the manufacturer.

The annual time of manufacture depends on orders given by the Government. The growers and merchants make the most profit when the date is early. Only two manufacturers are licensed, and one hundred and fifty growers. The quantity to be manufactured is also limited. In 1895 it was 15,000 *catties* of red ginseng and 3,000 of "beards." The terms "beards" and "tails" are used to denote different parts of the root, which eventually has a grotesque resemblance to a headless man ! It is possible that this likeness is the source of some of the almost miraculous virtues which are attributed to it. Everything about the factories is scrupulously clean, and would do credit to European management. The row of houses used by what we should call the excisemen are well built and comfortable. There are two officials sent from Seoul by the Agricultural Department for the "season," with four policemen and two attendants, whose expenses are paid by the manufacturers, and each step of the manufacture and the egress of the workmen are carefully watched. Mr. Yi was sent by the Customs to make special inquiries in connection with the revenue derived.

Ginseng is steamed for twenty-four hours in large earthen jars over iron pots built into furnaces, and is then partially dried in a room kept at a high temperature by charcoal. The final drying is effected by exposing the roots in elevated flat baskets to the rays of the bright winter sun. The human resemblance survives these processes, but afterwards the "beards" and "tails," used chiefly in Korea, are cut off, and the trunk, from 3 to 4 inches long, looks like a piece of clouded amber. These trunks are carefully picked over, and being classified according to size, are neatly packed in small oblong baskets containing about five *catties* each, twelve or fourteen of these being packed in a basket, which is waterproofed and matted, and stamped and sealed by the Agricultural Department as ready for exportation. A basket, according to quality, is worth from $14,000 to $20,000 ! In a good season the grower makes about fifteen times his outlay. Ginseng was a Royal monopoly, but times have changed. This medicine, which has such a high and apparently partially deserved reputation throughout the Far East, does not suit Europeans, and is of little account with European doctors.

A Post Office had been established in Song-do under Korean management, and I not only received but sent a letter, which reached its destination safely! Buddhism still prevails to some extent in this city, and large sums are expended upon the services of sorcerers. In Song-do I saw, what very rarely may be seen in Seoul and elsewhere, a " Red Door." These are a very high honor reserved for rare instances of faithfulness in widows, loyalty in subjects, and piety in sons. When a widow (almost invariably of the upper class) weeps ceaselessly for her husband, maintains the deepest seclusion, attends loyally to her father- and mother-in-law, and spends her time in pious deeds, the people of the neighborhood, proud of her virtues, represent them to the Governor of the province, who conveys their recommendation to the King, with whom it rests to confer the " Red Door." The distinction is also given to the family of an eminently loyal subject, who has given his life for the King's life.

The case of a son whose father has reached a great age is somewhat different, and the honor is more emphatic still. His filial virtue is shown by such methods as these. He goes every morning to his father's apartments, asks him how his health is, how he has slept, what he has eaten for breakfast, and how he enjoyed the meal—if he has any fancies for dinner, and if he shall go to the market and buy him some *tai* (the best fish in Korea), and if he shall come back and assist him to take a walk? The reader will observe how extremely material the pious son's inquiries are. Such assiduity continued during a course of years, on being represented to the King, may receive the coveted red portal. In former days, these matters used to be referred to the Suzerain, the Emperor of China. In Song-do, as in the villages, a straw fringe is frequently to be seen stretched across a door, either plain or with bits of charcoal knotted into it.   The former denotes the birth of a girl, the latter that of a boy.   A girl is not specially welcome, nor is the occasion one of festivity, but neither is it, as in some countries, regarded as a calamity, although, if it be a firstborn, the friends of the father are apt to write letters of condolence to him, with the consoling suggestion that "the next will be a boy."

CHIL-SUNG MON, SEVEN STAR GATE.

CHAPTER XXVI

THE PHYÖNG-YANG BATTLEFIELD

GLORIOUS weather favored my departure from the ancient Korean capital. The day's journey lay through pretty country, small valleys, and picturesquely shaped hills, on which the vegetation, whatever it was, had turned to a purple as rich as the English heather blossom, while the blue gloom of the pines emphasized the flaming reds of the dying leafage. The villages were few and small, and cultivation was altogether confined to the valleys. Pheasants were so abundant that the *mapu* pelted them out of the cover by the roadside, and wild ducks abounded on every stream. The one really fine view of the day is from the crest of a hill just beyond O-hung-suk Ju, where there is a second defensive gate, with a ruinous wall carried along a ridge for some distance on either side. The masonry and the gate-house are fine, and the view down the wild valley beyond with its rich autumn coloring was almost grand. It was evident that officials were expected, for the road was being repaired everywhere—that is, spadefuls of soft soil were being taken from the banks and roadsides, and were being thrown into the ruts and holes to deepen the quagmire which the next rain would produce. From four to seven men were working at each spade! A great part of the male population had turned out; for when an official of rank is to travel, every family in the district must provide one male member or a substitute to put the road in order. The repairs of the roads and bridges devolve entirely on the country people.

The following day brought a change of weather. My room

had no hot floor and the mercury at daybreak was only 20°!
When we started, a strong northwester was blowing, which increased to a gale by noon, the same fierce gale in which at
Chemulpo H.M.S. *Edgar* lost her boat with forty-seven men.
My pony and I would have been blown over a wretched bridge
had not four men linked themselves together to support us;
and later, on the top of a precipice above a river, a gust came
with such force that the animals refused to face it, and one of
them was as nearly lost as possible. By noon it was impossible
to sit on our horses, and we fought the storm on foot. When
Im lifted me from my pony I fell down, and it took several
men shouting with laughter to set me on my feet again. When
Mr. Yi and I spoke to each other, our voices had a bobbery
clatter, and sentences broke off halfway in an insane giggle. I
felt as if there were hardly another "shot in the locker," but
if a traveller "says die," the men lose all heart, so I summoned up all my pluck, took a photograph after the noon halt,
and walked on at a good pace.

But the wind, with the mercury at 26°, was awful, gripping
the heart and benumbing the brain. I have not felt anything
like it since I encountered the "devil wind" on the Zagros
heights in Persia. At some distance from our destination Mr.
Yi, Im, and the *mapu* begged me to halt, as they could no
longer face it, though the accommodation for man and beast
at Tol Maru, where we put up, was the worst imaginable, and
the large village the filthiest, most squalid, and most absolutely
poverty-stricken place I saw in that land of squalor. The
horses were crowded together, and their baffled attempts at
fighting were only less hideous than the shouts and yells of the
mapu, who were constantly being roused out of a sound sleep
to separate them.

My room was 8 feet by 6, and much occupied by the chattels of the people, besides being alive with cockroaches and
other forms of horrid life. The dirt and discomfort in which
the peasant Koreans live are incredible.

An uninteresting tract of country succeeded, and some time was occupied in threading long treeless valleys, cut up by stony beds of streams, margined by sandy flats, inundated in summer, and then covered chiefly with withered reeds, asters, and artemisia, a belated aster every now and then displaying its untimely mauve blossom. All these and the dry grasses and weeds of the hillsides were being cut and stacked for fuel, even brushwood having disappeared. This work is done by small boys, who carry their loads on wooden saddles suited to their size. That region is very thinly peopled, only a few hamlets of squalid hovels being scattered over it, and cultivation was rare and untidy, except in one fine agricultural valley where wheat and barley were springing. No animals, except a breed of pigs not larger than English terriers, were to be seen.

One of the most dismal and squalid " towns " on this route is Shur-hung, a long rambling village of nearly 5,000 souls, and a magistracy, built along the refuse-covered bank of a bright, shallow stream. As if the Crown official were the upas tree, the town with a *yamen* is always more forlorn than any other. In Shur-hung the large and once handsome *yamen* buildings are all but in ruins, and so is the Confucian temple, visited periodically, as all such temples are, by the magistrate, who bows before the tablet of the " most holy teacher " and offers an animal in sacrifice.

The Korean official is the vampire which sucks the life-blood of the people. We had crossed the Tao-jol, the boundary between the provinces of Kyöng-hwi and Hwang-hai, and were then in the latter. Most officials of any standing live in Seoul for pleasure and society, leaving subordinates in charge, and as their tenure of office is very brief, they regard the people within their jurisdiction rather with reference to their squeezeableness than to their capacity for improvement.

Forty Japanese soldiers found a draughty shelter within the tumble-down buildings of the *yamen*. As I walked down the street one of them touched me on the shoulder, asking my nationality, whence I came, and whither I was going, not quite politely, I thought. When I reached my room a dozen of them came and gradually closed round my door, which I could not shut, standing almost within it. A trim sergeant raised his cap to me, and passing on to Mr. Yi's room, asked him where I came from and whither I was going, and on hearing, replied, "All right," raised his cap to me, and departed, withdrawing his men with him. This was one of several domiciliary visits, and though they were usually very politely made, they suggested the query as to the right to make them, and to whom the mastership in the land belonged. There, as elsewhere, though the people hated the Japanese with an intense hatred, they were obliged to admit that they were very quiet and paid for everything they got. If the soldiers had not been in European clothes, it would not have occurred to me to think them rude for crowding round my door.

A day's ride through monotonous country brought us to Pong-san, where we halted in the dirtiest hole I had till then been in. As soon as my den was comfortably warm, myriads of house flies, blackening the rafters, renewed a semi-torpid existence, dying in heaps in the soup and curry, filling the well of the candlestick with their singed bodies, and crawling in hundreds over my face. Next came the cockroaches in legions, large and small, torpid and active, followed by a great army of fleas and bugs, making life insupportable. To judge from the significant sounds from the public room, no one slept all night, and when I asked Mr. Yi after his welfare the next morning, he uttered the one word "miserable." Discomforts of this nature, less or more, are inseparable from the Korean inn.

The following day, at a large village, we came upon the weekly market. It is usual to inquire regarding the trade of a district, and as the result of my inquiries, I assert that "trade" in the ordinary sense has no existence in a great part of Central and Northern Korea, i.e. there is no exchange of commodities between one place and another, no exports, no imports by resident merchants, and no industries supplying more than a local demand. Such are to be found to some extent in Southern Korea, and specially in the province of Chul-la. Apart from Phyöng-yang, "trade" does not exist in the region through which I travelled.

Reasons for such a state of things may be found in the debased coinage, so bulky that a pony can only carry £10 worth of it, the entire lack of such banking facilities as even in Western China render business transactions easy; the general mutual distrust; prejudices against preparing hides and working leather; caste prejudices; the general insecurity of earnings, ignorance absolutely inconceivable, and the existence of numerous guilds which possess practical monopolies.

Under Japanese influence, however, the superb silver *yen* has made its way slowly into the interior, and instead of having to carry a load of *cash*, as on my former journey, or to be placed in great difficulties by the want of it, this large silver coin was readily taken at all the inns, although I did not see a single specimen of the new Korean coinage.

"Trade," as I became acquainted with it, is represented by Japanese buyers, who visit the small towns and villages, buying up rice, grain, and beans, which they forward to the ports for shipment to Japan, and by an organized corporation of *pusang* or pedlars, one of the most important of the many guilds which have been among the curious features of Korea.

There are no shops in villages, and few, where there are any, even in small towns. It is, in fact, impossible to buy anything except on the market-day, as no one keeps any stock of anything. At the weekly market the usual melancholy dulness of a Korean village is exchanged for bustle, color, and crowds of men. From an early hour in the morning the paths leading to the officially appointed centre are thronged with peasants bringing in their wares for sale or barter, chiefly fowls in coops, pigs, straw shoes, straw hats, and wooden spoons, while the main road has its complement of merchants, *i.e.* pedlars, mostly fine, strong, well-dressed men, either carrying their heavy packs themselves or employing porters or bulls for the purpose. These men travel on regular circuits to the village centres, and are industrious and respectable. A few put up stalls, specially those who sell silks, gauzes, cords for girdles, dress shoes, amber, buttons, silks in skeins, small mirrors, tobacco-pouches, dress combs of tortoise-shell for men's topknots, tape girdles for trousers, boxes with mirror tops, and the like. But most of the articles, from which one learns a good deal about the necessaries and luxuries required by the Korean, are exposed for sale on low tables or on mats on the ground, the merchant giving the occupant of the house before which he camps a few *cash* for the accommodation.

On such tables are sticks of pulled candy as thick as an arm, some of it stuffed with sesamum seeds, a sweetmeat sold in enormous quantities, and piece goods, shirtings of Japanese and English make, Victoria lawns, hempen cloth, Turkey-red cottons, Korean flimsy silks, dyes, chiefly aniline, which are sold in great quantities, together with saffron, indigo, and Chinese Prussian blue. On these also are exposed long pipes, contraband in the capital, and Japanese cigarettes, coming into great favor with young men and boys, with leather courier bags and lucifer matches from the same country, wooden combs, hairpins with tinsel heads, and, such is the march of ideas, purses for silver! Paper, the best of the Korean manufactures, in its finer qualities produced in Chul-la Do, is honored by stalls. Every kind is purchasable in these markets, from the beautiful, translucent, buff, oiled paper, nearly equal to vellum in appearance and tenacity, used for the floors of middle- and upper-class houses, and the stout paper for covering walls, to the thin, strong film for writing on, and a beautiful fabric, a sort of frothy gauze, for wrapping up delicate fabrics, as well as the coarse fibrous material, used for covering heavy packages, and intermediate grades, applied to every imaginable purpose, such as the making of string, almost all manufactured from the paper mulberry.

On mats on the ground are exposed straw mats, straw and string shoes, flints for use with steel, black buckram dress hats, coarse, narrow cotton cloth of Korean manufacture, rope muzzles for horses (much needed), sweeping whisks, wooden *sabots*, and straw, reed, and bamboo hats in endless variety. On these also are rough iron goods, family cooking-pots, horseshoes, spade-shoes, door-rings, nails, and carpenter's tools, when of native manufacture, as rough as they can be; and Korean roots and fruits, tasteless and untempting, great hard pears much like raw parsnips, chestnuts, peanuts, persimmons which had been soaked in water to take the acridity out of them, and ginger. There were coops of fowls and piles of pheasants, brought down by falcons, gorgeous birds, selling at six for a *yen* (about 4d. each), and torn and hacked pieces of bull beef.

One prominent feature of that special market was the native pottery, both coarse and brittle ware, clay, with a pale green glaze rudely applied, small jars and bowls chiefly, and a coarser ware, nearly black and slightly iridescent, closely resembling iron. This pottery is of universal use among the poor for cooking-pots, water-jars, refuse-jars, receptacles for grain and pulse, and pickle-jars 5 feet high, roomy enough to hold a man, two of which are a bull's load. At that season these jars were in great request, for the peasant world was occupied, the men in digging up a great hard white radish weighing from 2 to 4 lbs., and the women in washing its great head of partially blanched leaves, which, after being laid aside in these jars in brine, form one great article of a Korean peasant's winter diet.

Umbrella hats, oiled paper, hat covers, pounded capsicums, rice, peas, and beans, bean curd, and other necessaries of Korean existence, were there, but business was very dull, and the crowds of people were nearly as quiet as the gentle bulls which stood hour after hour among them. Late in the afternoon, the pedlars packed up their wares and departed *en route* for the next centre, and a good deal of hard drinking closed the day. I have been thus minute in my description because the peripatetic merchant really represents the fashion of Korean trade, and the wares which are brought to market are both the necessaries and luxuries of Korean existence.

The reader will agree with me that, except for a certain amount of insight into Korean customs which can only be gained by mixing freely with Koreans, the journey from Seoul to Phyöng-yang tends to monotony, though at the time Mr. Yi's brightness, intelligence, sense of fun, and unvarying good-nature made it very pleasant. Among the few features of interest on the road are the "Hill Towns," of which three are striking objects, specially one on the hill opposite to the magistracy of Pyeng-san, the hilltop being surrounded by a battlemented wall two miles in circuit, enclosing a tangled thicket containing a few hovels and the remains of some granaries. Unwalled towns are supposed to possess such strongholds, with stores of rice and *soy*, as refuges in times of invasion or rebellion, but as they have not been required for three centuries, they are now ruinous. The one on a high hill above Sai-nam, where the last Chinese gate occurs, is imposing from its fine gateway and the extent of ground it encloses.

Two days before reaching Phyöng-yang we crossed the highest pass on the road, and by a glen wooded with such deciduous trees, shrubs, and trailers as ash, elæagnus, euonymus, horn-beam, oak, lime, *Acanthopanax ricinifolia*, actinidia with scarlet berries, clematis, *Ampelopsis Veitchii*, etc., descended to the valley of the Nam-chhon, a broad but shallow stream which joins the Tai-döng. On the right bank, where the stream, crossed by a dilapidated bridge, is 128 yards wide, the town of Whang Ju is picturesquely situated, 36 *li* from the sea, at the base of two low fir-crowned hills, which terminate in cliffs above the Nam-chhon.

A battlemented wall 9 *li* in circumference, with several fine towers and gateways, encloses the town, and being carried along the verge of the cliff and over the downs and ups of the hills, has a very striking appearance. It was a singularly attractive view. The Korean sky was at its bluest, and the winding Nam-chhon was seen in glimpses here and there through the broad fertile plain in reaches as blue, and the broken sparkle of its shallow waters flashed in sapphire gleams against the gray rock and the gray walls of the city. On the wall, and grouped in the handsome Water Gate, were a number of Japanese soldiers watching a crowd of Koreans spearing white fish with three-pronged forks from rafts made of two bundles of reeds with a cask lashed between them, and from the bridge the ruinous state of the walls and towers could not be seen.

Whang Ju is memorable to me as being the first place I saw which had suffered from the ravages of recent war. There the Japanese came upon the Chinese, but there was no fighting at that point. Yet whatever happened has been enough to reduce a flourishing town with an estimated population of 30,000 souls to one of between 5,000 and 6,000, and to destroy whatever prosperity it had.

I passed through the Water Gate into a deplorable scene of desolation. There were heaps of ruins, some blackened by fire, others where the houses had apparently collapsed "all of a heap," with posts and rafters sticking out of it. There are large areas of nothing but this and streets of deserted houses, sadder yet, with doors and windows gone for the bivouac fires of the Japanese, and streets where roofless mud walls alone were standing. In some parts there were houses with windows gone and torn paper waving from their walls, and then perhaps an inhabited house stood solitary among the deserted or destroyed, emphasizing the desolation. Some of the destruction was wrought by the Chinese, some by the Japanese, and much resulted from the terrified flight of more than 20,000 of the inhabitants.

North of Whang Ju are rich plains of productive, stoneless, red alluvium, extending towards the Tai-döng for nearly 40 miles. On these there were villages partly burned and partly depopulated and ruinous, and tracts of the superb soil had passed out of cultivation owing to the flight of the cultivators, and there was a total absence of beasts, the splendid bulls of the region having perished under their loads *en route* for Manchuria.

It was a dreary journey that day through partially destroyed villages, relapsing plains, and slopes denuded of every stick which could be burned. There were no wayfarers on the roads, no movement of any kind, and as it grew dusk the *mapu* were afraid of tigers and robbers, and we halted for the night at the wretched hamlet of Ko-moun Tari, where I obtained a room with delay and difficulty, partly owing to the unwillingness of the people to receive a foreigner. They had suffered enough from foreigners, truly!

The concluding day's march was through a pleasant country, though denuded of trees, and the approach to a great city was denoted by the number of villages, dæmon shrines, and refreshment booths on the road, the increased traffic, and eventually, by a long avenue of stone tablets, some of them under highly decorated roofs, recording the virtues of Phyöng-yang officials for 250 years!

The first view of Phyöng-yang delighted me. The city has a magnificent situation, taken advantage of with much skill, and at a distance merits the epithet "imposing." It was a glorious afternoon. All the low ranges which girdle the rich plain through which the Tai-döng winds were blue and violet, melting into a blue haze, the crystal waters of the river were bluer still, brown-sailed boats drifted lazily with the stream, and above it the gray mass of the city rose into a dome of unclouded blue.

It is built on lofty ground rising abruptly from the river, above which a fine wall climbs picturesquely over irregular, but always ascending altitudes, till it is lost among the pines of a hill which overhangs the Tai-döng. The great double-roofed Tai-döng *Mön* (river gate), decorated pavilions on the walls, the massive curled roofs of the Governor's *yamen*, a large Buddhist monastery and temple on a height, and a fine temple to the God of War, prominent objects from a distance, prepare one for something quite apart from the ordinary meanness of a Korean city.

Crossing the clear flashing waters of the Tai-döng with our ponies in a crowded ferry-boat, we found ourselves in the slush of the dark Water Gate, at all hours of the day crowded with water-carriers. There are no wells in the city, the reason assigned for the deficiency being that the walls enclose a boat-shaped area, and that the digging of wells would cause the boat to sink ! The water is carried almost entirely in American kerosene tins. I lodged at the house of a broker, and had nice clean rooms for myself and Im, quite quiet, and with a separate access from the street. It was truly a luxury to have roof, walls, and floor papered with thick oiled paper much resembling varnished oak, but there was no hot floor, and I had to rely for warmth solely on the " fire bowl."

Taking a most diverting boy as my guide, I went outside the city wall, through some farming country to a Korean house in a very tumble-to-pieces compound, which he insisted was the dwelling of the American missionaries ; but I only found a Korean family, and there were no traces of foreign occupation in glass panes let into the paper of the windows and doors. Nothing daunted, the boy pulled me through a smaller compound, opened a door, and pushed me into what was manifestly posing as a foreign room, gave me a chair, took one himself, and offered me a cigarette !

I had reached the right place. It was a very rough Korean room, about the length and width of a N.W. Railway saloon carriage. It had three camp-beds, three chairs, a trunk for a table, and a few books and writing materials, as well as a few articles of male apparel hanging on the mud walls. I waited more than an hour, every attempt at departure being forcibly as well as volubly resisted by the urchin, imagining the devotion which could sustain educated men year after year in such surroundings, and then they came in hilariously, and we had a most pleasant evening. I shall say more of them later. It was a weird walk through ruins which looked ghostly in the starlight to my curious quarters in the densest part of the city by the Water Gate, where at intervals through the night I heard the beat of the sorcerer's drum and the shrieking chant of the *mu-tang*.

It may be taken for granted that every Korean winter day is splendid, but the following day in Phyöng-yang was heavenly. Three Koreans called on me in the morning, very courteous persons, but as Mr. Yi and I had parted company for a time on reaching the city, the interpretation was feeble, and we bowed and smiled, and smiled and bowed with tedious iteration without coming to much mutual understanding, and I was glad when the time came for seeing the city and battlefield under Mr. Moffett's guidance.

On such an incomparable day everything looked at its very best, but also at its very worst, for the brilliant sunshine lit up desolations sickening to contemplate,—a prosperous city of 80,000 inhabitants reduced to decay and 15,000—four-fifths of its houses destroyed, streets and alleys choked with ruins, hill slopes and vales once thick with Korean crowded homesteads, covered with gaunt hideous remains—fragments of broken walls, *kang* floors, *kang* chimneys, indefinite heaps in which roofs and walls lay in unpicturesque confusion—and still worse, roofs and walls standing, but doors and windows all gone, suggesting the horror of human faces with their eyes put out. Everywhere there were the same scenes, miles of them, and very much of the desolation was charred and blackened, shapeless, hideous, hopeless, under the mocking sunlight.

Phyöng-yang was not taken by assault; there was no actual fighting in the city, both the Chinese who fled and the Japanese who occupied posed as the friends of Korea, and all this wreck and ruin was brought about not by enemies, but by those who professed to be fighting to give her independence and reform. It had gradually come to be known that the " wojen (dwarfs) did not kill Koreans," hence many had returned. Some of these unfortunate fugitives were picking their way among the heaps, trying to find indications which might lead them to the spots where all they knew of home once existed; and here and there, where a family found their walls and roof standing, they put a door and window into one room and lived in it among the ruins of five or six.

When the Japanese entered and found that the larger part of the population had fled, the soldiers tore out the posts and woodwork, and often used the roofs also for fuel, or lighted fires on house floors, leaving them burning, when the houses took fire and perished. They looted the property left by the fugitives during three weeks after the battle, taking even from Mr. Moffett's house $700 worth, although his servant made a written protest, the looting being sanctioned by the presence of officers. Under these circumstances the prosperity of the most prosperous city in Korea was destroyed. If such are the results of war in the " green tree," what must they be in the " dry "?

During the subsequent occupation the Japanese troops behaved well, and all stores obtained in the town and neighborhood were scrupulously paid for. Intensely as the people hated them, they admitted that quiet and good order had been preserved, and they were very apprehensive that on their withdrawal they would suffer much from the *Kun-ren-tai*, a regiment of Koreans drilled and armed by the Japanese, and these had already begun to rob and beat the people, and to defy the civil authorities. The main street on my second visit had assumed a bustling appearance. There was much building up and pulling down, for Japanese traders had obtained all the eligible business sites, and were transforming the small, dark, low, Korean shops into large, light, airy, dainty Japanese erections, well stocked with Japanese goods, and specially with kerosene lamps of every pattern and price, the Defries and Hinckes patents being unblushingly infringed.

Phyöng-yang has a truly beautiful situation on the right or north bank of the clear, bright Tai-döng, 400 yards wide at the ferry. It occupies an undulating plateau, and its wall, parallel for two miles and a half, rises from the river level at the stately Water Gate, and following its windings, mounts escarped hills to a height of over 400 feet, turning westwards at the crest of the cliff at a sharp angle marked by a pavilion, one of several, and follows the western ridge of the plateau, where it falls steeply down to a fertile rolling plain where the one real battle of the late war was fought.

This wall, which is in excellent repair, is a loopholed and battlemented structure, 20 feet high, pierced by several gates with gate towers. The city, large as it was, was once much larger, for the old wall on the west side encloses a far larger area than the modern one. The walk over the grassy undulations within the wall and up to the northern pine-clothed summit is entrancing, and the views, even in winter, are exquisite—eastwards over a rich plain to the mountains through which the Tai-döng cuts its way, or northwest to one of its affluents and the great battlefield over which in 1593 the joint forces of Chinese and Koreans poured to recover Phyöng-yang from the Japanese, or seawards where the clear bright waters wind through fertile and populous country, or the hilly area within the walls where pine-clothed knolls conceal the devastations, and the Governor's *yamen*, temples, and monasteries make a goodly show.

Between the city and the Chinese frontier is the largest and richest plain in Korea; to the east where the violet shadows lay are the valleys of the two branches of the Tai-döng, rich in silk, iron, and cotton, while within 10 miles there are at least five coal-mines,[1] and for all produce there is easy communication with the sea, 36 miles distant, for vessels of light draught, by means of the river which flows below the city wall. Timber is rafted down the Tai-döng in summer. The Peking road, which I had followed thus far, and which for centuries has linked Phyöng-yang with the outer world and the capital, is another element in the former prosperity of the city. It was to photograph for the widow and family of General Tso of Mukden, the commander of the best-disciplined and best-equipped cavalry brigade in the Chinese army, the scenes connected with his last days and death that I visited the hill within the wall.

The river wall of Phyöng-yang, after 2 miles of an undulating ascent, turns sharply at a pavilion, outside of which the ground falls precipitously, to rise again in a knife-like ridge, the three highest points of which are crowned with Chinese forts. From this pavilion the wall, following the lie of the hill, slopes rapidly down to a very picturesque and narrow gate, the *Chil-sung Mön* or Seven Star Gate, after which it trends in a northwesterly direction to the *Potong Mön*.

[1] There are five coal-mines at distances varying from 10 to 30 *li* from Phyöng-yang, those of Yang-tang, 15 *li* away, producing the best quality. With rich iron ore close to the river bank at Kai Chhön, about 36 *li* off, the elements of prosperity are ready to hand. The "coal-owners" have no proper appliances for working the coal, relying chiefly on Korean axes, and the "output" is very small. Much money has been spent in trying to get the coal, and in two mines they cannot proceed any farther with their present tools. The difficulties of transport are great, and there is no demand for any quantity in Phyöng-yang itself, but the mineral is there in abundance and of good quality, and only awaits capital and enterprise. A tax of 5 per cent. is levied on all coal sent away from the mines. The total export for 1895 was only 652 tons, valued at 4 dols. 20 cts. per ton (9s.).

In the pine wood, at the highest part of the angle formed by the wall, General Tso had built three mud forts or camps with walls 10 feet high. The ground under the trees is dotted with the stone-lined cooking holes of his men, blackened with the smoke of their last fires. On the afternoon of the 15th of September, 1894, General Tso and his force, which mustered 5,000 men when it left Mukden, but must have been greatly diminished by desertion and death, made his fatal sally, passing through the *Chil-sung Mön* and down the steep zigzag descent below it to the plain, meeting his death probably within 300 yards of the gate. The Koreans say that some of his men took up the body, but were shot by the Japanese while removing it, and that it was lost in the slaughter which ensued. A neat obelisk, railed round, was erected by the Japanese at the supposed spot, bearing on one face the inscription :—

Tso Pao-kuei, commander-in-chief of the Feng-tien division. Place of death.

And on the other——

Killed while fighting with the Japanese troops at Phyöng-yang.

A graceful tribute to their ablest foe.

General Tso's troops, demoralized by his death, sought refuge everywhere from the deadly fire of the Japanese, a part flying back to their forts within the wall, while many, probably blinded and desperate, rode along the pine woods which densely cover the broken ground outside, by a path along a wide dry moat, which, three weeks later, when Mr. Moffett returned, was piled with the dead bodies of their horses.

In the bright moonlight night which followed that day, the Japanese stormed and took by assault the three Chinese forts on the three summits of the ridge, which were the key of the position, enabling them to throw their shell into the Chinese forts and camps within the wall. The beautiful pavilion at the angle of the wall is much shattered, and big fragments of shell are embedded in its pillars and richly carved woodwork.

So desperately hurried was the flight of the vanquished from the last fort which held out, that they were mown down in numbers as they ran down the steep hill, falling face foremost with their outstretched hands clutching the earth.

All was then lost, and why that doomed army, numbering then perhaps 12,000 men, did not surrender unconditionally, I cannot imagine. During the night, abandoning guns and all war material, the remains of Tso's brigade and all the infantry and unwounded men passed through the deserted and silent city, surged out of the *Potong Mön*, crossed a shallow stream, and emerged upon a plain girdled by low hills, and intersected by the Peking road, the eastern extremity being occupied by some Chinese forts and breastworks. Tso's cavalry attempted to cross the plain and gain the shelter of some low hills, while great numbers of the infantry took to the Peking road.

The horrors of that night will never be accurately known. The battle of Phyöng-yang was lost and won when the forts were taken. What remained was less of a battle than a massacre. Before the morning, this force, the flower of the Chinese army as to drill and equipment, had perished, those who escaped never reappearing as an organized body. It is estimated that from 2,000 to 4,000 men were slain, with thousands of horses and bulls, the cavalry being literally mown down in hundreds, and lying, men and horses, heaped "in mounds." For the Japanese had girdled the plain with a ring of fire. Mr. Moffett, who was there three weeks later, described the scene even then as one of "indescribable horror." Still, there were "mounds" of men and horses stiffened in the death-agony, many having tried vainly to extricate themselves from the pile above them. There were blackened corpses in hundreds lying along the Peking road, ditches filled up with bodies of men and animals, fields sprinkled with them, and rifles, muskets, paper umbrellas, fans, coats, hats, swords belts, scabbards, cartridge boxes, sleeves, and everything that could be cast away in a desperate flight strewing the ground.

Numbers of the wounded crept into the deserted houses and died there, some of the bodies showing indications of suicide from agony, and throughout this mass of human relics which lay blackening and festering in the hot sun, dogs, left behind by their owners, were holding high carnival. Even in my walks over the battlefield, though the grain of another year had ripened upon it, I saw human skulls, spines with ribs, spines with the pelvis attached, arms and hands, hats, belts, and scabbards.

On a lofty knoll within the wall, the Japanese have erected a fine monolith to the memory of the 168 men they lost. They turned the temple of the God of War into a hospital, and there, *cela va sans dire*, their wounded were admirably treated, and in another building the Chinese wounded were carefully attended to, though naturally not till many of them had died of their wounds on the battlefield. A ghastly retribution followed the neglect to bury the Chinese dead, for typhus fever broke out, and its ravages among the Japanese troops may be partially estimated by the long lines of graves in the military cemetery at Chemulpo.

Outside the wall, in beautifully broken ground, roughly wooded with the *Pinus sinensis*, there are still bullets in the branches, many of which were splintered by the iron hail, and the temple at the tomb of Kit-ze, the founder of Korean civilization, must have been the centre of a deadly fight, for its woodwork is riddled with bullets and damaged by shell, and on its floor are great dark stains, where, when the fight was over, the Japanese wounded lay in pools of blood.

At some points, specially at the mud forts by the ferry, the Chinese made a very determined stand for ten hours, so that the Japanese troops wavered, and were only recovered by a gallant dash made by General Oshima. Probably the battle of Phyöng-yang decided the fate of the campaign.

Mr. Yi found an old book in eighteen vols. for sale, which gives a history of this city. Most Korean matters are lost in

ALTAR AT TOMB OF KIT-ZE.

obscurity after one or two centuries, but the story of Phyöng-yang takes a bold backward leap and deals fearlessly with the events of centuries B. C. Kit-ze, whose fine reputed tomb and temples in the wood are still regarded with so much reverence that a stone tablet on the road below warns equestrians to dismount in passing so sacred a place, and who is said to have emigrated from China in 1122 B. C., and to have founded a dynasty which lasted for seven centuries, made Phyöng-yang his capital. The temple at his reputed grave, though full of bullets, is in admirable repair, and its rich decorations have lately been renovated, a phenomenon in Korea. Near the city is the standard of land measurement which he introduced, illustrated by ditches and paths cut, it is said, by himself.

The temple to the God of War at the foot of the hill is perhaps the finest in Korea. Frescoes, as in the temple to the same god outside the South Gate of Seoul, but on a far grander scale, cover the walls of the corridors of one of the courtyards, and the gigantic figures round the altar, with the sacrificial utensils, hangings, and dresses, are costly and magnificent. Not far from this is a large and wealthy Buddhist monastery.

CHAPTER XXVII

NORTHWARD HO !

FOR the northern journey simple preparations only were needed, consisting of the purchase of candles and two blankets for Im, in having two pheasants cooked, in dispensing with one pony, leaving us the moderate allowance of two baggage animals, and in depositing most of my money with Mr. Moffett. For there were rumors of robbers on the road, and Mr. Yi left his fine clothes and elegant travelling gear also behind.

On a brilliant morning (and when are Korean mornings not brilliant?), passing through the gate out of which General Tso made his last sally, and down the steep declivity on which it opens, we travelled for a time along the An Ju road, skirting the base of the hill on which the Chinese cavalry made their desperate attack on an intrenched position, and near the ruins of two intrenched camps, where they fell in hundreds before the merciless fire of the enemy, and where human bones were still lying about. But where Death reaped that ghastly harvest magnificent grain crops had recently been secured, and the mellow sunlight shone on miles of stubble.

Shortly we turned off on a road untouched by the havoc of war, and saw no more of the gaunt ruins or charred remains of cottages. In that pleasant region ranges of hills with pines on their lower slopes girdle valleys of rich stoneless alluvium, producing abundantly cotton, tobacco, caster oil, wheat, barley, peas, beans, and most especially, the red and white millet. Wherever a lateral valley descends upon the one through which the road passes, there is a village of thatched

RUSSIAN SETTLER'S HOUSE.

houses, pretty enough at a distance and embowered in fruit trees, while clumps of pines, oaks, elms, and zelkawas denote the burial-places of its dead, who are the guardians of the only fine timber which is suffered to exist.

The hamlets along the road were cheerfully busy. Millet was stacked in the village roadways, leaving only room for one laden animal to pass at a time, and as all the threshing of rice and grain is done with double flails also in the village street, one actually rides over the threshed product. The red or large millet is nearly as useful to the Korean as is the bamboo to the Chinese. Its stalks furnish fuel, material for mats and thick woven fences, and even for houses, for in Phyöng-an Do the walls are formed of bundles of millet stalks 8 feet high for the uprights, across which single stalks are laid, the interstices being filled up with mud.

After two days of somewhat monotonous prettiness, beyond Shou-yang-yi the country became really beautiful. Some of the larger valleys were specially attractive, with abundance of fruit and other deciduous trees below the dark *Pinus sinensis* on the hill slopes, and there were plenty of large villages with a general look of prosperity, everything, clothing included, being much cleaner than usual. There were fine views of lofty dog-tooth peaks, and of serrated ranges running east and west. Nearly every valley has its bright, rapid stream, on which the hills descend on one side in abrupt and much caverned limestone cliffs, the other side being level and fertile. The people there, and doubtless everywhere, were taken up entirely with their own concerns, the new system of taxation under which a fixed tax in money is levied on the assessed value of the land meeting with their approval. Events in Seoul had no interest for them. The recent murder of the Queen and the imprisonment of the King did not concern them, as there were no effects of either on their circumstances. After crossing the pass of Miriok Yang, 816 feet in altitude, in a romantic region, we entered poorer country with stony soil, often piled with large shingle by the violence of streams then perfectly dry.

By misdirection, misunderstanding, or complexity or complete illegibility of the track, we spent much of the day in losing and retracing our way, scrambling up steep rock-ladders, etc., and when we reached Kai-pang after dusk we were for some time refused admission to the inn. The owner said he could not take in any one travelling with so many *mapu* (four) and a soldier. He was terrified. He said we should go away in the morning without paying him, and should beat him when he asked to be paid! However, the *mapu* gave me such an excellent character that at last he consented, and I had an excellent room,—that is, the walls and roof were cream-washed, which gave it a look of cleanliness. The timid innkeeper was old, and this brought out the fact that when a local migistrate has aged parents, it is customary for him to invite to an entertainment everybody in his district between the ages of 60 and 100, and it is usual for the old men to take their oldest grandsons with them as testimonies to their old age. As every guest has to be accompanied fittingly, the company often numbers 200.

At Ka-chang and elsewhere the pigsties are much more solid than the houses, being regular log cabins with substantial roofs for the protection of their inmates from tigers, or in that neighborhood from wolves (?). These pigs, of which every country family in Korea possesses some, are of an absurdly small black breed, a full-grown animal not weighing more than 26 lbs.

During the two days' journey from the market-place of Sian-chöng, we passed the magistracies of Cha-san and Un-san, ferrying the Tai-döng just beyond Cha-san, where it is a fine stream 317 yards broad, and is said by the ferrymen to be 47 feet deep. All that region is well peopled and fertile. There are no resident *yang-bans* in the province of Phyöng-an. Gold is obtained by a simple process all round the country, specially at Keum san. At Wol-po, a prettily situated village, and elsewhere, a quantity of the coarser descriptions of paper is made. Paper and tobacco were the goods that were on the move, bound for Phyöng-yang.

Paper is used for a greater variety of purposes in Korea than anywhere else, and its toughness and durability render it invaluable. The coarser sorts are made from old rags and paper, the finer from the paper mulberry. Paper is the one article of Korean manufacture which is exported in any quantity to China, where it is used for some of the same purposes.

Oil paper about a sixth of an inch in thickness is pasted on the floors instead of carpets or mats. It bears washing, and takes a high polish from dry rubbing. In the Royal Palaces, where two tints are used carefully, it resembles oak parquet. It is also used for walls. A thinner quality is made into the folding, conical hat-covers which every Korean carries in his sleeve, and into waterproof cloaks, coats, and baggage covers. A very thick kind of paper made of several thicknesses beaten together is used for trunks, which are strong enough to hold heavy articles. Lanterns, tobacco-pouches, and fans are made of paper, and the Korean wooden latticed windows from the palace to the hovel are " glazed " with a thin, white, tough variety, which is translucent. Much prized, however, were my photographic glass plates when cleaned. Many a joyful householder let one into his window, giving himself an opportunity of amusement and *espionage* denied to his neighbors.

The day's journey from Ka-chang to Tok Chhön is through very attractive scenery with grand mountain views. After crossing a low but severe pass, we came down upon a large affluent of the Tai-döng, which for want of a name I designate as the Ko-mop-so, flowing as a full-watered, green stream between lofty cliffs of much caverned limestone, fantastically buttressed, and between hills which throw out rocky spurs, terminating or thinning down into high limestone walls, resembling those of ruinous fortifications.

Again losing the way and our time, a struggle over a rough pass brought us in view of the Tai-döng, with the characteristics of its mountain course, long rapids with glints of foam and rocks, long reaches of deep, still, slow-gliding jagged translucent green water broad and deep, making constant abrupt turns, and by its volume suggesting great powers of destructiveness when it is liberated from its mountain barriers. In about a fortnight it would be frozen for the winter. Diamond-flashing in the fine breeze, below noble cliffs and cobalt mountains, across which cloud shadows were sailing in indigo, under a vault of cloud-flecked blue, that view was one of those dreams of beauty which become a possession for ever.

From that pass the road, if it can be called such, is shut in with the Tai-döng for 30 *li*. In some places there is not room even for the narrowest bridle track, and the ponies scramble as they may over the rough boulders which margin the water, and climb the worn, steep, and rocky steps, often as high as their own knees, by which the break-neck track is taken over the rocky spurs which descend on the river. It is one of the worst pieces of road I ever encountered, and it was not wonderful that we did not meet a single traveller, and that there should be only about nine a year! We made by our utmost efforts only a short mile an hour, and it took us five hours of this severe work to reach the wretched hamlet of Huok Kuri, a few hovels dumped down among heaps of stones and great boulders, some of which served as backs for the huts. Poverty-stricken, filthy, squalid, the few inhabitants subsisted entirely on red millet! Poor Mr. Yi, who had had a wakeful night owing to vermin, said woefully as he dismounted stiffly, "Sleepy, tired, cold, hungry,"—and there was nothing to eat, and little for the ponies either, which may have been the reason that they got up a desperate fight, of which they bore the traces for some days.

The track continued shut in by the high mountains which line the Tai-döng till within a mile of Tok Chhön, forcing the

UPPER TAI-DONG.

ponies to climb worn rock-ladders, or to pick a perilous way among sharp-pointed rocks. I had not thought that Korea could produce anything so emphatic! As the road occasionally broke up in face of some apparently impassable spur, we occasionally got into impassable places, and lost time so badly that we were benighted when little more than halfway, but as there were no inhabitants we pushed on as a matter of necessity. When we got to better going the *mapu*, inspired by the double terror of robbers and wild animals, hurried on the ponies, yelling as they drove, and by the time we reached the Tok Chhön ferry a young moon had risen, and the mountains in shadow, and the great ferry-boat full of horses, men in white, and bulls, in relief against the silvered water, made a beautiful night scene. I sent on the ponies, and Im to prepare my room, fully expecting comfort, as at Phyöng-yang, for though I could never find anybody who had been at Tok Chhön, it was always spoken of as a sort of metropolis.

It is indeed a magistracy, with a remarkably ruinous *yamen* and a market-place, and is the chief town of a very large region. It is entered from the river by stepping-stones, through abominable slush, by a long narrow street, from which we were directed on and on till we came to a wide *place*, where the inns of the town are. There in the moonlight a great masculine crowd had collected, and in the middle of it were our *mapu*, with the loads still on their ponies, raging at large, and Im rushing hither and thither like a madman. For they had been refused accommodation, and every door had been barred against them on the ground that I was a foreigner! They said, truly or falsely, that no foreigner had ever profaned Tok Chhön by his presence, that they lived in peace, and did not want to be "implicated with a foreigner" (all foreigners being Japanese). It is most disagreeable to force oneself in even the slightest degree on any one, but I had been twelve hours in the saddle, it was 8 P. M., there was snow on the ground, and it was freezing hard! The yard door of one inn was opened a chink for a moment, our men rushed for it, but it was at once barred, and we were all again left standing in the street, the centre of a crowd which increased every moment.

Our men eventually forced open the door of one inn and got their ponies in. Then the paper was torn off two doors, and Im was visible against the light from within tearing about like a black dæmon. We had then stood like statues for two hours with our feet in freezing slush, the great crowd preserving a ring round us, staring stolidly, but not showing any hostility. At last Im appeared at an open door, waving my chair, and we got into a high, dark lumber-room; but the crowd was too quick for us, and came tumbling in behind us till the place was full. Then the landlord closed the doors, but they were smashed in, and he had no better luck when he weakly besought the people to look at him and not at the stranger, for his entreaty only produced an ebullition of Korean wit, by no means complimentary. An official from the *yamen* arrived and inquired if I had any complaint to make, but I had none, and he sat down and took a prolonged stare on his own account, not making any attempt to disperse the crowd.

So I sat facing the door, Mr. Yi not far off smoking endless cigarettes, while Im battled for a room, after one he had secured had its doors broken down by the crowd. I sat for two hours longer in that cold, ruinous, miserable place, two front and three back doorways filled up with men, the whole male population of Tok Chhön, and, never moved a muscle or showed any sign of dissatisfaction! Some sat on the doorsill, little men were on the shoulders of big ones, all, inside and outside, clamoring at once.

The situation might have been serious had a European man been with me, and the experiences of Mr. Campbell of the Consular Service, at Kapsan might have been repeated. No Englishman could have kept his temper in such circumstances from 8 P. M. till midnight. He would certainly have knocked somebody down, and then there would have been a fight. The ill-bred curiosity tires but does not annoy me, though it exceeded all bounds that night. Fortunately for me, a Korean gentleman is taught from his earliest boyhood that he must never lose his temper, and that it is a degradation to him to touch an inferior, therefore he must never strike a servant or one of the lower orders.

At midnight, probably weary of our passivity, and anxious for sleep, the inn people consented to give me a room in the back-yard if I did not object to one "prepared for sacrifice," and containing the ancestral tablets. The crowd then filled the back-yard, and attempted to pour into my room, when Im's sorely-tried patience gave way for only the second time, and he knocked people down right and left. This, and the contents of a fire-bowl which was upset in the scrimmage, helped to scatter the crowd, but it was there again at daylight, attempting to enter every time Im opened the door!

The "room prepared for sacrifice" in aspect was a small barn, fearfully dirty and littered with rubbish, and bundles of rags, rope, and old shoes were tucked away among the beams and rafters. My camp-bed cut it exactly in half. In the inner half there was a dusty table, and behind it on a black stand a dusty black shrine, at the back of which was a four-leaved screen covered with long strips of paper, on which were poems in praise of the deceased. In front, dividing the room, and falling from the roof to the floor, was a curtain made of two widths of very dirty foreign calico. Among the poor, instead of setting food before the ancestral shrine twice or thrice daily during the three years of mourning for a parent, it is only placed there twice a month. In a small white wooden tablet within the shrine popular belief places the residence of the third soul of the deceased, as I have mentioned before.

I spent two days at Tok Chhön. Properly speaking, the Tai-döng is never navigable to that point, owing to many and dangerous rapids, and any idea of the possibility of this highly picturesqe stream becoming "a great commercial highway" may be utterly dismissed. Small boats can ascend it at all seasons to Mou-chin Tai, about 140 *li* lower down, and during two summer months, when the water is high, a few with much difficulty get up to Tok Chhön, and even a few *li* farther, and at the same season rafts descend from the forests of the Yung-wön district, from 30 to 40 *li* higher; but owing to severe rapids, shallows, and sandbanks which shift continually, the river is not really navigable higher than Phyöng-yang, and all commercial theories built upon it are totally chimerical. For 30 *li* above Tok Chhön the river scenery is far grander than below, the perpendicular walls of limestone rock rising from 800 to 1,000 feet, with lofty mountains above them, the peaks of which, even so early as the end of November, were crested with new-fallen snow. I had been assured in Phyöng-yang that boats could be hired at Tok Chhön, and I had planned to descend the river; but there are no boats, except a few ferry scows, higher than Mou-chin Tai.

Tok Chhön and its district are lamentably poor. The people said that the war had made the necessaries of life dearer, and that they had only the same produce to barter or buy with. The reforms which were being carried out farther south had not reached that region, and "squeezing" was still carried on by the officials. Rice, the ordinary staff of Korean life, is brought from An Ju, but is used only by the rich, *i.e.* the officials. The poor live on large and small millet. Potatoes and wheat are grown, but the soil is poor and stony. A little trade, chiefly in dried fish and seaweed, is done with Wön-san. A few silk lenos and gauzes of very poor quality are made, the industry having been introduced by the Chinese. Piece goods are only a few *cash* dearer than at Phyöng-yang. Those displayed on the market-day were nearly all Japanese. It was the dullest market I have seen. The pedlars carried away nearly as much as they brought. The country is absolutely denuded of wood. There are no deciduous trees, and the region owes its few groves of dwarfed and distorted pines to the horseshoe graves on the hillsides. A *yamen* which only hangs together from force of habit, a Confucian temple, and a Buddhist temple on a height are the only noteworthy buildings.

The district magistrate returned while I was in Tok Chhön, and the people showed a degree of interest in the event. Runners lined the river-bank by the ferry, blowing horns, forty men in black gauze coats over their white ones, and a few singing girls met his chair and ran with it to the *yamen*, and a few men looked on apathetically. A more squalid retinue could not be imagined.

Some magistrates had a thousand of such retainers paid by this impoverished country. In a single province, there were at that time 44 district mandarins, with an average staff of 400 men each, whose sole duties were those of police and tax-collecting, their food alone, at the rate of two dollars per month, costing $392,400 a year.[1] This army of 17,600 men, not receiving a "living wage," "squeezed" on its own account the peasant, who in Korea has neither rights nor privileges, except that of being the ultimate sponge. As an illustration of the methods of proceeding I give the case of a village in a southern province. Telegraph poles were required, and the Provincial Governor made a requisition of 100 *cash* on every house. The local magistrate increased it to 200, and his runners to 250, which was actually paid by the people, the runners getting 50 *cash*, the magistrate 100, and the Governor 100, a portion of which sum was expended on the object for which it was levied. An edict abolishing this attendance, and reducing the salaries of magistrates, had recently been promulgated. At Tok Chhön, the ruin and decay of official buildings, and the filth and squalor of the private dwellings, could go no farther.

[1] My authority for this statement is Mr. W. K. Carles, formerly H.B. M.'s Vice-Consul in Korea.

CHAPTER XXVIII

OVER THE AN-KIL YUNG PASS

FINDING the Tai-döng totally impracticable, and being limited as to time by the approach of the closing of the river below Phyöng-yang by ice, I regretfully turned southwards, and journeyed Seoul-wards by another route, of much interest, which touches here and there the right bank of the Tai-döng.

As I sat amidst the dirt, squalor, rubbish, and odd and endism of the inn yard before starting, surrounded by an apathetic, dirty, vacant-looking, open-mouthed crowd steeped in poverty, I felt Korea to be hopeless, helpless, pitiable, piteous, a mere shuttlecock of certain great powers, and that there is no hope for her population of twelve or fourteen millions, unless it is taken in hand by Russia, under whose rule, giving security for the gains of industry as well as light taxation, I had seen Koreans in hundreds transformed into energetic, thriving, peasant farmers in Eastern Siberia.

The road, which was said, and truly, to be a very bad one, crosses a small plain, and passing under a roofed gateway between two hills which are scarred by remains of fortifications running east and west, enters upon really fine scenery, which becomes magnificent in about 30 *li*, at first a fertile mountain-girdled basin, whose rim is spotted with large villages, and then a narrowing valley with stony soil, and a sparse population, walled in by savage mountains of emphatic forms, swinging apart at times, and revealing loftier peaks and ranges then glittering with new-fallen snow.

In crossing the plain at a point where the road was good, I

RUSSIAN OFFICERS, HUN-CHUN.

was remarking to Mr. Yi what a pleasant and prosperous journey we had had, and hoping our good fortune might continue, when there was a sudden clash and flurry, I was nearly kicked off my pony, and in a moment we were in the midst of disaster. One baggage pony was on his back on his load, pawing the air in the middle of a ploughed field, his *mapu* helpless for the time, lamed by a kick above the knee, sobbing, blood and tears running down his face; the other baggage animal, having divested himself of Im, was kicking off the rest of his load; and Im, who had been thrown from the top of the pack, was sitting on the roadside, evidently in intense pain—all the work of a moment. Mr. Yi called to me that the soldier had broken his ankle, and it was a great relief when he rose and walked towards me. Everything breakable was broken except my photographic camera, which I did not look at for two days for fear of what I might find !

Leaving the men to get the loads and ponies together, we walked on to a hamlet so destitute as not to be able to provide either wood or wadding for a splint ! I picked up a thick faggot, however, which had been dropped from a load, and it was thinned into being usable with a hatchet, the only tool the village possessed, and after padding it with a pair of stockings and making a six-yard bandage out of a cotton garment, I put up Im's right arm, which was broken just above the wrist, in splints, and made a sling out of one of the two towels which the rats had left to me. I should have been glad to know Korean enough to rate the gossiping *mapu*, three men to two horses, who allowed the accident to happen.

The animals always fight if they are left to themselves, and loads and riders are nowhere. One day Mr. Yi had a bit of a finger taken off in a fight, and if a strange brute had not kicked my stirrup iron (which was bent by the blow) instead of myself, I should have had a broken ankle. When we halted at midday the villagers tried hard to induce Im to have his arm " needled " to " let out the bad blood," a most risky surgical proceeding, which often destroys the usefulness of a limb for life, and he was anxious for it, but yielded to persuasion.

Being delayed by this accident, it was late when we started to cross the pass of An-kil Yung, regarded as "the most dangerous in Korea," owing to its liability to sudden fogs and violent storms, 3,346 feet in altitude, and said to be 30 *li* long.

The infamous path traverses a wild rocky glen with an impetuous torrent at its bottom, and only a few wretched hamlets, in which the hovels are indistinguishable from the millet and brushwood stacks, along its length of several miles. Poverty, limiting the people to the barest necessaries of life, is the lot of the peasant in that region, but I believe that his dirty and squalid habits give an impression of want which does not actually exist. I doubt much whether any Koreans are unable to provide themselves with two daily meals of millet, with clothes sufficient for decency in summer and for warmth in winter, and with fuel (grass, leaves, twigs, and weeds) enough to keep their miserable rooms at a temperature of 70° and more by means of the hot floor.

To the west the valley is absolutely closed in by a wall of peaks. The bridle-path, a well-engineered road, when it ascends the very steep ridge of the watershed in many zigzags, rests for 100 feet, and descends the western side by seventy-five turns. Except in Tibet, I never saw so apparently insurmountable an obstacle, but it does not present any real difficulty. The ascent took seventy minutes. Rain fell very heavily, but the superb view to the northeast was scarcely obscured. At the top, which is only 100 feet wide, there is a celebrated shrine to the dæmon of the past. To him all travellers put up petitions for deliverance from the many malignant spirits who are waiting to injure them, and for a safe descent. The shrine contains many strips of paper inscribed with the names of those who have made special payments for special prayers, and a few wreaths and posies of faded paper flowers. The woman who lives in the one hovel on the pass makes a good living by receiving money from travellers, who offer rice cakes and desire prayers. The worship is nearly all done by proxy, and the rice cakes do duty any number of times.

Besides the shrine and a one-rooomed hovel, there are some open sheds made of millet stalks to give shelter during storms. The An-kil Yung pass is blocked by snow for three months of the year, but at other times is much used in spite of its great height. Excellent potatoes are grown on the mountain slopes at an altitude exceeding 3,000 feet, and round Tok Chhŏn they are largely cultivated and enter into the diet of the people, never having had the disease.

Darkness came on prematurely with the heavy rain, and we asked the shrine-keeper to give us shelter for the night, but she said that to take in six men and a foreign woman was impossible, as she had only one room. But it was equally impossible for us to descend the pass in the darkness with tired ponies, and after half an hour's altercation the matter was arranged, Im, who retained his wits, securing for me a degree of privacy by hanging some heavy mats from a beam, giving me, I am sure, the lion's share of the apartment. Really the accommodation was not much worse than usual, but though the mercury fell to the freezing point, the hot floor kept the inside temperature up to 83°, and the dread of tigers on the part of my hostess forbade my having even a chink of the door open !

The rain cleared off in time for the last sunset gleam on the distant mountains, which, when darkness fell on the pass, burned fiery red against a strip of pale green sky, taking on afterwards one by one the ashy look of death as the light died off from their snows. All about An-kil Yung the mountains are wooded to their summits with deciduous trees, the ubiquitous *Pinus sinensis* being rare ; but to the northward in the direction of Paik-tu San the character of the scenery changes, and peaks and precipices of naked rock, and lofty mountain monoliths, with snow-crowned ranges beyond, form by far the grandest view that I saw in this land of hill and valley.

Then Im had to be attended to, and though I was very anxious about him, I could not be blind to the picturesqueness of the scene in the hovel, Mr. Yi sitting in my chair holding the candle, the soldier, with his face puckered with pain, squatting on the floor with his swollen arm lying on a writing board on my lap, and no room to move. I failed there as elsewhere to get a better piece of wood for the splint, which was too short, and I could only get wadding for padding it by taking some out of Im's sleeve, and all the time and afterwards I was very anxious for fear that I had put the bandage on too tightly or too loosely, and that my want of experience would give the poor fellow a useless right arm. He was in severe pain all that night, but he was very plucky about it, made no fuss, and never allowed me to suffer in the slightest degree from his accident. Indeed, he was even more attentive than before. He said to Mr. Yi, "The foreign woman looked so sorry, and touched my arm as if I had been one of her own people, I shall do my best "—and so he did. I had indulged in a long perspective of pheasant curries, and I must confess that when the prospect faded I felt a little dismal. To a traveller who carries no "foreign food," it makes a great difference to get a nice, hot, stimulating dish (even though it is served in the pot it is cooked in) after a ten hours' cold ride. To my surprise, I was never without curry for dinner, and though before the accident I had only cold rice for tiffin, after it I was never without something hot.

The descent of An-kil Yung is very grand. The road leads into a wide valley with a fine stream, one side of which looks as if the mountains had dumped down all their available stones upon it, while the other is rich alluvial soil. Gold washing is carried on to a great extent along this stream,

which is a tributary of the Tai-döng, and some of the work-
ings show more care and method than usual, being pits neatly
lined with stone in their upper parts. Eighty cents per day is
the average earning of a gold-seeker there. This valley terminates in pretty, broken country, with fine mountain views,
and picturesque cliffs along the river, on which the dark blue
gloom of pines was lighted by the fading scarlet of the maple,
and crimson streaks of the *Ampelopsis Veitchii* brightened
the russet into which the countless trailers which draped the
rocks had passed. The increased fertility of the soil was denoted by the number of villages and hamlets on the road, and
foot passengers in twos and threes gave something of life and
movement. But it was remarkable that so soon after the harvest, and when the roads were in their best condition, there
were no goods in transit except such local productions as paper
and tobacco—no strings of porters or ponies carrying goods
into the interior from Phyöng-yang, no evidence of trade but
that given by the pedlars going the round of the market-places.

Along that road and elsewhere near the villages there are
tall poles branching at the top into a V, which are erected in
the belief that they will guard the inhabitants from cholera
and other pestilences. On that day's journey, at a crossroad,
a small log with several holes like those of a mouse-trap, one
of them plugged doubly with bungs of wood, was lying on the
path, and the *mapu* were careful to step over it and lead their
ponies over it, though it might easily have been avoided. Into
the bunged hole the *mu-tang* or sorceress by her arts had in-
veigled a dæmon which was causing sickness in a family, and
had corked him up ! It is proper for passers-by to step over
the log. At nightfall it is buried. That afternoon's ride was
through extremely attractive country—small valley basins of
rich stoneless soil, with brown hamlets nestling round them in
calm, pine-sheltered folds of hills, which though not high are
shapely, and were etherealized into purple beauty by the sinking sun, which turned the lake-like expanse of the Tai-döng at

Mou-chin Tai, the beautifully situated halting-place for the night, into a sheet of gold.

With a splendid climate, an abundant, but not superabundant, rainfall, a fertile soil, a measure of freedom from civil war and robber bands, the Koreans ought to be a happy and fairly prosperous people. If "squeezing," *yamen* runners and their exactions, and certain malign practices of officials can be put down with a strong hand, and the land tax is fairly levied and collected, and law becomes an agent for protection rather than an instrument of injustice, I see no reason why the Korean peasant should not be as happy and industrious as the Japanese peasant. But these are great " ifs " ! *Security for the gains of industry*, from whatever quarter it comes, will, I believe, transform the limp, apathetic native. Such ameliorations as have been made are owed to Japan, but she had not a free hand, and she was too inexperienced in the rôle which she undertook (and I believe honestly) to play, to produce a harmonious working scheme of reform. Besides, the men through whom any such scheme must be carried out are nearly universally corrupt both by tradition and habit. Reform was jerky and piecemeal, and Japan irritated the people by meddlesomeness in small matters and suggested interferences with national habits, giving the impression, which I found prevailing everywhere, that her object is to denationalize the Koreans for purposes of her own.

Travellers are much impressed with the laziness of the Koreans, but after seeing their energy and industry in Russian Manchuria, their thrift, and the abundant and comfortable furnishings of their houses, I greatly doubt whether it is to be regarded as a matter of temperament. Every man in Korea knows that poverty is his best security, and that anything he possesses beyond that which provides himself and his family with food and clothing is certain to be taken from him by voracious and corrupt officials. It is only when the exactions of officials become absolutely intolerable and encroach upon his means of providing the necessaries of life that he resorts to the only method of redress in his power, which has a sort of counterpart in China. This consists in driving out, and occasionally in killing, the obnoxious and intolerable magistrate, or, as in a case which lately gained much notoriety, roasting his favorite secretary on a wood pile. The popular outburst, though under unusual provocation it may culminate in deeds of regrettable violence, is usually founded on right, and is an effective protest.

Among the modes of squeezing are forced labor, doubling or trebling the amount of a legitimate tax, exacting bribes in cases of litigation, forced loans, etc. If a man is reported to have saved a little money, an official asks for the loan of it. If it is granted, the lender frequently never sees principal or interest; if it is refused, he is arrested, thrown into prison on some charge invented for his destruction, and beaten until either he or his relations for him produce the sum demanded. To such an extent are these demands carried, that in Northern Korea, where the winters are fairly severe, the peasants, when the harvest has left them with a few thousand *cash*, put them in a hole in the ground, and pour water into it, the frozen mass which results then being earthed over, when it is fairly safe both from officials and thieves.

CHAPTER XXIX

SOCIAL POSITION OF WOMEN

MOU-CHIN TAI is a beautifully situated village, and has something of a look of comfort. Up to that point small boats can come up at all seasons, but there is almost no trade. The Tai-döng expands into a broad sheet of water, on which the hills descend abruptly. There is a ferry, and we drove our ponies into the ferryboat and yelled for the ferryman. After a time he appeared on the top of the bank, but absolutely declined to take us over "for any money." He would have "nothing so do with a foreigner," he said, and he would not be "implicated with a Japanese"! So we put ourselves across, and the *mapu* were so angry that they threw his poles into the river.

Passing through very pretty country, and twice crossing the Tai-döng, we halted at the town of Sun-chhön, a magistracy with a deplorably ruinous *yamen*. All these official buildings have seen better days. Their courts are spacious, and the double-roofed gateways, with their drum towers, as well as the central hall of the *yamen*, still retain a certain look of stateliness, though paint, lacquer, and gilding have long ago disappeared from the elaborately arranged beams and carved wood of the roofs, and the fretwork screening the interiors is always shabby and broken.

About the Sun-chhön *yamen*, and all others, there are crowds of "runners," writers, soldiers in coarse ragged uniforms, young men of the *yang-ban* class in spotless white garments, lounging, or walking with the swinging gait befitting their position, while the decayed and forlorn rooms in the courtyard are filled with

338

petty officials, smoking long pipes and playing cards. To judge from the crowds of attendants, the walking hither and thither, the hurrying in various directions with manuscripts, and the din of drums and fifes when the great gate is opened and closed, one would think that nothing less than the business of an empire was transacted within the ruinous portals.

Soldiers, writers, *yamen* runners, and men of the *yang-ban* and literary classes combined with the loafers of the town to compose a crowd which by its buzzing and shouting, and tearing off the paper from my latticed door, gave me a fatiguing and hideous two hours, a Korean crowd being only *un*bearable when it is led by men of the literary class, who, as in China, indulge in every sort of vulgar impertinence. Eventually I was smuggled into the women's apartments, where I was victimized in other ways by insatiable curiosity.

The women of the lower classes in Korea are ill-bred and unmannerly, far removed from the gracefulness of the same class in Japan or the reticence and kindliness of the Chinese peasant women. Their clothing is extremely dirty, as if the men had a monopoly of their ceaseless laundry work, which everywhere goes on far into the night. Every brookside has its laundresses squatting on flat stones, dipping the soiled clothes in the water, laying them on flat stones in tightly rolled bundles and beating them with flat paddles, a previous process consisting of steeping them in a ley made of wood ashes. Bleached under the brilliant sun and very slightly glazed with rice starch, after being beaten for a length of time with short quick taps on a wooden roller with club-shaped "laundry sticks," common white cotton looks like dull white satin, and has a dazzling whiteness which always reminds me of St. Mark's words concerning the raiment at the Transfiguration, "so as no fuller on earth can white them." This wearing of white clothes, and especially of white wadded clothes in winter, entails very severe and incessant labor on the women. The coats have to be unpicked and put together again each time that they are washed, and though some of the long seams are often joined with paste, there is till much sewing to be done.

Besides this the Korean peasant woman makes all the clothing of the household, does all the cooking, husks and cleans rice with a heavy pestle and mortar, carries heavy loads to market on her head, draws water, in remote districts works in the fields, rises early and takes rest late, spins and weaves, and as a rule has many children, who are not weaned till the age of three.

The peasant woman may be said to have no pleasures. She is nothing but a drudge, till she can transfer some of the drudgery to her daughter-in-law. At thirty she looks fifty, and at forty is frequently toothless. Even the love of personal adornment fades out of her life at a very early age. Beyond the daily routine of life it is probable that her thoughts never stray except to the dæmons, who are supposed to people earth and air, and whom it is her special duty to propitiate.

It is really difficult to form a general estimate of the position of women in Korea. Absolute seclusion is the inflexible rule among the upper classes. The ladies have their own courtyards and apartments, towards which no windows from the men's apartments must look. No allusion must be made by a visitor to the females of the household. Inquiries after their health would be a gross breach of etiquette, and politeness requires that they should not be supposed to exist. Women do not receive any intellectual training, and in every class are regarded as beings of a very inferior order. Nature having in the estimation of the Korean man, who holds a sort of dual philosophy, marked woman as his inferior, the *Youth's Primer*, *Historical Summaries*, and the *Little Learning* impress this view upon him in the schools, and as he begins to mix with men this estimate of women receives daily corroboration.

The seclusion of women was introduced five centuries ago by the present dynasty, in a time of great social corruption,

for the protection of the family, and has probably been continued, not, as a Korean frankly told Mr. Heber Jones, because men distrust their wives, but because they distrust each
other, and with good reason, for the immorality of the cities
and of the upper classes almost exceeds belief. Thus all young
women, and all older women except those of the lowest class,
are secluded within the inner courts of the houses by a custom
which has more than the force of law. To go out suitably
concealed at night, or on occasions when it is necessary to
travel or to make a visit, in a rigidly closed chair, are the only
" outings " of a Korean woman of the middle and upper
classes, and the low-class woman only goes out for purposes of
work.

The murdered Queen told me, in allusion to my own Korean
journeys, that she knew nothing of Korea, or even of the capital, except on the route of the *Kur-dong*.

Daughters have been put to death by their fathers, wives by
their husbands, and women have even committed suicide, according to Dallet, when strange men, whether by accident or design, have even touched their hands, and quite lately a serving-
woman gave as her reason for remissness in attempting to save
her mistress, who perished in a fire, that in the confusion a
man had touched the lady, making her not worth saving !

The law may not enter the women's apartments. A noble
hiding himself in his wife's rooms cannot be seized for any
crime except that of rebellion. A man wishing to repair his
roof must notify his neighbors, lest by any chance he should
see any of their women. After the age of seven, boys and
girls part company, and the girls are rigidly secluded, seeing
none of the male sex except their fathers and brothers until
the date of marriage, after which they can only see their own
and their husband's near male relations. Girl children, even
among the very poor, are so successfully hidden away, that in
somewhat extensive Korean journeys I never saw one girl who
looked above the age of six, except hanging listlessly about in

the women's rooms, and the brightness which girl life contributes to social existence is unknown in the country.

But I am far from saying that the women fret and groan under this system, or crave for the freedom which European women enjoy. Seclusion is the custom of centuries. Their idea of liberty is peril, and I quite believe that they think that they are closely guarded because they are valuable chattels. One intelligent woman, when I pressed her hard to say what they thought of our customs in the matter, replied, " We think that your husbands don't care for you very much " !

Concubinage is a recognized institution, but not a respected one. The wife or mother of a man not infrequently selects the cuncubine, who in many cases is looked upon by the wife as a proper appendage of her husband's means or position, much as a carriage or a butler might be with us. The offspring in these cases are under a serious social stigma, and until lately have been excluded from some desirable positions. Legally the Korean is a strict monogamist, and even when a widower marries again, and there are children by the second marriage, those of the first wife retain special rights.

There are no native schools for girls, and though women of the upper classes learn to read the native script, the number of Korean women who can read is estimated at two in a thousand. It appears that a philosophy largely imported from China, superstitions regarding dæmons, the education of men, illiteracy, a minimum of legal rights, and inexorable custom have combined to give woman as low a status in civilized Korea as in any of the barbarous countries in the world. Yet there is no doubt that the Korean woman, in addition to being a born *intrigante*, exercises a certain direct influence, especially as mother and mother-in-law, and in the arrangement of marriages.

Her rights are few, and depend on custom rather than law. She now possesses the right of remarriage, and that of remaining unmarried till she is sixteen, and she can refuse permission

to her husband for his concubines to occupy the same house
with herself. She is powerless to divorce her husband, conjugal fidelity, typified by the goose, the symbolic figure at a
wedding, being a feminine virtue solely. Her husband may
cast her off for seven reasons—incurable disease, theft, child-
lessness, infidelity, jealousy, incompatibility with her parents-
in-law, and a quarrelsome disposition. She may be sent back
to her father's house for any one of these causes. It is believed, however, that desertion is far more frequent than
divorce. By custom rather than law she has certain recognized rights, as to the control of children, redress in case of
damage, etc. Domestic happiness is a thing she does not look
for. The Korean has a house, but no home. The husband
has his life apart; common ties of friendship and external interest are not known. His pleasure is taken in company with
male acquaintances and *gesang ;* and the marriage relationship
is briefly summarized in the remark of a Korean gentleman in
conversation with me on the subject, "We marry our wives,
but we love our concubines."

CHAPTER XXX

EXORCISTS AND DANCING WOMEN

AT Cha san, a magistracy, we rejoined the road from which we had diverged on the northward journey. It is a quiet, decayed place, though in a good agricultural country. As I had been there before, the edge of curiosity was blunted, and there was no mobbing. The people gave a distressing account of their sufferings from the Chinese soldiers, who robbed them unscrupulously, took what they wanted without paying, and maltreated the women. The Koreans deserted, through fright, the adjacent ferry village of Ou-Chin-gang, where we previously crossed the Tai-döng, and it was held by 53 Chinese, being an important post. Two Japanese scouts appeared on the other side of the river, fired, and the Chinese detachment broke and fled! At Cha san, as elsewhere, the people expressed intense hatred of the Japanese, going so far as to say that they would not leave one of them alive; but, as in all other places, they bore unwilling testimony to the good conduct of the soldiers, and the regularity with which the commissariat paid for supplies.

The Japanese detachments were being withdrawn from the posts along that road, and we passed several well-equipped detachments, always preceded by bulls loaded with red blankets. The men were dressed in heavy gray ulsters with deep fur-lined collars, and had very thick felt gloves. They marched as if on parade, and their officers were remarkable for their smartness. When they halted for dinner, they found everything ready, and had nothing to do but stack their arms and eat! The peasant women went on with their avocations as usual. In that district and in the region about Tok Chhön, the women seclude themselves in monstrous hats like our wicker garden sentry-boxes, but without bottoms. These extraordinary coverings are 7 feet long, 5 broad, and 3 deep, and shroud the figure from head to foot. Heavy rain fell during the night, and though the following day was beautiful, the road was a deep quagmire, so infamously bad that when only two and a half hours from Phyöng-yang we had to stop at the wayside inn of An-chin-Miriok, where I slept in a granary only˙ screened from the stable by a bamboo mat, and had the benefit of the squealing and vindictive sounds which accompanied numerous abortive fights. If possible, the next day exceeded its predecessors in beauty, and though the drawbacks of Korean travelling are many, this journey had been so bright and so singularly prosperous, except for Im's accident, which, however, brought out some of the best points of Korean character, that I was even sorry to leave the miserable little hostelry and conclude the expedition, and part with the *mapu*, who throughout had behaved extremely well. The next morning, crossing the battlefield once more and passing through the desolations which war had wrought, I reached my old, cold, but comparatively comfortable quarters at Phyöng-yang, where I remained for six days.

While the river remained open, a small Korean steamer of uncertain habits, the *Hariong*, plied nominally between Phyöng-yang and Chemulpo, but actually ran from Po-san, a point about 60 *li* lower down the Tai-döng, which above it is too shallow and full of sandbanks for vessels of any draught, necessitating the˙transhipment of all goods not brought up by junks of small tonnage. There was, however, no telegraph between Po-san and Phyöng-yang, no one knew when the steamer arrived except by cargo coming up the river, and she only remained a few hours; so that my visit to Phyöng-yang was agitated by the fear of losing her, and having to make a long land journey when time was precious. There was no

Korean post, and the Japanese military post and telegraph office absolutely refused to carry messages or letters for civilians. Wild rumors, of which there were a goodly crop every hour, were the substitute for news.

A subject of special interest and inquiry at Phyöng-yang was mission work as carried on by American missionaries. At Seoul it is far more difficult to get into touch with it, as, being older, it has naturally more of religious conventionality. But I will take this opportunity of saying that longer and more intimate acquaintance only confirmed the high opinion I early formed of the large body of missionaries in Seoul, of their earnestness and devotion to their work, of the energetic, hopeful, and patient spirit in which it is carried on, of the harmony prevailing among the different denominations, and the cordial and sympathetic feeling towards the Koreans. The interest of many of the missionaries in Korean history, folklore, and customs, as evidenced by the pages of the valuable monthly, the *Korean Repository*, is also very admirable, and a traveller in Korea must apply to them for information vainly sought elsewhere.

Christian missions were unsuccessful in Phyöng-yang. It was a very rich and very immoral city. More than once it turned out some of the missionaries, and rejected Christianity with much hostility. Strong antagonism prevailed, the city was thronged with *gesang*, courtesans, and sorcerers, and was notorious for its wealth and infamy. The Methodist Mission was broken up for a time, and in six years the Presbyterians only numbered 28 converts. Then came the war, the destruction of Phyöng-yang, its desertion by its inhabitants, the ruin of its trade, the reduction of its population from 60,000 or 70,000 to 15,000, and the flight of the few Christians.

Since the war there had been a very great change. There had been 28 baptisms, and some of the most notorious evil livers among the middle classes, men shunned by other men for their exceeding wickedness, were leading pure and right-

eous lives.   There were 140 catechumens under instruction,
and subject to a long period of probation before receiving baptism, and the temporary church, though enlarged during my
absence, was so overcrowded that many of the worshippers
were compelled to remain outside.   The offertories were liberal.[1]   In the dilapidated extra-mural premises occupied by
the missionaries, thirty men were living for twenty-one days,
two from each of fifteen villages, all convinced of the truth of
Christianity, and earnestly receiving instruction in Christian
fact and doctrine.   They were studying for six hours daily
with teachers, and for a far longer time amongst themselves,
and had meetings for prayer, singing, and informal talk each
evening.   I attended three of these, and as Mr. Moffett interpreted for me, I was placed in touch with much of what was
unusual and interesting, and learned more of missions in their
earlier stage than anywhere else.

Besides the thirty men from the villages, the Christians and
catechumens from the city crowded the room and doorways.
Two missionaries sat on the floor at one end of the room with
a kerosene lamp mounted securely on two wooden pillows in
front of them—then there were a few candles on the floor,
centres of closely-packed groups.   Hymns were howled in
many keys to familiar tunes, several Koreans prayed, bowing
their foreheads to the earth in reverence, after which some
gave accounts of how the Gospel reached their villages,
chiefly through visits from the few Phyŏng-yang Christians,
who were "scattered abroad," and then two men, who seemed

[1] The Seoul *Christian News*, a paper recently started, gave its readers
an account of the Indian famine, with the result that the Christians in the
magistracy of Chang-yang raised among themselves $84 for the sufferers
in a land they had hardly heard of, some of the women sending their solid
silver rings to be turned into *cash*.   In Seoul the native Presbyterian
churches gave $60 to the same fund, of which $20 were collected by a
new congregation organized entirely by Koreans.   I am under the impression that the liberality of the Korean Christians in proportion to their
means far exceeds our own.

very eloquent as well as fluent, and riveted the attention of all, gave narratives of two other men who they believed were possessed with devils, and said the devils had been driven out a few months previously by united prayer, and that the "foul spirits" were adjured in the name of Jesus to come out, and that the men trembled and turned cold as the devils left them, never to return, and that both became Christians, along with many who saw them.

A good many men came from distant villages one afternoon to ask for Christian teaching, and in the evening one after another got up and told how a refugee from Phyöng-yang had come to his village and had told them that they were both wicked and foolish to worship dæmons, and that they were wrongdoers, and that there is a Lord of Heaven who judges wrongdoing, but that He is as loving as any father, and that they did not know what to think, but that in some places twenty and more were meeting daily to worship "the Highest," and that many of the women had buried the dæmon fetishes, and that they wanted some one to go and teach them how to worship the true God.

A young man told how his father, nearly eighty years old, had met Mr. Moffett by the roadside, and hearing from him "some good things," had gone home saying he had heard "good news," "great news," and had got "the Books," and that he had become a Christian, and lived a good life, and had called his neighbors together to hear "the news," and would not rest till his son had come to be taught in the "good news," and take back a teacher. An elderly man, who had made a good living by sorcery, came and gave Mr. Moffett the instruments of his trade, saying he "had served devils all his life, but now he knew that they were wicked spirits, and he was serving the true God."

On the same afternoon four requests for Christian teaching came to the missionaries, each signed by from fifteen to forty men. At all these evening meetings the room was crammed within and without by men, reverent and earnest in manner, some of whom had been shunned for their wickedness even in a city "the smoke of which" in her palmy days was said "to go up like the smoke of Sodom," but who, transformed by a power outside themselves, were then leading exemplary lives. There were groups in the dark, groups round the candles on the floor, groups in the doorways, and every face was aglow except that of poor, bewildered Im.   One old man, with his forehead in the dust, prayed like a child that, as the letter bearing to New York an earnest request for more teachers was on its way, "the wind and sea might waft it favorably," and that when it was read the eyes of the foreigners[1] might be opened "to see the sore need of people in a land where no one knows anything, and where all believe in devils, and are dying in the dark."

As I looked upon those lighted faces, wearing an expression strongly contrasting with the dull, dazed look of apathy which is characteristic of the Korean, it was impossible not to recognize that it was the teaching of the Apostolic doctrines of sin, judgment to come, and divine love which had brought about such results, all the more remarkable because, according to the missionaries, a large majority of those who had renounced dæmon worship, and were living in the fear of the true God, had been attracted to Christianity in the first instance by the hope of gain !   This, and almost unvarying testimony to the same effect, confirm me in the opinion that when people talk of "nations craving for the Gospel," "stretching out pleading hands for it," or "athirst for God," or "longing for the living waters," they are using words which in that connection have no meaning.   That there are "seekers after righteousness" here and there I do not doubt, but I believe that the one "craving" of the far East is for money—that "unrest" is only in the east a synonym for poverty, and that the spiritual instincts have yet to be created.

[1] The American Presbyterian Board of Foreign Missions.

On the Sunday I went with Dr. Scranton of Seoul to the
first regular service ever held for women in Phyöng-yang.
There were a number present, all dæmon-worshippers, some
of them attracted by the sight of a "foreign woman." It was
impossible to have a formal service with people who had not the
most elementary ideas of God, of prayer, of moral evil, and of
good. It was not possible to secure their attention. They
were destitute of religious ideas. An elderly matron, who
acted as a sort of spokeswoman said, "They thought perhaps
God is a big dæmon, and He might help them to get back
their lost goods." That service was "mission work" in its
earliest stage.

On returning from a service in the afternoon where there
were crowds of bright intelligent-looking worshippers, we
came upon one of the most important ceremonies connected
with the popular belief in dæmons—the exorcism of an evil
spirit which was supposed to be the cause of a severe illness.
Never by night or day on my two visits to Phyöng-yang had I
been out of hearing of the roll of the sorcerer's drum, with
the loud vibratory clash of cymbals as an intermittent accompaniment. Such sounds attracted us to the place of exorcism.

In a hovel with an open door a man lay very ill. The space
in front was matted and enclosed by low screens, within which
were Korean tables loaded with rice cakes, boiled rice, stewed
chicken, sprouted beans and other delicacies. In this open
space squatted three old women, two of whom beat large
drums, shaped like hour-glasses, while the third clashed large
cymbals. Facing them was the *mu-tang* or sorceress, dressed
in rose-pink silk, with a buff gauze robe, with its sleeves trailing much on the ground, over it. Pieces of paper resembling
the Shinto *gohei* decorated her hair, and a curious cap of buff
gauze with red patches upon it, completed the not inelegant
costume. She carried a fan, but it was only used occasionally
in one of the dances. She carried over her left shoulder a stick,
painted with bands of bright colors, from which hung a gong

which she beat with a similar stick, executing at the same time a slow rhythmic movement accompanied by a chant. From time to time one of the ancient drummers gathered on one plate pieces from all the others and scattered them to the four winds for the spirits to eat, invoking them, saying, "Do not trouble this house any more, and we will again appease you by offerings."

The *mu-tang* is, of course, according to the belief of those who seek her services, possessed by a powerful dæmon, and by means of her incantations might induce this dæmon to evict the one which was causing the sickness by aiding her exorcisms, but where the latter is particularly obstinate, she may require larger fees and more offerings in order that she may use incantations for bringing to her aid a yet more powerful dæmon than her own. The exorcism lasted fourteen hours, until four the next morning, when the patient began to recover. A crowd, chiefly composed of women and children, stood round the fence, the children imbibing devilry from their infancy.

I was not at a regular inn in Phyŏng-yang but at a broker's house, with a yard to myself nominally, but which was by no means private. Im generally, and not roughly, requested the people to "move on," but he made two exceptions, one being in favor of a madwoman of superior appearance and apparel who haunted me on my second visit, hanging about the open front of my room, and following me to the mission-house and elsewhere. She said that I was her grandmother and that she must go with me everywhere, and, like many mad people, she had an important and mysterious communication to make which for obvious reasons never reached me. She was the concubine of a late governor of the city, and not having escaped before its capture, went mad from horror at seeing the Chinese spitted on the bayonets of the Japanese. She carried a long bodkin, and went through distressing pantomimes of running people through with it !

The other exception was in favor of *gesang*, upon whose

presence Im looked quite approvingly, and evidently thought I
did.

Phyŏng-yang has always been famous for the beauty and
accomplishments of its *gesang*, singing and dancing girls,
resembling in many respects the *geishas* of Japan, but correctly speaking they mostly belong to the Government, and
are supported by the Korean Treasury. At the time of my
two first sojourns in Seoul, about seventy of them were attached to the Royal Palace. They were under the control of
the same Government department as that with which the official
musicians are connected.

As a poor man gifted with many sons, for whom he cannot
provide, sometimes presents one to the government as a
eunuch, so he may give a girl to be a *gesang*. The *gesang*
are trained from a very early age in such accomplishments as
other Korean women lack, and which will ensure their
attractiveness, such as playing on various musical instruments,
singing, dancing, reading, reciting, writing, and fancy work.
As their destiny is to make time pass agreeably for men of the
upper classes, this amount of education is essential, though a
Korean does not care how blank and undeveloped the mind of
his wife is. The *gesang* are always elegantly dressed, as they
were when they came to see me, even through the mud of the
Phyŏng-yang streets, and as they have not known seclusion,
their manners with both sexes have a graceful ease. Their
dancing, like that of most Oriental countries, consists chiefly
of posturing, and is said by those foreigners who have seen it,
to be perfectly free from impropriety.

Dr. Allen, Secretary to the U.S. Legation at Seoul, in a
paper in the *Korean Repository* for 1886, describes among
the dances which specially interest foreigners at the entertainments at the Royal Palace one known as the " Lotus Dance."
In this, he writes, " A tub is brought in containing a large
lotus flower just ready to burst open. Two imitation storks
then come in, each one being a man very cleverly disguised.

These birds flap their wings, snap their beaks, and dance round in admiration of the beautiful bud which they evidently intend to pluck as soon as they have enjoyed it sufficiently in anticipation. Their movements all this time are very graceful, and they come closer and closer to the flower keeping time to the soft music. At last the proper time arrives, the flower is plucked, when, as the pink petals fall back, out steps a little *gesang* to the evident amazement of the birds, and to the intense delight of the younger spectators."

The Sword and Dragon dances are also extremely popular, and on great occasions the performance is never complete without "Throwing the Ball," which consists in a series of graceful arm movements before a painted arch, after which the *gesang* march in procession before the King, and the successful dancers receive presents.

Though the most beautiful and attractive *gesang* come from Phyöng-yang, they are found throughout the country. From the King down to the lowest official who can afford the luxury, the presence of *gesang* is regarded at every entertainment as indispensable to the enjoyment of the guests. They appear at official dinners at the Foreign Office, and at the palace are the chief entertainers, and sing and dance at the many parties which are given by Koreans at the picnic resorts near Seoul, and though attached to the prefectures, and various other departments, may be hired by gentlemen to give fascination to their feasts.

Their training and non-secluded position place them, however, outside of the reputable classes, and though in Japan *geishas* often become the wives of nobles and even of statesmen, no Korean man would dream of raising a *gesang* to such a position.

Dr. Allen, who has had special opportunities of becoming acquainted with the inner social life of Korea, says that they are the source of much heartburning to the legal but neglected wife, who in no case is the wife of her husband's choice, and that Korean folklore abounds with stories of discord arising in families from attachments to *gesang*, and of ardent and prolonged devotion on the part of young noblemen to these girls, who they are prevented from marrying by rigid custom. There is a Korean tale called *The Swallow King's Rewards* in which a man is visited with the " ten plagues of Korea," for maltreating a wounded swallow, and in it *gesang* are represented along with *mu-tang* as " among the ten curses of the land."

Dr. Allen, to whom I owe this fact writes, " Doubtless they are so considered by many a lonely wife, as well as by the fathers who mourn to see their sons wasting their substance in riotous living, as they doubtless did themselves when they were young."

The house in which I had quarters was much resorted to by merchants for whom my host transacted brokerage business, and entertainments were the order of the day. Mr. Yi was invited to dinner daily, and on the last evening entertained all who had invited him. Such meals cost per head as much as a dinner at the St. James's restaurant! Noise seems essential to these gatherings. The men shout at the top of their voices.

There is an enormous amount of visiting and entertaining among men in the cities. Some public men keep open house, giving their servants as much as $60 a day for the entertainment of guests. Men who are in easy circumstances go continually from one house to another to kill time. They never talk politics, it is too dangerous, but retail the latest gossip of the court or city and the witticisms attributed to great men, and tell, hear, and invent news. The front rooms of houses in which the men live are open freely to all comers. In some circles, though it is said to a far less extent than formerly, men meet and talk over what we should call " questions of literary criticism," compare poetic compositions, the ability to compose a page of poetry being the grand result of Korean education, and discuss the meaning of celebrated works—all literature being in Chinese.

The common people meet in the streets, the house fronts, and the inns. They ask each other endless questions, of a nature that we should think most impertinent, regarding each other's business, work, and money transactions, and for the latest news. It is every man's business to hear or create all the news he can. What he hears he embellishes by lies and exaggerations. Korea is the country of wild rumors. What a Korean knows, or rather hears, he tells. According to Père Dallet, he does not know the meaning of reserve, though he is utterly devoid of frankness. Men live in company in each others' houses. Domestic life is unknown. The women in the inner rooms receive female visitors, and the girl children are present. The boys at a very early age are removed to the men's apartments, where they learn from the conversation they hear that every man who respects himself must regard women with contempt.

We left Phyöng-yang for Po-san in a very small boat in which six people and their luggage were uncomfortably packed and cramped. One of the two boatmen was literally "down with fever," but with one and the strong ebb-tide we accomplished 20 miles in six hours, and were well pleased to find the *Hariong* lying at anchor, as we had not been able to get any definite information concerning her, and I never believed in her till I saw her. The Tai-döng has some historic interest, for up its broad waters sailed Ki-ja or Kit-ze with his army of 5,000 men on the way to found Phyöng-yang and Korean civilization, and down it fled Ki-jun, the last king of the first dynasty from the forces of Wei-man descending from the north. Phyöng-yang impressed me as it did Consul Carles with its natural suitability for commerce, and this Tai-döng, navigable up to the city for small junks, is the natural outlet for beans and cotton, some of which find their way to Newchwang for shipment, for the rich iron ore which lies close to the river banks at Kai Chhön, for the gold of Keum-san only 20 miles off, for the abounding coal of the immediate neighborhood;

for the hides, which are now carried on men's backs to Chemulpo, and for the products of what is said to be a considerable silk industry.

In going down the river something is seen of the original
size of Phyöng-yang, for the "earth wall" on solid masonry,
built, it is said, by Kit-ze 3,000 years ago, follows the right
bank of the Tai-döng for about four miles before it turns away
to the north, to terminate at the foot of the hill on which is the
reputed grave of its builder. This extends in that direction
possibly three miles beyond the present wall.

The plain through which the river runs is fertile and well
cultivated, though the shining mud flats at low tide are anything but prepossessing. Various rivers, enabling boats of light
draught to penetrate the country, most of them rising in the picturesque mountain ranges which descend on the plain, specially
on its western side, join the Tai-döng.

Much had been said of the *Hariong*. I was told I "should
be all right if I could get the *Hariong*," that "the *Hariong's*
a most comfortable little boat—she has ten staterooms," and
as we approached her in the mist, very wet, and stiff from the
length of time spent in a cramped position, I conjured up visions of comfort and even luxury which were not to be realized.

She was surrounded by Japanese junks, Japanese soldiers
crowded her gangways, and Japanese officers were directing
the loading. We hooked on to the junks and lay in the rain
for an hour, nobody taking the slightest notice of us. Mr. Yi
then scrambled on board and there was another half-hour's delay, which took us into the early darkness. He reappeared,
saying there was no cabin and we must go on shore. But there
was no place to sleep on shore and it was the last steamer, so I
climbed on board and Im hurried in the baggage. It was rain-
ing and blowing, and we were huddled on the wet deck like
steerage passengers, Japanese soldiers and commissariat officers there as elsewhere in Korea, masters of the situation. Mr.
Yi was frantic that he, a Government official, and one from

whom "the Japanese had to ask a hundred favors a month" should be treated with such indignity! The vessel was hired by the Japanese commissariat department to go to Nagasaki, calling at Chemulpo, and we were really, though unintentionally, interlopers!

There was truly no room for me, and the arrangement whereby I received shelter was essentially Japanese. I lived in a minute saloon with the commissariat officers, and fed precariously, Im dealing out to me, at long intervals, the remains of a curry which he had had the forethought to bring. There was a Korean purser, but the poor dazed fellow was "nowhere," being totally superseded by a brisk young manikin who, in the intervals of business, came to me, notebook in hand, that I might help him to enlarge his English vocabulary. The only sign of vitality that the limp, displaced purser showed was to exclaim with energy more than once, "I hate these Japanese, they've taken our own ships."

Fortunately the sea was quite still, and the weather was dry and fine; even Yön-yung Pa-da, a disagreeable stretch of ocean off the Whang Hai coast, was quiet, the halt of nearly a day off the new treaty port of Chin-nam-po where the mud flats extend far out from the shore, was not disagreeable, and we reached the familiar harbor of Chemulpo by a glorious sunset on the frosty evening of the third day from Po-san, the voyage in a small Asiatic transport having turned out better than could have been expected.

ITINERARY

Seoul to—

	Li.
Ko-yang	40
Pa Ju	40
O-mok	40
Ohur-chuk Kio	30
Song-do	10
O-hung-suk Ju	30
Kun-ko Kai	30

Seoul to—

	Li.
Tol Maru	35
An-shung-pa Pal	25
Shur-hung	30
Hung-shou Wan	30
Pong-san	40
Whang Ju	40
Kur-moun Tari	30
Chi-dol-pa Pal	40
Phyöng-yang	30
Mori-ko Kai	30
Liang-yang Chang	30
Cha-san	30
Shou-yang Yi	40
Ha-kai Oil	35
Ka Chang	35
Hu-ok Kuri	40
Tok Chhön	30
Shur-chong	30
An-kil Yung	20
Shil-yi	40
Mou-chin Tai	25
Sun Chhön	35
Cha-san	30
Siang-yang Chhön	40
An-chin Miriok	30
Phyöng-yang	20

Total land journey 1060

CHAPTER XXXI

THE HAIR-CROPPING EDICT

THE year 1896 opened for Korea in a gloom as profound as that in which the previous year had closed. There were small insurrections in all quarters, various officials were killed, and some of the rebels threatened to march on the capital. Japanese influence declined, Japanese troops were gradually withdrawn from the posts they had occupied, the engagements of many of the Japanese advisers and controllers in departments expired and were not renewed, some of the reforms instituted by Japan during the period of her ascendency died a natural death, there was a distinctly retrograde movement, and government was disintegrating all over the land.

The general agitation in the country and several of the more serious of the outbreaks had a cause which, while to our thinking it is ludicrous, shows as much as anything else the intense conservatism of *pung-kok* or custom which prevails among the Koreans. The cause was an attack on the " Top Knot" by a Royal Edict on 30th December, 1895 ! This set the country aflame ! The Koreans, who had borne on the whole quietly the ascendency of a hated power, the murder of their Queen, and the practical imprisonment of their King, found the attack on their hair more than they could stand. The topknot is more to a Korean than the queue is to a Chinese. The queue to the latter may be a sign of subjugation or of loyalty to the Government and that is all, and the small Chinese boy wears it as soon as his hair is long enough to plait.

To the Korean the Top Knot means nationality, antiquity (some say of five centuries, others of 2,000 years), sanctity derived from antiquity, entrance on manhood socially and legally, even though he may be a child in years, the assumption of two names by which in addition to his family name he is afterwards known, and by which he is designated on the ancestral tablets, marriage is intimately bound up with it, as is ancestral worship, and as has been mentioned in the chapter on marriage, a Korean without a Top Knot, even if in middle life, can only be treated as a nameless and irresponsible boy. In a few cases a Korean, to escape from this stage of disrespect, scrapes together enough to pay for the Top Knot ceremonies and the *mang-kun*, hat, and long coat, which are their sequence, though he is too poor to support a family, but the Top Knot in ninety-nine cases out of a hundred is only assumed on marriage, without which the wearer has the title of " a half man " bestowed on him !

The ceremonies at the "Investiture of the Top Knot" deserve a brief notice as among the most important of the singularities of the nation. When the father and family have decided that a boy shall be "invested," which in nearly all cases is on the verge of his marriage, men's clothes, the hat, *mang-kun*, etc., are provided to the limits of the family purse, and the astrologers are consulted, who choose a propitious day and hour for the ceremony, as well as the point of the compass which the chief actor is to face during its progress. The fees of the regular astrologer are very high, and in the case of the poor, the blind sorcerer is usually called in to decide on these important points.

When the auspicious day and hour arrive the family assembles, but as it is a family matter only, friends are not invited. Luck and prosperity and a number of sons are essential for the Master of the Ceremonies. If the father has been so blessed he acts as such, if not, an old friend who has been more lucky acts for him. The candidate for the distinction and privileges of manhood is placed in the middle of the room, seated on the floor, great care being taken that he faces the point of the compass which has been designated, otherwise he would have bad luck from that day forward. With much ceremony and due deliberation the Master of the Ceremonies proceeds to unwind the boy's massive plait, shaves a circular spot three inches in diameter on the crown of his head, brings the whole hair up to this point, and arranges it with strings into a firm twist from two and a half to four inches in length, which stands up from the head slightly forwards like a horn. The *mang-kun*, fillet, or crownless skullcap of horsehair gauze, coming well down over the brow, is then tied on, and so tightly as to produce a permanent groove in the skin, and headaches for some time. The hat, secured by its strings, is then put on, and the long wide coat, and the boy rises up a man.[1] The new man bows to each of his relations in regular order, beginning with his grandfather, kneeling and placing his hands, palms downward, on the floor, and resting his forehead for a moment upon them.

He then offers sacrifices to his deceased ancestors before the ancestral tablets, lighted candles in high brass candlesticks being placed on each side of the bowls of sacrificial food or fruit, and bowing profoundly, acquaints them with the important fact that he has assumed the Top Knot. Afterwards he calls on the adult male friends of his family, who for the first time receive him as an equal, and at night there is a feast in his honor in his father's house, to which all the family friends who have attained to the dignity of Top Knots are invited.

The hat is made of fine " crinoline " so that the Top Knot may be seen very plainly through it, and weighs only an ounce and a half. It is a source of ceaseless anxiety to the Korean. If it gets wet it is ruined, so that he seldom ventures to stir abroad without a waterproof cover for it in his capacious sleeve, and it is so easily broken and crushed, that when not in use it must be kept or carried in a wooden box, usually

---

[1] In chapter ix. p. 114, there is a short notice of what is involved in the transformation.

much decorated, as obnoxious in transit as a lady's bandbox. The keeping on the hat is a mark of respect.   Court officials appear in the sovereign's presence with their hats on, and the Korean only takes it off in the company of his most intimate friends.   The *mang-kun* is a fixture.   The Top Knot is often decorated with a bead of jade, amber, or turquoise, and some of the young swells wear expensive tortoise-shell combs as its ornaments.   There is no other single article of male equipment that I am aware of which plays so important a part, or is regarded with such reverence, or is clung to so tenaciously, as the Korean Top Knot.

On an "institution" so venerated and time-honored, and so bound up with Korean nationality (for the Korean, though remarkably destitute of true patriotism, has a strongly national instinct), the decree of the 30th of December, 1895, practically abolishing the Top Knot, fell like a thunderbolt. The measure had been advocated before, chiefly by Koreans who had been in America, and was known to have Japanese support, and had been discussed by the Cabinet, but the change was regarded with such disgust by the nation at large that the Government was afraid to enforce it.   Only a short time before the decree was issued, three chief officers of the *Kun-ren-tai* entered the Council Chamber with drawn swords, demanding the instantaneous issue of an edict making it compulsory on every man in Government employment to have his hair cropped, and the Ministers, terrified for their lives, all yielded but one, and he succeeded for the time in getting the issue of it delayed till after the Queen's funeral.   Very shortly afterwards, however, the King, practically a prisoner, was compelled to endorse it, and he, the Crown Prince, the Tai-Won-Kun, and the Cabinent were divested of their Top Knots, the soldiers and police following suit.

The following day the *Official Gazette* promulgated a decree, endorsed by the King, announcing that he had cut his hair short, and calling on all his subjects, officials and common people alike, to follow his example and identify themselves with the spirit of progress which had induced His Majesty to take this step, and thus place his country on a footing of equality with the other nations of the world !

The Home Office notifications were as follows :—

Translation

The present cropping of the hair being a measure both advantageous to the preservation of health and convenient for the transaction of business, our sacred Lord the King, having in view both administrative reform and national aggrandizement, has, by taking the lead in his own person, set us an example. All the subjects of Great Korea should respectfully conform to His Majesty's purpose, and the fashion of their clothing should be as set forth below :—

1. During national mourning the hat and clothing should, until the expiration of the term of mourning, be white in color as before.

2. The fillet (*mang-kun*) should be abandoned.

3. There is no objection to the adoption of foreign clothing.

(Signed) YU-KIL CHUN,
Acting Home Minister.

11th moon, 15th day.

No. 2

In the Proclamation which His Majesty graciously issued to-day (11th moon, 15th day) are words, " We, in cutting Our hair, are setting an example to Our subjects. Do you, the multitude, identify yourselves with Our design, and cause to be accomplished the great work of establishing equality with the nations of the earth."

At a time of reform such as this, when we humbly peruse so spirited a proclamation, among all of us subjects of Great Korea who does not weep for gratitude, and strive his utmost? Earnestly united in heart and mind, we earnestly expect a humble conformity with His Majesty's purposes of reformation.

(Signed) YU-KIL CHUN,
Acting Home Minister.

504th year since the founding of the Dynasty,
11th moon, 15th day.

Among the reasons which rendered the Top Knot decree detestable to the people were, that priests and monks, who, instead of being held in esteem, are regarded generally as a nuisance to be tolerated, wear their hair closely cropped, and the Edict was believed to be an attempt instigated by Japan to compel Koreans to look like Japanese, and adopt Japanese customs. So strong was the popular belief that it was to Japan that Korea owed the denationalizing order, that in the many places where there were Top Knot Riots it was evidenced by overt acts of hostility to the Japanese, frequently resulting in murder.

The rural districts were convulsed. Officials even of the highest rank found themselves on the horns of a dilemma. If they cut their hair, they were driven from their lucrative posts by an infuriated populace, and in several instances lost their lives, while if they retained the Top Knot they were dismissed by the Cabinet. In one province, on the arrival from Seoul of a newly-appointed mandarin with cropped hair, he was met by a great concourse of people ready for the worst, who informed him that they had hitherto been ruled by a Korean man, and would not endure a " Monk Magistrate," on which he prudently retired to the capital.

All through the land there were Top Knot complexities and difficulties. Countrymen, merchants, Christian catechists, and others, who had come to Seoul on business, and had been shorn, dared not risk their lives by returning to their homes. Wood and country produce did not come in, and the price of the necessaries of life rose seriously. Many men who prized the honor of entering the Palace gates at the New Year feigned illness, but were sent for and denuded of their hair. The click of the shears was heard at every gate in Seoul, at the Palace, and at the official residences ; even servants were not exempted, and some of the Foreign Representatives were unable to present themselves at the Palace on New Year's Day, because their chairmen were unwilling to meet the shears. A father poisoned himself from grief and humiliation because his two sons had submitted to the decree. The foundations of social order were threatened when the Top Knot fell !

People who had had their hair cropped did not dare to venture far from Seoul lest they should be exposed to the violence of the rural population. At Chun Chhön, 50 miles from the capital, when the Governor tried to enforce the ordinance, the people rose *en masse* and murdered him and his whole establishment, afterwards taking possession of the town and surrounding country. As policemen with their shears were at the Seoul gates to enforce the decree on incomers, and peasants who had been cropped on arriving did not dare to return to their homes, prices rose so seriously by the middle of January, 1896, that "trouble" in the capital was expected, and another order was issued that "country folk were to be let alone at that time."

Things went from bad to worse, till on the 11th of February, 1896, the whole Far East was electrified by a sensational telegram—"The King of Korea has escaped from his Palace, and is at the Russian Legation."

On that morning the King and Crown Prince in the dim daybreak left the Kyeng-pok Palace in closed box chairs, such as are used by the Palace waiting-women, passed through the gates without being suspected by the sentries, and reached the Russian Legation, the King pale and trembling as he entered the spacious suite of apartments which for more than a year afterwards offered him a secure asylum. The Palace ladies who arranged the escape had kept their counsel well, and had caused a number of chairs to go in and out of the gates early and late during the previous week, so that the flight failed to attract any attention. As the King does much of his work at night and retires to rest in the early morning, the ever vigilant Cabinet, his jailers, supposed him to be asleep, and it was not until several hours later that his whereabouts became known, when the organization of a new Cabinet was progressing, and Korean dignitaries began to be summoned into the Royal presence.

The King, on gaining security, at once reassumed his long-lost prerogatives, which have never since been curbed in the slightest degree. The irredeemable Orientalism of the two following proclamations which were posted over the city within a few hours of his escape warrants their insertion in full :—

ROYAL PROCLAMATION

Translation

Alas! alas! on account of Our unworthiness and mal-administration the wicked advanced and the wise retired. Of the last ten years, none has passed without troubles. Some were brought on by those We had trusted as the members of the body, while others, by those of Our own bone and flesh. Our dynasty of five centuries has thereby been often endangered, and millions of Our subjects have thereby been gradually impoverished. These facts make Us blush and sweat for shame. But these troubles have been brought about through Our partiality and self-will, giving rise to rascality and blunders leading to calamities. All have been Our own fault from the first to the last.

Fortunately, through loyal and faithful subjects rising up in righteous efforts to remove the wicked, there is a hope that the tribulations experienced may invigorate the State, and that calm may return after the storm. This accords with the principle that human nature will have freedom after a long pressure, and that the ways of Heaven bring success after reverses. We shall endeavor to be merciful. No pardon, however, shall be extended to the principal traitors concerned in the affairs of July, 1894, and of October, 1895. Capital punishment should be their due, thus venting the indignation of men and gods alike. But to all the rest, officials or soldiers, citizens or coolies, a general amnesty, free and full, is granted, irrespective of the degree of their offences. Reform your hearts; ease your minds; go about your business, public or private, as in times past.

As to the cutting of the Top Knots—what can We say? Is it such an urgent matter? The traitors, by using force and coercion, brought about the affair. That this measure was taken against Our will is, no doubt, well known to all. Nor is it Our wish that the conservative subjects throughout the country, moved to righteous indignation, should rise up, as they have, circulating false rumors, causing death and injury to one another, until the regular troops had to be sent to suppress the disturbances by force. The traitors indulged their poisonous nature in everything.

Fingers and hairs would fail to count their crimes. The soldiers are Our children. So are the insurgents. Cut any of the ten fingers, and one would cause as much pain as another. Fighting long continued would pour out blood and heap up corpses, hindering communications and traffic. Alas! if this continues the people will all die. The mere contemplation of such consequences provokes Our tears and chills Our heart. We desire that as soon as orders arrive the soldiers should return to Seoul and the insurgents to their respective places and occupations.

As to the cutting of Top Knots, no one shall be forced as to dress and hats. Do as you please. The evils now afflicting the people shall be duly attended to by the Government. This is Our own word of honor. Let all understand.

By order of His Majesty,
(Signed)   PAK-CHUNG YANG,
Acting Home and Prime Minister.

11th day, 2nd moon, 1st year of Kon-yang.

PROCLAMATION TO THE SOLDIERS

On account of the unhappy fate of Our country, traitors have made trouble every year. Now We have a document informing us of another conspiracy. We have therefore come to the Russian Legation. The Representatives of different countries have all assembled.

Soldiers! come and protect us. You are Our children. The troubles of the past were due to the crimes of chief traitors. You are all pardoned, and shall not be held answerable. Do your duty and be at ease. When you meet the chief traitors, viz. Cho-hui Yen, Wu-pom Sun, Yi-tu Hwong, Yi-pom Nai, Yi-chin Ho, and Kon-yong Chin, cut off their heads at once, and bring them.

You (soldiers) attend us at the Russian Legation.

11th day, 2nd moon, 1st year of Kon-yang.
Royal Sign.

Following on this, on the same day, and while thousands of people were reading the repeal of the hair-cropping order, those of the Cabinet who could be caught were arrested and beheaded in the street—the Prime Minister, who had kept his place in several Cabinets, and the Minister of Agriculture and Commerce. The mob, infuriated, and regarding the Premier as the author of the downfall of the Top Knot, gave itself up to unmitigated savagery, insulting and mutilating the dead bodies in a manner absolutely fiendish. Another of the Cabinet was rescued by Japanese soldiers, and the other traitorous members ran away. A Cabinet, chiefly new, was installed, prison doors were opened, and the inmates, guilty and innocent alike, were released, strict orders were given by the King that the Japanese were to be protected, one having already fallen a victim to the fury of the populace, and before night fell on Seoul much of the work of the previous six months had been undone, and the Top Knot had triumphed.[1]

How the Korean King, freed from the strong influence of the Queen and the brutal control of his mutinous officers, used his freedom need not be told here. It was supposed just after his escape that he would become "a mere tool in the hands of the Russian Minister," but so far was this from being the case, that before a year had passed it was greatly desired by many that Mr. Waeber would influence him against the bad in statecraft and in favor of the good, and the cause of his determination not to bias the King in any way remains a mystery to this day.

The roads which led to the Russian Legation were guarded by Korean soldiers, but eighty Russian marines were quartered in the compound and held the gates, while a small piece of artillery was very much *en évidence* on the terrace below the King's windows! He had an abundant *entourage*. For some months the Cabinet occupied the ballroom, and on the terrace and round the King's apartments there were always numbers of Court officials and servants of all grades, eunuchs, Palace women, etc., while the favorites, the ladies Om and Pak, who assisted in his escape, were constantly to be seen in his vicinity.

Revelling in the cheerfulness and security of his surround-

[1] When I last saw the King this national adornment seemed to have resumed its former proportions.

ings, the King shortly built a Palace (to which he removed in the spring of 1897), surrounding the tablet-house of the Queen, and actually in Chong-dong, the European quarter, its grounds adjoining those of the English and U. S. Legations. To the security of this tablet-house the remains of the Queen, supposed to consist only of the bones of one finger, were removed on a lucky day chosen by the astrologers with much pomp.

On this occasion a guard of eighty Russian soldiers occupied a position close to the Royal tent, not far from one in which the Foreign Representatives, with the noteworthy exception of the Japanese Envoy, were assembled. Rolled-up scroll portraits of the five immediate ancestors of the King, each enclosed in a large oblong palanquin of gilded fretwork, and preceded by a crowd of officials in old Court costume, filed past the Royal tent, where the King did obeisance, and the Russian Guard presented arms. This was only the first part of the ceremony.

Later a colossal catafalque, containing the fragmentary remains of the murdered Queen, was dragged through the streets from the Kyeng-pok Palace by 700 men in sackcloth, preceded and followed by a crowd of Court functionaries, also in mourning, and escorted by Korean drilled troops. The King and Crown Prince received the procession at the gate of the new Kyeng-wun Palace, and the hearse, after being hauled up to the end of a long platform outside the Spirit Shrine, was tracked by ropes (for no hand might touch it) to the interior, where it rested under a canopy of white silk, and for more than a year received the customary rites and sacrifices from the bereaved husband and son. The large crowd in the streets was orderly and silent. The ceremony was remarkable both for the revival of picturesque detail and of practices which it was supposed had become obsolete, such as the supporting of officials on their ponies by retainers, or when on foot by having their arms propped up.

In July, 1896, Mr. J. M'Leavy Brown, LL.D., Chief Com-

missioner of Customs, received by Royal decree the absolute
control of all payments out of the Treasury, and having gained
considerable insight into the complexities of financial corruption, addressed himself in earnest to the reform of abuses, and
with most beneficial results.

In September a Council of State of fourteen members was
substitued for the Cabinet of Ministers organized under Japanese auspices, a change which was to some extent a return to
old methods.

Many of the attempts made by the Japanese during their ascendency to reform abuses were allowed to lapse. The country
was unsettled, a "Righteous Army" having replaced the Tong-
haks. The Minister of the Household and other Royal favorites resumed the practice of selling provincial and other posts
in a most unblushing manner after the slight checks which had
been imposed on this most deleterious custom, and the sovereign himself, whose Civil List is ample, appropriated public
moneys for his own purposes, while, finding himself personally safe, and free from Japanese or other control, he reverted
in many ways to the traditions of his dynasty, and in spite of
attempted checks upon his authority, reigned as an absolute
monarch—his edicts law, his will absolute. Meanwhile Japan
was gradually effacing herself or being effaced, and whatever
influence she lost in Korea, Russia gained, but the advantages
of the change were not obvious.

CHAPTER XXXII

THE REORGANIZED KOREAN GOVERNMENT [1]

THE old system of Government in Korea, which, with but a few alterations and additions, prevailed from the founding of the present dynasty until the second half of 1894, was modelled on that of the Ming Emperors of China. The King was absolute as well in practice as in theory, but to assist him in governing there was a *Eui-chyeng Pu*, commonly translated Cabinet, composed of a so-called Premier, and Senior and Junior Ministers of State, under whom were Senior and Junior Chief Secretaries, and Senior and Junior Assistant Secretaries, with certain minor functionaries, the Government being conducted through Boards as in China, viz. Civil Office, Revenue, Ceremonies, War, Punishment, and Works, to which were added after the opening of the country to foreigners, Foreign and Home Offices. During the present reign the Home Office, under the Presidency of a powerful and ambitious cousin of the Queen, Min Yeng-chyun, began to draw to itself all administrative power, while Her Majesty's and his relations, who occupied the chief positions throughout the country, fleeced the people without restraint. Of the remaining offices which

[1] The chapters on the Reorganized Korean Government—Education, Trade, and Finance—and Dæmonism are intended to aid in the intelligent understanding of those which precede them. The reader who wishes to go into the subject of the old and the reorganized systems of Korean Government will find a mass of curious and deeply interesting detail in a volume entitled, *Korean Government*, by W. H. Wilkinson, Esq., lately H.B.M.'s Acting Vice-Consul at Chemulpo, published by the Statistical Department of the Chinese Imperial Maritime Customs at Shanghai in March, 1897. To it I am very greatly indebted.

were seated in the Metropolis the chief were the Correctional Tribunal, an office of the first rank which took cognizance of the offences of officials, and the Prefecture of Seoul which had charge of all municipal matters.

Korea was divided into eight Provinces, each under the control of a Governor, aided by a Civil and Military Secretary. Magistrates of different grades according to the size of the magistracies were appointed under him, five fortress cities, however, being independent of provincial jurisdiction. The principal tax, the land-tax, was paid in kind, and the local governments had very considerable control over the local revenues. There were provincial military and naval forces with large staffs of officers, and Boards, Offices, and Departments innumeral under Government, each with its legion of supernumeraries.

The country was eaten up by officialism. It is not only that abuses without number prevailed, but the whole system of Government was an abuse, a sea of corruption without a bottom or a shore, an engine of robbery, crushing the life out of all industry. Offices and justice were bought and sold like other commodities, and Government was fast decaying, the one principle which survived being its right to prey on the governed.

The new order of things, called by the Japanese the " Reformation," dates from the forcible occupation of the Kyeng-pok Palace by Japanese troops on the 23rd of July, 1894. The constitutional changes which have subsequently been promulgated (though not always carried out) were initiated by the Japanese Minister in Seoul, and reduced to detail by the Japanese " advisers " who shortly arrived; and Japan is entitled to the credit of having attempted to cope with and remedy the manifold abuses of the Korean system, and of having bequeathed to the country the lines on which reforms are now being carried out. It was natural, and is certainly not blameworthy, that the Japanese had in view the assimilation of Korean polity to that of Japan.

To bring about the desired reorganization, Mr. Otori, at that time the Japanese Minister, induced the King to create an Assembly, which, whatever its ultimate destiny, was to form meanwhile a Department for "the discussion of all matters grave and trivial within the realm." The Prime Minister was its President, and the number of its members was limited to twenty Councillors. A noteworthy feature in connection with it was that it invited suggestions from outsiders in the form of written memoranda.

It met for the first time on the 30th of July, 1894, and for the last on the 29th of October of the same year. It was found impossible, either by payment or Royal orders, to secure a quorum ; and after the Vice-Minister of Justice, one of the few Councillors who took an active part in the proceedings, was murdered two days after the last meeting, as was believed, by an agent of the reactionary party, it practically expired, and was dissolved by Royal Decree on the 17th of December, 1894, and a reconstituted Privy Council took its place. Those of its Resolutions, however, which had received the Royal assent became law, and unless repealed or superseded are still binding.

These Resolutions appeared in the *Government Gazette*, an institution of very old standing, imitated, like most things else, from China. This was prepared by the Court of Transmission, a Palace Department, the senior members of which formed the channel of communication between the King and the official body at large, and who, while other high officials could only reach the throne by means of personal memorials or written memoranda, were privileged to address the King *viva voce*, and through whom as a rule his commands were issued. Each day this Department collected the various memoranda and memorials, the Royal replies and the lists of appointments, copies of which when edited by it formed the

Gazette, which was furnished in MS. to officials throughout the kingdom. The Royal Edicts when published in this paper became law in Korea.

In July, 1894, Mr. Otori made the useful innovation of publishing the *Gazette* in clear type, and in the following January it appeared in a mixture of Chinese hieroglyphs and *En-mun*, the "vulgar script" of Korea, and became intelligible to the common people. No special change was made at that time, except that the Resolutions of the Deliberative Assembly were included in it. Later changes have assimilated it farther to the Government *Gazette* of Japan, and it has gained rather than lost in importance. Gradually a diminution of the power of the Court of Transmission began to show itself. Its name was changed to the Receiving Office, and members of the Cabinet and the Correctional Tribunal began to enjoy direct access to the King. In April, 1895, a farther change in a Japanese direction, and one of great significance in Korean estimation, was made, the date of the *Gazette* being given thus:—

"No. 1.—504th year of the Dynasty, 4th moon, 1st day, Wood-day."[1]

Two months later farther changes in the official *Gazette* were announced, and the programme then put forward has been adhered to, paving the way for many of the changes which have followed. It is difficult to make the importance of the *Gazette* intelligible, except to foreigners who have resided in China and Korea. The reason for dwelling so long upon it is, that for several centuries the publication in it of Royal Edicts has given them the force of law and the currency of Acts of Parliament.

In the pages which follow a brief summary is given of the outlines of the scheme for the reorganization of the Korean

[1] Wood-day is the term adopted by the Japanese for Thursday, their week, which has now been imposed on the Koreans, being Sun-day, Moon-day, Fire-day, Water-day, Wood-day, Metal-day, and Earth-day.

Government, which was prepared for the most part by the Japanese advisers, honorary and salaried, who have been engaged on the task since 1894, and which has been accepted by the King.

The first change raised the status of the King and the Royal Family to that of the Imperial Family of China. After this, it was enacted, following on the King's Oath of January, 1895, that the Queen and Royal Family were no longer to interfere in the affairs of State, and that His Majesty would govern by the advice of a Cabinet, and sign all ordinances to which his assent is given. The Cabinet, which was, at least nominally, located in the Palace, had two aspects—a Council of State, and a State Department, presided over by the Premier.

I.—As the Council of State

The members of the Cabinet or Ministers of State were the Premier, the Home Minister, the Minister for Foreign Affairs, the Finance Minister, the War Minister, the Minister of Education, the Minister of Justice, and the Minister of Agriculture, Trade and Industry. A Foreign Adviser is supposed to be attached to each of the seven Departments.

Ministers in Council were empowered to consider—the framing of laws and ordinances; estimates and balance-sheets of yearly revenue and expenditure; public debt, domestic and foreign; international treaties and important conventions; disputes as to the respective jurisdictions of Ministers; such personal memorials as His Majesty might send down to them; supplies not included in the estimates; appointments and promotions of high officials, other than legal or military; the retention, abolition, or alteration of old customs; abolition or institution of offices, and, without reference to their special relations to any one Ministry, their reconstruction or amendment; the imposition of new taxes or their alteration; and the control and management of public lands, forests, buildings, and vessels. All ordinances after being signed and sealed by the King required the countersign of the Premier.

The second function of the Cabinet as a Department of State it is needless to go into.

A Privy Council was established at the close of 1894 to take the place of the Deliberative Assembly which had collapsed, and is now empowered, when consulted by the Cabinet, to inquire into and pass resolutions concerning :—

I. The framing of laws and ordinances.

II. Questions which may from time to time be referred to it by the Cabinet.

The Council consists of a President, Vice-President, not more than fifty Councillors, two Secretaries, and four Clerks. The Councillors are appointed by the Crown on the recommendation of the Premier, and must either be men of rank, or those who have done good service to the State, or are experts in politics, law, or economics. The Privy Council is prohibited from having any correspondence on public matters with private individuals, or with any officials but Ministers and Vice-Ministers. The President presides. Two-thirds of the members must be present to form a quorum. Votes are given openly, resolutions are carried by a majority, and any Councillor dissenting from a resolution so carried has a right to have his reasons recorded in the minutes.

In the autumn of 1896 some important changes were made. A Decree of the 24th of September condemned in strong language the action of "disorderly rebels, who some three years ago revolutionized the Constitution," and changed the name of the King's advising body. The decree ordained that the old name, translated Council of State, "should be restored, and declared that new regulations would be issued, which, while adhering to ancient principles, would confirm such of the enactments of the previous three years as in the King's judgment were for the public good." The Council of State was organized by the first ordinance of a new series, and the preamble, as well as one at least of the sections, marks a distinctly retrograde movement and a reversion to the absolutism renounced in the King's Oath of January, 1895.[1] It is distinctly stated that "any motion debated at the Council may receive His Majesty's assent, without regard to the number of votes in its favor, by virtue of the Royal prerogative; or should the debates on any motion not accord with His Majesty's views, the Council may be commanded to reconsider the matter." Resolutions which the King approves, on publication in the *Gazette*, become law.

Thus perished the checks which the Japanese sought to impose on the absolutism of the Crown, and at the present time the Royal will (or whim) can and does override all else.

This *Eui-chyeng Pu* or Council, like the *Nai Kak*, its predecessor, is both a 'Council of State, and a State Department presided over by the Chancellor. The members of the Council of State are the Chancellor, the Home Minister, who is, *ex officio*, Vice-Chancellor, the Ministers of Foreign Affairs, Finance, War, Justice, and Agriculture, five Councillors, and the Chief Secretary. As a State Department under the Chancellor, the staff consists of the "Director of the General Bureau," the Chancellor's Private Secretary, the Secretary, and eight clerks.

The Council of State, as now constituted, is empowered, to pass resolutions concerning the enactment, abrogation, alteration, or interpretation of laws or regulations; peace and war and the making of treaties; restoration of domestic order; telegraphs, railways, mines, and other undertakings, and questions of compensation arising therefrom; the estimates and special appropriations; taxes, duties, and excise; matters sent down to the Council by special command of the Sovereign; publication of laws and regulations approved by the King.

The King, if he so pleases, is present in person, or may send the Heir-Apparent to represent him. The Chancellor

[1] See p. 250.

presides, two-thirds of the members from a quorum, motions are carried by a numerical majority, and finally a memorial stating in outline the debate and its issue is submitted by the Chancellor to the King, who issues such commands as may seem to him best, for, as previously stated, His Majesty is not bound to acquiesce in the decision of the majority.

The *Eui-chyeng Pu* as a Department of State through the " Director of the General Bureau" has three sections— Archives, Gazette, and Accounts, and is rather a recording than an initiating office.

The scheme for the reconstruction of the Provincial and Metropolitan Governments has introduced many important changes and retrenchments. The thirteen Provinces are now divided into 339 Prefectures, Seoul having a Government of its own. The vast *entourage* of provincial authorities has been reduced, and a Provincial Governor's staff is now limited, nominally at least, to six clerks, two chief constables, thirty police, ten writers, four ushers, fifteen messengers, eight coolies, and eight boys. Ordinances under the head of " Local Government" define the jurisdiction, powers, duties, period of office, salaries, and etiquette [1] of all officials, along with

---

[1] *Official Intercourse.* Ord. 45 amends some old practices regulating the intercourse and correspondence of officials. The etiquette of the official call by a newly appointed Prefect on the Governor, on the whole, is retained, although it is in some respects simplified. The old fashion obliged the Magistrate to remain outside the *yamen* gate, while a large folded sheet of white paper inscribed with his name, was sent in to the Governor. The latter thereupon gave orders to his personal attendants or ushers to admit the Magistrate. The *t'oin*, as they were commonly styled, called out " *Sa-ryeng*," to which the servants chanted a reply. The Governor being seated, the Magistrate knelt outside the room and bowed to the ground. To this obeisance the Governor replied by raising his arms over his head. The Magistrate was asked his name and age, given some stereotyped advice, and dismissed. The Governor is for the future to return the bow of the Prefect, and conversation is to be conducted in terms of mutual respect, the Magistrate describing himself as *ha-koan* (" your subordinate "), and addressing the Governor by his title.

many minor matters. It is in this Department that the reforms instituted by the Japanese are the most sweeping. Very many offices were abolished, and all Government property belonging to the establishments of the officials holding them was ordered to be handed over to officers of the new *régime*. A Local Government Bureau was established with sections, under which local finance in cities and towns and local expenditure of every kind were to be dealt with. An Engineering Bureau dealing with civil engineering and a Land Survey, a Registration Bureau dealing with an annual census of the population and the registration of lands, a Sanitary Bureau, and an Accounts Bureau form part of the very ambitious Local Government scheme, admirable on paper, and which, if it were honestly carried out, would strike at the roots of many of the abuses which are the curse of Korea. The whole provincial system as reorganized is under the Home Office.

An important part of the new scheme is the definition of the duties and jurisdiction of the Ministers of State. The Cabinet Orders dealing with the duties and discipline of officials at large so far issued are :—

Order 1. General rules for the conduct of public business.
   "   2. Memorabilia for officials.
   "   3. Resumption of office after mourning.
   "   4. Reprimand and correction.
   "   5. Obligation to purchase the *Gazette*.
   "   6. Memorials to be on ruled paper.

The management of public offices under the new system is practically the same as the Japanese.

The *Memorabilia for Officials* are as follows :—

(*a*) No official must trespass outside his own jurisdiction.

(*b*) Where duties have been deputed to a subordinate, the latter must not be continually interfered with.

(*c*) A subordinate ordered to do anything which in his opinion is irregular or irrelevant should expostulate with his senior. If the latter holds by his opinion, the junior must conform.

(*d*) Officials must be straightforward and outspoken, and not give outward acquiescence while privately criticising or hindering their superiors.

(*e*) Officials must not listen to suggestions from outsiders or talk with them on official business.

(*f*) Officials must be frank with one another, and not form cliques.

(*g*) No official must wilfully spread false rumors about another or lightly credit such.

(*h*) No official must absent himself from office without permission during office hours, or frequent the houses of others.

Resolution 88, passed some months earlier, was even more explicit :—

Officials are thereby forbidden to divulge official secrets even when witnesses in a court of law, unless specially permitted to do so; or to show despatches to outsiders. They are not allowed to become directors or managers in a public company; to accept compensation from private individuals or gifts from their subordinates; to undertake, without permission, extra work for payment; or to put to private use Government horses. They may receive honors or presents from foreign Sovereigns or Governments only with the special sanction of His Majesty.

An ordinance restored the use of the uniforms worn prior to the " Reformation," whether Court dress, full dress, half-dress, or undress, and announced that neither officials nor private persons were to be compelled any longer to wear black.

Each Department is presided over by a Minister, who is empowered to issue Departmental Orders, as Instructions to the local officials and police, and Notifications to the people. His jurisdiction over the police and local officials is concurrent with that of his colleagues, who must also be consulted by him before recommending to the Throne the promotion or degradation of the higher officials of his Departmental Staff.

Under the Minister is a Vice-Minister, empowered to act for him on occasion, and, when doing so, possessing equal privileges. The Vice-Minister is usually the head of the Minister's Secretariat, which deals with " confidential matters, promotions, custody of the Minister's and Departmental Seals, receipt

and despatch of correspondence, and consultation of prec-
edents, preparation of statistics, compilation and preservation
of archives.''

In addition to the Secretariats, there are a number of Bureaux,
both Secretariats and Bureaux being, for convenience, subdi-
vided into sections, each of which has its special duties.

The Departments of Government are as follows:—

HOME OFFICE

The Home Minister has charge of matters concerning local
government, police, jails, civil engineering, sanitation, shrines
and temples, surveying, printing census, and public charity, as
well as the general supervision of the local authorities and the
police.

FOREIGN OFFICE

The Foreign Minister is vested with the control of international affairs, the protection of Korean commercial interests
abroad, and the supervision of the Diplomatic and Consular
Services.

THE TREASURY

'' The Minister for Finance, being vested with the control
of the finances of the Government, will have charge of all
matters relating to accounts, revenue, and expenditure, taxes,
national debts, the currency, banks, and the like, and will
have supervision over the finances of each local administration '' (Ord. 54, § 1).

Under this Minister there is a Taxation Bureau with three
sections—Land Tax, Excise, and Customs.[1]   The ordinances

[1] The finances of Korea are now practically under British management,
Mr. J. M'Leavy Brown, LL. D., of the Chinese Imperial Maritime Customs, and Chief Commissioner of Customs for Korea, having undertaken
in addition the post of Financial Adviser to the Treasury, and a Royal
Edict having been issued that every order for a payment out of the national purse, down to the smallest, should be countersigned by him.

connected with the remodelled system of taxation and the salaries and expenses of officials are very numerous and minute. The appropriation actually in money for the Sovereign's Privy Purse was fixed at $500,000.

WAR OFFICE

The Minister for War, who must be a general officer, has charge of the military administration of an army lately fixed at 6,000 men, and the chief control of men and matters in the army, and is to exercise supervision over army divisions, and all buildings and forts under his Department. The new military arrangements are very elaborate.

MINISTRY OF EDUCATION

In this important Department, besides the Minister and Vice-Minister and heads of Bureaux and Sections, there are three special Secretaries who act as Inspectors of Schools, and an official specially deputed to compile and select text-books.

Besides the Minister's Secretariat, there are the *Education Bureau*, which is concerned with primary, normal, intermediary, foreign language, technical and industrial schools, and students abroad; and a *Compilation Bureau*, concerned with the selection, translation, and compilation of text-books; the purchase, preservation, and arrangement of volumes, and the printing of books.

Under this Department has been placed the Confucian College, an institution of the old *régime*, the purpose of which was to attend to the Temple of Literature, in which, as in China, the Memorial Tablets of Confucius, Mencius, and the Sages are honored, and to encourage the study of the classical books. The subjects for study are the "Three Classics," "Four Books and Popular Commentary," Chinese Composition, Outlines of Chinese History—of the Sung, Yüan, and Ming Dynasties. To meet the reformed requirements, this College has been reorganized, and the students, who must be between the ages of twenty and forty, "of good character, persevering, intelligent, and well acquainted with affairs," are in addition put through a course of Korean and foreign annals, Korean and foreign geography, and arithmetic.

MINISTRY OF JUSTICE

The Minister of Justice has charge of judicial matters, pardons and restorations to rank, instructions for public prosecution, and supervision over Special Courts, High Courts, and District Courts; and the Department forms a High Court of Justice for the hearing of certain appeals.

MINISTRY OF AGRICULTURE, TRADE, AND INDUSTRY

The Minister of Agriculture has charge of all matters relating to agriculture, commerce, industries, posts, telegraphs, shipping, and marine officers.

In this Department, besides the Minister's Secretariat, there are Bureaux of Agriculture, Communications, Trade, Industry, Mining, and Accounts. The Bureau of Agriculture contains Agricultural, Forest, and Natural Products sections; that of Communications, Post, Telegraph, and Marine sections; and that of Trade and Industry deals with Commerce, Trading Corporations, Weights and Measures, Manufactures, and Factories. The Mining Bureau has sections for Mines and Geology, and the Bureau of Accounts deals with the inventories and expenditure of the Department.

THE VILLAGE SYSTEM

Besides the Reorganization of these important Departments of State, a design for a "Village System," organized as follows, is to supersede that which had decayed with the general decay of Government in Korea.

The country is now divided into districts (*Kun*), each *Kun* containing a number of *myen* or cantons, each of which includes a number of *ni* or villages. The old posts and titles are abolished, and each village is now to be provided with the following officers :—

1. *Headman.*—He must be over thirty years of age, and is elected for one year by the householders. The office is honorary.

2. *Clerk.*—He holds office under the same conditions as the Headman, under whom he keeps the books and issues notices.

3. *Elder.*—Nominated by the householders, he acts for the Headman as occasion demands.

4. *Bailiff.*—Elected at the same time as the Headman he performs the usual duties of a servant or messenger, and holds office for a year on good behavior.

The corresponding officers of the canton (commune) are a *Mayor*, a *Clerk*, a *Bailiff*, and a *Communal Usher* who is irremovable except for cause given, and is, like the other officials, elected by the canton.

A Village Council is composed of the Headman and one man from each family, and is empowered to pass resolutions on matters connected with education, registration of households or lands, sanitation, roads and bridges, communal grain exchanges, agricultural improvements, common woods and dykes, payment of taxes, relief in famine or other calamity, adjustment of the *corvée*, savings associations, and by-laws. The Headman, who acts as chairman, has not only a casting vote, but the power to veto. A resolution passed over the veto of the Headman has to be referred to the Mayor, and over the veto of the Mayor to the Prefect. If passed twice over the veto of the Prefect, reference may be made to the Governor. All resolutions, however, must be submitted twice a year to the Home Office, through the Prefect and Governor ; and it is incumbent on the Prefectural Council to sit at least twice in the year.

Taxes are by a law of 13th October, 1895, classified as Land-Tax, Scutage, Mining Dues, Customs Dues, and Excise. Excise is now made to include, besides ginseng dues, what are known as "Miscellaneous Dues," viz. rent of glebe lands, tax on rushes used in mat-making, market dues on firewood and tobacco, tax on kilns, tax on edible seaweed, tax on grind-stones, up-river dues, and taxes on fisheries, salterns, and boats. All other imposts have been declared illegal. The first Korean Budget under the reformed system was published in January, 1896, and showed an estimated revenue from all sources of $4,809,410.

The Palace Department underwent reorganization, nomi-nally at least, and elaborate schemes for the administration of Royal Establishments, State Temples, and Mausolea were de-vised, and the relative rank of members of the Royal Clan, including ladies, was fixed—the ladies of the King's Seraglio being divided into eight classes, and those of the Crown Prince into four. The number of Court officials attached to the different Royal Households, though diminished, is legion.

Various ordinances brought the classification of Korean officials into line with those of Japan. Every class in the country, private and official, has come into the purview of the Reorganizers, and finds its position (*on paper*) more or less altered.

Among the more important of the Edicts which have nom-inally become law are the following :—

Agreements with China cancelled. Distinctions between Patrician and Plebeian abolished. Slavery abolished. Early Marriages prohibited. Remarriage of widows permitted. Bribery to be strictly forbidden. No one to be arrested with-out warrant for civil offences. Couriers, mountebanks, and butchers no longer to be under degradation. Local Councils to be established. New coinage issued. Organization of Police force. No one to be punished without trial. Irregular taxation by Provincial Governments forbidden. Extortion of money by officials forbidden. Family of a criminal not to be involved in his doom. Great modifications as to torture.

Superfluous Paraphernalia abolished. School of Instruction in Vaccination. Hair-cropping Proclamation. Solar Calendar adopted. "Drilled Troops" (*Kun-ren-tai*) abolished. Legal punishments defined. Slaughter-Houses licensed. Committee of Legal Revision appointed. Telegraph Regulations. Postal Regulations. Railways placed under Bureau of Communications. These ordinances are a selection from among several hundred promulgated since July, 1894.

Of the reforms notified during the last three and a half years several have not taken effect; and concerning others there has been a distinctly retrograde movement, with a tendency to revert to the abuses of the old *régime;* and others which were taken in hand earnestly, have gradually collapsed, owing in part to the limpness of the Korean character, and in part to the opposition of all in office and of all who hope for office to any measures of reform. Some, admirable in themselves, at present exist only on paper; but, on the whole, the reorganized system, though in many respects fragmentary, is a great improvement on the old one; and it may not unreasonably be hoped that the young men, who are now being educated in enlightened ideas and notions of honor, will not repeat the iniquities of their fathers.

CHAPTER XXXIII

EDUCATION AND FOREIGN TRADE

KOREAN education has hitherto failed to produce patriots, thinkers, or honest men. It has been conducted thus. In an ordinary Korean school the pupils, seated on the floor with their Chinese books in front of them, the upper parts of their bodies swaying violently from side to side or backwards and forwards, from daylight till sunset, vociferate at the highest and loudest pitch of their voices their assigned lessons from the Chinese classics, committing them to memory or reciting them aloud, writing the Chinese characters, filling their receptive memories with fragments of the learning of the Chinese sages and passages of mythical history, the begoggled teacher, erudite and supercilious, rod in hand and with a book before him, now and then throwing in a word of correction in stentorian tones which rise above the din.

This educational mill grinding for ten or more years enabled the average youth to aspire to the literary degrees which were conferred at the *Kwa-ga* or Royal Examinations held in Seoul up to 1894, and which were regarded as the stepping-stones to official position, the great object of Korean ambition. There is nothing in this education to develop the thinking powers or to enable the student to understand the world he lives in. The effort to acquire a difficult language, the knowledge of which gives him a mastery of his own, is in itself a desirable mental discipline, and the ethical teachings of Confucius and Mencius, however defective, contain much that is valuable and true, but beyond this little that is favorable can be said.

Narrowness, grooviness, conceit, superciliousness, a false

387

pride which despises manual labor, a selfish individualism, destructive of generous public spirit and social trustfulness, a slavery in act and thought to customs and traditions 2,000 years old, a narrow intellectual view, a shallow moral sense, and an estimate of women essentially degrading, appear to be the products of the Korean educational system.

With the abolition of the Royal Examinations; a change as to the methods of Government appointments; the working of the Western leaven; the increased prominence given to *En-mun*, and the slow entrance of new ideas into the country, some of the desire for this purely Chinese education has passed away, and it has been found necessary to stimulate what threatened to become a flagging interest in all education by new educational methods and forces, the influence of which should radiate from the capital.

There are now (October, 1897) Government Vernacular Schools, a Government School for the study of English, Foreign Language Schools, and Mission Schools. Outside the Vernacular and Mission Schools there is the before-mentioned Royal English School, with 100 students in uniform, regularly drilled by a British Sergeant of Marines, and crazy about football! These young men, in appearance, manners, and rapid advance in knowledge of English, reflect great credit on their instructors. After this come Japanese, French, and Russian Schools, at present chiefly linguistic. Mr. Birukoff, in charge of the Russian School, was a captain of light artillery in the Russian army, and in both the Russian and French schools the students are drilled daily by Russian drill instructors.

Undoubtedly the establishment which has exercised and is exercising the most powerful educational, moral, and intellectual influence in Korea is the Pai Chai College (" Hall for the rearing of Useful Men "), so named by the King in 1887. This, which belongs to the American Methodist Episcopal Church, has had the advantage of the services of one Principal, the Rev. H. G. Appenzeller, for eleven years. It has a

Chinese-*En-mun* department, for the teaching of the Chinese classics, Sheffield's *Universal History*, etc., a small theological department, and an English department, in which reading, grammar, composition, spelling, history, geography, arithmetic, and the elements of chemistry and natural philosophy are taught.   Dr. Jaisohn, a Korean educated in America, has recently lectured once a week at this College on the geographical divisions of the earth and the political and ecclesiastical history of Europe, and has awakened much enthusiasm.   A patriotic spirit is being developed among the students, as well as something of the English public school spirit with its traditions of honor.   This College is undoubtedly making a decided impression, and is giving, besides a liberal education, a measure of that broader intellectual view and deepened moral sense which may yet prove the salvation of Korea.   Christian instruction is given in Korean, and attendance at chapel is compulsory.   The pupils are drilled, and early in 1897, during the military craze, adopted a neat European military uniform. There is a flourishing industrial department, which includes a tri-lingual press and a book-binding establishment, both of which have full employment.

Early in 1895 the Government, recognizing the importance of the secular education given in this College, made an agreement by which it could place pupils up to the number of 200 there, paying for their tuition and the salaries of certain tutors.

There are other schools for girls and boys, in which an industrial training is given, conducted with some success by the same Mission, and the American Presbyterians have several useful schools, and pay much attention to the training of girls.

The *Société des Missions Etrangères* has in Seoul an Orphanage and two Boys' Schools, with a total of 262 children. The principal object is to train the orphans as good Roman Catholics.   In the Boys' Schools the pupils are taught to read and write Chinese and *En-mun*, and to a limited extent they study the Chinese classics.   The religious instruction is given in *En-mun*.   They aim at providing a primary education for the children of Korean converts.

The boys in the Orphanage are taught *En-mun* only, and at thirteen are adopted by Roman Catholics in Seoul or the country, and learn either farming or trades, or, assuming their own support, enter a trade or become servants.   The elder girls learn *En-mun*, sewing, and housework, and at fifteen are married to the sons of Roman Catholics.   At Riong San near Seoul there is a Theological Seminary for the training of candidates for the priesthood.

Besides these there is a school established in 1896 by the "Japanese Foreign Educational Society," which is composed chiefly of "advanced" Japanese Christians.   The course of study embraces the Chinese classics, *En-mun*, composition, the study of Japanese as a medium for the study of Western learning, and lectures on science and religion.   This school was intended by its founders to work as a Christian propaganda.

In 1897 there were in Seoul nearly 900 students, chiefly young men, in Mission and Foreign Schools, inclusive of 100 in the Royal English School, which has English teachers.   In the majority of these the students are trained in Christian morality, fundamental science, general history, and the principles of patriotism.   A certain amount of denationalization is connected with most of the Boys' Schools, for the students necessarily receive new ideas, thoughts, and views of life, which cannot be shaken out of them by any local circumstances, changing their standpoints and the texture of their minds for life.   When they replace the elder generation better things may be expected for Korea.

The Korean reformed ideas of education, which had their origin during the Japanese reform era, embrace the creation of a primary school system, an efficient Normal College, and Intermediate Schools.   Actually existing under the Department of Education are a revived Confucian School, the Royal English School, and the Normal College, placed in May, 1897, under the very efficient care of the Rev. H. B. Hulbert, M.A., a capable and scholarly man, some of whose contributions to our knowledge of Korean poetry and music have enriched earlier chapters of these volumes.   Text-books in *En-mun* and teachers who can teach them have to be created.   It is hoped and expected that supply will follow demand, and that in a few years the larger provincial towns will possess Intermediate or High Schools, and the villages attain the advantages of elementary schools, all using a uniform series of text-books in the vernacular.   Chinese finds its place in the curriculum, but not as the medium for teaching Korean and general history, or geography and arithmetic, which must be acquired through the native tongue.

In spite of the somewhat spasmodic and altogether unscientific methods of the Education Department, it has succeeded in getting the revived Normal College under way, as well as a fair number of primary schools, where over 1,000 boys are learning the elements of arithmetic, geography, and Korean history, with brief outlines of the systems of government in other civilized countries.   Seventy-seven youths are studying in Japan at Government expense, and have made fair progress in languages, but are said to show a lack of mathematical aptitude and logical power.   Altogether the Korean educational outlook is not without elements of hopefulness.

Though the Foreign Trade of Korea only averages something less than £1,500,000 annually, the potential commerce of a country with not less than 12,000,000 of people, all cotton-clad, ought not to be overlooked.   The amount of foreign trade which exists is the growth of thirteen years only, but when we remember that Korea is a purely agricultural country of a very primitive and backward type, that many of her finest valleys are practically isolated by mountain ranges, traversed by nearly impassable roads, that the tyranny of custom is strong, that the Korean farmer is only just learning that a profitable and almost unlimited demand exists for his ricc and beans across the sea, that the serious cost of his cotton clothing can be kept down by importing foreign yarn or piece goods, and that his comfort can be increased by the introduction of articles of foreign manufacture, and that such facts are only slowly entering the secluded valleys of the Hermit Kingdom, the actual bulk of the trade is rather surprising, and its possibilities are worth considering. The net imports of foreign goods have increased from the value of $2,474,189 in 1886 to $6,531,324 in 1896.[1] Measured in dollars, the trade of 1896 exceeds that of any previous year except 1895, when the occupation of Korea by Japanese troops, with their large following of transport coolies, created an artificial expansion.

Among Korean exports, which chiefly consist of beans, fish (dried manure), cow-hides, ginseng, paper, rice, and seaweed, there are none which are likely to find a market elsewhere than in China and Japan, but Korea, so far as rice goes, is on the way to become the granary of the latter country, her export in 1890 having reached the value of £271,000.

With imports, European countries, India, and America are concerned. Without, I think, being over sanguine, I anticipate a time when, with improved roads, railroads, and enlightenment, together with security for the earnings of labor from official and patrician exactions, the Korean will have no further occasion for protecting himself by an appearance of squalid poverty, and when he will become on a largely increased scale a consumer as well as a producer, and will surround himself with comforts and luxuries of foreign manufacture, as his brethren are already doing under the happier rule of Russia. Under the improved conditions which it is reasonable to expect, I should not be surprised if the value of the Foreign Trade of Korea were to reach £10,000,000 in another quarter of a century, and the share which England is to have of it is an important question.

[1] For detailed statistics of Korean Foreign Trade, see Appendix C.

Our great competitor in the Korean markets is Japan, and we have to deal not only with a rival within twenty hours of Korean shores, and with nearly a monopoly of the carrying trade, but with the most nimble-witted, adaptive, persevering, and pushing people of our day. It is inevitable that British hardware and miscellaneous articles must be ousted by the products of Japanese cheaper labor, and that the Japanese will continue to supply the increasing demand for scissors, knives, matches, needles, hoes, grass knives, soap, perfumes, kerosene lamps, iron cooking pots, nails, and the like, but the loss of the trade in cotton piece goods would be a serious matter, and the possibility of it has to be faced.

The value of the import trade in 1896 was £708,461 as against £875,816 for 1895 (an exceptional year), and the larger part of this reduction took place in articles of British manufacture, the decrease of £134,304 in the value of cotton imports falling almost entirely on cottons of British origin, the Japanese import not only retaining its position in spite of adverse circumstances, but showing a slight increase. Japanese sheetings showed a substantial increase, more than counterbalanced by the diminished import of the British and American article, and Japanese cotton yarn continued to arrive in larger quantities, and is gradually driving British and Indian yarn out of the Korean market. It can be sold at a considerably lower price than the British article, and practically at the same price as the Indian, with which its improved quality enables it to compete on very favorable terms.

As the result of inquiries carried on during my two journeys in the interior, as well as at the treaty ports, it does not appear to me that Japanese success is even chiefly caused by proximity, and in 1896 she had to compete with the enterprise and energy of the Chinese, who, having returned after the war to the benefits of British protection, were pushing the distribution of Manchester goods imported from Shanghai.

Rather I am inclined to think that the success of our rival is

mainly due to causes which I have seen in operation in Persia
and Central Asia as well as in Korea, and which embrace not
only imperfect knowledge of the tastes and needs of customers,
but the neglect to act upon information supplied by consular
and diplomatic agents, a groovy adherence to British methods
of manufacture, and the ignoring of native desires as to colors,
patterns, and the widths and makes which suit native clothing
and treatment, and the size of bales best suited to native
methods of transport.   I do not allude to the charge ofttimes
made against our manufacturers of supplying inferior cottons,
because I have never seen any indications of its correctness,
nor have I heard any complaints on the subject either in Korea
or China, but of the ignoring of the requirements of customers
there is no doubt.   It is everywhere a grievance and source of
loss, and is likely to lose us the prospective advantages of the
Korean market.

The Japanese success, putting the advantages of proximity
aside, is, I believe, mainly due to the accuracy of the information obtained by their keen-witted agents, who have visited all
the towns and villages in Korea, and to the carefulness with
which their manufacturers are studying the tastes and requirements of the Korean market.   Their goods reach the shore in
manageable bales, which do not require to be adapted after
arrival to the minute Korean pony, and their price, width,
length, and texture commend them to the Korean consumer.
The Japanese understand that cotton 18 inches wide is the
only cotton from which Korean garments can be fashioned
without very considerable waste, and they supply the market
with it; and on the report of the agents of the importing
firms, the weavers of Osaka and other manufacturing towns
with adroitness and rapidity closely adapted the texture, width,
and length of their cottons to those of the hand-loom cotton
goods made in South Korea, which are deservedly popular for
their durability, and have succeeded not only in producing an
imitation of Korean cotton cloth, which stands the pounding

and beating of Korean washing, but one which actually deceives the Korean weavers themselves as to its origin, and which has won great popularity with the Korean women. If Korea is to be a British market in the future, the lost ground must be recovered by working on Japanese lines, which are the lines of commercial common sense.

To sum up, I venture to express the opinion that the circumstances of the large population of Korea are destined to gradual improvement with the aid of either Japan or Russia, that foreign trade must increase more or less steadily with increased buying powers and improved means of transport, and that the amount which falls to the share of Great Britain will depend largely upon whether British manufacturers are willing or not to adapt their goods to Korean tastes and convenience.

As instances of the aptitude of the Koreans for taking to foreign articles which suit their needs, it may be mentioned, on the authority of a report from the British Consul-General to the British Foreign Office on Trade and Finance in Korea for 1896, presented to Parliament July, 1897, that the import of lucifer matches reached the figure of £11,386,[1] while that of American and Russian kerosene exceeded £36,000.

In 1896 the export of gold increased, and was $1,390,412, one million dollars' worth being exported from Wön-san alone. The gold export included, the excess of Korean imports over exports was only about £50,000, and as it is estimated that only one half of the gold actually leaving the country is declared, it may be assumed that Korea is able to pay for a larger supply of foreign goods than she has hitherto taken. The statistics of Korean Foreign Trade which are to be found in the Appendix are the latest returns, supplied to me by the courtesy of the Korean Customs' Department,[2] the returns of shipping and of principal articles of export and import being taken from

[1] This seems incredible, and compels one to suppose that £ is a misprint for $.

[2] See Appendix B.

H.B.M.'s. Consul-General's Report for 1896, presented to Parliament July, 1897.[1] With reference to the shipping returns, it must be observed that the British flag is practically unrepresented in Korean waters, even a chartered British steamer being rarely seen. The monopoly of the carrying trade which Japan has enjoyed has only lately been broken into by the establishment of a Russian subsidized line as a competitor.

In addition to the trade of the three ports open to Foreign Trade in 1896, to which the returns given refer exclusively, there is that carried on by the non-treaty ports, and on the Chinese and Russian frontiers.

In concluding this brief notice of the Foreign Trade of Korea, I may remark that Japanese competition, so far as it consists in the ability to undersell us owing to cheaper labor, is likely to diminish year by year, as the conditions under which goods can be manufactured gradually approximate to those which exist in England ; the rapidly increasing price of the necessaries of life in Japan, the demand for more than " a living wage," and an appreciation of the advantages of combination all tending in this direction.

On the subject of Finance there is little to be said. The principal items of revenue are a land tax of six dollars on a fertile *kyel*, and five dollars on a mountain *kyel*, a house tax of 60 cents annually, from which houses in the capital are exempt, the ginseng tax, and the gold dues, making up a budget of about 4,000,000 dollars, a sum amply sufficient for the legitimate expenditure of the country. The land tax is extremely light. Only about a third of the revenue actually collected reaches the National Treasury, partly owing to the infinite corruption of the officials through whose hands it passes, and partly because provincial income and expenditure are to a certain extent left to local management. If the Government is in earnest in the all important matter of educating

[1] See Appendix C.

the people, the increased expenditure can readily be met by imposing taxation on such articles of luxury as wine and tobacco, which are enormously consumed, Seoul alone possessing 475 wine shops and 1,100 tobacco shops. But even without resorting to any new source of revenue, with strict supervision and regular accounts the income of the Central Government is capable of considerable expansion.

In spite of the awful official corruption which has been revealed, and the chaos which up to 1896 prevailed in the Treasury, the Korean financial outlook is a hopeful one. At the close of 1895 the King persuaded Mr. M'Leavy Brown, LL.D., the Chief Commissioner of Customs, to undertake the thankless office of Adviser to the Treasury, confirming his position some months later by the issue of an edict making his signature essential to all orders for payments out of the national purse. Korean imagination and ingenuity are chiefly fertile in devising tricks and devices for getting hold of public money, and anything more hydra-headed than the dishonesty of Korean official life cannot be found, so that it is not surprising that as soon as the foreign adviser blocks one nefarious proceeding another is sprung upon him, and that the army of useless drones, deprived of their " vested interests " by the judicious retrenchments which have been made, as well as thousands who are trembling for their ill-gotten gains, should oppose financial reform by every device of Oriental ingenuity.

However, race, as represented by the honor and capacity of one European, is carrying the day, and Korean Finance is gradually being placed on a sound basis. With careful management, judicious retrenchments of expenditure, the reduction of the chaos in the Treasury to an orderly system of accounts, and a different method of collecting the land tax, which is now being remitted with tolerable regularity to the Treasury, an actual financial equilibrium was established and maintained during the year 1896, which closed with a considerable surplus, and in April, 1897, one million dollars of the Japanese loan of three millions was repaid to Japan, and there is every prospect that the remaining indebtedness might be paid off out of income in 1899, leaving Korea in the proud position of a country without a national debt, and with a surplus of income over expenditure !

The prosperous financial conclusion of 1896 is all the more remarkable because of certain exceptional expenditures. Two new regiments were added to the army, the old Arsenal, a disused costly toy, was put into working order, with all necessary modern improvements, under the supervision of a Russian machinist, the Kyeng-wun Palace was built, costly ceremonies and works connected with the late Queen's prospective funeral were paid for, and a considerable area of western Seoul was recreated. All civil Government *employés* (and they are legion), as well as soldiers and police, are paid regularly every month, and sinecures are very slowly disappearing.

A Korean silver, copper, and brass coinage, convenient as well as ornamental, is coming into general circulation, and as it gradually displaces *cash*, is setting trade free from at least one of the conditions which hampered it, and increased banking facilities are tending in the same direction.

CHAPTER XXXIV

DÆMONISM OR *SHAMANISM*

KOREAN cities without priests or temples; houses without "god shelves"; village festivals without a *mikoshi* or idols carried in festive procession; marriage and burial without priestly blessing; an absence of religious ceremonials and sacred books to which real or assumed reverence is paid, and nothing to show that religion has any hold on the popular mind, constitute a singular Korean characteristic.

Putting aside Buddhism with its gross superstitions, practised chiefly in remote places, and the magisterial homage before the Confucian tablets to the memory of the Great Teacher, the popular cult—I dare not call it a religion—consists of a number of observances dictated by the dread of bodiless beings created by Korean fancy, and representing chiefly the mysterious forces of nature. It may be assumed, taking tradition for a guide, as certain of the litanies used in exorcism and invocation were introduced along with Buddhism from China, that Korean imagination has grafted its own fancies on those which are of foreign origin, and which are of by no means distant kinship to those of the *Shamanism* of northern Asia.

The external evidences of this cult are chiefly heaps of stones on the tops of passes, rude shrines here and there containing tawdry pictures of mythical beings, with the name in Chinese characters below, strings from which depend small bags of rice, worn-out straw shoes, strips of dirty rags, and, though rarely, rusty locks of black hair. Outside of many villages are high posts (not to be confounded with the distance posts) with their tops rudely carved into heads and faces half human, half dæmonic, from which straw ropes, with dependent straw tassels, recalling the Shintoism of Japan, are stretched across the road. There are large or distorted trees also, on which rags, ricebags, and old shoes are hung, and under which are heaps of stones at which it is usual for travellers to bow and expectorate. On the ridge poles of royal buildings and city gates, there are rows of grotesque bronze or china figures for the purpose of driving away evil dæmons, and at crossroads a log of wood perforated like a mouse-trap, and with one hole bunged up, over which travellers step carefully, may sometimes be seen. In cities the beating of drums accompanied by the clashing of cymbals vies with the laundry sticks in breaking the otherwise profound stillness of night, and in travelling through the country, the *mu-tang* or sorceress is constantly to be seen going through various musical and dancing performances in the midst of a crowd in front of a house where there is sickness.

I have referred to these things in earlier chapters, but the subject is such an important one, and the influence on Korean life of the belief in dæmons is so strong and injurious, that I feel justified in laying before my readers at some length such details of *Dæmonism* as have hitherto been ascertained. There is an unwillingness to speak to foreigners on this topic, and inquirers may have been purposely misled, but enough has been gained to make it likely that further inquiry will be productive of very valuable results.[1] The superstitions already mentioned, however trivial in themselves, point to that which underlies all religion, the belief in something outside ourselves which is higher or more powerful than ourselves.

[1] I desire again to express my indebtedness to the Rev. G. Heber Jones, of Chemulpo, for the loan of, and the liberty to use, his very careful and painstaking notes on the subject of Korean dæmonism, and also to a paper on *The Exorcism of Spirits in Korea*, by Dr. Landis of Chemulpo. Apart from the researches of these two Korean scholars, the results of my own inquiry and observation would scarcely have been worth publishing.

It is indeed asserted by many of the so-called educated class that the only cult in Korea is ancestor worship, and they profess to ridicule the rags, cairns, shrines, and the other paraphernalia of dæmon-worship, as the superstition of women and coolies, and it is probable that in Seoul, at least, few men of the upper class are believers, or patronize the rites otherwise than as unmeaning customs which it would be impolitic to discontinue, but it is safe to say that from the Palace to the hovel all women, and a majority of men, go through the forms which, influencing Buddhism, and possibly being modified by it, have existed in Korea for more than fifteen centuries.

Without claiming any degree of scientific accuracy for the term *Shamanism*, as applied to this cult in Korea, it is more convenient to use it, the word dæmon having come to bear a popular meaning which prohibits its use where good spirits as well as bad are indicated. So far as I know, *Shamanism* exists only in Asia, and flourishes specially among the tribes north of the Amur, the Samoyedes, Ostiaks, etc., as well as among hill tribes on the southwestern frontier of China. The term *Shaman* may be applied to all persons, male or female, whose profession it is to have direct dealings with dæmons, and to possess the power of securing their good will and averting their malignant influences by various magical rites, charms, and incantations, to cure diseases by exorcisms, to predict future events, and to interpret dreams.

Korean *Shamanism* or Dæmonism differs from that of northern Asia in its mildness, possibly the result of early Buddhist influence. It is the cult of dæmons not necessarily evil, but usually the enemies of man, and addicted to revenge and caprice. Though the *Shamans* are neither an order, nor linked by a common organization, they are practically recognized as a priesthood, in so far as it is through their offices that the dæmons are approached and propitiated on behalf of the people. It is supposed that the *Shaman* or wizard was one of the figures in the dawn of Korean history, and that

Dæmonism in its early stage was marked by human sacrifices. *Shamans* in the train of royalty, and as a part of the social organization of the Peninsula, figure in very early Korean story, and they appear to have been the chief, if not the only, "religious" instructors.

One class among the *Shamans* is incorporated into one of those guilds which are the Trades Unions of Korea, and the Government has imposed registration on another class.[1] There are now two principal classes of *Shamans*, the *Pan-su* and the *mu-tang*. The *Pan-su* are blind sorcerers, and those parents are fortunate who have a blind son, for he is certain to be able to make a good living and support them in their old age. The *Pan-su* were formerly persons of much distinction in the kingdom, but their social position has been lowered during the present dynasty, though in the present reign their influence in the Palace, and specially with the late Queen, has wrought much evil. The chief officials of the *Pan-su* Guild in Seoul hold the official titles of *Cham-pan*[2] and *Seung-ji* from the Government, which gives prestige to the whole body. In order to guard their professional interests, the *Pan-su* have local guilds, and in the various sections "clubhouses" built out of their own funds. The central office of the *Pan-su* guild in Seoul was built and maintained by Government, and the two chief officials of the guild hold, or held, *quasi*-official rank.

It appears that admission into the fraternity is only granted to an applicant on his giving proof of proficiency in the knowledge of a cumbrous body of orally transmitted *Shaman* tradition, wisdom and custom, much of it believed by the people to be 4,000 years old, and embracing scraps of superstition

[1] What is true in Korea to-day may be untrue to-morrow. One month there was a police raid in Seoul upon the *mu-tang* or sorceresses, another the sisterhood was flourishing, and so the pendulum swings.

[2] *Cham-pan* is a title of officials of a certain rank in Government Departments in Seoul, and might be rendered Secretary of Department. *Seung-ji* probably has the same meaning.

from the darkest arcana of Buddhism, as well as fragments of Confucianism. The neophyte has to learn of "the existence, nature, and power of dæmons, their relations with man, the efficacy of exorcism through a magic ritual, and the genuine and certain character of the results of divination." He must meditate on "the customs, habits, and weaknesses of every class in Korean society in order to deal knowingly with his clients. A slight acquaintance with Confucianism must enable him to give a flavor of learning to his speech, and he must be well drilled in the methods of exorcisms, incantations, magic spells, divination, and the manufacture of charms and amulets."

The services of sorcerers or geomancers are invariably called for in connection with the choice of sites for houses and graves, in certain contracts, and on the occasion of unusual calamities, sickness, births, marriages, and the purchase of land. The chief functions of the *Shaman* are, the influencing of dæmons by ritual and magical rites, propitiating them by offerings, exorcisms, and the procuring of oracles. In their methods, dancing, gesticulations, a real or feigned ecstasy, and a drum play an important part. The fees of the *Shaman* are high, and it is believed that at the lowest computation, Dæmonism costs Korea two million five hundred thousand dollars annually! In order to obtain favors or avert calamities, it is necessary to employ the *Shamans* as mediators, and it is their fees, and not the cost of the offerings which press so heavily on the people.

Among the reasons which render the *Shaman* a necessity are these. In Korean belief, earth, air, and sea, are peopled by dæmons. They haunt every umbrageous tree, shady ravine, crystal spring, and mountain crest. On green hill slopes, in peaceful agricultural valleys, in grassy dells, on wooded uplands, by lake and stream, by road and river, in north, south, east, and west they abound, making malignant sport out of human destinies. They are on every roof, ceiling, fireplace, *kang* and beam.   They fill the chimney, the shed, the living room, the kitchen—they are on every shelf and jar.   In thousands they waylay the traveller as he leaves his home, beside him, behind him, dancing in front of him, whirring over his head, crying out upon him from earth, air, and water.   They are numbered by *thousands of billions*, and it has been well said that their ubiquity is an unholy travesty of the Divine Omnipresence.[1]   This belief, and it seems to be the only one he has, keeps the Korean in a perpetual state of nervous apprehension, it surrounds him with indefinite terrors, and it may truly be said of him that he " passes the time of his sojourning here in fear."   Every Korean home is subject to dæmons, here, there, and everywhere.   They touch the Korean at every point in life, making his well-being depend on a continual series of acts of propitiation, and they avenge every omission with merciless severity, keeping him under this yoke of bondage from birth to death.

The phrase " dæmon-worship " as applied to Korean *Shamanism* is somewhat misleading.   These legions of spirits which in Korean belief peopled the world, are of two classes, the first alone answering to our conception of dæmons.   These are the self-existent spirits, unseen enemies of man, whose designs are always malignant or malicious, and spirits of departed persons, who, having died in poverty and manifold distresses, are unclothed, hungry, and shivering vagrants, bringing untold calamities on those who neglect to supply their wants.   It is true, however, that about 80 per cent. of the legions of spirits are malignant.   The second class consists also of self-existent spirits, whose natures are partly kindly, and of departed spirits of prosperous and good people, but even these are easily offended and act with extraordinary capriciousness.   These, however, by due intercessions and offerings, may be induced to assist man in obtaining his desires, and may aid him to escape from the afflictive power of the evil dæmons.

[1] Rev. G. H. Jones.

The comfort and prosperity of every individual depend on his ability to win and keep the favor of the latter class.

Koreans attribute every ill by which they are afflicted to dæmoniacal influence. Bad luck in any transaction, official malevolence, illness, whether sudden or prolonged, pecuniary misfortune, and loss of power or position are due to the malignity of dæmons. It is over such evils that the *Pan-su* is supposed to have power, and to be able to terminate them by magical rites, he being possessed by a powerful dæmon, whose strength he is able to wield.

As an example of the *modus operandi*, exorcism in sickness which is believed to be the work of an unclean dæmon may be taken. The *Pan-su* arrives at the house, and boldly undertakes the expulsion of the foul spirit, the process being divided into four stages.[1]

1. By a few throws from the tortoise divining box, the sorcerer discovers the dæmon's nature and character, after which he seeks for an auspicious hour and makes arrangements for the next stage.

2. Gaining control of the dæmon follows. The *Pan-su* equips himself with a wand of oak or pine a foot and half long, and a bystander is asked to hold this in an upright position on an ironing stone. Magic formulas are recited till the rod begins to shake and even dance on the stone, this activity being believed to be the result of the dæmon having entered the wand. At this stage a talk takes place to test the accuracy of the divination of the dæmon's name and nature, and of the cause of the affliction. The *Pan-su* manages the questions so dexterously that a simple yes is indicated by motion in the wand, while no is expressed by quiescence. At this stage the dæmon is given the choice of quietly disappearing; after which, if he is obstinate, the *Pan-su* proceeds to dislodge him.

3. The third stage involves the aid of certain familiars of

---

[1] This detailed account is from notes kindly lent to me by the Rev. G. H. Jones.

the *Pan-su*. A special wand, made of an eastern branch of a peach tree, which has much repute in expelling dæmons, is taken, and is held on a table in a vertical position by an assistant. The *Pan-su* recites a farther part of his magic ritual, its power being shown by acute movements in the wand in spite of attempts to keep it steady. A parley takes place with the *Chang-gun*, the spirit who has been summoned to find out his objects. He promises to catch the *Chang-kun*, the malignant dæmon, and after preparations and offerings have been made he is asked to search for him. The man who holds the wand is violently dragged by a supernatural power out of the house to the place where the *Chang-kun* is. Then the *Chang-gun* is supposed to seize him, and the wand-holder is dragged back to the house.

4. A bottle with a wide mouth is put on the floor, and alongside it a piece of paper inscribed with the name of the unclean dæmon, which has been obtained by divination and parley. The paper being touched with the magic wand jumps into the bottle, which is hastily corked and buried on the hillside or at the crossroads.

This singular form of exorcism has a long and unintelligible ritual, in the cases of those who can afford to pay for it, occupying some days, and at greater or lesser length is repeated daily by the *Shamans* throughout Korea. It is usually succeeded by a form known as the Ritual Pacification, which takes a whole night. This is for the purpose of restoring order among the household dæmons, who have been much upset by the previous proceedings, cleaning the house, and committing it and its inmates to the protection of the most powerful members of the Korean dæmoniacal hierarchy.

The instruments of exorcism used by the *Pan-su* are offerings to be made at various stages of the process, a drum, cymbals, a bell, a divination box, and a wand or wands.

The *Shamans* claim to have derived many of their very numerous spells and formulas from Buddhists, who on their side assert that dæmon-worship was practised in Korea long before the introduction of Buddhism, and a relic of this worship is pointed out in the custom which prevails in the Korean magistracies of offering to guardian spirits on stone altars on the hills, pigs, or occasionally sheep, before sowing time and after harvest, as well as in case of drought, or other general calamity. This sacrifice is offered by the local magistrate in the king's name, and though identical in form with that offered to *Hananim* (the Lord of Heaven), is altogether distinct from it. Most of the formulæ recited by the *Shamans* have the reputation of being unsafe for ordinary people to use, but in consideration of the possibility of a great emergency, one is provided, which is pronounced absolutely safe. This consists of fifty-six characters which must be recited forwards, backwards, and sideways, and is called "The twenty-eight stars formula."[1]

Divination is the second function of the *Pan-su*, and consists in a forecast of the future by means of rituals, known only to himself, associated with the use of certain paraphernalia. This is used also for finding out the result of a venture, or the cause of an existing trouble, and for casting a man's horoscope, *i.e.* "The four columns of a man's future," these being the hour, day, month, and year of his birth, or rather their four combinations. This horoscope is the crowning function of divination. In these "four columns" the secret of a man's life is hidden, and their relations must govern him in all his actions. When a horoscope contains an arrow, which denotes ill-luck, the *Pan-su* corrects the misfortune by formulæ used with a bow of peach, with which during the recital he shoots arrows made of a certain reed into a "non-prohibited" quarter. One of the great duties of divination is to cast the horoscope of a bride and bridegroom for an auspicious day for the

---

[1] The twenty-eight constellations, or stellar mansions, referred to in the *Shu King*, one of the Chinese classical books, showing the close connection between Chinese and Korean superstition.—W. C. H.

wedding, for an unlucky one would introduce dæmons to the ruin of the new household.

The great strongholds of divination are the "Frog-Boxes" and dice boxes, manufactured for this purpose. The frog box is made like a tortoise, having movable lips, and contains three *cash*, over which the *Pan-su* repeats a very ancient invocation, which has been translated thus : "Will all you people grant to reveal the symbols." The coins are thrown three times, and the three falls present him with the combinations of characters, out of which he manufactures his oracle. The second implement of divination is a bamboo or brass tube closed at both ends, but with a small hole in one to allow of the exit of small bamboo splinters of which it contains eight. The same thing is to be seen on innumerable altars in China. Each splinter has from one to eight notches on it, and stands for a symbol of certain signs on that divining table 3,000 years old, called the *Ho-pai*, which is implicitly believed in by the Chinese. Two of these splinters give two sets of characters, eight being connected with each symbol. When the *Pan-su* has obtained these he is ready to evolve his oracle.

Great reliance is placed on the charms which the *Pan-su* make and sell. Proabably there are few adults or children who do not wear these as amulets. They are generally made in the form of insects, or consist of Chinese characters. They are written on specially prepared yellow paper in red ink, and are regarded as being efficacious against illness and other calamities. Amulets are made of the wood of trees struck by lightning, which is supposed to possess magical qualities.

CHAPTER XXXV

NOTES ON DÆMONISM CONCLUDED

THE second and larger division of the *Shamans* consists of the *mu-tang*. Though the *Pak-su Mu*, who are included among the *mu-tang*, are men, the female idea prevails so largely that these wear female clothing in performing their functions, and the whole class has the name of *mu-tang*, and is spoken of as female.

The *mu-tang* is universally prevalent, and her services are constantly and everywhere sought. She enters upon an office regarded as of high importance with very little ceremonial, requiring only a little instruction from some one who has practised magic, and the "supernatural call." This call, of which much is made, consists in the assurance of dæmoniacal possession, the dæmon being supposed to seize upon the woman, and to become in fact her *döppel ganger*, so completely is his personality superimposed on hers. The dæmon is almost invariably a member of the Korean "*Dæmoneon.*" Mr. Jones mentions a woman who claims that her indwelling dæmon is known as the spirit *Chil-song Shin*, supposed to come from the constellation of *Ursa Major*, and he brought with him a legion of other dæmons, from which the *mu-tang* derive their honorific title, *Man-shin*, a Legion of Spirits. This woman in her early married life was ill for three years, and had frequent visions of the spirit, and heard but resisted the "call." When at last she yielded she was immediately cured, and was received into favor with the spirit !

On obeying a dæmon call the woman snaps every tie of custom or relationship, deserts parents, husband, or children, and obeys the "call" alone. Her position from that hour is a peculiar one, for while she is regarded as indispensable to the community she is socially an outcast. In the curious relations of the Shamanate, the *Pan-su* is obviously the Master of the Dæmons, gaining power by cabalistic formulæ or ritual to drive them off, or even bury them, while the *mu-tang* supplicates and propitiates them. It is impossible to live in a place which has not a *mu-tang Shaman*.

The functions of the *mu-tang* are more varied than those of the *Pan-su*, but on a par with his exorcisms may be placed her *Kauts* or Pacifications and Propitiations of dæmons, which are divided into the occasional and periodic, the latter being Dæmon Festivals, one public the other private. The public one is a triennial *festa* celebrated either by a large village or by an aggregation of hamlets, and occupies three or four days. Its object is the tutelary dæmon of the neighborhood, and its methods are sacrifice, petition, worship, and thanksgiving. The villagers choose two of their number to take entire charge of the festival, and by them a tax for expenses is levied on the vicinity. They also choose the festival day, hire the *mu-tang*, and arrange for the paraphernalia and the offerings to the dæmons. It is essential that the festival day should be chosen by divination, by either a *Sön-li* or a *Pan-su* acquainted with magic, and that the sorcerers should bathe frequently and abstain from animal food for seven previous days.

The village dæmon festival has a resemblance at some points to the Shinto *matsuri* of Japan. On the *festa* day a booth, much decorated with tags of brilliant color, is erected near the dæmons' shrine, and with an accompaniment of *mu-tang* music, dancing, and lavish and outlandish gesticulations, the offerings are presented to the spirits. The popular belief is that the dæmons become incarnate in the *mu-tang*, who utter oracles called *Kong-su Na-ta*, and the people bring them bowls of uncooked rice, and plead for a revelation of their future during the following three years. A common "test" at this festival is the burning a tube of very thin white paper in a bowl. Its upper end is lighted by the *mu-tang*, who recites her spells as it burns. When it reaches the rim of the bowl, if the augury for the future be unfavorable, the paper burns away in the bowl, if favorable, the paper lifts itself and is blown away.

The private *festa*, the *Chöl-muri Kaut*, one of thanksgiving to the household dæmons, is necessary to secure a continuance of their good offices. The expenditure of the family resources on this occasion is so lavish as frequently to impoverish the household for a whole year. This *festa* may be biennial or triennial. At the time a pig is sacrificed, offerings are made, *mu-tang* are hired, and the fetishes of the dæmons are renewed or cleaned. The Ritual for these occasions, if unabbreviated, lasts several days, but among the poor only a selection from it is used. Its stages consist of rituals of invocation, petition, offering, and purification. While these are being recited a household spirit becomes incarnate in the *mu-tang*, and through her makes oracular revelations of the future. At another stage deceased parents and ancestors appear in the *mu-tang*, and her personation of them is described by an eyewitness as both "pathetic and ludicrous." At Seoul this festival is observed by families at the dæmon shrines outside the city walls, and not in private houses.

One of the very common occasions which requires the presence of a *mu-tang* is the ceremonial known as the Rite of Purification, defilement being contracted by a birth or death or any action which brings in an unclean dæmon, whose obnoxious entrance moves the guardian or friendly dæmons to leave the house. A wand cut from a pine tree to the *east* of the house is used to bring about their return. It is set working by the muttered utterance of special spells or formulæ by the *mu-tang*, the *mont-gari*, or tutelary spirit is found, and by means of prayers and offerings is induced to resume his place, and the unclean dæmon is exorcised and expelled. The beating of a drum and the frequent sprinkling of pure water are portions of this rite.

The utterance of oracles is another great function of the *mu-tang*. In spite of the low opinion of women held by the Koreans, so strong is the belief in the complete dæmoniacal possession of the *mu-tang*, and their consequent elevation above their sex, that the Koreans refer fully as much to them as to the *Pan-su* for information regarding the outcome of commercial ventures, and of projects of personal advancement, as well as for the hidden causes of the loss of wealth or position, or of adversity or illness. The *mu-tang*, by an appeal to her familiar dæmon, in some cases obtains a direct answer, and in others a reply by the divining chime, or the rice divination. The latter consists of throwing down some grains of rice on a table and noting the combinations which result. The " divining chime " is a hazel wand with a circle of bells at one end. These are shaken violently by the *mu-tang*, and in the din thus created she hears the utterance of the dæmon.

The arranging for the sale of children to dæmons is a farther function of the *mu-tang*, and is carried on to a very great extent. The Korean father desires prosperity and long life for his boy (a girl being of little account), and the sale of the child to a spirit is he believes the best way of attaining his object. When the so-called sale has been decided on, the father consults the sorceress as to when and where it shall be made. The place chosen is usually a boulder near home, and the child is there " consecrated " to the dæmon by the *mu-tang* with fitting rites. Thenceforward, on the 15th day of the 1st moon, and the 3rd day of the 3rd moon, worship and sacrifice are offered to the boulder. After this act of sale the name of the dæmon becomes part of the boy's name. It is not an unusual thing for the sale to be made to the *mu-tang* herself, who as the proxy of her dæmon accepts the child in case she learns by a magic rite that she may do so. She takes in its stead one of its rice bowls and a spoon, and these, to-

SOUTH GATE.

gether with a piece of cotton cloth on which the facts concerning the sale of the child are written, are laid up in her own house in the room devoted to her dæmon.   There is a famous *mu-tang*, whose house I have been in just outside the south gate of Seoul, who has many of these, which are placed on tables below the painted daubs of dæmons ordinarily, but which, on great occasions, are used as banners.   At the Periodic Festivals offerings are made on behalf of these children, who, though they live with their parents, know the sorceress or *mu-tang* as *Shin*, and are considered her children.

The *mu-tang* rites are specially linked with the house dæmon and with *Mama* the smallpox dæmon.   The house dæmon is on the whole a good one, being supposed to bring health and happiness, and if invited with due ceremony he is willing to take up his abode under every roof.   He cannot always keep off disease, and in the case of contagious fevers, etc., he disappears until the rite of purification has been accomplished and he has been asked to return.   The ceremonies attending his recall deserve notice.   On this great occasion the *mu-tang* in office ties a large sheet of paper round a rod of oak, holds it upright, and goes out to hunt him.   She may find him near, as if waiting to be invited back, or at a considerable distance, but in either case he makes his presence known by shaking the rod so violently that several men cannot hold it still, and then returns with the *mu-tang* to the house, where he is received with lively demonstrations of joy.   The paper which was round the stick is folded, a few *cash* are put into it, it is soaked in wine, and is then thrown up against a beam in the house to which it sticks, and is followed by some rice which adheres to it.   That special spot is the abiding place of the dæmon.   This ceremony involves a family in very considerable expense.

The universal belief that illness is the work of dæmons renders the services of a *Pan-su* or *mu-tang* necessary wherever it enters a house, and in the case of smallpox, the universal scourge of Korean childhood, the dæmon, instead of being exorcised, bottled, or buried, is treated with the utmost respect. The name by which the disease is called, "*Mama*," is the dæmon's name. It is said that he came from South China, and has only infested Korea for 1,000 years. On the disease appearing, the *mu-tang* is called in to honor the arrival of the spirit with a feast and fitting ceremonial. Little or no work is done, and if there are neighbors whose children have not had the malady, they rest likewise, lest, displeased with their want of respect, he should deal hardly with them. The parents do obeisance (worship) to the suffering child, and address it at all times in honorific terms. Danger is supposed to be over after the 12th day, when the *mu-tang* is again summoned, and a farewell banquet is given. A miniature wooden horse is prepared, and is loaded for the spirit's journey with small bags of food and money, fervent and respectful adieus are spoken, and he receives hearty good wishes for his prosperous return to his own place!

In the course of many centuries the office of the *mu-tang* has undergone considerable modification. Formerly her power consisted in the foretelling of events by the movements of a turtle on the application of hot iron to his back, and by the falling of a leaf of certain trees. Her present vocation is chiefly mediatorial. It is also becoming partially hereditary, her daughter or even daughter-in-law taking up her work. The "call" is considered a grave calamity. Ordinarily these women are of the lower class. They are frequently worshippers of Buddha, after the gross and debased cult which exists in Korea, and place his picture along with those of the dæmons in the small temples in their houses.

Taking the male and female Shamanate together, the *Shamans* possess immense power over the people, from the clever and ambitious Korean queen, who resorted constantly to the *Pan-su* on behalf of the future of the Crown Prince, down to the humblest peasant family. They are in intimate contact with the people in all times of difficulty and affliction, their largest claims are conceded, and they are seldom out of employment.

The dæmons whose professed servants the *Shamans* are, and whose yoke lies heavy on Korea, are rarely even mythical beings, who might possibly have existed in human shape. They are legion. They dwell in all matter and pervade all space. They are a horde without organization, destitute of genus, species, and classification, created out of Korean superstitions, debased Buddhism, and Chinese mythical legend. There have been no native attempts at their arrangement, and whatever has been done in this direction is due to the labors of Mr. G. H. Jones and Dr. Landis, from whose lists a few may be chosen as specimens.

The *O-bang-chang-kun* are five, and some of the more important preside over East Heaven, South, West, North, and Middle. In *Shaman's* houses shrines are frequently erected to them, bearing their collective name to which worship is paid. They are held in high honor and are prominent in *Pan-su* rites. At the entrance of many villages on the south branch of the Han the villagers represent them by posts with tops rudely carved into hideous caricatures of humanity, which are ofttimes decorated with straw tassels, and receive offerings of rice and fruit as village protectors.

The *Shin-chang* are dæmon generals said to number 80,000, each one at the head of a dæmon host. They fill the earth and air, and are specially associated with the *Pan-su*, who are capable of summoning them by magic formulæ to aid in divination and exorcism. Shrines to single members of this militant host occur frequently in Central Korea, each one containing a highly-colored daub of a gigantic mediæval warrior, and the words, "I, the Spirit—dwell in this place."

The Tok-gabi are the most dreaded and detested, as well as the best known of all the dæmon *horde*. Yet they seem nondescripts, and careful and patient examination has only succeeded in relegating them to the class of such myths as the Will o' the Wisp, and Jack o' Lantern, elevated, however, in Korea to the status of genuine devils with fetishes of their own. They are regarded as having human originals in the souls of those who have come to sudden or violent ends. They are bred on execution grounds and battlefields, and wherever men perish in numbers. They go in overwhelming legions, and not only dwell in empty houses but in inhabited villages, terrifying the inhabitants. They it was who, by taking possession of the fine Audience Hall of the Mulberry Palace in Seoul, rendered the buildings untenable, frightful tales being told and believed of nocturnal dæmon orgies amidst those doleful splendors. People leave their houses and build new ones because of them. Their fetishes may be such things as a *mapu's* hat or the cloak of a *yamen* clerk, rotten with age and dirt, enshrined under a small straw booth. Besides the devilry attributed to the *Tok-gabi* they are accused of many pranks, such as placing the covers of iron pots inside them, and pounding doors and windows all night, till it seems as if they would be smashed, yet leaving no trace of their work.

The actually unclean spirits, the *Sagem*, the criminal class of the vast "*Dæmoneon*," infest Korean life like vermin, wandering about embracing every opportunity of hurting and molesting man. Against these both *Pan-su* and *mu-tang* wage continual war by their enchantments, the *Pan-su* by their exorcisms, either driving them off or catching them and burying them in disgrace, while the *mu-tang* propitiate them and send them off in honor.

Another great group of dæmons is the *San-Shin Ryŏng*—the spirits of the mountains. I found their shrines in all the hilly country, along both branches of the Han, by springs and streams, and specially under the shade of big trees, and on *ampelopsis* covered rocks, a flat rock being a specially appropriate site from its suitability for an altar, and thus specially "fortunate." The dæmon who is the tutelary spirit of *gin-*

seng, the most valuable export of Korea, is greatly honored. So also is the patron dæmon of deer hunters, who is invariably represented in his shrine as a fierce looking elderly man in official dress riding a tiger. Surrounding him are altars to his harem, and there are also female dæmons, mountain spirits, who are pictured as women, frequently Japanese.

The tiger which abounds in Central and Northern Korea is understood to be the confidential servant of these mountain dæmons, and when he commits depredations, the people, believing the dæmon of the vicinity to be angry, hurry with offerings to his nearest shrine. The Koreans consider it a good omen when they see in their dreams the mountain dæmon, either as represented in his shrine, or under the form of his representative, the tiger. These mountain dæmons are specially sought by recluses, and people ofttimes retire into solitary mountain glens, where by bathing, fasting, and offerings they strive to gain their favor. These spirits, believed to be very powerful, are much feared by farmers, and by villagers living near high mountains. They think that if when they are out on the hillsides cutting wood they forgot to cast the first spoonful of rice from the bowl to the dæmon, they will be punished by a severe fall or cut, or some other accident. These spirits are capricious and exacting, and for every little neglect take vengeance on the members of a farmer's household or on his crops or cattle.

The *Long-shin,* or Dragon dæmons, are water spirits. They have no shrines, but the *Shamans* conduct a somewhat expensive ceremony by the sea and riversides in which they present them with offerings for the repose of the souls of drowned persons.

The phase of Dæmonolatry which is the most common and the first to arrest a traveller's attention is also the most obscure. The *Söng Whoang Dan* (altar of the Holy Prince), the great Korean altar, rudely built of loose stones under the shade of a tree, from the branches of which are suspended such worthless *ex votos* as strips of paper, rags, small bags of rice, old clouts, and worn-out shoes, look less like an altar than a decaying cairn of large size.[1] A peculiarity of the *Söng Whoang Dan* is that they are generally supposed to be frequented by various dæmons, though occasionally they are crowned by a shrine to a single spirit. Korean travellers make their special plea to a travellers' dæmon who is supposed to be found there, and hang up strips of their goods in the overhanging branches, and the sailor likewise regards the altar as the shrine of his guardian dæmon, and bestows a bit of old rope upon it. Further than this, when some special bird or beast has destroyed insects injurious to agriculture, the people erect a shrine to it on these altars or cairns, on which may frequently be seen the rude daub of a bird or animal.

Two spirits, the *To-ti-chi Shin* and the *Chon-Shin*, are regarded as local dæmons, and occupy spots on the mountain sides. They receive worship at funerals, and a sacrifice similar to that offered in ancestral worship is made to them before the body is laid in the earth. Two *Shamans* preside over this, and one of them intones a ritual belonging to the occasion. The shrine of *Chon-Shin* is a local temple, a small decayed erection usually found outside villages. In Seoul he has a mud or plaster shrine is which his picture is enshrined with much ceremony, but in the country his fetish is usually a straw booth set up over a pair of old shoes under a tree. For the observances connected with him all the residents in a neighborhood are taxed. He may be regarded as the chief dæmon in every district, and it is in his honor that the *mutang* celebrate the triennial festival formerly described.

The Household Spirits are the last division of the Korean *Dæmoneon*. Söng Ju, the spirit of the ridge pole who pre-

---

[1] Mr. G. H. Jones suggests the idea that these uncouth heap of stones were originally munitions of war over which tutelary dæmons were supposed to brood, and thinks that the transition to an altar would be a very natural one.

sides over the home, occupies a sort of imperial position with regard to the other household spirits.

His fetish consists of some sheets of paper and a paper bag containing as many spoonfuls of rice as the household is years old on the day when the *mu-tang* suspends it to the crossbeam of the house.

The ceremony of his inauguration was conducted as follows in the case of a householder who was at once a scholar, a noble, a rich man, and the headman of a large village. A lucky day having been chosen by divination, the noble, after grading the site for his house, erected the framework, and with great ceremony attached such a fetish, duly prepared by the *Pan-su*, to the crossbeam. Prostrations and invocations marked this stage. When the building of the house was completed, an auspicious day was again chosen by divination, and a great ceremony was performed by the *mu-tang* for the enshrining of the dæmon in the home. The *mu-tang* arranged the ceremonial and prepared the offerings, and then with a special wand only used on these occasions, called the spirit who is supposed to be under her control, and returning to the house solemnly enshrined him in the fetish, to which it is correct to add a fresh sheet of paper every year. After *Söng Ju* was supposed to have had time to feed spiritually on the offerings, they were placed before the guests, and a great entertainment followed.

Ti Ju, or the lord of the site, is the next great dæmon, but investigations regarding him have been very resultless. Little is known, except that offerings are presented to him at some spot on the premises, but not inside the house. These offerings, which are of food, are made on the 1st, 2nd, 3rd, and 15th of each month. This food is afterwards eaten by the family, and a continual offering is represented by a bit of cloth or a scrap of old rope. His fetish is a bundle of straw, empty inside, placed on three sticks, but in some circumstances a flower pot with some rice inside is substituted.

Op Ju, the kitchen dæmon, is the third of the trio which is permanently attached to the house. His fetish is a piece of cloth or paper nailed to the wall above the cooking place.

After these come the dæmons who are attached to the family and not the house, the first of them being *Cho Wang*, a spirit of the constellation of the Great Bear, a very popular spirit. His shrine is outside the wall, and his fetish, to which worship is paid, is a gourd full of cloth and paper. *Cho Wang* is often the dæmon familiar of a *mu-tang*.

Ti Ju, No. 2, is the fate or luck of the family, and every household is ambitious to secure him. His fetish is a straw booth three feet high, in which is a flower pot containing some rice covered with a stone and paper.

The greatest of the family dæmons is an ancient and historical dæmon, *Chöi Sok*, who is regarded as the grandfather of *San Chin-chöi Sök*, the dæmon of nativity. His fetish, unless it becomes rotten or is accidentally destroyed, descends from father to son. He has several fetishes, and when he receives homage at the Triennial Festival, the *mu-tang* puts on the dress of an official. He is the dæmon of nativity and the giver of posterity, and is a triple dæmon. Korean women hearing of the Christian Trinity have been known to say that *San chin* enables them to understand the mystery! He is believed to have the control of all children up to the age of four. He avenges ceremonial defilement such as the sight by an expectant mother of a mourner or a dead object, and outside a house where there has been a recent birth, a notice warning visitors not to enter is often put up on his behalf. He imposes on plebeian mothers a period of seclusion for twenty-one days after a birth, but for noble mothers one hundred days, for which period the rays of the sun are rigidly excluded from both mother and child.

Pa-mul, the dæmon of riches, is the Japanese *Daikoku* and the British *Mammon*. He is worshipped in the granary, and thanks are offered to him as well as petitions.   His fetish is a paste jar set up on two decorated bags of rice.   A man in Chemulpo, now a Christian, had a very famous fetish, which was originally a jar of beans, but these were changed into clear water, and a mysterious improvement in the fortunes of the family set in from that date, the jar becoming an object of grateful worship.   One day it was found broken and the water lost, and from that time his fortunes declined.

Kol-lip is the dæmon who takes charge of the external fortunes of the family, and is also the mercury of the household dæmons.   His fetish is enshrined over the gate house, and consists of a mass of rubbish, old straw shoes for wearing on his travels, *cash* for spiritual funds, and a fragment of grass cloth for travelling outfit.   There is also the dæmon of the gate whose fetish hangs over the entrance.

Dr. Landis has classified the Korean dæmons as follows:—

Spirits high in rank

1. Spirits of the Heavens.
2. Spirits of the Earth.
3. Spirits of the Mountains and Hills.
4. Spirits of the Dragons.
5. Guardian Spirits of the District.
6. Spirits of the Buddhist Faith (?)

Spirits of the House

7. Spirit of the ridge pole.   This is the chief of all the spirits of the House.
8. Spirit of goods and furniture.
9. Spirit dæmon of the Yi family.
10. Spirit of the kitchen.
11. Attendant spirits of No. 9.
12. Spirits which serve one's ancestors.
13. The Guards and servants of No. 9.
14. The Spirits which aid jugglers.
15. Spirits of goods and chattels, like No. 8, but inferior in rank.
16. Spirits of smallpox.
17. Spirits which take the forms of animals.

18. Spirits which take possession of young girls and change them into exorcists.

19. Spirits of the seven stars which form the Dipper.

20. Spirits of the house site.

Various kinds of Spirits

21. Spirits which make men brave.

22. Spirits which reside in trees. Any gnarled shrub or malformed tree is supposed to be the residence of one of these spirits. Spirits which cause persons to meet either a violent death or to die young. Any one who has died before reaching a cycle (*i.e.* 60 years) is supposed to have died owing to the influence of one of these spirits. It is needless to say that they are all evil.

23. Spirits which cause tigers to eat men.

24. Spirits which cause men to die on the road.

25. Spirits which roam about the house causing all sorts of calamities.

26. Spirits which cause a man to die away from home.

27. Spirits which cause men to die as substitutes for others.

28. Spirits which cause men to die by strangulation.

29. Spirits which cause men to die by drowning.

30. Spirits which cause women to die in childbirth.

31. Spirits which cause men to die by suicide.

32. Spirits which cause men to die by fire.

33. Spirits which cause men to die by being beaten.

34. Spirits which cause men to die by falls.

35. Spirits which cause men to die by pestilence.

36. Spirits which cause men to die by cholera.

The belief in the efficacy of the performances of the *mu-tang* is enormous. In sickness the very poor half starve themselves and pawn their clothing to pay for her exorcisms. Her power has been riveted upon the country for hundreds, if not thousands, of years. The order is said to date back 4,000 years, to have been called in China, where it was under official regulations, *mu-ham*. Five hundred years ago the founder of the present dynasty prohibited *mu-tang* from living within the walls of Seoul—hence their houses and temples are found outside the city walls.

Women are not *mu-tang* by birth, but of late years it has become customary for the girl children of a sorceress to go out with her and learn her arts, which is tending to give the profession a hereditary aspect.   It is now recruited partly in this fashion, partly from among hysterical girls, and partly for a livelihood, but outside of these sources, a dæmon may take possession of any woman, wife, maid, or widow, rich or poor, plebeian or patrician, and compel her to serve him.   At the beginning of the possession she becomes either slightly or seriously ill, and her illness may last four weeks or three years, during which time she dreams of a dragon, a rainbow, peach trees in blossom, or of a man in armor who is suddenly metamorphosed into an animal.   Under the influence of these dreams she becomes like an insane person, and when awake sees many curious things, and before long speaks as an oracle of the spirits.

She then informs her family that messengers from Heaven, Earth, and the Lightning have informed her that if she is not allowed to practise exorcism, they or their domestic animals will die.   Should they insist on secluding her, her illness shortly terminates fatally.   If a daughter of a noble family becomes possessed, they probably make away with her, in the idea that if madness takes this turn, the disgrace would be indelible.

But things usually go smoothly, and on being allowed to have her own way the first thing she does is to go into a vacant room and fill it with flowers as an offering to the dæmons. Then she must obtain the clothing and professional paraphernalia of a deceased *mu-tang*.   The clothing may be destroyed after the dæmon has taken full possession of his new recruit, but the drums and other instruments must be retained.   After the possessions of the deceased *mu-tang* have been bestowed on the new one who claims them, she proceeds to exorcise such bad spirits as may be infesting the donor's house, so as to enable his family to live in peace, after which she writes his name on a tablet, and placing it in a small room invokes blessings on him for three years.

After this ceremonial has been observed the *mu-tang*, fully possessed by a dæmon, begins to exercise her very important and lucrative profession.   Her equipment consists of a number of dresses, some of them very costly, a drum shaped like an hourglass, four feet in length, copper cymbals, a copper rod, with tinklers suspended from it by copper chains, strips of silk and paper banners which float round her as she dances, fans, umbrellas, wands, images of men and animals, brass or copper gongs, and a pair of telescope-shaped baskets for scratching, chiefly used in cases of cholera, which disease is supposed to result from rats climbing about in the human interior.   The scratching sound made by a peculiar use of these baskets, which resembles the noise made by cats, is expected to scare and drive away these rodents.

The preliminaries of exorcism are that the *mu-tang* must subject herself to certain restraints varying from a month to three days, during which time she must abstain from flesh and fish, and must partially fast.   Before an exorcism ashes are steeped in water and the sorceress takes of this, and sprinkles it as she walks round the house, afterwards taking pure water and going through the same ceremony.

The almost fabulous sums squeezed by the *mu-tang* out of the people of Seoul are given in a previous chapter.   It will be observed that in Korea sickness is always associated with dæmoniacal possession, and that the services of the *Pan-su*, or *mu-tang*, are always requisitioned.   European medicine and surgery are the most successful assailants of this barbarous and degrading system which holds the whole nation, in many respects highly civilized, in bondage, and the influence of both as practised in connection with " Medical Missions " is tending increasingly in the direction of emancipation.

It would be impossible to say how far the *mu-tang* is self-deceived.   In some of her dances, especially in one in which she exorcises " The dæmon of the Yi family," one of the most powerful and malignant of the dæmon hierachy, she works herself into such a delirious frenzy that she falls down foaming at the mouth, and death is occasionally the result of the frantic excitement.

The " Dæmon of the Yi Family " is invoked in every district once in three years by the *mu-tang* in a formula which has been translated thus—" Oh Master and Mistress of our Kingdom, may you ever exist in peace.   Once in every three years we invoke you with music and dancing.   Oh make this house to be peaceful."   If this malignant spirit arrives at a house he can only be appeased by the death of a man, an ox, or a pig.   Therefore when the *mu-tang* becomes aware that he has come to a house or neighborhood, a pig is at once killed, boiled, and offered up entire—the exorcist takes two knives and dances a sword dance, working herself into a " fine frenzy," after which a box is made and a Korean official hat and robes are placed within it, as well as a dress suitable for a palace lady.   The box is then placed on the top of the family clothes chest, and sacrifices are frequently offered there.   This dæmon is regarded as the spirit of a rebellious Crown Prince, the sole object of whose dæmon existence is to injure all with whom he can come into contact.

A man sometimes marries a *mu-tang*, but he is invariably "a fellow of the baser sort," who desires to live in idleness on the earnings of his wife.   If, as is occasionally the case, the *mu-tang* belongs to a noble family, she is only allowed to exorcise spirits in her own house, and when she dies she is buried in a hole in a mountain side with the whole paraphernalia of her profession.   Some *mu-tang* do not go abroad for purposes of exorcism.   These may be regarded as the aristocracy of their profession, and many of them are of much repute and live in the suburbs of Seoul.   Those who desire their services send the necessary money and offerings, and the *mu-tang* exorcise the spirits in their own houses.

The use of straw, ropes, and of pieces of paper resembling the Shinto *gohei*, during incantations, with a certain similarity between the Shinto and the *Shaman* ceremonies, might suggest a common origin, but our knowledge of the Dæmonism of Korea is so completely in its infancy, that any speculations as to its kinships can be of little value, and it is only as a very slight contribution to the sum of knowledge of an obscure but very interesting subject, that I venture to present these chapters to my readers.

The Koreans, it must be remarked, have no single word for Dæmonism or Shamanism. The only phrase in use to express their belief in dæmons who require to be propitiated is, *Kursin wi han-nan Köt* (the worship of Spirits). *Pulto* is Buddhism, *Yuto* Confucianism, and *Sönto* Taoism, but the termination *To*, "doctrine," has not yet been affixed to Dæmonism.

CHAPTER XXXVI

SEOUL IN 1897 [1]

IT was midnight when, by the glory of an October full moon, I arrived from Chemulpo at the foot of the rugged slope crowned with the irregular, lofty, battlemented city wall and picturesque double-roofed gateway of the Gate of Staunch Loyalty which make the western entrance to the Korean capital so unique and attractive. An arrangement had been made for the opening of the gate, and after a long parley between the faithful Im and the guard, the heavy iron-bolted door creaked back before the united efforts of ten men, and I entered Seoul, then under the authority of Ye Cha Yun, an energetic and enlightened Governor, under whose auspices the western part of the city has lost the refuse heaps and foulness, with their concomitant odors, which were its chief characteristic. In the streets and lanes not a man, dog, or cat stirred, and not a light glimmered from any casement; but when I reached Chongdong, the foreign quarter, I observed that the lower extremity of every road leading in the direction of the Russian Legation was irregularly guarded by several slouching Korean sentries, gossiping in knots as they leaned on their rifles.

The grounds of my host's house open on those of the King's new palace, and the King and Crown Prince, attended by large retinues, were constantly carried through them on their way from their asylum in the Russian Legation to perform the

[1] I left Korea for China at Christmas, 1895, and after spending six months in travelling in the Chinese Far West, and three months among the Nan-tai San mountains in Japan, returned in the middle of October, 1896, and remained in Seoul until late in the winter of 1896-97.

427

customary rites at the spirit shrine, to which the fragmentary remains of the murdered Queen had been removed, to wait until the geomancers could decide on an "auspicious" site for her grave, the one which had been prepared for her at an enormous expense some miles outside the city having just been pronounced "unlucky."

A few days after my arrival the King went to the Kyeng-wun Palace to receive a Japanese prince, and courteously arranged to give me an audience afterwards, to which I went, attended, as on the last occasion, by the British Legation interpreter. The entrances were guarded by a number of slouching sentries in Japanese uniforms. Their hair, which had been cropped at the time of the abolition of the "topknot," had grown again, and hung in heavy shocks behind their ears, giving them a semi-barbarous appearance. At the second gate I alighted, no chair being permitted to enter, and walked to a very simple audience hall, then used for the first time, about 20 feet by 12 feet, of white wood, with lattice doors and windows, both covered with fine white paper, and with fine white mats on the floor.

The King and Crown Prince, both of whom were in deep mourning, *i.e.* in pure white robes with sleeveless dresses of exquisitely fine buff grass-cloth over them, and fine buff crinoline hats, stood together at the upper end of the room, surrounded by eunuchs, court ladies, including the reigning favorites, the ladies *Pak* and *Om*, and Court functionaries, all in mourning, the whole giving one an impression of absolute spotlessness. The waists of the voluminous white skirts of the ladies, which are a yard too long for them all round, were as high up as it is possible to place them.

The King and Crown Prince bowed and smiled. I made the required three curtseys to each, and the interpreter adopted the deportment required by Court etiquette, crouching, looking down, and speaking in an awe-struck whisper. I had not seen the King for two years, a period of great anxiety and vicissi-

SEOUL AND PALACE ENCLOSURE.

tude to him, but he was not looking worn or older, and when I congratulated him on his personal security and the assumption of his regal functions he expressed himself cordially in reply, with an air of genuine cheerfulness. In the brief conversation which followed the Crown Prince took part, and showed a fair degree of intelligence, as well as a much improved physique.

Later I had two informal audiences of the King in his house in the centre of the mass of the new buildings of the Kyeng-wun Palace. It is a detached Korean dwelling of the best Korean workmanship, with a deep-eaved, tiled roof, the carved beams of which are elaborately painted, and their terminals decorated with the five-petalled plum blossom, the dynastic emblem. The house consists of a hall with a *kang* floor, divided into one large and two small rooms by sliding and removable partitions of fretwork, filled in with fine tissue paper, the windows which occupy the greater part of both sides being of the same construction. The very small rooms at each end are indicated as the sleeping apartments of the King and his son by pale blue silk mattresses laid upon the fine white mats which cover the whole floor. The only furniture was two ten-leaved white screens. The fastenings of the windows and partitions are of very fine Korean brasswork. Simplicity could not go further.

Opposite is the much-adorned spirit shrine of the late Queen, connected with the house by a decorated gallery. The inner palace enclosure, where these buildings are, is very small, and behind the King's house rises into a stone terrace. Numerous as is the King's guard, it is evident that he fears to rely upon it solely, for of two gates leading from his house one opens into quarters occupied by Russian officers, who arrived in Seoul in the autumn of 1890, at the King's request, for purposes of military organization; and the other into small barracks occupied by the Russian drill instructors of the Korean army. Through the former he could reach the grounds of the English Legation in one minute, and after his former experiences possibilities of escape must be his first consideration. The small buildings of this new palace were already crowded like a rabbit warren, and when completed will contain over 1,000 people, including the bodyguard, eunuchs, and Court officials innumerable, writers, readers, palace ladies, palace women, and an immense establishment of cooks, runners, servants, and all the superabundant and useless *entour ge* of an Eastern Sovereign, to whom crowds and movement represent power. This congeries of buildings was carefully guarded, and even the Korean soldier who attended on me was not allowed to pass the gate.

The King had given me permission to take his photograph for Queen Victoria, and I was arranging the room for the purpose when the interpreter shouted " His Majesty," and almost before I could step back and curtsey, the King and Crown Prince entered, followed by the Officers of the Household and several of the Ministers, a *posse* of the newfangled police crowding the veranda outside. The Sovereign, always courteous, asked if I would like to take one of the portraits in his royal robes. The rich crimson brocade and the gold embroidered plastrons on his breast and shoulders became him well, and his pose was not deficient in dignity. He took some trouble to arrange the Crown Prince to the best advantage but the result was unsuccessful. After the operation was over he examined the different parts of the camera with interest, and seemed specially cheerful.

At a farewell audience some weeks later the King reverted to the subject of a British Minister, accredited solely to Korea; and the interpreter added, as an aside, " His Majesty is very anxious about this." He hardly seemed to realize that even if a change in the representation were contemplated, it could scarcely be carried out while Sir Claude Macdonald, who is accredited to both Courts, remains Minister at Peking.

The King was for more than a year the guest of the Russian Legation, an arrangement most distasteful to a large number

THE KING OF KOREA.

of his subjects, who naturally regarded it as a national humiliation that their Sovereign should be under the protection of a foreign flag. Rumors of plots for removing him to the Palace from which he escaped were rife, and there were days on which he feared to visit the Queen's tablet-house unless Russian officers walked beside his chair.

Mr. Waeber, the Russian Minister, had then been in Korea twelve years. He is an able and faithful servant of Russia. He was trusted by the King and the whole foreign community, and up to the time of the *Hegira* had been a warm and judicious friend of the Koreans. His guidance might have prevented the King from making infamous appointments and arbitrary arrests, from causelessly removing officials who were working well, and from such reckless extravagances as a costly Embassy to the European Courts and a foolish increase of the army and police force. But he remained passive, allowing the Koreans to "stew in their own juice," acting possibly under orders from home to give Korea "rope enough to hang herself," a proceeding which might hereafter give Russia a legitimate excuse for interference. Apart from such instructions, it must remain an inscrutable mystery why so excellent a man and so capable a diplomatist when absolutely master of the situation neglected to aid the Sovereign with his valuable advice, a course which would have met with the cordial approval of all his colleagues.

Be that as it may, the liberty which the King has enjoyed at the Russian Legation and since has not been for the advantage of Korea, and recent policy contrasts unfavorably with that pursued during the period of Japanese ascendency, which, on the whole, was in the direction of progress and righteousness.

Old abuses cropped up daily, Ministers and other favorites sold offices unblushingly, and when specific charges were made against one of the King's chief favorites, the formal demand for his prosecution was met by making him Vice-Minister of

Education ! The King, freed from the control of the mutinous officers and usurping Cabinet of 8th October, 1895, from
the Queen's strong though often unscrupulous guidance, and
from Japanese ascendency, and finding himself personally safe,
has reverted to some of the worst traditions of his dynasty,
and in spite of certain checks his edicts are again law and his
will absolute.   And it is a will at the mercy of any designing
person who gets hold of him and can work upon his fears and
his desire for money—of the ladies *Pak* and *Om*, who assisted
him in his flight, and of favorites and sycophants low and
many, who sell or bestow on members of their families offices
they have little difficulty in obtaining from his pliable good
nature.   With an ample Civil List and large perquisites he is
the most impecunious person in his dominions, for in common
with all who occupy official positions in Korea he is surrounded by hosts of grasping parasites and hangers-on, for
ever clamoring " Give, Give."

Men were thrown into prison without reason, some of the
worst of the *canaille* were made Ministers of State, the mur-
derer of *Kim Ok-yun* was appointed Master of Ceremony,
and a convicted criminal, a man whose life has been one
career of sordid crime, was made Minister of Justice.   Consequent upon the surreptitious sale of offices, the seizure of
revenue on its way to the Treasury, the appointment of men to
office for a few days, to give them " rank " and to enable
them to quarter on the public purse a host of impecunious relations and friends, and the custom among high officials of
resigning office on the occasion of the smallest criticism, the
administration is in a state of constant chaos, and the ofttimes
well-meaning but always vacillating Sovereign, absolute without an idea of how to rule, the sport of favorites usually unworthy, who work upon his amiability, the prey of greedy
parasites, and occasionally the tool of foreign adventurers,
paralyzes all good government by destroying the elements of
permanence, and renders economy and financial reform diffi-

cult and spasmodic by consenting to schemes of reckless extravagance urged upon him by interested schemers. Never has the King made such havoc of reigning as since he regained his freedom under the roof of the Russian Embassy.

I regret to have to write anything to the King's disadvantage. Personally I have found him truly courteous and kind, as he is to all foreigners. He has amiable characteristics, and I believe a certain amount of patriotic feeling. But as he is an all-important element of the present and future condition of Korea, it would be misleading and dishonest to pass over without remark such characteristics of his character and rule as are disastrous to Korea, bearing in mind in extenuation of them that he is the product of five centuries of a dynastic tradition which has practically taught that public business and the interests of the country mean for the Sovereign simply getting offices and pay for favorites, and that statesmanship consists in playing off one Minister against another.

Novelties in the Seoul streets were the fine physique and long gray uniforms of Colonel Putiata and his subordinates, three officers and ten drill-instructors, who arrived to drill and discipline the Korean army, the American military adviser having proved a failure, while the troops drilled by the Japanese were mutinous and rapacious, and the Japanese drill-instructors had retired with the rest of the *régime*. This "Military Commission" was doing its work with characteristic vigor and thoroughness, and the flat-faced, pleasant-looking, non-commissioned officers, with their drilled slouch, serviceable uniforms, and long boots were always an attraction to the crowd. A novelty, too, was the sight of the Korean cadet *corps* of thirty-seven young men of good families and seven officers, marching twice daily between the drill ground of the Korean troops close to the Kyeng-pok Palace and their own barracks behind the Russian Legation, with drums beating and colors flying. These young men, who are to receive a two years' military education from Russian officers, are under severe discipline, and were greatly surprised to find that servants were a prohibited luxury, and that their training involved the cleaning and keeping bright of their own rifles and accoutrements, and hard work for many hours of the day. The army now consists of 4,300 men in Seoul, 800 of whom are drilled as a bodyguard for the King, and 1,200 in the provinces, in Japanese uniforms, and equipped (so far as they go) with 3,000 Berdan rifles presented by Russia to Korea. The drill and words of command are Russian.

A standing army of 2,000 men would have been sufficient for all purposes in Korea, and as far as her need goes an army of 6,000 is an unblushing extravagance and a heavy drain on her resources. It is most probable that a force drilled and armed by Russia, accustomed to obey Russian orders and animated by an intense hereditary hatred of Japan, would prove a valuable *corps d'armée* to Russia in the event of war with that ambitious and restless empire.

The old *kesu* or *gens d'armes* with their picturesque dresses and long red plumes are now only to be seen, and that rarely, in attendance on officials of the Korean Government. Seoul is now policed, much overpoliced, for it has a force of 1,200 men, when a quarter of that number would be sufficient for its orderly population. Everywhere numbers of slouching men on and off duty, in Japanese semi-military uniforms, with shocks of hair behind their ears and swords in nickel-plated scabbards by their sides, suggest useless and extravagant expenditure. The soldiers and police, by an unwise arrangement made by the Japanese, and now scarcely possible to alter, are enormously overpaid, the soldiers receiving five dollars and a half a month, "all found," and the police from eight to ten, only finding their food. The Korean army is about the most highly paid in the world. The average Korean in his great baggy trousers, high, perishable, broad-brimmed hat, capacious sleeves, and long flapping white coat, is usually a docile and harmless man; but European clothes

KOREAN CADET CORPS AND RUSSIAN DRILL INSTRUCTORS.

and arms transform him into a truculent, insubordinate, and ofttimes brutal person, without civic sympathies or patriotism, greedy of power and spoil. Detachments of soldiers scattered through the country were a terror to the people from their brutality and marauding propensities early in 1897, and unless Russian officers are more successful than their predecessors in disciplining the raw material, an overpaid army, too large for the requirements of the country, may prove a source of weakness and frequent disorder.

Seoul in many parts, specially in the direction of the south and west gates, was literally not recognizable. Streets, with a minimum width of 55 feet, with deep stone-lined channels on both sides, bridged by stone slabs, had replaced the foul alleys, which were breeding-grounds of cholera. Narrow lanes had been widened, slimy runlets had been paved, roadways were no longer "free coups" for refuse, bicyclists "scorched" along broad, level streets, "express wagons" were looming in the near future, preparations were being made for the building of a French hotel in a fine situation, shops with glass fronts had been erected in numbers, an order forbidding the throwing of refuse into the streets was enforced,—refuse matter is now removed from the city by official scavengers, and Seoul, from having been the foulest is now on its way to being the cleanest city of the Far East !

This extraordinary metamorphosis was the work of four months, and is due to the energy and capacity of the Chief Commissioner of Customs, ably seconded by the capable and intelligent Governor of the city, Ye Cha Yun, who had acquainted himself with the working of municipal affairs in Washington, and who with a rare modesty refused to take any credit to himself for the city improvements, saying that it was all due to Mr. M'Leavy Brown.

Old Seoul, with its festering alleys, its winter accumulations of every species of filth, its ankle-deep mud and its foulness, which lacked the redeeming element of picturesqueness, is

being fast improved off the face of the earth. Yet it is chiefly
a restoration, for the dark, narrow alleys which lingered on till
the autumn of 1896 were but the result of gradual encroachments on broad roadways, the remains of the marginal channels of which were discovered.

What was done (and is being done) was to pull down the
houses, compensate their owners, restore the old channels, and
insist that the houses should be rebuilt at a uniform distance
behind them. Along the fine broad streets thus restored tiled
roofs have largely replaced thatch, in many cases the lower
parts of the walls have been rebuilt of stone instead of wattle,
and attempts at decoration and neatness are apparent in many
of the house and shop fronts, while many of the smoke-holes,
which vomit forth the smoke of the *kang* fires directly into the
street, are now fitted with glittering chimneys, constructed out
of American kerosene tins.

Some miles of broad streets are now available as promenades,
and are largely taken advantage of; business looked much
brisker than formerly, the shops made more display, and there
was an air of greater prosperity, which has been taken advantage of by the Hong-Kong and Shanghai Bank, which has
opened a branch at Chemulpo, and will probably erelong appear in the capital.

It is not, however, only in the making of broad thoroughfares that the improvement consists. Very many of the narrow
lanes have been widened, their roadways curved and gravelled,
and stone gutters have been built along the sides, in some cases
by the people themselves. Along with much else the pungent,
peculiar odor of Seoul has vanished. Sanitary regulations are
enforced, and civilization has reached such a height that the
removal of the snow from the front of the houses is compulsory
on all householders. So great is the change that I searched in
vain for any remaining representative slum which I might
photograph for this chapter as an illustration of Seoul in 1894.

SOUTH STREET, SEOUL.

It must be remarked, however, that the capital is being recon-
structed on Korean lines, and is not being Europeanized.

Chong-dong, however, the quarter devoted to Foreign Legations, Consulates, and Mission agencies, would have nearly
ceased to be Korean had not the King set down the Kyeng-
won Palace with its crowded outbuildings in the midst of the
foreign residences. Most of the native inhabitants have been
bought out. Wide roads with foreign shops have been constructed. The French have built a Legation on a height,
which vies in grandeur with that of Russia, and the American
Methodist Episcopal Mission has finished a large red brick
church, which, like the Roman Cathedral, can be seen from
all quarters.

The picturesque Peking Pass, up and down whose narrow,
rugged pathway generations of burdened baggage animals
toiled and suffered, and which had seen the splendors of successive Chinese Imperial Envoys at the accession of the
Korean Kings, has lost its identity. Its rock ledges, holes,
and boulders have disappeared—the rocky gash has been
widened, and the sides chiselled into smoothness, and under
the auspices of the Russian Minister a broad road, with retaining walls and fine culverts, now carries the traffic over the
lowered height.

Many other changes were noticeable. The Tai-won Kun,
for so many years one of the chief figures in Korean politics,
was practically a prisoner in his own palace. The Eastern and
Western Palaces, with their enormous accommodation and immense pleasure-grounds, were deserted, and were already beginning to decay. The Japanese soldiers had vacated the
barracks so long occupied by them close to the Kyeng-pok
Palace, and, reduced to the modest numbers of a Legation
guard, were quartered in the Japanese settlement; parties of
missionaries who had hived off from Chong-dong were occupying groups of houses in various parts of the capital, and there
was a singular "boom" in schools, accompanied by a military

craze, which affected not the scholars only, but the boys of Seoul generally.

But it must be remarked in connection with education in Korea that so lately as the close of 1896 a book, called *Confucianist Scholars' Handbook of the Latitudes and Longitudes*, had been edited by Sin Ki Sun, Minister of Education, prefaced by two Councillors of the Education Department, and published at Government expense, in which the following sentences occur :—

P. 52 : " Europe is too far away from the centre of civilization, *i.e.* the Middle Kingdom ; hence Russians, Turks, English, French, Germans, and Belgians look more like birds and beasts than men, and their languages sound like the chirping of fowls."

Again : " According to the views of recent generations, what westerners call the Christian Religion is vulgar, shallow, and erroneous, and is an instance of the vileness of Barbarian customs, which are not worthy of serious discussion. . . . They worship the heavenly spirits, but do not sacrifice to parents, they insult heaven in every way, and overturn the social relations. This is truly a type of Barbarian vileness, and is not worthy of treatment in our review of foreign customs, especially as at this time the religion is somewhat on the wane.

" Europeans have planted their spawn in every country of the globe except China. All of them honor this religion (!), but we are surprised to find that the Chinese scholars and people have not escaped contamination by it."

On p. 42 it is said : " Of late the so-called *Ye Su Kyo* (Christianity) has been trying to contaminate the world with its barbarous teachings. It deceives the masses by its stories of Heaven and Hell : it interferes with the rites of ancestral worship, and interdicts the custom of bowing before the gods of Heaven and Earth. These are the ravings of a disordered intellect, and are not worth discussing."

P. 50 : " How grand and glorious is the Empire of China, the Middle Kingdom ! She is the largest and richest in the world. The grandest men of the world have all come from the Middle Empire."

This tirade from an official pen was thought worthy of a remonstrance from the foreign representatives.

The graceful *Pai-low*, near the Peking Pass, at which generations of Korean kings had publicly acknowledged Chinese suzerainty by awaiting there the Imperial Envoy who came to invest them with regal rights, was removed, and during my sojourn the foundation of an arch to commemorate the assumption of Independence by Korea in January, 1895, was laid near the same spot, in presence of a vast concourse of white-robed men. An Independence Club, with a disused Royal Pavilion near the stumps of the *Pai-low* for its Club House, had been established to commemorate and conserve the national autonomy, and though the entrance fee is high, had already a membership of 2,000.

After a number of patriotic speeches had been made on the occasion of the laying of the foundation of the independence arch, the Club entertained the Foreign Legations and all the foreign residents at a *récherché* " collation " in this building ; speeches were made both by Koreans and the Foreign Representatives, and an extraordinary innovation was introduced. Waiters were dispensed with, and the Committee of the Club, the Governor of Seoul, and several of the Ministers of State themselves attended upon the guests with much grace and courtesy.

One of the most important events in Seoul was the establishment in April, 1896, by Dr. Jaisohn of the *Independent*, a two-page tri-weekly newspaper in English and the Korean script, enlarged early in 1897 to four pages, and published separately in each language. Only those who have formed some idea of the besotted ignorance of the Korean concerning current events in his own country, and of the credulity which makes

him the victim of every rumor set afloat in the capital, can appreciate the significance of this step and its probable effect in
enlightening the people, and in creating a public opinion
which shall sit in judgment on regal and official misdeeds. It
is already fulfilling an important function in unearthing abuses
and dragging them into daylight, and is creating a desire for
rational education and reasonable reform, and is becoming
something of a terror to evil-doers. Dr. Jaisohn (So Chia
P'il) is a Korean gentleman educated in America, and has the
welfare of his country thoroughly at heart.

The sight of newsboys passing through the streets with bundles of a newspaper in *En-mun* under their arms, and of men
reading them in their shops, is among the novelties of 1897.
Besides the *Independent*, there are now in Seoul two weeklies
in *En-mun* the *Korean Christian Advocate*, and the *Christian
News;* and the Korean Independence Club publishes a
monthly magazine, *The Chosen*, dealing with politics, science,
and foreign news, which has 2,000 subscribers. Seoul has
also a paper, the *Kanjo Shimbo*, or *Seoul News*, in mixed
Japanese and Korean script, published on alternate days, and
there are newspapers in the Japanese language, both in Fusan
and Chemulpo. All these, and the admirable *Korean Repository*, are the growth of the last three years.

The faculty of combination, by which in Korea as in China
the weak find some measure of protection against the strong,
is being turned to useful account. This *Kyei*, or principle of
association, which represents one of the most noteworthy
features of Korea, develops into insurance companies, mutual
benefit associations, money-lending syndicates, tontines, marriage and burial clubs, great trading guilds, and many others.

With its innumerable associations, only a few of which I
have alluded to, Korean life is singularly complex; and the
Korean business world is far more fully organized than ours,
nearly all the traders in the country being members of guilds,
powerfully bound together, and having the common feature of

mutual helpfulness in time of need. This habit of united action, and the measure of honesty which is essential to the success of combined undertakings, supply the framework on which various joint-stock companies are being erected, among which one of the most important is a tannery. Korean hides have hitherto been sent to Japan to be manufactured, owing to caste and superstitious prejudices against working in leather. The establishment of this company, which brought over Japanese instructors to teach the methods of manufacture, has not only made an end of a foolish prejudice, in the capital at least, but is opening a very lucrative industry, and others are following.

As may be expected in an Oriental country, the administration of law in Korea is on the whole infamous. It may be said that a body of law has yet to be created, as well as the judges who shall administer it equably. A mixed Committee of Revision has been appointed, but the Korean members show a marked tendency to drop off, and no legal reform, solely the work of foreigners, would carry weight with the people. Mr. Greathouse, a capable lawyer and legal adviser to the Law Department, has been able to prevent some infamous transactions, but on the whole the Seoul Law Court does little more than administer injustice and receive bribes. Of the two Law Courts of the capital the Supreme Court, under the supervision of the Minister and Vice-Minister of Justice, and in which the foreign adviser sits with the judges to advise in important cases, is the most hopeful; yet one of the most disgraceful of late appointments has been in connection with this department. The outrageous decisions, the gross bribery, and the actual atrocities of the Seoul Court are likely to bring about its abolition, and I will not enlarge upon them.

One of the most striking changes introduced into the Seoul of 1897 is the improvement in the prison, which is greatly owing to Mr. A. B. Stripling, formerly of the Shanghai Police, who, occupying a position as adviser to the Police Department, is carrying out prison reforms, originally suggested by the Japanese, in a humane and enlightened manner. Torture has disappeared from the great city prison, but there were dark rumors that some of the political prisoners, so lately as January, 1897, were subjected to it elsewhere.

My experience of Eastern prisons, chiefly in Asia Minor, China, Persia, and a glimpse of a former prison in Seoul, have given me a vivid impression of the contrast presented by the present system. Surrounding a large quadrangle, with the chief jailer's house in the centre, the rooms, not to be called cells, are large, airy, light, and well ventilated, with boarded floors covered with mats, and plenty of air space below. It is true that on the day I visited them some of the prisoners were shivering, and shivered more vigorously as an appeal to my compassion, but then the mecury was at 18° F., and this is not a usual temperature. They have a large bathroom with a stove on the Japanese plan. Their diet consists of a pint of excellent soup twice a day, with a large bowl of rice, and those who go out to work get a third meal. This ample diet cost 1¼d. per day.

There were from twelve to eighteen prisoners in each ordinary room, and fifty were awaiting trial in one roomy hall. A few under sentence, two of them to death, wore long wooden *cangues*, but I did not see any fetters. They are allowed to bring in their own mattresses, mats, and pillows for extra comfort. On the whole they were clean, cleaner than the ordinary coolies outside. A perforated wooden bar attached to the floor, with another with corresponding perforations above it, secures the legs of the prisoners at night. The sick were lying thickly on the hot floor of a room very imperfectly lighted, but probably the well would have been glad to change with them.

There were 225 prisoners altogether, all men. Classification is still in the future. Murderers and pilferers occupied the same room, and colonels of regiments accused of a serious conspiracy were with convicted felons, who might or might not be acting as spies and informers ; a very fine-looking man, sentenced for life, the first magistrate in Korea ever convicted and punished for bribery, and that on the complaint of a simple citizen, was in a "cell" with criminals wearing *cangues.* Some of the sentences seemed out of proportion to the offences, as, for instance, a feeble old man was immured for three years for cutting and carrying off pine brush for fuel, and an old blind man of some position was incarcerated for ten years for the violation of a grave under circumstances of provocation.

Much has been done in the way of prison reform, and much remains to be done, specially in the direction of classification, but still the great Seoul prison contrasts most favorably with the prisons of China and other unreformed Oriental countries. Torture is at least nominally abolished, and brutal exposures of severed heads and headless trunks, and beating and slicing to death, were made an end of during the ascendency of Japan. After an afternoon in the prison of Seoul, I could hardly believe it possible that only two years before I had seen several human heads hanging from tripod stands and lying on the ground in the throng of a business street, and headless bodies lying in their blood on the road outside the East Gate.

To mention the changes in Seoul would take another chapter. Dr. Allen, now U.S. Minister to Korea, said that the last four months of 1896 had seen more alterations than the previous twelve years of his residence in the country, and the three months of my last visit brought something new every week.

As a foil to so much that is indicative of progress, I conclude this chapter by mentioning, on the authority of the Governor of Seoul, that in January, 1897, there were in the capital a thousand *mu-tang*, or sorceresses, earning on an average fifteen dollars a month each, representing an annual expenditure by that single city of a hundred and eighty thousand dollars on dealings with the spirits, exclusive of the large sums paid to the blind sorcerers for their services, and to the geomancers, whose claims on the occasion of the interment of any one of rank and wealth are simply monstrous.

KOREAN POLICEMEN

Old *Régime*   New *Régime*

CHAPTER XXXVII

LAST WORDS ON KOREA

THE patient reader has now learned with me something of Korean history during the last three years, as well as of the reorganized methods of Government, and the education, trade, and finance of the country. He has also by proxy travelled in the interior, and has lived among the peasant farmers, seeing their industries, the huckstering which passes for trade, something of their domestic life and habits, and the superstitions by which they are enslaved, and has acquired some knowledge of the official and patrician exactions under which they suffer. He has seen the Koreans at home, with their limpness, laziness, dependence, and poverty, and Koreans under Russian rule raised into a thrifty and prosperous population. He can to some extent judge for himself of the prospects of a country which is incapable of standing alone, and which could support double its present population, and of the value of a territory which is possibly coveted by two Powers. Having acted as his guide so far, I should like to conclude with a few words on some of the subjects which have been glanced at in the course of these volumes.

Korea is not *necessarily* a poor country. Her resources are undeveloped, not exhausted. Her capacities for successful agriculture are scarcely exploited. Her climate is superb, her rainfall abundant, and her soil productive. Her hills and valleys contain coal, iron, copper, lead, and gold. The fisheries along her coast-line of 1,740 miles might be a source of untold wealth. She is inhabited by a hardy and hospitable race, and she has no beggar class.

445

On the other hand, the energies of her people lie dormant. The upper classes, paralyzed by the most absurd of social obligations, spend their lives in inactivity. To the middle class no careers are open ; there are no skilled occupations to which they can turn their energies. The lower classes work no harder than is necessary to keep the wolf from the door, for very sufficient reasons. Even in Seoul, the largest mercantile establishments have hardly risen to the level of shops. Everything in Korea has been on a low, poor, mean level. Class privileges, class and official exactions, a total absence of justice, the insecurity of all earnings, a Government which has carried out the worst traditions on which all unreformed Oriental Governments are based, a class of official robbers steeped in intrigue, a monarch enfeebled by the seclusion of the palace and the pettinesses of the Seraglio, a close alliance with one of the most corrupt of empires, the mutual jealousies of interested foreigners, and an all-pervading and terrorizing superstition have done their best to reduce Korea to that condition of resourcelessness and dreary squalor in which I formed my first impression of her.

Nevertheless the resources are there, in her seas, her soil, and her hardy population.

A great and universal curse in Korea is the habit in which thousands of able-bodied men indulge of hanging, or "sorning," on relations or friends who are better off than themselves. There is no shame in the transaction, and there is no public opinion to condemn it. A man who has a certain income, however small, has to support many of his own kindred, his wife's relations, many of his own friends, and the friends of his relatives. This partly explains the rush for Government offices, and their position as marketable commodities. To a man burdened with a horde of hangers-on, the one avenue of escape is official life, which, whether high or low, enables him to provide for them out of the public purse. This accounts for the continual creation of offices, with no other real object than the pensioning of the relatives and friends of the men who rule the country. Above all, this explains the frequency of conspiracies and small revolutions in Korea. Principle is rarely at stake, and no Korean revolutionist intends to risk his life in support of any conviction.

Hundreds of men, strong in health and of average intelligence, are at this moment hanging on for everything, even their tobacco, to high officials in Seoul, eating three meals a day, gossiping and plotting misdeeds, the feeling of honorable independence being unknown. When it is desirable to get rid of them, or it is impossible to keep them longer, offices are created or obtained for them. Hence Government employment is scarcely better than a "free coup" for this class of rubbish. The factious political disturbances which have disgraced Korea for many years have not been conflicts of principle at all, but fights for the Government position which gives its holder the disposal of offices and money. The suspiciousness which prevents high officials from working together is also partly due to the desire of every Minister to get more influence with the King than his colleagues, and so secure more appointments for his relations and friends. The author of the Korean Dictionary states that the word for *work* in Korean is synonymous with "loss," "evil," "misfortune," and the man who leads an idle life proves his right to a place among the gentry. The strongest claim for office which an official puts forward for a *protégé* is that he cannot make a living. Such persons when appointed do little, and often nothing, except draw their salaries and "squeeze" where they can!

I have repeated almost *ad nauseam* that the cultivator of the soil is the *ultimate sponge*. The farmers work harder than any other class, and could easily double the production of the land, their methods, though somewhat primitive, being fairly well adapted to the soil and climate. But having no security for their gains, they are content to produce only what will feed and clothe their families, and are afraid to build better houses or to dress respectably. There are innumerable peasant farmers who have gone on reducing their acreage of culture year by year, owing to the exactions and forced loans of magistrates and *yang-bans*, and who now only raise what will enable them to procure three meals a day. It is not wonderful that classes whose manifest destiny is to be squeezed, should have sunk down to a dead level of indifference, inertia, apathy, and listlessness.

In spite of reforms, the Korean nation still consists of but two classes, the Robbers and the Robbed,—the official class recruited from the *yang-bans*, the licensed vampires of the country, and the *Ha-in*, literally "low men," a residuum of fully four-fifths of the population, whose *raison d'être* is to supply the blood for the vampires to suck.

Out of such unpromising materials the new nation has to be constructed, by education, by protecting the producing classes, by punishing dishonest officials, and by the imposition of a labor test in all Government offices, *i.e.* by paying only for work actually done.

That reforms are not hopeless, if carried out under firm and capable foreign supervision, is shown by what has been accomplished in the Treasury Department in one year. No Korean office was in a more chaotic and corrupt condition, and the ramifications of its corruption were spread all through the Provinces. Much was hoped when Mr. M'Leavy Brown accepted the thankless position of Financial Adviser, from his known force of character and remarkable financial capacity, but no one would have ventured to predict what has actually occurred.

Although his efforts at financial reform have been thwarted at every turn, not alone by the rapacity of the King's male and female favorites, and the measureless cunning and craft of corrupt officials, who incite the Sovereign to actions concerning money which are subversive of the fairest schemes of financial rectitude, but by chicane, fraud, and corruption in every department; by the absence of trustworthy subordinates; by infamous traditional customs; and the fact that every man in office, and every man hoping for office, is pledged by his personal interest to oppose every effort at reform actively or passively, Korean finance stands thus at the close of 1897.

In a few months the Augean stable of the Treasury Department in Seoul has been cleansed; the accounts are kept on a uniform system, and with the utmost exactitude; " value received" precedes payments for work; an army of drones, hanging on to all departments and subsisting on public money, has been disbanded; a partial estimate has been formed of the revenue which the Provinces ought to produce; superfluous officials unworthily appointed find that their salaries are not forthcoming; every man entitled to receive payment is paid at the end of every month; nothing is in arrears; great public improvements are carried out with a careful supervision which ensures rigid economy; the accounts of every Department undergo strict scrutiny; no detail is thought unworthy of attention, and instead of Korea being bankrupt, as both her friends and enemies supposed she would be in July, 1896, she closed the financial year in April, 1897, with every account paid and a million and a half in the Treasury, out of which she has repaid one million of the Japanese loan of three millions. If foreign advisers of similar calibre and capacity were attached to all the departments of State similar results might in time be obtained.

One thing is certain, that the war and the period of the energetic ascendency of Japan have given Korea so rude a shake, and have so thoroughly discredited various customs and institutions previously venerated for their antiquity, that no retrograde movements, such as have been to some extent in progress in 1897, can replace her in the old grooves.

Seoul is Korea for most practical purposes, and the working of the Western leaven, the new impulses and modes of thought introduced by Western education, the inevitable contact with foreigners, and the influence of a free Press are through Seoul slowly affecting the nation. Under the shadow of Chinese suzerainty the Korean *yang-ban* enjoyed practically unlimited opportunities for the extortions and tyrannies which were the atmosphere of patrician life. Japan introduced a new theory on this subject, and practically gave the masses to understand that they possess rights which the classes are bound to respect, and the Press takes the same line.

It is slowly dawning upon the Korean peasant farmer through the medium of Japanese and Western teaching, that to be an ultimate sponge is not his inevitable destiny, that he is entitled to civil rights, equality before the eye of the law, and protection for his earnings.

The more important of the changes during the last three years which are beneficial to Korea may be summarized thus: The connection with China is at an end, and with the victories of Japan the Korean belief in the unconquerable military power of the Middle Kingdom has been exploded, and the alliance between two political systems essentially corrupt has been severed. The distinction between patrician and plebeian has been abolished, on paper at least, along with domestic slavery, and the disabilities which rendered the sons of concubines ineligible for high office. Brutal punishments and torture are done away with, a convenient coinage has replaced *cash*, an improved educational system has been launched, a disciplined army and police force has been created, the Chinese literary examinations are no longer the test of fitness for official employment, a small measure of judicial reform has been granted, a railroad from Chemulpo to the capital is being rapidly pushed to completion, the pressure of the Trades Guilds is relaxed, a postal system efficiently worked and commanding confidence has been introduced into all the Provinces, the finances of the country are being placed on a sound basis, the change from a land-tax paid in kind to one which is an assessment in money on the value of the land greatly diminishes the opportunities for official "squeezing," and large and judicious retrenchments have been carried out in most of the metropolitan and provincial departments.

Nevertheless, the Government *Gazette* of the 12th of August, 1897, contains the following Royal Edicts:—

I

We have been looking into the condition of the country. We have realized the imminent danger which threatens the maintenance of the nation. But the people of both high and low classes do not seem to mind the coming calamity and act indifferently. Under the circumstances the country cannot prosper. We are depending upon Our Ministers for their advice and help, but they do not respond to our trust. How are we going to bring the nation out of its chaotic condition? We desire them to pause and to think that they cannot enjoy their homes unless the integrity of the nation is preserved. We confess that We have not performed our part properly, but Our Ministers and other officials ought to have advised Us to refrain from wrongdoing as their ancestors had done to Our forefathers. We will endeavor to do what is right and proper for our country hereafter, and We trust Our subjects will renew their loyalty and patriotism in helping Us to carry out Our aim. Our hope is that every citizen in the land will consider the country's interest first before thinking of his private affairs. Let Us all join Our hearts to preserve the integrity of Our country.

II

The welfare of Our people is our constant thought. We realize that since last year's disturbance Our people have been suffering greatly on account of lack of peace and order. The dead suffers as much as the living, but the Government has not done anything to ameliorate the existing condition. This thought makes Us worry to such an extent that the affluence by which We are surrounded is rather uncomfortable. If this fact is known to Our provincial officials they will do their best to ameliorate the condition of the people. Compulsory collection of unjust taxes and thousands of lawless officials and Government agents rob the helpless masses upon one pretence or another. Why do they treat Our people so cruelly? We hereby order the provincial officials to look into the various items of illegal taxes now being collected, and abolish them all without reservation. Whoever does not heed this edict will be punished according to the law.[1]

Though the Koreans of to-day are the product of centuries of disadvantages, yet after nearly a year spent in the country, during which I made its people my chief study, I am by no means hopeless of their future, in spite of the distinctly retrograde movements of 1897. Two things, however, are essential.

I. As Korea is incapable of reforming herself from within, that she must be reformed from without.

II. That the power of the Sovereign must be placed under stringent and permanent constitutional checks.

Hitherto I have written exclusively on Korean internal affairs, her actual condition, and the prospects of the social and commercial advancement of the people. I conclude with a few remarks on the political possibilities of the Korean future, and the relations of Korea with certain other powers.

The geographical position of Korea, with a frontier conterminous with those of China and Russia, and divided from Japan by only a narrow sea, has done much to determine her political relationships. The ascendency of China grew naturally out of territorial connection, and its duration for many centuries was at once the cause and effect of a community in philosophy, customs, and to a great extent in language and religion. But Chinese control is at an end, and China can scarcely be regarded as a factor in the Korean situation.

Japan having skilfully asserted her claim to an equality of rights in Korea, after several diplomatic triumphs and marked success in obtaining fiscal and commercial ascendency, eventually, by the overthrow of her rival in the late war, secured political ascendency likewise ; and the long strife between the

[1] The good intentions of the Korean Sovereign, as well as the weakness which renders them ineffective, are typically illustrated in these two pathetic documents.

two empires, of which Korea had been the unhappy stage, came to an end.

The nominal reason for the war, to which the Japanese Government has been careful to adhere, was the absolute necessity for the reform of the internal administration of a State too near the shores of Japan to be suffered to sink annually deeper into an abyss of misgovernment and ruin. It is needless to speculate upon the ultimate object which Japan had in view in undertaking this unusual task. It is enough to say that she entered upon it with great energy; and that, while the suggestions she enforced introduced a new *régime*, struck at the heart of privilege and prerogative, revolutionized social order, and reduced the Sovereign to the position of a "salaried automaton," the remarkable ability with which her demands were formulated gave them the appearance of simple and natural administrative reforms.

I believe that Japan was thoroughly honest in her efforts; and though she lacked experience, and was ofttimes rough and tactless, and aroused hostile feeling needlessly, that she had no intention to subjugate, but rather to play the *rôle* of the protector of Korea and the guarantor of her independence.

For more than a year, in spite of certain mistakes, she made fair headway, accomplished some useful and important reforms, and initiated others; and it is only just to her to repeat that those which are now being carried out are on the lines which she laid down. Then came Viscount Miura's savage *coup*, which discredited Japan and her diplomacy in the eyes of the civilized world. This was followed by the withdrawal of her garrisons, and of her numerous advisers, controllers, and drill instructors, and the substitution of an apparently *laissez-faire* policy for an active dictatorship. I write "apparently," because it cannot for a moment be supposed that this sagacious and ambitious Empire recognized the unfortunate circumstances in Korea as a finality, and retired in despair!

The landing of Japanese armies in Korea, and the subsequent declaration of war with China, while they gave the world the shock of a surprise, were, as I endeavored to point out briefly in chapter xiii., neither the result of a sudden impulse, nor of the shakiness of a Ministry which had to choose between its own downfall and a foreign war. The latter view could only occur to the most superficial student of Far Eastern history and politics.

Japan for several centuries has regarded herself as possessing vested rights to commercial ascendency in Korea. The harvest of the Korean seas has been reaped by her fishermen, and for 300 years her colonies have sustained a more or less prosperous existence at Fusan. Her resentment of the pretensions of China in Korea, though debarred for a considerable time from active exercise, first by the policy of seclusion pursued by the Tokugawa House, and next by the necessity of consolidating her own internal polity after the restoration, has never slumbered.

To deprive China of a suzerainty which, it must be admitted, was not exercised for the advantage of Korea; to consolidate her own commercial supremacy; to ensure for herself free access and special privileges; to establish a virtual protectorate under which no foreign dictation would be tolerated; to reform Korea on Japanese lines, and to substitute her own liberal and enlightened civilization for the antique Oriental conservatism of the Peninsula, are aims which have been kept steadily in view for forty years, replacing in part the designs which had existed for several previous centuries.

In order to judge correctly of the action or inaction of Japan during 1896 and 1897, it must be borne in mind not only that her diplomacy is secret and reticent, but that it is steady; that it has not hitherto been affected by any great political cataclysms at home; that it has less of opportunism than that of almost any other nation, and that the Japanese have as much tenacity and fixity of purpose as any other race. Also, Japanese policy in Korea is still shaped by the same remarkable statesmen, who from the day that Japan emerged upon the international arena have been recognized by the people as their natural leaders, and who have guided the country through the manifold complications which beset the path of her enlightened progress with a celerity and freedom from disaster which have compelled the admiration of the world.

The assassination of the Korean Queen under the auspices of Viscount Miura, and the universal horror excited by the act, rendered it politic for Japan to keep out of sight till the storm which threatened to wreck her *prestige* in Korea had blown over. This temporary retirement was arranged with consummate skill. There were no violent dislocations. The garrisons which were to be withdrawn quietly slipped away, and were replaced by guards only sufficient for the protection of the Japanese Legation, the Japanese telegraph, and other property. The greater number of the Japanese in Korean Government employment fell naturally out of it as their contracts expired, and quietly retired from the country. Ministers of experience, proved ability, and courtesy of demeanor, have succeeded to the post once occupied by Mr. Otori and Viscount Miura. There has been scarcely any recent interference with Korean affairs, and the Japanese colonists who were much given to bullying and blustering are on greatly improved behavior, the most objectionable among them having been recalled by orders from home. Diplomatically, Japan has carefully avoided friction with the Korean Government and the representatives of the other Powers. But to infer from this that she has abandoned her claims, or has swerved from her determination to make her patronage essential to the well-being of Korea would be a grave mistake.

It has been said that whatever Japan lost in Korea Russia gained. It is true that the King in his terror and apprehension threw himself upon the protection of the Russian Minister, and remained for more than a year under the shelter of the Russian flag, and that at his request a Russian Military Commission arrived to reorganize and drill the Korean army, that Russia presented 3,000 Berdan rifles to Korea, that a Russian financier spent the autumn of 1896 in Seoul investigating the financial resources and prospects of the country, and that the King, warned by disastrous experiences of betrayal, prefers to trust his personal safety to his proximity to the Russian military quarters.

But "Russian Ascendency," in the sense of " *Control* " in which Japanese ascendency is to be understood, has never existed. The Russian Minister used the undoubtedly influential position which circumstances gave him with unexampled moderation, and only brought his influence to bear on the King in cases of grave misrule. The influence of Russia, however, grew quietly and naturally, with little of external manifestation, up to March, 1897, when the publication of a treaty, concluded ten months before between Russia and Japan,[1] caused something of a revulsion of feeling in favor of the latter country, and Russia has been slowly losing ground. Her policy is too pacific to allow of a quarrel with Japan, and a quarrel would be the inevitable result of any present attempt at dictatorship in Korea. So far, she has pursued a strictly opportunist policy, taking no steps except those which have been forced upon her; and even if the Korean pear were ready to drop into her mouth, I greatly doubt if she would shake the tree.

At all events, Russia let the opportunity of obtaining ascendency in Korea go by. It is very likely that she never desired it. It may be quite incompatible with other aims, at which we can only guess. At the same time, the influence of Japan is quietly and steadily increasing. Certainly the great object of the triple intervention in the treaty negotiations in Shimonoseki was to prevent Japan from gaining a foothold on the mainland of the Asiatic Continent; but it does not seem

[1] See Appendix E.

altogether impossible that, by playing a waiting game and profiting by previous mistakes, she, without assuming a formal protectorate, may be able to add, for all practical purposes of commerce and emigration, a mainland province to her Empire. Forecasts are dangerous things,[1] but it is safe to say that if Russia, not content with such quiet, military developments as may be in prospect, were to manifest any aggressive designs on Korea, Japan is powerful enough to put a brake on the wheel! Korea, however, is incapable of standing alone, and unless so difficult a matter as a joint protectorate could be arranged, she must be under the tutelage of either Japan or Russia.

If Russia were to acquire an actual supremacy, the usual result would follow. Preferential duties and other imposts would practically make an end of British trade in Korea with all its large potentialities. The effacement of British political influence has been effected chiefly by a policy of *laissez-faire*, which has produced on the Korean mind the double impression of indifference and feebleness, to which the dubious and hazy diplomatic relationship naturally contributes. If England has no contingent interest in the political future of a country rich in undeveloped resources and valuable harbors, and whose possession by a hostile Power might be a serious peril to her interests in the Far East, her policy during the last few years has been a sure method of evidencing her unconcern.

Though we may have abandoned any political interest in Korea, the future of British trade in the country remains an important question. Such influence as England possesses, being exercised through a non-official channel, and therefore necessarily indirect, is owing to the abilities, force, and diplomatic tact of Mr. M'Leavy Brown, the Chief Commissioner

---

[1] As " it is the unexpected which happens," it would not be surprising if certain moves, ostensibly with the object of placing the independence of Korea on a firm basis, were made even before these volumes are published.

of Customs, formerly of H.B.M.'s Chinese Consular Service. So long as he is in control at the capital, and such upright and able men as Mr. Hunt, Mr. Oiesen, and Mr. Osborne are Commissioners at the treaty ports (Appendix D), so long will England be commercially important in Korean estimation.

The Customs revenue, always increasing, and collected at a cost of 10 per cent. only, is the backbone of Korean finance; and everywhere the ability and integrity of the administration give the Commissioners an influence which is necessarily in favor of England, and which produces an impression even on corrupt Korean officialism.   That this service should remain in our hands is of the utmost practical importance.   In the days of Japanese ascendency there was a great desire to upset the present arrangement, but it was frustrated by the tact and firmness of the Chief Commissioner.   The next danger is that it should pass into Russian hands, which would be a severe blow to our *prestige* and interests.   Some of the leading Russian papers are agitating this question, and the *Novoie Vremia* of 9th September, 1897, in writing of the opening of the ports of Mok-po and Chi-nam-po to foreign trade, says:— "These encroachments are chiefly due to the cleverness of the British officials who are at the head of the Financial and Customs Departments of the Korean administration." It adds, "If Russia tolerates any further increase in this policy . . . Great Britain will convert the country into one of her best markets." The *Novoie Vremia* goes on to urge "the Russian Government to exercise, before it is too late, a more searching surveillance than at present, to take steps to reduce the number of British officials in the Korean Government (the Customs), and to compel Japan to withdraw what are practically the military garrisons which she has established in Korea."

Such, in brief outline, is the position of political affairs in Korea at the close of 1897.   Her long and close political connection with China is severed; she has received from Japan a gift of independence which she knows not how to use;

England, for reasons which may be guessed at, has withdrawn from any active participation in her affairs; the other European Powers have no interests to safeguard in that quarter; and her integrity and independence are at the mercy of the most patient and the most ambitious of Empires, whose interests in the Far East are conflicting, if not hostile.

It is with great regret that I take leave of Korea, with Russia and Japan facing each other across her destinies. The distaste I felt for the country at first passed into an interest which is almost affection, and on no previous journey have I made dearer and kinder friends, or those from whom I parted more regretfully. I saw the last of Seoul in snow in the blue and violet atmosphere of one of the loveliest of her winter mornings, and the following day left Chemulpo in a north wind of merciless severity in the little Government steamer *Hyenik* for Shanghai, where the quaint Korean flag excited much interest and questioning as she steamed slowly up the river.

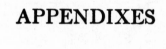

APPENDIXES

Name of Mission.	Year of beginning work in Korea.	Number of married male Missionaries.	Number of unmarried male Missionaries.	Number of unmarried female Missionaries.	Number of stations where Missionaries reside.	Number of out stations where no Missionaries reside.	Number of organized churches.	Number of churches wholly self-supporting.	Number of churches partially self-supporting.	Number of communicants received during past year.	Number of catechumens or probationers received during past year.	Number dismissed during past year.	Number of deaths during past year.	Present membership.
American Presbyterian Mission (North)	1884	11	2	5	4	25	13	8	5	210	635	3	2	510
American Presbyterian Mission (South)	1892	4	2	2	3									
Australian Presbyterian Mission . .	1891	1		3	1									
Y.M.C.A. Mission of Canada . . .	1889	1			1									
American Meth. Epis. Mission (North) .	1885	8	7	7	4	4	7		7	57	588		2	266
American Meth. Epis. Mission (South) .	1896	1												
Ella Thing Memorial Mission (Baptist) .	1895	1	1	1	1						3			1
Society for the Propagation of the Gospel	1890		9	7	3									
Société des Missions-Étrangères . .	1784		26	8	19	466	18			1,250			515	28,802

* Besides much in labor and in contributions for support of native evangelists,

FOR KOREA, 1896.

Number of Sabbath schools.	Number of pupils in Sabbath schools.	Number of day schools.	Number of pupils in day schools.	Number of boarding-schools for boys.	Number of boarding-schools for girls.	Number of pupils in boarding-schools for boys.	Number of pupils in boarding-schools for girls.	Number of theological schools.	Number of theological students.	Number of native ministers.	Number of unordained preachers and helpers.	Number of Bible-women.	Number of hospitals.	Number of in-patients treated during past year.	Number of dispensaries.	Number of patients treated during past year.	Native contributions for all purposes during past year.
		7	139	1	1	50	35				13	4	3	339	7	20,295	$796.44*
10	783										2	1			1	2,000	
				1			9				1	1					
7	512	4	121	1	1	110	50				10	5	2	116	4	7,778	$647.37
																	$.60
													3	795	3	29,786	
		21	204	2		271		1	24	3	16						

schools, and the enlargement and construction of Church edifices.

APPENDIX B

Direct Foreign Trade of Korea, 1886–96

(*i.e.* net value of foreign goods imported in foreign, or foreign-type, vessels into the Treaty Ports, and taken cognizance of by the foreign Customs ; and of native goods similarly exported and re-exported from the Treaty Ports to foreign countries.)

Year.	Net imports of Foreign Goods (*i.e.* exclusive of Foreign Goods re-exported to Foreign Countries).	Exports and Re-exports[1] of Native Goods to Foreign Countries.	Total.
1886	$2,474,185	$ 504,225	$2,978,410
1887	2,815,441	804,996	3,620,437
1888	3,046,443	867,058	3,913,501
1889	3,377,815	1,233,841	4,611,656
1890	4,727,839	3,550,478	8,278,317
1891	5,256,468	3,366,344	8,622,812
1892	4,598,485	2,443,739	7,042,224
1893	3,880,155	1,698,116	5,578,271
1894	5,831,563	2,311,215	8,142,778
1895	8,088,213	2,481,808	10,570,021
1896	6,531,324	4,728,700	11,260,024

Note.—The increase in the foreign trade of Korea between 1886 and 1896 may not have been so great as the above figures without explanation would imply. It is generally stated that side by side with the trade in foreign vessels at the Treaty Ports a considerable traffic has been carried on by junk between non-Treaty ports in Korea and ports in China and Japan. This junk trade was probably much larger in the earlier years of the period the figures of which are compared, and the rapid development shown in the table may be partly due to the increasing transfer of traffic from native craft to foreign-type vessels which offer greater regularity and safety and less delay.

[1] *i.e.* including native goods imported from another Korean port and re-exported to a foreign country.

COMPARATIVE TABLE OF THE NET DUES AND DUTIES COLLECTED
AT THE THREE PORTS FOR THE YEARS 1884–96

Year.	Import Duties.	Export Duties.	Tonnage Dues.	Total.
1884	$79,373.71	$19,234.74	$3,478.19	$102,086.64
1885	119,364.41	19,602.22	2,996.90	141,963.53
1886	132,757.12	24,812.11	2,708.75	160,277.98
1887	203,271.68	40,384.52	3,045.12	246,701.32
1888	219,759.81	43,330.62	4,124.55	267,214.98
1889	213,457.49	61,835.23	4,707.04	279,999.76
1890	327,460.11	178,552.14	8,587.90	514,600.15
1891	372,022.07	168,096.36	8,940.26	549,058.69
1892	308,954.13	123,212.24	6,247.05	438,413.42
1893	262,679.28	85,720.22	5,717.16	354,116.66
1894	357,828.34	115,779.33	7,398.64	481,006.31
1895	601,588.06	124,261.22	15,448.20	741,297.48
1896	448,137.16	226,342.45	17,304.75	691,784.36

COMPARAVIVE STATEMENT OF THE JAPANESE AND NON-JAPANESE COTTON
GOODS IMPORTED INTO KOREA DURING THE YEAR 1896

Description.	Classification of Quantity.	Japanese.		Non-Japanese.		Total.	
		Quantity.	Value.	Quantity.	Value.	Quantity.	Value.
Shirtings—Gray Plain	Pieces	6,715	$ 23,660	428,911	$ 1,567,967	435,626	$ 1,591,627
Shirtings—White	,,	31	121	5,445	21,768	5,476	21,889
T-Cloths	,,	1,211	2,719	1,660	4,177	2,871	6,896
Drills	,,	163	634	11,583	47,998	11,746	48,632
Turkey-Red Cloths	,,	1,652	3,663	7,519	17,349	9,171	21,012
Sheetings	,,	30,184	115,914	14,793	58,455	44,977	174,369
Cotton Flannel	,,	762	2,870	1,432	3,927	2,194	6,797
Cotton Blankets	Pairs	1,625	3,883			1,625	3,883
Cotton Yarn and Thread	Piculs	12,821	368,064	1,795	71,386	14,616	439,450
	Value		521,528		1,793,027		2,314,555
Cotton Goods, Unclassed	,,	[1]	644,671		[2]379,319		1,023,990
Total	Value		1,166,199		2,172,346		3,338,545

[1] Chiefly narrow-width cloth, gray or white, checked or plain.   [2] Including $2,549 Chinese Cottons.

APPENDIX C

RETURN of Principal Articles of Export (net) to Foreign Countries for the Years 1896–95

Articles.	Chemulpo.		Fusan.		Wön-san.	
	1896.	1895.	1896.	1895.	1896.	1895.
Beans . . .	£48,485	£45,679	£65,731	£22,337	£24,132	£32,049
Fish (dried manure)	..	..	4,296	639	4,394	312
Cowhides . .	8,789	14,036	11,077	37,225	4,424	6,152
Ginseng . .	29,739	575	..	..	..	..
Paper . .	2,326	1,785	1,806	2,236	24	9
Rice . . .	92,444	62,390	178,852	17,646	549	..
Seaweed . .	55	40	6,705	3,809	..	..
Sundries . .	12,713	8,992	13,633	9,361	2,101	3,590
Total . .	£194,551	£133,497	£282,100	£93,253	£35,624	£42,112

	1896.		1895.	
	Currency.	Sterling.	Currency.	Sterling.
Total exports from Korea . . .	$4,728,700	£512,275	$2,481,808	£268,862

RETURN of Principal Articles of Foreign Import (net : *i.e.* excluding Re-exports) to Open Ports of Korea during the Years 1896–95.

Articles.	Chemulpo.		Fusan.		Wön-san.	
	1896.	1895.	1896.	1895.	1896.	1895.
Cotton goods—						
Shirtings....................	£103,196	£172,549	£51,920	£54,911	£21,982	£55,190
Lawns and muslins.....	6,956	11,554	10,670	8,183	1,072	2,066
Sheetings—						
Japanese.....	12,508	7,199	......	......	40	1,330
English and American	6,736	8,594	......	......	23	4,500
Japanese piece-goods....	14,015	20,129	24,944	19,432	30,867	38,608
Yarn—						
Japanese....................	27,271	26,098	11,018	3,886	1,590	3,483
English and Indian.....	5,634	4,876	222	......	1,871	4,364
Other cottons................	14,394	29,065	6,363	4,836	8,732	15,125
Total.....................	£190,710	£280,064	£105,137	£91,238	£66,177	£124,666
Woolens........................	3,266	4,933	578	884	182	333
Metals............................	7,172	8,620	15,253	10,342	7,690	6,217
Sundries—						
Dyes	4,818	10,794	2,363	3,084	777	1,667
Grass-cloths................	22,358	13,641	3,546	1,402	2,241	3,154
Matches......................	4,798	3,575	4,571	3,348	2,018	1,680
Kerosene oil—						
American.................	20,035	9,819	9,560	7,479	6,463	3,990
Russian....................	9,312	457	4,513	478	69	1
Provisions...................	5,717	3,859	2,358	2,024	381	......
Saké...........................	3,018	9,639	2,972	2,818	1,203	1,176
Silk piece-goods..........	28,943	65,057	8,167	5,606	4,058	12,848
Other articles.............	89,417	111,902	50,828	38,859	26,241	30,884
Total.....................	£188,416	£228,743	£88,878	£65,098	£43,451	£55,400
Grand total...........	£382,203	£522,360	£209,846	£167,562	£117,500	£186,616
Less excess of re-exports over imports in some articles..................	1,088	596	......	......	......	126
Net total	£381,115	£521,764	£209,846	£167,562	£117,500	£186,490

	1896.		1895.	
	Currency.	Sterling.	Currency.	Sterling.
Total for Korea................................	$6,539,630[1]	£708,461	$8,084,465[1]	£875,816

[1] 1 dollar = 2s. 2d.

RETURN of all Shipping Vessels Entered at the Open Ports of Korea during the Year 1896.

Nationality.	Chemulpo. Sailing.		Chemulpo. Steam.		Fusan. Sailing.		Fusan. Steam.		Wŏn-san. Sailing.		Wŏn-san. Steam.		Korea. Total.	
	No. of Vessels	Tons.	No. of Vessels	Tons.	No. of Vessels	Tons.	No. of Vessels	Tons.	No. of Vessels	Tons.	No. of Vessels	Tons.	No. of Vessels	Tons.
American . .	2	158	.....	.....	.....	.....	.....	.....	.....	.....	.....	.....	2	158
British . .	.....	.....	3	3,381	.....	.....	5	5,635	.....	.....	5	5,635	13	14,651
Chinese . .	56	557	.....	.....	.....	.....	.....	.....	.....	.....	.....	.....	56	557
German . .	.....	.....	1	808	.....	.....	5	4,732	.....	.....	4	3,612	10	9,152
Japanese . .	307	10,278	154	118,145	537	17,035	292	210,645	41	3,227	58	65,654	1,389	424,984
Norwegian .	.....	.....	2	1,082	.....	.....	.....	.....	.....	.....	.....	.....	2	1,082
Russian . .	.....	.....	2	2,202	9	500	13	10,381	.....	.....	10	10,234	25	22,817
Korean . .	111	3,572	51	10,375	.....	.....	16	5,900	8	572	28	4,840	223	25,759
Total . .	476	14,565	213	135,993	546	17,535	331	237,293	49	3,799	105	89,975	1,720	499,160
" for 1895 .	531	14,449	242	108,021	497	14,300	272	180,784	61	5,029	93	83,547	1,696	406,130

APPENDIX D

The population of the three Korean treaty ports was as follows in January, 1897 :—

	Chemulpo Settlement.
Japanese	3,904
Chinese	404
British	15
German	12
American	7
French	7
Norwegian	3
Greek	3
Italian	1
Portuguese	1
Total	4,357
Estimated native population	6,756

	Fusan Settlement.
Japanese	5,508
Chinese	34
British	10
American	7
German	2
Danish	1
French	1
Italian	1
Total	5,564
Estimated native population of Fusan City and the Prefecture of Túng-nai	33,000

	Wŏn-san Settlement.
Japanese	1,299
Chinese	39
American	8
German	3
British	2
French	2
Russian	2
Danish	1
Norwegian	1
Total	1,357
Estimated native population	15,000

APPENDIX E

TREATY BETWEEN JAPAN AND RUSSIA WITH REPLY OF H.E. THE KOREAN MINISTER FOR FOREIGN AFFAIRS

MEMORANDUM

The Representatives of Russia and Japan at Seoul, having conferred under the identical instructions from their respective Governments, have arrived at the following conclusions:—

While leaving the matter of His Majesty's, the King of Korea, return to the Palace entirely to his own discretion and judgment, the Representatives of Russia and Japan will friendly advise His Majesty to return to that place, when no doubts could be entertained concerning his safety.

The Japanese Representative, on his part, gives the assurance, that the most complete and effective measures will be taken for the control of Japanese *soshi*.

The present Cabinet Ministers have been appointed by His Majesty by his own free will, and most of them have held ministerial or other high offices during the last two years and are known to be liberal and moderate men.

The two Representatives will always aim at recommending His Majesty to appoint liberal and moderate men as Ministers, and to show clemency to his subjects.

The Representative of Russia quite agrees with the Representative of Japan that at the present state of affairs in Korea it may be necessary to have Japanese guards stationed at some places for the protection of the Japanese telegraph line between Fusan and Seoul, and that these guards, now consisting of three companies of soldiers, should be withdrawn as soon as possible and replaced by gendarmes, who will be distributed as follows: fifty men at Fusan, fifty men at Ka-heung, and ten men each at ten intermediate posts between Fusan and Seoul.

This distribution may be liable to some changes, but the total number of the gendarme force shall never exceed two hundred men, who will afterwards gradually be withdrawn from such places, where peace and order have been restored by the Korean Government.

For the protection of the Japanese settlements at Seoul and the open ports against possible attacks by the Korean populace, two companies of Japanese troops may be stationed at Seoul, one company at Fusan and one at Wŏn-san, each company not to exceed two hundred men. These troops will be quartered near the settlements, and shall be withdrawn as soon as no apprehension of such attacks could be entertained.

For the protection of the Russian Legation and Consulates the Russian Government may also keep guards not exceeding the number of Japanese troops at those places, and which will be withdrawn as soon as tranquillity in the interior is completely restored.

(Signed)   C. WAEBER,
Representative of Russia.
J. KOMURA,
Representative of Japan.

SEOUL, 14*th May*, 1896.

PROTOCOL

The Secretary of State, Prince Lobanow-Rostovskey, Foreign Minister of Russia, and the Marshal Marquis Yamagata, Ambassador Extraordinary of His Majesty the Emperor of Japan, having exchanged their views on the situation of Korea, agreed upon the following articles :—

I

For the remedy of the financial difficulties of Korea, the Governments of Russia and Japan will advise the Korean Government to retrench all superfluous expenditure, and to establish a balance between expenses and revenues. If, in consequence of reforms deemed indispensable, it may be necessary to have recourse to foreign loans, both Governments shall by mutual consent give their support to Korea.

II

The Governments of Russia and Japan shall endeavor to leave to Korea, as far as the financial and economical situation of that country will permit, the formation and maintenance of a national armed force and police of such proportions as will be sufficient for the preservation of the internal peace, without foreign support.

III

With a view to facilitate communications with Korea, the Japanese Government may continue (*continuera*) to administer the telegraph lines which are at present in its hands.

It is reserved to Russia (the rights) of building a telegraph line between Seoul and her frontiers.

These different lines can be repurchased by the Korean Government, so soon as it has the means to do so.

IV

In case the above matters should require a more exact or detailed explanation, or if subsequently some other points should present themselves upon which it may be necessary to confer, the Representatives of both Governments shall be authorized to negotiate in a spirit of friendship.

(Signed)   LOBANOW.
YAMAGATA.

MOSCOW, 9th June, 1896.

The following is the exact translation of the reply sent to the Japanese Minister by the Korean Minister of Foreign Affairs, concerning the Russo-Japanese Convention :—

MINISTRY OF FOREIGN AFFAIRS,
Mar. 9th, 2nd year of Kun-yang (1897).

SIR—I have the honor to acknowledge the receipt of your despatch of the 2nd instant, informing me that, on the 14th day of May last, a memorandum was signed at Seoul by H.E. Mr. Komura, the former Japanese Minister Resident, and the Russian Minister, and that, on the 4th of June of the same year, an Agreement was signed at Moscow, by H.E. Marshal Yamagata, the Japanese Ambassador, and the Minister for Foreign Affairs of Russia; and that these two documents have been laid publicly before the Imperial Diet. You further inform me that on the 26th ultimo you received a telegram from your Government, pointing out that the above-mentioned Agreement and memorandum in no way reflect upon, but, on the contrary, are meant to strengthen, the independence of Korea,—this being the object which the Governments of Japan and Russia had in view,—and you cherish the confident hope that my Government will not fail to appreciate this intention. In accordance with telegraphic instructions received from the Imperial Minister of Foreign Affairs you enclose copies of the Agreements referred to.

I beg to express my sincere thanks for your despatch and the information it conveys. I would observe, however, that as my Government has not joined in concluding these two Agreements, its freedom of action as an independent Power cannot be restricted by their provisions.—I have, etc.,

(Signed)   YE WANYONG,
Minister of State for Foreign Affairs.
H.E. MR. KATO,
Minister of Japan, etc.

INDEX

MORE ABOUT KPI BOOKS

If you would like further information about books available from KPI please write to

> The Marketing Department
> KPI Limited
> Routledge & Kegan Paul Plc
> 14 Leicester Square
> London WC2H 7PH

In the USA write to

> The Marketing Department
> KPI Limited
> Routledge & Kegan Paul
> 9 Park Street
> Boston
> Mass 02108

In Australia write to

> The Marketing Department
> KPI Limited
> Routledge & Kegan Paul
> c/o Methuen Law Book Company
> 44 Waterloo Road
> North Ryde, NSW 2113
> Australia

KPI